PILGRIMS, PICKERS AND HONKY-TONK HEROES

PILGRIMS, PICKERS AND HONKY-TONK HEROES

My Personal Time with Music City Friends and Legends in Rock 'n' Roll, R&B, and a Whole Lot of Country

TIM GHIANNI

Foreword by Peter Cooper
Preface by Bobby Bare

Backbeat
Books
Essex, Connecticut

Backbeat Books

An imprint of Globe Pequot, the trade division of
The Rowman & Littlefield Publishing Group, Inc.
4501 Forbes Blvd., Ste. 200
Lanham, MD 20706
www.rowman.com

Distributed by NATIONAL BOOK NETWORK

British Library Cataloguing in Publication Information Available

Library of Congress Cataloging-in-Publication Data

Names: Ghianni, Tim, author.
Title: Pilgrims, pickers and honky-tonk heroes / Tim Ghianni ; foreword by Peter
   Cooper.
Identifiers: LCCN 2022042065 (print) | LCCN 2022042066 (ebook) | ISBN
   9781493072156 (paperback) | ISBN 9781493072163 (ebook)
Subjects: LCSH: Musicians—Tennessee—Nashville—Anecdotes. | Country musicians—
   Tennessee—Nashville—Anecdotes.
Classification: LCC ML385 .G48 2023 (print) | LCC ML385 (ebook) | DDC
   780.9768/55—dcundefined
LC record available at https://lccn.loc.gov/2022042065
LC ebook record available at https://lccn.loc.gov/2022042066

∞™ The paper used in this publication meets the minimum requirements of
American National Standard for Information Sciences—Permanence of Paper for
Printed Library Materials, ANSI/NISO Z39.48-1992.

For the people in this book, friends who should never be forgotten: Thanks for your time and love. Also, for my wife, Suzanne; my children, Emily and Joe; and grandson Roman. And, as always, thanks to John, Paul, George, and Ringo for a lifetime of love, peace, encouragement, support, and rock 'n' roll.

Contents

Acknowledgments

I'D LIKE TO RECOGNIZE some of those who helped bring this book to reality. The top of the list is John Cerullo, the acquisition editor for Rowman & Littlefield/Globe Pequot, who read and pitched the book and got the go-ahead for it to be published by the Backbeat Books imprint.

Also, massive thanks to Barbara Claire, editorial assistant at Rowman & Littlefield/Globe Pequot, who worked diligently and patiently to help me get through the process.

I also need to thank great music biographer Peter Guralnick for his encouragement and support. He was the first person I contacted for direction on getting this to a publisher. He directed me to pros in the book-publishing industry, including literary agent David Dunton. While this book wasn't necessarily in his ballpark, he read a long sample and recommended I contact John Cerullo. He also told me to use his name for a recommendation.

I'd also like to acknowledge those who helped make this book come to life in pictures: John Partipilo, Bill Steber, Cary Mark Passeroff, Shannon Bare, Shannon Pollard, Melissa Lawrence Buck, Rebekah Speer, Thurman Mullins, Monty Combs (courtesy of the Blue Ridge Music Hall of Fame), Mike Keller (courtesy of the West Virginia Music Hall of Fame), Tod Ellsworth, photographer Eric Glasnapp and music historian Dan Fiorentino from the National Association of Music Merchants, photographer Dick Cooper and Mickey J. Lollar (courtesy of the Alabama Music Hall of Fame), Dean Smith and the other children of Carl Smith and Goldie Hill, the Americana Music Association, the Musicians Hall of Fame and Museum, Billy Cannon, Steven C. Pesant/Authentic Hendrix, Amanda Sizemore, Joe Viglione, Jim McGuire, Nashville's WeGo Public Transit, the Country

Music Hall of Fame and Museum, George Hamilton V, Ken Gray, Sandy Knox, Johnny Kristofferson, Kris Kristofferson Jr., Lisa Kristofferson, Jane Rose, and Keith Richards. I shot some also.

Special thanks to John Partipilo, who got up in the middle of the night to meet me on Nashville's Lower Broadway for the cover and author photographs.

And, once more, I want to thank my various employers, from the *Leaf-Chronicle* in Clarksville, Tennessee, to the old *Nashville Banner*, *The Tennessean*, the *Nashville Ledger*, *Living Blues*, and the *Journal of Country Music* as well as the *Nashville Scene*, Reuters, and various websites with whom I have been affiliated during the last half century and who put me in the position to meet the people in this book.

And, especially, I could not have done this book without the love of and for the people who fill its pages.

Foreword

THERE IS NO SUCH THING as impartiality. Or, God forbid, there is such a thing. If so, we're screwed. Impartiality is robotic, metronomic, and exactly the opposite of everything that writing should be.

Everything in the world is subjective. There are people who worship the sun, and that's fine. A favorite (see, I am impartial) songwriter of mine, Malcolm Holcombe, sings, "I like the shade, where it's cool and green."

I want to hear Malcolm sing about the shade, not about the sun. I want to hear Tom T. Hall sing, "Those clear Kentucky streams, they are always in my dreams/I think that is something you should know."

I don't want to hear Tom T. objectively compare Kentucky streams to West Virginia streams.

I want to hear Kris Kristofferson sing, "Take the ribbon from your hair/Shake it loose and let it fall," and I don't want to hear him give an impartial guide of ways that someone might secure their hair.

I don't want to hear that Hank Aaron hit .268 with 20 home runs in 1974. I want to hear the story of how he changed everything that year by hitting a towering blow off Al Downing of the Los Angeles Dodgers on April 8 that made him the all-time home run king.

(He still is, in my partial opinion, though cold statistics and easy research will tell you that the homer crown is shared by Barry Bonds and performance-enhancing drugs.)

None of this is to say that facts are inconsequential. You can't get 'em wrong, or you'll lose credibility. But facts are an essential but incomplete part of our stories.

Where are you from? Who are you, really? These questions are often related. The answers are inherently different. I've never met anyone from Ironton, Ohio, who reminds me of native hero Bobby Bare, and I've spent some time in Ironton.

I'm partial to Tim Ghianni, in no small part because he's anything but impartial. He sees people for who they are, not for their statistics. He values humanity and humility over scoreboard-lit accomplishments. If you want to know what these people did, you can look it up yourself (it's simple these days). If you want to know who these people are or who they were, you can't find it anywhere but here.

Tim's writing provides a window into people you will treasure.

If you want to know who Tim Ghianni is, you'll find that here, too. And, partially speaking, it's a finding far worth the journey.

Peter Cooper
Nashville, Tennessee

Preface

I HAVE BEEN A FAN of the great journalist Tim Ghianni for more than 30 years. He should have won a Pulitzer by now for all he has written about Nashville and country music. Underline Pulitzer and underline Tim Ghianni.

Tim has written a book of up-close-and-personal chapters about country superstars who have changed the direction of the way country music has been perceived.

This unique style of writing gives an insight into all the personalities and quirks, good and bad, of a lot of famous people—from Shel Silverstein to Eddy Arnold, Charlie Daniels, Johnny Cash, and Kris Kristofferson—and so many more magic revelations during a period of time that will never be forgotten.

Being the notoriously great human being that he is, Tim Ghianni is respected by all, close friends with many, and, to a few others like myself, a best friend.

Bobby Bare
Grammy-winning member of the Country Music Hall of Fame
Nashville, Tennessee

Introduction

I STARTED WRITING THIS BOOK about Kris Kristofferson. Ended up writing about Bobby Bare. And Johnny Cash. Little Jimmy Dickens. Funky Donnie Fritts. Mac Wiseman. Earl Scruggs. Charlie Daniels. Billy Joe Shaver. Tom T. and Dixie Hall had a lot to do with it.

Above, I'm kind of adapting for my purposes the rumbling, rambling introduction to Kris Kristofferson's "The Pilgrim, Chapter 33" as a way of beginning my explanation for why I've spent more than a year reliving my time with some of Nashville's great musical figures and committing those personal memories to paper. The names above are just a few of the people I have written about, folks who shared small slices of their lives with me.

The reason for the Kristofferson-style intro is that song and the album it's on, *The Silver Tongued Devil and I*, actually initiated what became a deep love of Nashville and Nashville musicians after I bought the album in the summer of 1971 between my sophomore and junior years at Iowa State University.

Kris's lyrics-rich chronicle of a lifestyle with which I could identify came on top of the fact I'd already been a devotee of *The Johnny Cash Show*, filmed at the Ryman Auditorium beginning in 1969. Cash was country, of course, but guests ran the gamut, with folks like Kristofferson, Bob Dylan, Neil Young, and Joni Mitchell.

During what turned out to be my last summer living in Chicagoland, where I'd grown up, I bought Kristofferson's albums as well as those by other acclaimed Nashville writers and artists. Bobby Bare, Cash, and Tom T. Hall became part of my soundtrack—joining The Beatles, The Rolling Stones, The Doors, Derek and the Dominos, Cream, and the Who—that blasted from my dorm room once school started. Other guys would play Sinatra if entertaining their dates. Me, well, I played Kristofferson.

I didn't know it at the time, but the taste for country music I was acquiring was preparing me for the summer of 1972. My parents moved to Nashville that winter, something I didn't expect the year before. So, when summer arrived, I climbed in my 1965 Ford Falcon Futura with the faded vinyl top and noisy hole in the manifold and drove down South.

I hated leaving Chicago, but I was ready to embrace Nashville, which I quickly realized was a weathered, sometimes wicked, but truly magnificent city and state of mind. It was during the summer of 1972 that I lived a life that laid the groundwork for this book.

I became a regular at Tootsie's Orchid Lounge, back when Hattie Bess used her knitting needle to "settle" arguments and country legends drank beer between sets at the Opry, which then was in the Ryman Auditorium, across the alley from the back door of that bar.

I also began hanging out on Music Row, walking the sidewalks near the studios, looking for stars, hoping for music. Not infrequently, to quote Kris, "I took myself down to the Tally-Ho Tavern to buy me a bottle of beer."

Most of how I became addicted to Nashville and its music can be surmised if you read the first chapter of this book, the one that features Bobby Bare, who, it turns out, has become one of my closest friends and a mentor. I'm a lucky man, indeed.

Of course, a guy can't make a living sitting on barstools, so when I got out of school in 1973, I first traveled the country in that old Falcon, then I settled into the life of a newspaperman, the only job I'd ever wanted.

I wrote about sports and Helter Skelter–style murders and kidnapping and maybe even cannibalism for a few years, but I was continuing to build my collection of country albums, and also, as my duties shifted, I began to meet and write about some of the musical heroes.

Because of my job, I was able to walk out of the newspaper building at 1100 Broadway in Nashville (the newspapers are no longer there) and take a left. In six blocks, I'd be in the honky-tonk district. Perhaps it was a day when I was meeting Kristofferson down there—or Willie Nelson or Funky Donnie Fritts. Five or six blocks in the other direction would take me to Music Row.

My profession also allowed me to learn about the other side of Nashville Music—rhythm and blues (R&B)—and get to know some of the men and women who shook their tail feathers, made love to their guitars. Or sang "Sunny."

These experiences and the friendships that evolved guided me as I spent much of the COVID pandemic year and beyond working on this book.

I had time, the computer, and memories. I figured it likely was the spirit of Mac Wiseman telling me to do this book. Or Eddy Arnold. Grandpa Jones. George Jones. Uncle Josh Graves. And, of course, Funky Donnie Fritts.

And I had a lot of encouragement from my friend Peter Cooper, who was on the receiving end of e-mailed rough drafts of many of these chapters.

This book is about the artists, not me. I'm just the guide, capturing anecdotes and quotes, the chatter and the laughter, and sharing it with readers.

This never was intended to be some sort of scholastic or rigid historic exploration of Nashville's music and musicians. Rather, it is very personal: the kid who hung out down on Lower Broadway a half century ago has aged. And his profession as a journalist helped him make a lot of famous friends and acquaintances.

It is the sounds and the sights, the sound bites, tears among the funeral lilies, hugs, the memories, the farewells, and the howdies.

Some incidents and characters recur in various chapters. That's normal because most of these people loved each other or at least knew and respected the others' abilities. I was working among a tight circle of brilliant people. A comment about Waylon and Willie and the boys, for example, could be used in discussions with their cohorts.

Long ago, I began the practice of calling these musical friends just to talk. Perhaps the first conversation would lead to a story. But they'd invariably end with the invitation to call back. And I did on a regular basis all the way until their funerals. Chet Atkins expected me to keep calling after he was dead, you'll find out in these pages.

I want to express my thanks to my profession and, especially, the newspapers and magazines that put me in the position to enter these lives and make friends with heroes who really are just good people.

I have worked full-time at three newspapers: the *Leaf-Chronicle* (in Clarksville, Tennessee), the *Nashville Banner* (RIP), and *The Tennessean* (Nashville's morning newspaper). All of those papers gave me written permission to reprint anything I've ever written for them. I didn't reprint those stories here, though perhaps I will do that in the future.

What I did here was go back through those old stories in the archives as well as dig through my old notes and notebooks, harvesting some of the information and applicable quotes.

I also harvested some of the quotes, facts, and old notes I collected during research for stories in *Living Blues* magazine and the *Nashville Ledger* weekly business-oriented newspaper, for which I wrote a biweekly column for about a decade. Again, I have permission for reprinting old stories but didn't do that this time.

This intentionally is a leisurely spin through time with some great people, written through stream of consciousness and from the heart in a way that allows me to make many related stops while telling a story about having coffee with Bobby Bare in his living room or more caffeine with Tom T. Hall in the cottage behind the main house. Or perhaps I'm just taking one of my regular visits to see Mac Wiseman. Or Uncle Josh Graves, where beans always were on the stove for visiting pilgrims and pickers.

Those were casual visits, personal time spent with friends, no notebook nor recorder on my knee. So when recapturing those happy days, I had to rely mostly on my memories, so forgive me if a verb or an object is left out of a quotation. The truth is here, though.

I hope you enjoy *Pilgrims, Pickers and Honky-Tonk Heroes*.

This is my love letter to all of them. People like these will not pass this way again.

Bobby Bare

T HE BEAR OF A MAN sitting by the picnic table in the garage hollers, "Hey, Tim. In here."

Well, maybe I should say Bare of a man.

I had just parked my 35-year-old Saab with the bad transmission and failed air conditioner in the cul-de-sac fronting his house in Hendersonville, smiling all the way because I was going to interview the guy I have long considered the best singer in country music. Well, Waylon was great, too, but not nearly as approachable as Bobby Bare, who offers a broad smile rather than an on'ry glare (more about that later).

Bobby worked his cell phone at the picnic table, stacked with his then newest album: *BARE: Things Change.*

I wasn't at his house just to talk about the album, as I'm no music critic, though I possess thousands of albums, including an ample section by Bare.

I'm just a writer about people of all stripes, and one of my very favorite folks in the world is the guy in the folding chair who is autographing the black CD covers with a silver Sharpie.

"Got more comin' in," he said, nodding toward the pile of CDs. He handed me one of the CDs and stretched out his legs, probably getting a bit more circulation into the feet that are covered by black New Balance walking shoes, identical to the ones I was wearing.

Bare long ago realized (as have I) that some sort of soft-soled shoe was a much better type of footwear than cowboy boots or whatever you want to call the footwear favored by most country singers when in full costume. And by guys who just kinda like to feel cool.

I'd worn boots for a long time myself, wearing the Acme Boot brands manufactured in Clarksville, Tennessee, where I lived many years and where I met and first befriended O. J. Simpson, who was the national spokesman for their Dingo line. I may write more about O. J. in this book, but I doubt it. Fact is, I liked the guy, even though, apparently, he took no great pride in being the first black person to play on the tennis courts at Clarksville Country Club. He just shrugged when I told him that fact.

He was kind to the black men and women who brought us iced tea, although I'm still not sure that he recognized the irony of his barrier breaking at the all-white club in what was then Tennessee's fifth-largest city. Or the fact all the servers were black and wore white tuxes on a steamy summer day, waiting on the football royalty and knife master.

Those boots once carried me to Johnny Cash's house, too. But I'm getting off course here, if there is a course to be had as I tell this story.

"These are comfortable, aren't they, Tim?" said Bare, noting our matching footwear, before he answered a phone call from the publicist who was pushing the record of mostly ballads displaying the still-great voice of the 80-plus-year-old man.

"You want to go in and get some coffee?" he asked me (or really told me) as he pulled himself to his feet and led the way into his house and spacious family room.

Sitting on the sofa, I looked over at him and realized he really hadn't changed all that much in the almost a half century since we crossed paths when my car was parked outside a peep show on a steamy Nashville late night.

"I've gotta watch how much coffee I drink," said Bare, filling my mug and half filling his own. "But I've got to have a half cup a day, or I get coffee withdrawal."

I've told him the story of our first meeting before, and he always laughs at it. He doesn't remember it happening, though he admits "that sounds like something me and Shel would do."

Back in the summer of 1972, when I was 20 years old, I was enjoying my first steamy months in Nashville. I loved the place, a low-slung, sweaty little city where the state capitol and a lighted Bruton Snuff factory sign were the main fixtures on the skyline.

My father's company had moved down to Nashville to centralize their locations. He'd been running the facility and operations out of Chicago while his best friend from World War II brought the rest of the water heater manufacturing company, founded by his own father and operating in Detroit, down to Music City.

It was sort of the first modern era of carpetbaggers, the beginning of a trend that since has turned the Nashville area into a polluted metropolis, stretching from Clarksville and Fort Campbell to the northwest all the way down past Murfreesboro to the southeast. And it's stretched every which way but loose, accommodating too much industry and too many people. And it turns out, in the decades since, it has created an "It City" market for too much crappy wannabe country music, while masters like Bobby Bare go underappreciated.

The big draw—as most of these new corporations from Japan or Silicon Valley (and earlier Detroit and Chicago) never heard of the Grand Ole Opry—is that Tennessee is a "fire at will" state. That's really not the term, but that's what it means. Union power that drained resources of corporations from the North (and even in California and out East) does not exist here. Workers don't need to join unions. And bosses don't have to have any real reason to fire a guy. There is a guy I know who was "let go" by a company simply because he was 56 years old. But that's another story and another book (I wrote it).

Anyway, as a rising senior at Iowa State University, where I was earning a degree in journalism and mass communication while drinking heavily and otherwise cavorting, I really didn't have any options that summer of 1972. I loved Chicago and the many afternoons I went with Jimmy Hart to see the Cubs. I knew my way around the city and also was a familiar sight to Ron Santo, Ernie Banks, and Ferguson Jenkins as they climbed from their cars and to the door into the clubhouse beneath the left-field bleachers.

But no one up in Chicago would take me in, and it would be really boring to spend the summer out in Ames, Iowa, so I drove my 1965 Falcon Futura Sports Coupe down from the cornfields to stay with my parents at their new house in open country, miles and ridges from "the city." That countryside, big horse farms and hay fields, have been gobbled up by McMansions in the decades since, but I liked my folks' house, although it's been busted, gutted, and turned "modern" by developers since my dad died in 2019.

Of course, I needed to earn money that summer of 1972, and I couldn't find work at either of the Nashville newspapers. There was a really good afternoon paper called the *Nashville Banner* and the morning *Tennessean* as well. I ended up working at both later in a life as a newspaperman.

But since there were no jobs in my field that summer, I went to work at the water heater factory. That meant I wrote press releases and worked on advertising. But my greatest achievement was that I learned how to fix a heater (I can't remember that now). Oh yeah, and when the plant went on strike, I spent my days on the assembly line, screwing the tops onto water heaters. The children of all the carpetbaggers did that, but, like I said, it was okay for nonunion labor to work in Tennessee. I'd chat with the guys on the picket line (I already had befriended them before the strike) on my way in and out of the grounds.

Nothing like mindless scab labor at a water heater plant to make a guy thirsty. And since the drinking age was 18, I spent many evenings down on Lower Broadway.

Today, Lower Broadway is a designer-neon, honky-tonk Disney World, designed specifically to get tourists, mostly conventioneers and bachelorette parties, drunk and sell all comers three pair of boots and massive hangovers for the price of one.

Aside from the occasional homeless busker, there is little worry down there. It is sanitized, kind of like a movie set maker's idea of what a bar district in a "country and western" film ought to be like.

In 1972, it was different. The Grand Ole Opry was down there at the Ryman Auditorium full-time. It provided most of the reason for people to go downtown. I also perfected the simple art of waiting until the sold-out shows started on weekend nights before slipping into the fire exit from the alley and into the auditorium.

Sometimes, I'd follow Lefty Frizzell or Ernest Tubb as they departed the alley door of Tootsie's Orchid Lounge—which fronted on Lower Broadway and backed up to the Ryman—after they enjoyed a few beers between performances. They would simply cross the alley and go into the unlocked door to the auditorium wings. If you look like you know what you are doing, you can get away with it, and I became an Opry regular, generally nudging my sweaty, jeans-covered butt into the edge of one of the church pew seats and acting like I owned the place. Since it was not air-conditioned, more and more people would leave before the show was done, giving me legroom and, I'm sure, allowing security to be pretty relaxed about stragglers sneaking in late.

Anyway, more of that stuff likely will come up when I get around to writing about Johnny Cash, but right now, we are talking about Bobby Bare, Shel Silverstein, and what I like to refer to as the "Great Nashville Brick Heist of Summer 1972."

My experiences at the Opry—and while sitting with Tex Ritter and Porter Wagoner near the back door of Tootsie's—had quickly opened my eyes to the squalid splendor that was Lower Broadway.

The bars and businesses (many furniture stores) were on an obvious downhill trek. There were dark storefronts and almost no neon. There were no Florida Georgia Lines, Luke Bryans, Blake Sheltons, and their ilk opening up new joints to peddle high-priced comfort food and syrupy drinks to fans. I think there were only three bars that were open then. And there were plenty of peep shows and prostitutes who beckoned a guy to the second floor of just about any business down there. I simply smiled and said, "No, thanks. Hope you get what you need," and sauntered on.

On a weeknight, if it was windy, newspapers and other portable litter would blow down the street like sagebrush in a spaghetti western. Even then, though, music pumped from the bars that were there. And the dreams of stardom that have made Nashville such a magnet for young punks existed back then, too.

There just were not so many of them performing in so many bars, where music now begins at 10 a.m. and the musicians take two-hour shifts until 2 or 3 in the morning.

Back then, they hoped their steel guitar-driven singing would be discovered by Chet Atkins or Eddy Arnold, who might come down to Lower Broadway on scouting missions.

Today, the homogenized and soundalike bands play mostly Eagles and Jimmy Buffett covers in the mini-Vegas–flavored strip and nurture hopes that John Rich or Kid Rock will be their booster.

There just were not so many venues back then. As a pilgrim in the summer of 1972, I picked one out (The Wheel, I think), next to a peep show that was at the corner of Fifth Avenue South and Lower Broadway, as my summertime destination. Sometimes, all it takes to make me happy is a very cold beer and raging guitars, and I found both. The guitar player who drew me down there night after night didn't show up one day. He was found with a needle in his arm at a nearby "residential" hotel. But I had sure enjoyed him while he was alive.

Sometimes, Opry performers—George Jones, Johnny Cash, Lefty, Tom T. Hall, Bare, or whoever was on the legendary radio show that night—would amble the half block to the bar and sing a set, taking a beer and applause as payment. "I just got back from a show in Des Moines, and I want to try this song out for you" or words to that effect would be uttered by the "guests" as they took over the microphones and the house band got ready to follow their lead.

I met Roger Miller that summer as he wrote songs late into the night over cigarettes and coffee at Linebaugh's, a blue-plate joint that long ago was replaced by a reproduction of a run-down joint that serves overpriced food to drunken tourists and guys with their prom dates. After it became "civilized" down there and I was at a newspaper, I went there after a special concert by Willie Nelson and friends. Willie was there and Toby Keith as well. I can't remember if special guest Keith Richards was there. I do remember missing Roger Miller, who by then was roller-skating in a heavenly buffalo herd.

This is where Bobby Bare comes into the picture, or at least he will pretty soon as I reflect more on my hot summer nights and water heater days.

Lower Broadway and the feeder streets emptying into it from the north and the south were made of bricks instead of asphalt back then.

It was pretty but bumpy and, I'm sure, expensive to keep up. You can't just toss a shovel of cold mix onto a trouble spot when the streets are bricks instead of asphalt.

So the Metro Nashville Council and, I think, Mayor Beverly Briley (the first male Beverly I ever knew before finding out it was relatively common among southern men) pushed through a program to cover all the streets with asphalt.

Now, these bricks had been there a long time. For all I knew, Andy Jackson had driven his carriage across these bricks. Surely, Hank Williams had walked or stumbled here, as had Cash, Grandpa Jones and Mother Maybelle, Kristofferson, Willie, Carl Smith, Scruggs, Bare, and Minnie Pearl.

It occurred to me at about 1:00 or so in the morning, as I sat in my favorite bar next to the peep show, that those bricks needed to be saved. Of course, there were thousands of bricks, too much of a task for a guy driving a Falcon.

But I'd do my part. I went out to Fifth and Broadway. About a half block south were huge gravel lots, free parking, and a great setup for getting mugged or propositioned.

Anyway, I walked the half block to my Falcon, noted that my tires had not been slashed, and drove north on Fifth, parking in the middle of the street just outside the peep show.

I pulled a screwdriver out of my trunk and began using it and my bare hands to loosen bricks, separate them from the rest, and begin loading them into my trunk—pretty tedious work on a late night in a hot city.

That's when I heard laughter coming to me up Fifth Avenue South, from the parking lots, as two men began emerging from the thick mist found on summer nights in a hot and low-slung river city.

"What are you doing?" asked one of the guys, a bald fellow with a big smile.

"I'm stealing bricks," I said as the two men drew near. "Tomorrow the city is going to pave over them, and I'm trying to save as many as I can."

"Sounds like a good plan," said the other fellow, who had a full head of hair but no cowboy hat. I don't know why I added that about the hat, but it seems to matter.

"Do you mind if we help you out?" said the bald guy.

"Yeah, we got time. We're just going over to Tootsie's, and you are doing important business," said the guy without the cowboy hat, adding he hoped to meet up with Willie at the Orchid Lounge. Or maybe he was going to meet Billy Joe Shaver or Funky Donnie Fritts.

"Let's do it, Bobby," said the bald guy, who turned out to be Shel Silverstein, the best friend of country star and freethinker Bobby Bare, who was the fellow with the hair and no cowboy hat. "Let's help this guy. It's important."

The two had been working on an album (they did a couple with Bare singing Shel's writing, and, in fact, a boxed set of Bare singing Shel was released a year or so ago). They were tired and were seeking refreshments.

I introduced myself to the men and showed them the screwdriver I was using. I then got down and began prying at the edges of bricks, loosening them so Bare and Shel could pull them up and put them in the trunk.

Several hundred pounds of bricks later, the trunk was full, and I thanked the men. "We enjoyed it," said Shel.

"Thank you for what you are doing, Tim," said Bare with a laugh that I even today hear when I call him or visit with him.

It was almost 2 a.m. when the two left me. "Hey, Bobby, let's go get that beer now," said Shel.

"Glad we could help you," said Bare.

As they jaywalked across deserted Broadway, I thanked the men, and they turned and waved. I don't know if they met up with Willie, Billy Joe, or Funky Donnie.

I have told this story many times since then, and I realize the dialogue has changed (I have an age-damaged memory, forgetting far too many conversations that occurred at 2 a.m. in a cloud of beer). But it is pretty close.

I didn't know it at the time, of course, but of all the people I've met in my years in Nashville, Bare (he calls himself that; I still call him "Bobby" most of the time, mainly because that's what Shel called him during that midsummer night's scheme) has become a guy whom I not only admire; he's also become a great friend. When we talk, which is frequently, it's more life than music.

He'll talk about his kids and grandkids and about his wife. I'll talk about my own family. More often, we'll talk about our health, good and bad, and our friends who have gone.

Sometimes, he'll just call to make sure I'm okay. And sometimes I make that same call. He's a true friend.

Music is a regular topic, as is reading. We both share a love of mystery novels, and he's even been encouraging me to follow one of my dreams and try my hand at the whodunit game.

Shel's dead, but my friendship with Bare, though it didn't really develop for decades later, may have been born during the great brick heist. At least, that tale gave me a lead-in to many relaxed, laugh-drenched interviews or conversations later when doing my job as a journalist.

For example, I wrote about him in 2012, when he was 77 and putting out *Darker Than Light*, an album of folk songs, something he'd always wanted to do.

Why'd it take so long for him to get that collection out?

"There's no demand for an old fart doing an album," the affable 77-year-old shrugged at me.

"I've been wanting to do this album for 20 to 25 years," Bare said.

"I just love these old folk songs. The melodies are so great, the songs are so far out and real. It's what happens: a guy would take his knife and stab his girlfriend, and he'd run. They'd go after him, catch him, and hang him."

His booming laugh exploded, and he added, "That's what about four of those songs are about."

"My friend Tom T. (our mutual friend, the great Tom T. Hall) said that folk songs back in their day was the CNN of that day. Every time they knew something had happened, they'd write words to it and put it to the tune of any other popular folk song.

"I'm not interested in doing what everybody else is doing, because by the time everybody else is doing something, I'm tired of it. I'm more than comfortable in doing the exact opposite," Bobby said in the story I wrote for a now extinct Nashville music and arts website. Some notes I've used here come from that story, some simply from my treasure trove of scribbled-in notebooks or notes on the computer, and others from random conversations between friends over the years.

"The record companies that exist now, nobody wanted to touch a record like this," said Bare of the folk album. "If you went to them and mention the fact 'I want to do an album of folk songs and treat them just like they are, really good songs, which they are,' that's not something that the modern-day record companies would have been interested in.

"The record companies, for all purposes, don't exist anymore, at least the way we know it . . . so it's time for somebody to come up with a new way to do it."

I took my dad, World War II infantry First Lieutenant Em J. Ghianni, with me when I went to hear Bare perform some of those folk songs for a streaming radio show called *Music City Roots*.

I introduced the men and also said hello to Shannon Pollard, the Plowboy Records label chief who put out the album. Shannon, a good guy, is

Eddy Arnold's grandson, and the late Tennessee Plowboy himself was the leader of a daily lunch group at the old Melpark (later Sylvan Park) restaurant in Berry Hill. Eddy always sat at the head of the table, and his friend Bare was among the music stars who pulled up chairs. The southern meat 'n' three, shabby, but comforting, was closed in 2015 and fiercely renovated into a Mexican restaurant that likely appeals more to the residents of the new condo towers that have risen around it.

Five decades ago, about the time I encountered Bobby and Shel and they self-enlisted in my great Nashville brick heist, outside-the-box thinking led to the founding of the Outlaws, a movement whose legend outshines its substance.

Bobby was at the head of that table because his Music Row office on 18th Avenue South then was a gathering place for what Billy Joe Shaver called "lovable losers and no-account boozers" (not to mention guitar pickers, pinball wizards, and knife throwers like Waylon Jennings, Tompall Glaser, Captain Midnight, and Billy Ray Reynolds).

Of that group, I knew them all, and Bare, Midnight, Billy Joe, and Billy Ray became particularly important to me personally.

"Midnight was always there," said Bare in a recent conversation that got around to my friendship with Roger Schutt (deejay Captain Midnight). "He really wanted to be a songwriter."

Midnight, a good guy, was not shy about his use of liquor and combining that with his work as a radio announcer or in his rambling conversations when he called me, sometimes fairly early in the morning, at the newspapers.

Bare, by the way, wasn't the pinball-all-night or knife-throwing type. He'd leave the office to his pals and go home and sleep. By the crack of noon the next day, he'd return to find Waylon and the guys still going at it.

I'll get to Waylon later, but he, of course, possessed what I would say was, other than Bare's, the best country voice of all time.

Anyway, back to Bobby Bare and his role as King of the Outlaws.

Music Row romantics might have bought into the notion that those men were revolting against the countrypolitan sound as mastered by Bobby Bare's friend (and my own) Eddy Arnold, but Bobby says it was "a promotional gimmick" hijacked by the marketers.

Regardless, he was responsible for its biggest accomplishment, as in his own search for artistic freedom, he bartered with Chet Atkins and RCA for the right to produce his own records, eventually allowing him to make a full collection of songs written by Shel Silverstein, the brick-heist accomplice, cartoonist, and children's book author. Chet and RCA stepped out of the way.

The resulting *Lullabys, Legends and Lies*, released in 1973, is in many ways similar to the folk album *Darker Than Light*, which Bare debuted at *Music City Roots*. While not a collection of classic folk songs, *Lullabys* does feature story songs from Shel's lively mind.

Another Bare/Shel record, *American Saturday Night*, was buried in the vaults of Music Row as part of a contract dispute, and it finally was released in 2020. Recorded likely during the same period when I was enlisting the services of Bare and Shel to help me pull off the brick heist, it's the best country record of that year.

Lullabys, Legends and Lies barely took a break from my turntable after I bought it in 1973. I went to a release show at Nashville's Exit/In, in which Bobby went through the whole album, with guitar help from Neil Young and Dickie Betts.

The club later became a massive concert barn, but back then, it was just a small listening room. I'd gotten there early enough to get a front table, where I nursed two fingers of whiskey and applauded wildly. Shel was at the next table. After the show, I caught Bare drinking coffee in the little restaurant near the "Exit" of the original Exit/In. He was joined by Shel. I complimented the show and then left him alone.

Frequently, when we talk, I'll toss in the brick heist recollection, and it launches him into anecdotes and adventures with Shel. Or maybe he'll decide that this time he wants to talk about his family—his beloved Jeannie and their kids and grandkids—and the life he desired when he "got tired" of the road and its young man's pursuits and wanted to become a husband, father, and grandfather.

Or perhaps he'll grow sober and talk about how much he misses his friends. Jim Ed Brown, Eddy Arnold, Midnight, Tom T., Waylon, Cash, and his high-speed running buddy Shel. "All gone," he'll say.

I can't leave this little tale about my favorite Nashville musician without visiting Thomm Jutz, who, born in 1969, is neither old nor dead enough to warrant a chapter on its own in this book.

I wrote about the connection between Bare and Thomm in the *Nashville Ledger* on March 24, 2017.

That column really was about Thomm and how his admiration (still unabated) of Bare drew him to America (Nashville really, or extreme southeastern Davidson County), where he wins awards for his bluegrass musicianship as well as his record producing.

And if awards were given for nice guys, well, he'd get one. I mean, he's no Bare, but he's a fine fellow.

Thomm and I were talking one day when he recalled sitting in the living room of his family's home in Germany's Black Forest, a dark fairy-tale

Babby Bare's TV broadcasts into Germany's Black Forest inspired Thomm Jutz (left) to follow the sound to Nashville. Jutz, shown here playing with Bare, has become an acclaimed musician, songwriter, and producer. PHOTO COURTESY KEN GRAY

setting for sure, where he became transfixed when he watched Bare's flickering image on television.

"I saw Bobby Bare on TV when I was 11 or 12," said Thomm, who has had many songs on the bluegrass charts and even has been a Grammy nominee, something he downplays, though he really should have won. He is so fine a musician that he should have a house full of Grammys.

Seeing Bare on TV while he sat in the Black Forest changed the direction and the continent of Thomm's existence.

I should mention that his unusually spelled first name was not the one his parents gave him when he was christened in Neusatz, his small hometown.

"My name is Thomas," he said, noting that somehow along the way, back when he was aspiring to be a rock-'n'-roll star and touring Europe with a variety of similarly bent fellows, his cohorts dubbed him "Thomm."

"It was a bad thing to do. Now people don't know how to spell my name. And my last name is already hard to pronounce," adds Thomm, whose names are pronounced "Tom Yewtz" or something similar.

A self-effacing man, he has worked his way to renown among the Nashville music community for his jaw-dropping guitar playing (he has classical guitar training and a folksinger's heart) as well as his songs and the recordings he has written or produced for others. In most cases, the songs he produces for others have this outstanding guitarist chipping in his delicate playing.

"Bobby Bare was on this German show called *Country Time with Freddie Quinn*—Freddie was an old 1950s movie star and singer. For every TV show, he'd bring over one or two American acts," Thomm said.

"Bobby Bare sang 'Pour Me Another Tequila' (aka 'Tequila Sheila') and 'Detroit City.' There was something special about the way the music sounded, the way he wore himself, the way his guitar looked. It connected with my soul," Thomm said when recounting the TV show and the music star who changed his life.

Bare and his musical posture and near-flawless singing entranced Thomm and, while he didn't know it at the time, pretty much orchestrated his future.

"My sister had been taking guitar lessons, so she had a guitar. I went and got it and started trying to play 'Detroit City.' In a couple of days, I had it."

He since has received the highest degree of guitar training, going all the way to the conservatory-like University of Stuttgart.

While learning classical intricacies, Thomm couldn't erase from his heart Bare's flat-picking mastery.

"I could hear [Bare's playing and singing] on American Forces Network," he said. "The sound of the music spoke to me."

To fuel that passion, he needed more than radio or TV shows: he needed records. "Remember back then there was no YouTube or internet where you could listen to and watch musicians?" he asked.

"I had a fairly limited access to records as well. I lived in a little village, and there was no record store. I only got to a [bigger city], where I could buy records, one or two times a year."

He made the most of that, though, and his love affair with country music, especially Bare's world-worn attitude, continued to grow. "It did something to me," Thomm said.

After wearing out the grooves of Bare songs like "The Streets of Baltimore," "Daddy What If," and "Rosalie's Good Eats Café," Thomm knew it was time to move near the source.

"I had fallen in love with country music," he said. "In my mid-20s, I came to Nashville for the first time."

His "affinity for folk, country, song-based music," like Bare's, had him ready to shed the life of backing up Elvis impersonators and the like and move to Nashville with his wife, Eva Stabenow. "We were married in 1998, but we have been together since I was 15 and she was 14.

"I knew I was going to stay here and not go back to Europe. I wanted to be a part of this country. I wanted to be able to vote. It was a logical step for me," he said. "I've always been interested in history and especially American history. And I'd always been interested in southern literature, southern culture, and southern food.

"I didn't grow up in a bluegrass environment," he said. "You can't define yourself as the real thing in that genre unless you come from here.

"I'm to some degree an active participant in that category, but it would be preposterous to say I was a bluegrass player. I have worked with players and worked in the field, though, and it influences everything I do. . . . When you hear music that speaks to your soul, you react emotionally to it."

Oh, and as a bonus, a guy whose voice first spoke to his soul and continues to do so, Bare, has become a friend.

"He is exactly what you want him to be."

As for Bare, well, he's humbled when I recount Jutz's praise.

"All I can say is I'm flattered," he said. "I'm just glad I had something to do with somebody, as brilliant as he is, coming here. He's likable, his heart is in it. He has the respect of the young, real musicians in town. He will be hugely successful."

I'm just struck with the image of a German kid, born in 1969, falling in love with the flickering TV image of the greatest outlaw that country has ever had, a man who has become a valuable confidante to me.

Of course, I met him outside a peep show back in 1972, when he and Shel helped me load up a trunk of bricks.

"Thank you for doing what you are doing, Tim," he told me as he disappeared into the hot summer night, jaywalking with Shel across Lower Broadway and hoping to meet up with Willie, Roger, or the boys at Tootsie's Orchid Lounge.

Johnny Cash

THE LAST TIME I SAW JOHNNY CASH ALIVE, he had just been helped by his children and grandchildren from his wheelchair to his feet, and he was clutching the side of June Carter Cash's casket for support and farewell.

Pain was obvious, tears rolling down cheeks that were almost completely covered by very thick, large eyeglasses. Only in melancholy whispers did he sound like Johnny Cash.

I put my hand on his shoulder and said, "I'm really sorry, man" or, perhaps, "I'm sorry, Mr. Cash." He nodded as he kept his eyes fixed on the casket, his hands on its edges.

I left him alone, as there were other mourners moving toward his "Ring of Fire" bride and the Man in Black, whose normal fashion was appropriate for this day in mid-May 2003.

I have to admit deep sorrow, hurt in my heart as I wandered away from the casket.

I was entertainment editor at Nashville's morning newspaper, and I was in First Baptist Church of Hendersonville with my friend and my chief entertainment writer Peter Cooper to cover the funeral.

Peter and I left the casket and went into the narthex, where we said hello to Tom T. and Dixie Hall. They were longtime Cash family associates. Tom T. liked me a lot, but Peter was among his best friends. Similarly, Dixie, who I've known for most of my years in Nashville, loved me. I still miss her. That's a story for elsewhere in this book or otherwise. I might even tell you about the wooden angel I'm looking at right now in my office.

Anyway, after the funeral, Peter and I stopped to talk to others from the music community, and I made sure to interrupt the actor Robert Duvall, who was having a conversation with Billy Joe Shaver. I liked Duvall a lot—an underrated actor and a really good guy. It was Billy Joe, though, who I wanted to hug, as he was one of my original country music heroes, having composed all but the last song of Waylon's magical *Honky Tonk Heroes* album. The last song on that concept album was "We Had It All" by my pal Funky Donnie Fritts, aka "The Alabama Leaning Man," and Troy Seals. Even now when I listen to that album, the last song doesn't seem to fit, although it is damn good.

There'll be more on Donnie and some of those guys later, and I have to admit I wanted to tell Duvall that Fredo was weak and stupid and that I loved the smell of napalm in the morning. It didn't seem like the time for wisecracks, so I let the consigliere continue his conversation with Billy Joe.

I also quickly shook hands with Kris Kristofferson, who had brought his family from Hawaii for the service. We had spoken on the phone previously, and both he and his beautiful-in-spirit wife, Lisa—who also had been in on prior conversations—seemed glad to see me. Again, another story.

Anyway, back to that day at the church or, really, on to another day in the exact same location.

You see, the next time I visited with Cash, he was in the casket in September of that same year.

I had been scheduled to see him alive a week or so before.

He hadn't been granting any interviews because of his frighteningly frail physical appearance. He was a prideful man who no longer possessed that Folsom Prison snarl.

But I would call his niece Kelly Hancock, who handled his local affairs, every couple of weeks to check on his rapidly declining health and try to get an interview. I'd been making that call for a year or two, and Kelly and I developed a friendship.

I'd promised not to dwell on her uncle's physical appearance. I mainly wanted to talk about his great Rick Rubin–produced "my-death-is-approaching-fast" collection of albums. If you don't own them, buy them. Be prepared for spiritual and emotional gut punches and tears.

One day, Kelly called me to say that John had agreed to see me and that I should come up to his house on Old Hickory Lake in the Nashville suburb of Hendersonville. It wasn't far from Twitty City, the self-indulgent theme park where Conway Twitty lived and greeted his worshippers. I didn't know him, though I loved his voice and visited his park the day after his death to talk with mourners.

I'd been to the Cash compound before for a party that included a private, June-conducted tour of the home.

And back in 1974, I had picked up John's dad, Ray. I didn't know who it was. I stopped simply because it was an anonymous old man walking through a storm on the deeply shaded road between the Cash compound and Gallatin Road, the main road through Hendersonville.

I later learned that Ray had been at the House of Cash, the family business office, on Gallatin Road and that he was walking home (he and his wife lived across the road from John and June) when the overcast sky birthed a violent storm. I just happened to be nearby for personal reasons: I worked in Hendersonville, and on my lunch hour, I'd go looking for Johnny Cash or other stars. Back then, barrels of coffee and nicotine sufficed for my lunch. I'm nothing if not a health nut.

I didn't know who the old man down the road was, but it was a nasty storm, the kind that happens many afternoons, helter-skelter, in the summer swelter of Tennessee's summer months.

I stopped my old 1965 Ford Falcon Futura Sports Coupe with the faded black vinyl roof and soldered-together engine manifold. I rolled down the window. That's back when windows had hand cranks.

The old man was getting soaked, so I offered him a ride to wherever he was bound.

"I live about a mile up here, but you can take me to my son's house," he said, his wet trousers slipping and sliding a bit as he pushed himself onto the black vinyl passenger seat of my car.

"My son's a singer. I don't know if you know him. His name's Johnny Cash," the old man said.

Since there was no air-conditioning in the Falcon—which, by the way, had been both my transportation and my frequent sleeping quarters for my "discovery of America" months-long journey in 1973—the windows steamed up as we chatted while I drove down the narrow road through the heavy storm.

"Let me off right over there, and you can just turn around there," said Ray, pointing me to the unoccupied guardhouse outside the eclectic log cabin residence his son occupied with June and with their son John Carter Cash. I reached out to shake his hand, and he covered it with both of his.

Enough about that first visit to John and June's house. I returned a couple times, once for a party.

I had been invited to that party by Acme Boot Company. John and June had become spokespeople for that boot company, located in Clarksville, Tennessee, where I lived some of my best years. Actually, I think they were representing the Dingo line of boots. That was when footwear was still made in America.

As columnist and an editor for the newspaper in Clarksville at the time, I attended functions where the Acme folks rubbed elbows with their spokespeople. I mentioned earlier that thanks to Acme, I became a "friend" of O. J. Simpson, who for a couple of years was their spokesman and had a penchant for really tight gloves.

At the party at John and June's house, Carlene Carter (who later would become a friend), the Carter Sisters, the Tennessee Three (which by then included Cash, bassist Marshall Grant, and guitar hero Carl Perkins, who took over when Luther Perkins died in a fire), and, if I remember right, Rosanne Cash, Rodney Crowell, and, I think, Marty Stuart all performed. June gave me and a couple others a tour of the home, which sadly burned down decades later after both Cashes died. Bee Gee Barry "Stayin' Alive" Gibb had purchased the home with the idea of restoring it to past glory, a musicians' retreat of sorts, but fire ended those dreams.

June was a kind and buoyant hostess back on that 1970s visit to the home. I sure liked her and was glad most of the Acme folks had not accompanied us on the home tour, as she was free speaking and as intimate as a best friend.

Oh, I have to mention one other Cash encounter back when I was night city editor at the old *Nashville Banner*. I would come to work at 2 or 3 p.m. Fridays (I worked until 6 a.m. Saturday) or something like that. The *Banner* city editor, Shaun Carrigan, told me that music writer Jay Orr had been chasing down rumors that Cash had checked himself into Cumberland Heights, the alcohol and drug rehab establishment that sprawls on land that overlooks the Cumberland River and is just off the Ashland City Highway outside Nashville.

Of course, Jay would be the one to write this story, and aside from the fact he was a music historian more than a deadline journalist, I had a lot of respect for him and knew he would do a great job.

It was about 5:30 or so, though, that Jay came out of the features department and sat down on the leather couch next to the horseshoe-shaped city desk/copy desk (in newspaper lingo, it was the "rim").

"I haven't been able to get it, but I'm sure he's there," said Jay (or words to that effect). "I've got to leave now, so I'll leave it to you."

If I remember correctly, he had "handed off" a skeleton of a story with the man's biography and the like in it for me to fill in if we ever got the information that Cash had checked in out there.

I called the rehab center and left my name in case Cash felt like talking. I informed night general assignment reporter L. Carole Ritchie that she'd better get ready because we might be getting a call from Johnny Cash. I gave her Jay's info, and we talked about the rumors and, of course, about Cash's self-proclaimed problems with drugs.

I guess it was 8 or so that the phone on the city desk rang. "Hello, this is Johnny Cash," he said to me. "I'm trying to reach Jay Orr. I'm out at Cumberland Heights" (or words to that effect).

I spoke with him briefly, explaining that a young reporter was handling the story by then, and he was gracious and asked to speak with her.

He was a nice, nice man, Carole told me later when I edited the lead story for the Saturday newspaper.

Oh, well, I guess I'd better get back to the "main" point after taking that long side trek into Cash visits and conversations past.

Let's jump back to 2003 and the call from Kelly Hancock, setting up my long-awaited interview at the Cash compound.

"He'd like it if you brought Peter Cooper, too," she said, noting that my friend and I were the journalists he trusted not to "out" him as a shriveled and crippled old man but rather to focus on what he was doing: the most incredible work of his career. And he seemed to be rushing to do it in those months after June died. He knew his time was short. I'm sure he wanted it that way.

"Just come up here Monday, after he gets back from the West Coast, where he's meeting with Rick Rubin," Kelly said. "Call Monday morning first."

It would have been great. The problem was that instead of going to the coast that weekend, Cash went into the hospital and died, four months after the death of his life's partner.

Peter and I did go cover the funeral, of course, and occasionally, if I'm in Hendersonville, I still drop by the graves of Cash and June and my old friend Merle Kilgore, who is buried nearby. I might even write a note about Merle later on. Oh, and I know I'll write about Kris Kristofferson, who was the eulogist and mournfully good-natured master of ceremonies as the music community and church congregation gathered to say farewell to the Man in Black, who occupied the same altar space as his wife had months before.

To be clear, though John liked me a lot and trusted me and vice versa, the relationship with Cash hadn't evolved into "friendship" yet or, as it turned out ever. We never had that interview that would have cemented it, no doubt.

I didn't know him well, but I did love his music, at least going back to June 7, 1969, when I tuned into the first episode of *The Johnny Cash Show*, mainly because I wanted to see his guest, Bob Dylan.

Johnny Cash and June Carter Cash enjoy some time together on the stage in this intimate portrait from 2002. They carried music with them to their graves the following year. © Bill Steber Photography

It was sometime around then that I bought my first Johnny Cash album: *Johnny Cash at San Quentin*.

It had been released earlier that year and was a follow-up to his *Johnny Cash at Folsom Prison*.

I eventually bought the latter, but *San Quentin* still occupies a huge piece of my musical heart because it was my first Cash album. Sure, I preferred to listen to songs about the Eggman or Jumpin' Jack Flash, but Cash's voice and song choices earned him a spot among my musical preferences.

I should add that I did befriend Marshall Grant, the Tennessee Three bassist. His Epiphone Newport bass's neck is featured poking toward Cash on the iconic *San Quentin* cover.

In my role as journalist, I had notified Marshall of the deaths of Carl Perkins, June, and then John. He said he loved that we were friends, but he was tired of my calls.

We did spend time together later, talking about all three of his late friends and about his own career. He picked me up at the newspaper office so I could help him haul his gear into the Musicians Hall of Fame and Museum in Nashville, where in 2006 he was among the first class of inductees.

Back in 1969, when I bought *San Quentin* and watched the barrier-breaking TV show, I was not a country fan. But over the decades, I have developed friendships and mutual admiration with folks like George Jones, Eddy Arnold, Chet Atkins, Mac Wiseman, Carl Smith, Goldie Hill, Earl and Louise Scruggs, Tom T. Hall, George Hamilton IV, Kris Kristofferson, Jerry Reed, Uncle Josh Graves, and many of their associates, and I have a huge collection of country albums and CDs. Some of those folks will appear elsewhere in this book.

But all of this is just a sidetrack. I'm talking about *San Quentin* here. With "I Walk the Line," "The Wreck of the Old 97," "A Boy Named Sue," and "Folsom Prison Blues," all done live for the inmates, this is actually more of a rock album than a country album anyway.

After all, John had come out of Sam Phillips's Sun Records stable with guys like Elvis, Roy Orbison, Jerry Lee Lewis, and Carl Perkins (who had replaced the late Luther Perkins in Cash's band by the time they got to San Quentin). I had the great fortune to spend some time with Carl, and, sadly, I wrote his obituary.

Of course, "A Boy Named Sue"—the inmates' favorite—was written by Bobby Bare's running mate Shel Silverstein, and, as noted earlier, those two gentlemen helped me requisition road bricks one early Nashville morning.

I could go on to talk about Cash and the fact that my mother had become such a fan because of the TV show that, when my folks moved to Nashville in 1972, she and Dad (and me if I was around) went to see John whenever or wherever he was playing here.

That meant that if he was on the *Grand Ole Opry* radio show or if he was performing a fund-raiser at Hendersonville High School or just a concert in a nearby town, we went.

I even took my folks with me to the Opry (I showed them how to sneak in the side door off the alley) the last night the radio show officially called the Ryman home back in 1974. Cash, June, the other Carter sisters, Mother Maybelle, Dobie Gray, and the Reverend Jimmie Snow officially said good-bye to that old building as the Opry moved out to the suburbs. "Will the Circle Be Unbroken" was the finale.

San Quentin is an album that transformed me and laid open the path that ended up with my falling in love with Nashville and its real music: country, rock, or otherwise.

I guess I'd like to explore a bit more my mom's feelings about Cash. We were midwesterners who had relocated to Nashville because of my dad's job.

We moved from Sylvan Lake, Michigan, to Grand Rapids and then the Chicago area, where I did most of my so-called growing up. My folks didn't play much country music on the old stereo. Eddy Arnold was the main exception back in the days when a guy would come home from work, grab the afternoon newspaper, fix a martini, and end his day with Perry Como, Sinatra, or Mancini on the turntable.

After they moved to Nashville in 1972, they started to go to some of the country nightclubs, particularly Boots Randolph's in Printer's Alley, the old club district, and the Opry. As a result, my dad had acquired a taste for not only Eddy Arnold but also Charlie McCoy, Charlie Rich, Danny Davis, Floyd Cramer, Roy Clark, and Cash.

As already noted, their appreciation of Cash, particularly my mom's (she already was a fan from the television show), had us on the road a lot of nights over the years.

One afternoon, I sat with Kristofferson on a retaining wall not far from the site of the old Tally-Ho Tavern, where he worked when he was struggling as a songwriter and where I went in my early visits to Nashville. I'd go in, sit myself down, and buy me a bottle of beer, to quote an old song.

It wasn't long after he had emceed the funeral of his friend and mentor, Johnny Cash, and Kris wanted to talk a little bit about him.

There is nothing revelatory, and I'll talk about Kris and our afternoon on the streets where the Tally-Ho once stood later.

I did tell Kris, who would become a close friend, that my mom was a huge fan of the Man in Black, who was, of course, Kris's hero, mentor, and benefactor.

"Maybe he's not the handsomest man, but he has that animal magnetism," my mom would say.

Kris just smiled and nodded. "Animal magnetism. That's true."

He looked across the street to the Sony building (formerly Columbia), where Cash made musical magic back when Kris was just a janitor cleaning ashtrays.

Eddy Arnold

EDDY ARNOLD WAS NOT ONLY a great human being, a wonderful singer, a generous soul, a friend of Hank Williams, one of Johnny Carson's favorite guest hosts, and a good family man but also the reason, at least indirectly, why my career in daily newspapers ended.

First of all, it needs to be mentioned that, among his many achievements, Richard Edward Arnold, who died on May 8, 2008, was the guy who put real class in country music.

And it was well recognized by the country music establishment, the hillbillies, the outlaws, and the honky-tonk heroes and even the historians and scholars, all of whom crowded the Hall of Fame rotunda while Eddy lay in state—in a black suit, of course (that's all he ever wore).

"Eddy Arnold put a tuxedo on country music," his biographer and friend Don Cusic said in the obituary written by Peter Cooper and Beverly Keel for *The Tennessean*. (Cusic's *I'll Hold You in My Heart* is a well-regarded look at the life of the country crooner.)

"Eddy Arnold was the biggest star in country music in the late 1940s and early 1950s. He sold more records than Hank Williams, Lefty Frizzell, or any other country artist. He also transcended Nashville and country music and had an impact on the American pop audience through his TV shows and appearances."

Cusic's is a pretty decent summation of the polished showbiz giant who has been both cursed and heralded for his transition from the rough-around-the edges West Tennessee country singer in overalls to the smooth, violin-soaked guy in the tux who helped country music jump from bitter tales of love lost, death, sin, drinking, and cheating to pop radio, where songs like "Make the World Go Away" converted fans and made him a perfect fit for the Vegas showrooms populated by Tony Bennett, the Rat Pack, Perry Como, and Liberace.

I remember when he decided to quit singing for pay because I have big ears.

Eddy was in Las Vegas, still delighting crowds, where his name shouted from the star-studded marquees.

As hinted above, I listened in while my music writer Jay Orr (I was entertainment editor of the newspaper and sat within easy earshot of the bearded reporter) talked long distance to Eddy, who had announced his retirement on May 11, 1999, in a press conference at the Orleans Hotel in Vegas. That was a Tuesday, and he said his final appearance would be Sunday, the day after his eighty-first birthday.

"I cried. I sure did," Eddy said, describing his emotional farewell to a gathering of the Sin City journalism corps. "All those things have to come. They have to come."

He had been pondering retirement for a while, he told Jay, for the story that was published in *The Tennessean* on the "local" front instead of the front page, as I had aggressively proposed to the editor. Eddy went on to say that open-heart surgery and "other things" convinced him it was time. "I get tired of getting on and off of planes and running somewhere."

His plans were to take short trips to Nashville-area lakes with his wife, Sally, and their boat and also to "stop and eat catfish" on the way home instead of running to go perform somewhere, as he had done for most of his adult life.

He also said he would maintain his office, which is where I spent time with him, both in my role as a journalist and as a writer seeking peace, friendly banter, and perhaps a little solo serenade after a day of dealing with prima donnas and corporate bullies at the newspaper. Now Eddy sure was rich. But he always acted like the common fellow from Henderson, a town of about 1,000 people at the time he was born in 1918 in southwestern Tennessee.

On his daily visits to his office, he went through his mail—screened I'm sure by his secretary, Miss Roberta (Roberta Edging)—and answered all that seemed reasonable. He had long said that staying in touch with his fans by answering every letter was well worth the time and postage. The fans are the ones who "made him" Eddy Arnold, the great showman with the easy demeanor both on- and offstage. And he appreciated them.

This probably is a good place to add a little info about Miss Roberta. I wrote about her death for a website called Brentwood Home Page, but I also thought of her as a friend.

Eddy Arnold ran his music and real estate businesses and answered all fan mail in this office. Grandson Shannon Pollard now runs his music and real estate ventures in the building, but Eddy's office is mostly untouched. Photo courtesy Shannon Pollard

I spoke with Eddy's grandson Shannon Pollard about Miss Roberta after her death on January 3, 2013.

He told me that her health had been deteriorating but that, as long as she could, she stayed on at the office, working her shift of 9 a.m. until 3 or 3:30 p.m. five days a week for years after Eddy's death, on May 8, 2008, which came just months after the March 11 death of his wife, Sally.

"She was absolutely devastated" when Eddy died, said Shannon of the woman who, as the computer age was well into high gear, continued to click-clack away on a typewriter. It was a sound that made this old news-hound, whose own career went deep into the manual typewriter years, happy.

"She kept coming in every day, even though I told her she didn't have to. I told her she was the boss now and she could come in whenever she wanted to," Shannon said.

"She thought that was really funny." In 2010, health issues got the better of her, and she stopped coming into the office she loved.

"She lived to come into that office," he continued. "That was her reason for being, especially after her husband died in the early 1990s. It was important for her to come into that office every day."

He told me that in his own latter years, as the great crooner slowed down, Miss Roberta and Eddy were inseparable. "Ninety-nine percent of the time when I stopped by, he was in her office, sitting in a chair, talking to her. He trusted her. She was part of our family."

Her desk was just outside Eddy's office, which was the width of an office building that he owned.

His operation's real estate and music enterprises were actually behind the storefront of a State Farm Insurance agency run by Tom Jones, who I'd known when he was an assistant football coach at Austin Peay State University in Clarksville, where I was a sports editor for the *Leaf-Chronicle* newspaper.

A visitor could step in off Franklin Road—Brentwood, Tennessee's, main street—and walk through the insurance agency to see Roberta's desk. I generally came in through the back door, which was up a steep set of stairs, and into Eddy's office.

This seems as good a place as any in this tale to mention that, for whatever reason, Eddy liked Hoss Cartwright.

"Paw, them fellas gonna hurt Little Joe," Eddy said suddenly on one of the afternoons I climbed up into his office in the town that Eddy pretty much built.

Eddy, whom I considered a friend and whom I had first met at the old "downtown" Brentwood Post Office back in 1972, was on this day in 2003 breaking into an impression of Dan Blocker, the big fella with the giant hat who played Hoss Cartwright on *Bonanza*, the moralistic cowboy show whose reruns Eddy watched with passion.

In a different interview with a far different man, George "Possum" Jones, at his house down in Franklin, I found out that country's older stars shared this passion for *Bonanza*.

"That's a good show," said Eddy. "I met Hoss. Met Little Joe. Met the actor that played Paw, too—Lorne Greene—when he was trying to make some records."

A friend of Gene Autry, Eddy had made a conscious decision not to wear cowboy hats while performing for fear of being typecast and having to sing "Tumbling Tumbleweeds" for the rest of his life. Still, a student of the Old West, Eddy found joy in antics and drama on the Ponderosa, site of the show that was the "must-see TV" of its day.

"Paw, them fellas gonna hurt Little Joe," Eddy said again in his Hoss voice. He laughed, showing at least as much delight as I did.

When this immortal singer, the key in the smooth "countrypolitan" style that swept through Nashville for a few decades, decided he could imitate (somewhat accurately) a TV cowboy actor during one of our quiet conversations behind the insurance agency, I knew he was at least as comfortable as I was. I'm sure he "did" Matt Dillon, too, but I never asked.

There are those who complain, without good basis in fact, that Eddy's smooth vocals were a detriment to country music, but far from it, he brought people into the genre via the crooning tales of love and heartache. Eventually, thanks to the so-called Outlaw movement that cussed at elaborate production, things evened out. A funny side note, at least to me, is that the guy most revered by the masses as an outlaw, Willie Nelson, has often, at least in recent decades, depended on elaborate production for his projects. And he is as good as Sinatra with his phrasing and pitch. God, I love Willie.

Regardless, if you need proof that Eddy was a respected hillbilly, besides the fact that his hometown of Henderson is no "bright lights, big city" locale, you don't have to go much further than Doc Watson, one of the most respected men in all of acoustic, hillbilly music.

Doc, the great Appalachian guitarist and songwriter, was talking to guitar great Merle Travis one day as they were working on *Will the Circle Be Unbroken*, the giant recording project and visit to classic country music that the Nitty Gritty Dirt Band organized in 1971 (the album came out the following year).

Most the greats of true country music were on hand for this album, which introduced potheads, Deadheads, and even Skynyrd and Stones fans to Appalachian sounds. Participants included Mother Maybelle Carter (the Carter family song gave the title to the album, obviously), Merle Travis, Doc Watson, Earl Scruggs, Vassar Clements, Bashful Brother Oswald (Pete Kirby), Roy Acuff, Jimmy Martin—the list goes on.

It was in the studio that Doc Watson first met Merle Travis. According to a conversation captured by Frye Gaillard in the groundbreaking book *Watermelon Wine*, Doc and Merle traded hellos.

Then Doc said, "You know, I named my son [the great guitar picker Eddy Merle Watson, known as Merle and the inspiration for the annual Merlefest bluegrass celebration] after you and Eddy Arnold."

"That's what I heard. I appreciate that," Merle Travis replied.

Doc went on to tell Travis, "Well I figured that, uh, a little of that good guitar pickin' might rub off on him."

Eddy Merle Watson, whom I was lucky enough to see and hear play with his dad long ago at Nashville's original Old-Time Pickin' Parlor, died in a tractor accident in 1985. He was only 36. But his playing of the guitar made his dad, as well as Merle Travis and the Tennessee Plowboy (who really was quite a guitar picker) proud.

Eddy's first "Living Stereo" record, it might be noted, was a 1958 LP called *Have Guitar Will Travel*, an album that had the old Tennessee Plowboy on the cover with a guitar in his right hand and luggage at his feet beneath the tail of an airplane. No, he wasn't Chet Atkins, but he knew how to play that thing. Bear Family Records, which specializes in archival releases, has a five-CD Eddy Arnold retrospective titled *Eddy Arnold: The Tennessee Plowboy and His Guitar*, and it offers a lot of fine country-and-western vocals, accompanied by his guitar playing.

And the Queen of Country Music, the marvelous Kitty Wells, now long deceased but whom I was lucky enough to interview at her Madison, Tennessee, home, was asked by my friend Peter Cooper, then newspaper writer but really a musician and historian, for her thoughts on the death of her friend Eddy Arnold.

"He was like Roy Acuff. He had a great impact on country music, and he had a great style, the way he sang. He was always one of our favorite singers," she said in the obituary.

Queen Kitty told Peter that she also enjoyed Arnold's sense of humor offstage.

"He had a funny sort of way about him sometimes," she said. "He would say something funny, [but] I think he was sincere. When he sang songs, he was sincere about it. He had much feeling in his singing."

It is probably worth noting again here that Eddy's grandson, Shannon Pollard, a fine drummer in his own right, runs an indie record label, Plowboy Records, and also oversees his real estate ventures from the building where Eddy's office and the insurance company had been located.

Shannon has taken over and renovated the entire building. He tried for a long while to keep his grandfather's office the way he left it, but I'm sure he has had to go through the clutter by now.

Anyway, back to Eddy's fondness for the show *Bonanza* and the actors from the show whom he met during his own Hollywood ventures.

His spot-on imitation of Hoss lamenting what was happening to Little Joe faded away that day when Eddy turned on the television, inserted an unmarked VHS tape, and settled back into his office chair. He turned down the lights.

"Life, you have been good to me/Why have you chosen me to give your blessings to . . . I dedicate this song to life," sang Eddy on that video recording.

The song "To Life"—a sort of toast and farewell to a good life, one well lived—played out on the TV, and the then 85-year-old crooner smiled and sang a few of the lines again just for me.

He told me that the video was going to be part of an exhibit at the Country Music Hall of Fame and Museum.

By the way, I might mention here before I go much further that Eddy insisted I call him by that name rather than the "Mr. Arnold" I first employed.

That Hall of Fame display, assembled pretty much by Eddy and Sally from their collection of keepsakes, "I'll Hold You in My Heart: The Eddy Arnold Collection" exhibit, was set to open the next week, in June 2003.

It would be open in time for Fan Fair, the annual gathering of thousands of country music fans roaming like dog packs through the streets, bars, museums, and gift shops of Music City. The following year, during the corporatization of Fan Fair, the branding folks, and so on changed the name of the gathering to CMA (Country Music Association) Music Fest. I think it was because they didn't want people to think that all the folks attending the events, including the big shows in the hockey arena and football stadium, were a bunch of people in too-tight Hawaiian shirts and near-bursting shorts, avid fans who came all the way from Vero Beach, Buffalo, or Des Moines to see oldies country shows.

I once spent most of an afternoon with a quadriplegic from Pittsburgh, at Fan Fair with his friends and brothers, who was waiting to see the "Achy-Breaky Heart" debut of country star wannabe Billy Ray Cyrus.

The CMA Music Fest branding change worked, and the four-day CMA Fest now is a polished celebration of the young, new, and sexy in country music. Think Carrie Underwood and Miranda Lambert rather than Kitty Wells and Tammy Wynette (who could have been described that way in their day). Before he became "Garth," Mr. Brooks signed autographs for fans for 25 hours straight during Fan Fair. Now the closest the fans will get to him is if he brings his pyrotechnic show to the city's National Football League stadium. Friends in low places are long in his past or dead.

But that's not what I'm writing about today.

Probably here is a good enough place to talk about how my friendship and semi-allegiance to Eddy Arnold and to the traditions of country music was one of the main reasons I lost my job as entertainment editor at *The Tennessean*.

You see, as editor of that section, it was my job to plan what went on the cover and the inside pages as well as to edit it, help write headlines, choose the photos, and so on. Sometimes, letting my writers know I was going to do it, I took over writing a story myself.

That's what led to my calling him (getting Miss Roberta first) and asking Eddy if I could spend the day with him at his office.

It wasn't genius but, rather, time that dictated this desire.

Since Eddy hadn't been interviewed in depth for years and since it was obvious that age was taking a toll on this great man, I decided to "lead" the entertainment section with this story, about his career and quips, and at the same time promote the Hall of Fame exhibit he and his wife and museum curators had toiled so hard to prepare.

But all that is beside the point. I thought my job as entertainment editor was to figure out what people might want to read or what might sell newspapers, perhaps promote an event folks could attend, and put out a good section. New exhibits at the Hall of Fame give readers the chance to participate in living history. And I knew Eddy's life was running almost on empty.

Trouble for me and my future came in the form of St. Louis rapper Nelly. His hit "Hot in Herre" was the pop-radio sensation that summer. My celebrity columnist, Brad Schmitt, would often walk into the office singing that song in a slower, physically drained, Broadway-schmaltz fashion.

You may remember that song from its brilliant chorus: "It's gettin hot in herre (so hot), so take off all your clothes, I am gettin so hot, I wanna take my clothes off."

And then there were such near-literary lyrics as "Why you at the bar if you ain't poppin the bottles? . . . What good is all the fame if you ain't [a harsher word than "poppin'"] the models?"

Well, we didn't run the lyrics, unintelligible on radio, in the newspaper, but I did run a feature story from one of the wire services about Nelly and his red-hot summer inside the section.

That was my big mistake. The next day (the morning of publication), I was called into the features editor's office and told I messed up. She was my direct boss, and she was gettin' so hot in there.

"Eddy Arnold? That should have been just a two or three-inch brief," she said, spreading her thumb and forefinger, self-righteous anger in her voice. "Nobody cares about him."

Then she turned to the inside page with Nelly on it and pointed at it. "This should have been your centerpiece. Not some old singer no one cares about."

I was also told I was too old to be entertainment editor because of that choice. I was told that there would be someone "younger" brought in who understood that demographic.

I asked her if we should have run the line about what to do with models as the headline.

The same day, the big editor of the paper (and I do mean *big*) came to the features department and called me into a conference room, where he told me I was too old to be entertainment editor.

I told both of them that as much as I like poppin' bottles, models, and the rest, I was of the feeling that "Make the World Go Away" by Eddy Arnold might have a longer life than that song they loved so much.

I don't think the Hall of Fame ever knew that choosing them and Eddy Arnold had torpedoed my career—for good. Full speed ahead, Mr. Boatswain. We're going down.

But it was all right with me. I learned my lesson well. You can't please everyone, so you got to please myself. And live with yourself also. And be able to sleep at night. I'm doing okay in those categories.

And I had done what was right and what was respectful of our readers and also promoted a big event coming at the Country Music Hall of Fame. So I disagreed with both of the bosses and took my whipping (that included no raise for the next year and my career solidly aimed at the "Exit" sign).

It wasn't until a few months later that I was told I was writing too many stories about black people. My history in the case against me began, again, with the Hall of Fame. They had a groundbreaking exhibit featuring the stars of Nashville's huge R&B scene "back in the day." I took it on myself to interview all of those old musicians who were still alive. An R&B exhibit at the Country Music Hall of Fame and Museum was a brave and great move by the folks at that massive showcase and archive facility.

This was good stuff to write about, to educate folks that this wasn't just a country town. Again, my long interviews of guys like Earl Gaines, Ted Jarrett, Billy Cox, and Bobby Hebb gave those guys one last time to tell their stories before they died. After about a dozen stories, I was told by my bosses to no longer feature the R&B artists on the section front. I was told that those stories and those people didn't attract our audience and that their faces needed to be on inside pages.

It was at about that time that the new entertainment editor arrived, and I was "made" senior entertainment writer. Among my duties—after I trained my own replacement, who came in better paid than I—was a weekly column for a local section that enabled me to write "slice-of-life" tales of urban Nashville. This again led to a lot of columns about black people, many of whom remain my friends.

It also ended up with my being called to the publisher's office and told "that's not our demographic" and into the office of the editor of that local section, who asked me, "Don't you know any white people?"

To cut to the chase, they killed the column. Then they said I could bring it back if I'd write about the young, white businesspeople out in the suburbs.

I declined their "offer" and quoted their favorite lyric about bottles and models and the like.

That's when I was cut down for good and dispatched to night cops, where the hope obviously was that I'd miss my family enough that I'd quit. I rode with the cops for several months and actually enjoyed it, especially the vice squad ride-alongs, until the newspaper paid me to go away.

I really don't need to go on other than to say that the Eddy Arnold story that caused such a professional downfall for me was his last long interview. He died in 2008, but he retreated pretty much from the public eye after his exhibit. I'd still go by to visit his office, but his health was going downhill, and his grandson was taking over his real estate business (the real part of the Arnold fortune). Besides that, he wanted to be stopping at roadside stands with Sally and eating catfish rather than talking with journalists.

Of course, Nelly's career continued to be hot for a long time, with such great songs as "Tilt Ya Head Back" with Christina Aguilera and "Pimp Juice." Compare those titles to "I'll Hold You in My Heart (Till I Can Hold You in My Arms)," "Make the World Go Away," and "The Cattle Call."

Dying newspapers figured the answer would be to appeal to the younger readers who enjoyed such classics as "Ride Wit Me" with its catchy chorus: "If you want to go and get high with me, smoke a L in the back of the Benz-E."

Eddy Arnold wasn't a part of the package they wanted to offer.

Of course, the newspaper bean counters were wrong. Younger people simply didn't want to read newspapers and were happy to learn the news from the internet, relying on both serious sources and Facebook, Twitter, Instagram, and the gang that has sprung up in the years since my untimely demise.

Anyway, I am proud of what I did, of my reaction, and of the fact that I not only wrote the last long interview of a great musician but also became a friend.

After singing part of "To Life" to this one-man audience that day in his office, Eddy admitted he knew he would appeal to only a certain demographic: classic country fans and old people. And he was a dash apologetic.

"I haven't done any singing in quite some time," he said. "I don't sing as well as I did."

He said that if he was going to record again, "I'd have to get in shape for it."

The cracks of emotion in that song help make it what it is, of course: an old man, pretty much saying good-bye, with the grace that he had worn throughout his career.

And, of course, he knew he was neither Nelly nor Tim McGraw, two hot acts who actually teamed up on one song, "Over and Over." I'm not going to print those lyrics here. They don't match the quality of "Ride Wit Me" or that monumental "Hot in Herre."

Eddy said that if there were any more songs to be coaxed out of his giant heart, "I'd have to realize that it's not going to make the charts. Still, there's nothing wrong with hearing a good song performed."

In truth, after his death in 2008, RCA rereleased "To Life," which had first come out on the album *After All These Years*, as a single. It spent just one week on the country chart at number 49, making Eddy the only artist with a hit song in every decade from the 1940s to the 2000s. By the time of this last interview in 2003, Eddy had charted 145 singles, including 28 that went to number 1, and sold more than 85 million records.

Those numbers will change over the years as record companies put out various compilations on their best artists.

He was far from some old man with a bitter grudge against Alan Jackson, Tim McGraw, George Strait, the Dixie Chicks, Kenny Chesney, or anyone else making music that did make the radio, instead of his own, back at the time of the interview.

"I like some of the country music now. The songs I can understand. I like that guy, Alan, oh, what's his name, the one who wrote that beautiful song about September 11? Alan Jackson! Now, he really sings good songs." He paused. "Alan sings songs!"

He added that he saw a bit of his friend Johnny Cash in his own situation.

"It's kind of like Johnny Cash," he said. "He just keeps recording, and he can't get on the radio. Two or three years ago, he won a Grammy for one of his records that no one would put on the radio.

"He bought this big ad in *Billboard* 'thanking' radio for its support. Remember this?" Eddy did his best impression of the memorable picture of a clench-jawed Cash "flipping off" the industry that failed to support one of its greatest artists.

"When I saw that, I called Johnny down in Jamaica. Of course, he's not well. I was told he was taking a nap. But then they asked who was calling, and, the next thing I know, Johnny's on the phone.

"I said, 'I just want to congratulate you for this.'"

Indeed, Cash, who died that autumn, had been failing for some time. His wife, June Carter Cash, had died the month before my interview with Eddy, and Cash died in September.

Eddy, who had bought a black suit (the only color he wore, as I noted earlier) for the unveiling of the display at the Hall of Fame, was planning to keep going until he stopped. Literally.

"I feel okay. I'm still walking. I walk about 1½ miles, five days a week," he told me, adding that another of his passions was going boating in his *Sally K.* luxury boat (named for his wife, Sally Katherine).

"We've taken that boat all the way to Florida," he said. "Fellas like me need a hobby, and that's a good hobby."

I noted that he sure had a lot of photos, postcards, and clippings of dogs in his office, and he said people knew he liked dogs, so they kept sending them to him. And he kept hanging them up.

A bit of melancholy came into his voice as he came to one picture of a dog named "Mr. Nuggles."

He was the Arnolds' last dog, and he had died in an accident in the driveway of the 60-acre Arnold estate off Nashville's Granny White Pike. Eddy's grandson Shannon has begun developing that property in the years since Eddy died. They are some of the nicest and most environmentally friendly upscale homes you can find in Nashville.

I need to revisit the idea of Eddy, the real estate man, here before we close up shop for the day.

People who move to Nashville now (and there are way too many of you by the way) know Brentwood, mostly south of Nashville in William- son County (a part of it juts into Metro Nashville Davidson County) as the place where the more wealthy settle.

And that's great. There are plenty of very nice homes in Brentwood (though there are the occasional older, middle-class homes, too).

When I first moved to Nashville in 1972, Brentwood consisted mainly of a smaller grocery store, a market, a B&C Hardware store, a white- gloved steakhouse, a motel, a Shell service station (the old-fashioned, full- service type), and a post office.

The rest of the area was mostly green. Oh, there was a black settlement (families who worked for the wealthy in Nashville) down along Church Street with their community church and dinner on the grounds. I can't remember his name anymore, but the pastor of that church, a long, slender man, was a newspaper carrier for the old *Nashville Banner* newspaper. He used to come to visit me at my desk when he was waiting for the papers to come off the press. I had to apologize if something I had done had made the paper late that day.

Occasionally, a new house would sprout up in Brentwood back in the 1970s, and then the big horse farm—across Old Hickory Boulevard from Waylon Jennings's Flying W compound and Johnny Rodriguez's house— became an office park that we now know as Maryland Farms.

And plenty of nice homes, some of the McMansion variety but many more just spacious and warm, began to fill the landscape to the point where

Brentwood now is a congested city, a nice enough speed trap and only the occasional murder and one famous bank robbery that ended in a shoot-out, but that's not part of this story.

When I first met Eddy Arnold back in 1972, the post office was right behind a market on Franklin Road, maybe 100 yards south of the Old Hickory Boulevard intersection.

I met him in the post office and introduced myself. I had, after all, seen him on Johnny Carson. He was just a casual guy in a golf shirt and khakis, and he was walking to the little market, so I tagged along.

I was going to get some smokes (I used to have nasty habits, cigarettes, tea at three, and so on that I miss to this day), and Eddy was just going in to say hello to the clerk/owner of the market. Thinking back, I imagine Eddy actually was the owner, but I didn't ask.

I can't remember what I spoke about with Eddy, but we continued to bump into each other regularly, and he always was pleasant.

He also was smart and had invested in real estate in the old farm community. And he began to develop it. You see, he was a part of the music community (probably the nicest member). And he knew that his "hillbilly" friends didn't have any place to build their homes.

Back then, Belle Meade—whose houses the artists, with their millions, could easily have afforded—did not welcome hillbillies. It was a strictly white, Old South, noses-in-the-air private city, an island of exclusivity and judgment inside Metro Nashville. It was the kind of place where wives planned all year for the Swan Ball and Iroquois Steeplechase. It still is, pretty much, except I think Vince Gill and Amy Grant live there. They can "pass" for society because of Amy's grace.

Well, the hillbillies back then, Eddy's colleagues, were white for the most part (other than the great DeFord Bailey). But they weren't deemed "good enough" for Belle Meade. It was a sort of "there goes the neighborhood" mantra, similar to the racist rants of white people when neighborhoods were integrated.

Eddy, of course, was gentlemanly enough to mingle with the Belle Meade crowd if he wanted to. But he was smart enough to know there was a market for property and homes for his hillbilly friends. So he pretty much developed what became Brentwood so that his colleagues could have places to call their own.

Of course, he made plenty of money along the way.

Over the years, others found the gold mine and developed even more homes and businesses out there, but if it hadn't been for Eddy Arnold, Brentwood would not exist the way we know it.

Even late in his life, I was at a Brentwood Planning Commission meeting at which Eddy was pleading for some sort of variance or whatever for a new development on some of his land. He got it, whooped, applauded, and went up front to hug the commissioners with his smile.

I fondly remember my visits to the office behind the insurance agency, Miss Roberta typing and Eddy signing autographs and singing.

And I'd see Eddy and Sally around Brentwood (I don't live there, but it is the closest shopping area to my house in Nashville) at the restaurants. The couple even had their own table at a meat 'n' three called Vittles.

After the Arnolds died, a photo of the two of them was displayed over the table, forever labeled as being his. Unfortunately, that restaurant is gone now, a victim, I think, of the COVID pandemic.

My greatest memory of Eddy Arnold, though, really has nothing to do with music, real estate wealth, and his cultural impact.

Late one afternoon and early evening, my wife, Suzanne, and I were taking our young children—Emily, probably 10, and Joe, 7—out to eat at O'Charley's, a "casual" dining restaurant, fit for families, right across the street from Waylon's compound.

In fact, a big mural of Waylon had been painted on one of the inside walls. It was joined by another mural of Tennessee Titans running back Eddie George, who must have been a regular customer as well.

It was a warm summer night, so I sat with my family outside on benches near the door as we waited for our name to be called, letting us know our table was ready.

Eddy Arnold, the man who sold 85 million records and changed country music, and his wife, Sally, came out of the restaurant. It was pretty early, so Eddy probably had gone in time to catch the end of the lunchtime pricing. He was a frugal man.

Eddy walked to our bench and said, "There they are!"

He grabbed the hands of both of my children (both adoptees from Romanian orphanages), and they danced a little circle around on the cement walk while Eddy hummed.

Kris Kristofferson

LOOKING TOWARD THE SPOT where the Tally-Ho stood, Kris Kristofferson and I locked arms over each other's shoulders. We both
laughed slightly.

It had been pretty spontaneous and simply was triggered by the location.

We both realized it at the same time. It had to be done as we landed on
this spot on a clear-blue-sky autumn day as we walked the Sunday afternoon sidewalks. There's something in a Sunday, of course, but this time,
this place was special to these two guys who long ago had been wasted on
these sidewalks in our jackets and our jeans.

> I took myself down to the Tally-Ho Tavern to buy me a bottle
> of beer,
> I sat myself down by a tender young maiden, her eyes were as
> dark as her hair . . .

This man and I were singing his song "The Silver Tongued Devil and
I" near the former location of the actual tavern where it was hatched over
the too many beers that were a part of Kris's compensation for being a
Tally-Ho beer slinger.

I have to admit that I stumbled a syllable or two while singing, but Kris
just looked at me and smiled as we finished out the song. Hell, to me it
was fun—I liked the guy—but I'd met him only a couple of hours before,
though we had conversed on the phone a time or two over the years.

It would have been sort of like standing next to Dylan and singing
"Isis" and not being nervous. But that's not the direction home today.

Even though I was nervous, I felt like I was in the embrace of a friend, one of two old pals creating sort of a ruckus on the sleepy city sidewalks, wishin' Lord that we were stoned, as the song goes. But there was no Sunday smell of someone fryin' chicken.

I've never been the type to have my picture taken with celebrities, at least not on purpose. I think it's pretty much bush league for people who want to live vicariously through those celebs or who think being photographed with celebs makes them important. It doesn't.

This time was different, though. I had asked Johnny Robert Kristofferson, the then 16-year-old son of Kris and his wife, Lisa, who is a dear friend, to snap this one. Johnny, who as Lisa puts it "was named after the man!" (Mr. Cash), with his middle name honoring Lisa's dad, was with us, by the way, for a school project. When he'd heard I was going to get his dad down to Music Row in the daylight for the first time in 30 years, he asked if he could tag along to do a video project for his Hawaiian high school. He had heard the stories, either from the source or from his records, but Johnny had never been on a guided tour of his dad's old battlefield, let alone with a scraggly newspaperman.

"The Silver Tongued Devil and I," the great song whose story line occurs in the Tally-Ho Tavern, is something I've "sung" to myself since the early 1970s, when the album by that name first came out. It's on an auto-play mental song list that includes "Help," "Satisfaction," "Heartbreak Hotel," "Working Class Hero," "Tweeter and the Monkey Man," "Bob Dylan's 115th Dream," and "Folsom Prison Blues." "Purple Haze" and "All Along the Watchtower" also sneak in, along with "My Generation" and "The Ballad of John and Yoko." And "Detroit City."

I first heard Kris sing this autobiographical song after I used my thumbnail to cut the cellophane along the "mouth" edge of the LP after picking it up at the department store near where we lived, at Chicago's edge.

I was a rock guy, though I had bought Johnny Cash's *Live at San Quentin*, largely because my family (my mom and dad) and I had been avid fans of the Man in Black's TV variety show.

Kristofferson and his songs did appear on that show, but it really was stuff I'd read about him—about his Oxford education, his helicopter antics at Cash's Hendersonville property, and his affair with Janis Joplin, whom I adored—that captured me. This album, *The Silver Tongued Devil and I*, was being praised by rock critics as pure poetry from a down-and-out street level. Figuring I'd "find myself" in that crushed-beer-can poetry, I went to the store (I can't remember the name of it, but it was like a Target, and it was in a plaza at the corner of Waukegan and Lake Cook roads). As usual, I went to the record department.

Only people my age will likely remember, but back in those days, a half century ago, every department store had a record department. It was where you went to spend time fingering through the alphabetically arranged LPs. You'd probably already bought the latest by The Beatles, The Rolling Stones, and probably Dylan, too. And depending on the smile in your heart, illegal or otherwise, perhaps you'd dabble in Vanilla Fudge or Iron Butterfly. The latter's drunken studio demo also plays in my head sometimes, especially if I have a headache: "In-A-Gadda-Da-Vida, honey, don't you know that I'm lovin' you."

Oh, and record stores and record departments were very male places. I don't say this in any sexist notion, and I really loved pretty girls (still do), but it was mostly guys who gathered there, examining the albums, trying to figure out which one to add to the collection today. You didn't have to buy anything to be in this club. You just had to be interested in music.

If you were in a real record store—and there was an incense/pot-scented one "downtown" on Deerfield Road—they would even let you take a record from its sleeve and go into a listening room before making the investment. That actually was a good way to spend an hour or two and not pay a nickel while enjoying the store's thick, pleasing aroma: "Incense and peppermints, meaningless nouns/Turn on, tune in, turn your eyes around." Love that song but never bought a thing by Strawberry Alarm Clock. "Little to win, but nothin' to lose."

I don't know why it was so male in the record world. I suppose it was because girls had better things to do. Maybe they were home reading or studying catechism or polishing the family menorah from religions well represented in my neighborhood.

Anyway, this department store was about half a mile from my house, just outside of Chicago. In fact, when I was a senior in high school back in 1969, I worked night stock at the Jewel Tea Company grocery store in the same plaza. I hated the hours, but I could walk there from my parents' house, and it gave me a little bit of spending money.

Some of it I spent on dates, like the ill-fated prom that ended up with my paying way too much for very little fun other than that I did get to see Baby Huey and the Babysitters as our prom band and that I took the girl to the city to see the Modern Jazz Quartet. I spent half the show with cramps so bad that the restroom attendant was worried about me. Maybe that's why, two days later, the girl went back to dating her boyfriend, who had come home from college. I didn't know about that part of her life. And now she's a Republican judge in Florida.

Any 1960s-era stock boys will remember that what you did was go to the back room, pull out this little two-tongued cart (kind of like a miniature forklift), and roll the front part beneath a flat filled with cans of baked beans, borscht, yams, or whatever and then crank up the handle, raising the flat.

Then you'd push it to its place in a store aisle (there were no customers, as stores closed no later than 7 p.m. back then), crank the flat to the ground, and pull out this little ink-stamp thing. You'd look up the price of the beans and dial the numbers and then "stencil" the cost onto the top of the cans before stacking them on the shelves.

I did save some for college, but most of my free money went to albums, a habit that actually began when I was about eight years old and bought Elvis's *Blue Hawaii* when my family lived in Grand Rapids, Michigan. I bought 45-rpm singles, an awful lot of Elvis, before then.

Anyway, back to Kris's record and the day I went to buy it. I went to the department store "New Releases" rack, where generally you could get an album for $2 if it was featured, and I rescued this "Silver Tongued Devil" of an album. It was in that same rack where I found stuff like Led Zeppelin's first album and *Steppenwolf*, unaware that decades later, the guy who yelled, "Get yer motor runnin', head out on the highway" would become a friend or at least a close acquaintance, a true nature's child at the very least.

This Kristofferson guy had been heralded by *Rolling Stone*—still a quarter-folded newspaper—as something of a Dylanesque songwriter. Of course, he's not; he's way different, sort of more blue collar and beer-breathed.

Now I'm a Nashvillian and proud of it and call this city my hometown because I've lived in this area for almost 50 years. If not for the Cubs, I really don't think much about my Chicago days anymore.

In fact, the first summer I lived in Nashville, in 1972, one of the things I did to begin my adventures in Music City was open the White Pages, the phone book. Younger people don't know what these were (nor should they), as everything is online today.

I looked up Kris Kristofferson and found his phone number and his address. I believe it was 1717 17th Avenue South, but I'm not sure. I can't double-check since the building that I found at that address, where Kris lived, was bulldozed long ago and I believe replaced by condos. Nashville's soul has been swallowed by condos. Bob Beckham, the publisher who mentored Kris, Dolly, Ray Stevens, and others, had a house next door where all of Kris's album covers were spotlighted day and night on the wall, a permanent display for anyone traveling Music Row. My now great friend Bobby Bare rented his first office in Beckham's building before he moved to the RCA building and finally to the gathering place for outlaws on 18th Avenue South. He was slender back then and enjoyed fun, but he went home to his family at night while the other outlaws spent the clock playing pinball and throwing knives.

I never got an answer when I dialed Kris's number in the summer of 1972, but I pretty much immersed myself in the beer-drinking, guitar-picking world of Nashville, which was a friendlier place back then. I'd often go down to Lower Broadway to see aspiring pickers play, often interrupted by the joyful guest appearances by the Tom T. Halls, Bobby Bares, and Willie Nelsons of the world. Lefty, E. T. Porter—they all were there.

Other times (or perhaps afterward), I'd go to Music Row, and one place I'd visit was the Tally-Ho Tavern. There, for a buck, you could get a beer and an education. Some days, if you were lucky, Funky Donnie Fritts, Billy Joe Shaver, Billy Swan, Hank Jr., Waylon, Willie, Kristof-ferson, Charlie Daniels, the Reverend Will Campbell, and others were sprawled around the picnic tables out back, passing around the guitar and swapping lyrics and songs. I wouldn't be surprised if Cash went there some, too, though I never saw him. Hell, Captain Midnight and Billy Ray Reynolds may have been throwing knives at a tree.

Many of those guys later became my friends. Back then, I didn't disturb their camaraderie. I just toasted it. And I was a content witness to the soul of the city.

Now some sort of Curb Records building occupies the Tally-Ho cor-ner—tidy brick and soulless, corporate America, of course.

I had, as I said earlier, "met" Kristofferson on the phone before our jaunt on Music Row. In July 2003, pretty much halfway between the deaths of June Carter Cash in May and John in September, I had been offered a standard press interview after a bit of prodding.

He had a new album, *Broken Freedom Song: Live from San Francisco*, coming out on John Prine's Oh Boy Records, and as entertainment edi-tor at *The Tennessean*, I contacted his publicist to see if I could get an interview.

The album sprung from a concert that had been recorded with the idea that the producers could cherry-pick a song or two for a charity benefit album. Those types of charity collaborative albums were big back then after the genre was pretty much hatched by Michael Jackson and Lionel Ritchie, who gathered the stars as the supergroup USA for Africa and the album *We Are the World* (and the single by the same name).

Lisa Kristofferson heard the whole concert recording Kris had done in San Francisco and suggested her husband release it as a live album.

"Actually, it's only about half of the concert," Kris told me. "I was thinking it would be longer, but I guess it's hard to market a double-record these days. . . . It's kind of hard for me to compare my own records, but I think I've done some pretty good ones, and this one compares to them."

The 15-minute allotted time turned into something near an hour by the time I got done having fun on the phone with this personal musical hero and his wife, who did jump in gleefully.

And when the story was published, Kris's wife, Lisa, called me from their home in Hawaii and said if they were in Nashville sometime, they'd give me a call and we could get together. She loved the feature, she said. And she handed the phone to her husband, who echoed those sentiments. I told him I'd love it if he had time while he was in town to go revisit Music Row and see the changes.

In the autumn of 2003, not that long after his mentor Johnny Cash had died on September 12 (June Carter Cash, a wonderful woman, had died the preceding May 15), I got a call from Lisa.

They were going to be coming back to Nashville for a couple of weeks for a Cash tribute special and some other business and she wondered if I had Sunday afternoon (I can't remember the date) open. "It'll be like Sunday afternoon coming down instead of Sunday morning coming down," she said after telling me Kris had nothing on the schedule that day. "Would you be able to pick him up at the hotel?"

This would be his first daytime visit to Music City Row (as he calls it) since the 1970s, when he and Billy Swan, Funky Donnie Fritts, Stephen Bruton, Terry Paul, and former Lovin' Spoonful coleader Zal Yanovsky took his songs to the world as the Border Lords. There were other players, like the great Norman Blake, at various times in that evolving roster. By the way, an almost unheard masterpiece is Kristofferson's third album, *Border Lord*. It wasn't "Silver Tongued Devil," but it has great songs, particularly the title tune about breakneck fame:

> Breakin' any ties before they bind you
> Takin' any comfort you can find
> Runnin' like you're runnin' out of time

When I'd picked him up at a fancy hotel near Nashville's Centennial Park that day in 2003, the sound system of the establishment was pounding "To Beat the Devil" from the lobby and out into the parking lot, where a valet had allowed me to wait.

The song, while not a part of my personal karaoke routine while driving, is probably Kris's best song: "My thirsty wanted whiskey, my hungry needed beans; but it'd been a month of paydays since I'd heard that eagle scream."

Answering my query about whether the song had been selected because of the famous guest, the hotel valet told me the song selection was purely random: the guy who beat the devil (or at least drank his beer for nothing and stole his song) semi-trotted toward the car with his son, Johnny, toting a video camera and tripod and climbing in the backseat behind his pop.

I'd driven my wife's minivan instead of my old 1985 Saab for this venture because Lisa had asked me if Johnny could come along, and Kris asked again when he found me.

"Tim?" Kris said as he approached the van. "Hope you don't mind. . . . This is my son, John. He's gonna come along and take some pictures or somethin'. If it's okay?"

Kris was just 67 then, and he'd beaten his own devils, in great part due to the love of a good and kind woman, Lisa, "the brains behind the beast."

I don't need to repeat everything that happened on that great (for me) afternoon. I do know that both my passengers seemed to enjoy it, and we were a trio of joking and laughing desperadoes, at least for the afternoon.

After driving through the neighborhood, to give my guests an overview, I nursed the car to the curb outside the building occupying the spot where a rotting apartment building had been replaced by modern architecture. Kris had lived upstairs from great civil rights activist and humanitarian the Reverend Will Campbell in the vanished building. Will had told me once that the floors were so thin that he expected Kris to fall right through—probably bedsprings and all, I figured.

Kris reflected that the $50-per-month apartment "had holes in the floor. Dirt floors on the second floor."

As we walked the sidewalks, Kris said that nothing much looked the same as the years when he was living the experiences that led to "Me and Bobby McGee," "Sunday Morning Coming Down," "Help Me Make It Through the Night," "The Silver Tongued Devil and I," and so many more.

The prototypical Music Row songwriter from the wild-eyed days planted his scuffed, barely brownish cowboy boots in the middle of the alley bisecting the block between 16th Avenue South and 17th Avenue South or, rather, Music Square East and Music Square West as they're now called.

I would see these same boots so many times over the years. I guess he wears the one pair that he wore only while getting where he was going and where he has gone. He probably can let the boots go on autopilot to get him home.

"My apartment was over there," he said, pointing toward the back side of the luxuriously modern building that has replaced the old apartment house.

While we were standing there, he remembered his address was on 17th rather than the 16th of his recollection. No matter: "I never came in the front door," he said with a laugh.

He didn't need to. From this alley, at the "back door" of the building that is long gone, it was about 50 yards or less, kitty-corner across a side street to the legendary and generally decrepit Tally-Ho.

"I can remember riding my motorcycle down there to get some whiskey or something," he said, pointing up the alley. Whatever he was doing back then, whether going for a 90-proof bottle or a bag of Ireland's steak and biscuits (a "legendary" treat from a now defunct old steakhouse nearby), this genial grandfather finally admitted he had no business doing it on a motorcycle. Of course, he could have been saying that only because his 16-year-old son, a truly fine young man, was watching us and recording every word for his class project.

Kris looked at the sign on this cross street connecting 16th and 17th. "Chet Atkins's Place? That what they calling this street now? Chet's office was way over there." He pointed three-quarters of a block to the RCA building, where Kristofferson often listened in as Mr. Guitar helped reinvent Nashville music. RCA's famous Studio B is on Roy Acuff Place, he's told. Oh yeah, and Atkins Place used to be South Street.

"They shoulda named this street for Mr. Acuff and the one up by RCA Studio B for Chet," said my new friend.

Those name changes came in the rebranding of Music Row to make it great for tourists. The problem is that, while they changed the street signs, they didn't do much to retain the music, and so much of it now is made in studios in East Nashville or Berry Hill, a pair of creative enclaves. Heck, a buddy of mine named Thomm Jutz—a great guitarist and producer who always wears a hat—has fine musicians driving way out into his countryside studio near the next county to the east to make music.

"There's a lot of memories. It's hard to see. It's changed so much," Kris said, scanning the few hundred yards that contained the apartment, Columbia (now Sony) Records, and the Tally-Ho. This is the turf he occupied back when he was creating the mold for "struggling singer-songwriter works odd day jobs and battles demons while chasing dreams."

Many have followed that pathway. You can even major in a PG version of it at a nearby university. But schooling doesn't replace the experience of runnin' like you're runnin' out of time.

Sure, other singer-songwriters made it out of here alive. But who else called Johnny Cash, Waylon Jennings, or Willie Nelson "hoss" or simply "friend"? How many shared love with Janis Joplin, who turned "Bobby McGee" into such a rock classic that when Kris sings it now, he does it with her phrasing, kind of like when Dylan sings "All Along the Watchtower" in the cadence created by Jimi Hendrix? None of them starred with Barbra Streisand in "A Star Is Born" (after Elvis refused the part due to Colonel Parker's manipulative soul). Who else was gunned down by James Coburn in *Pat Garrett & Billy the Kid*, which I think of as Kris's best movie? He's the Kid, of course. Coburn is his best friend, who is hired to kill him in the film that also has Slim Pickens dying while Dylan sings "Knockin' on Heaven's Door." (He wrote the movie soundtrack and also played one of Billy's buddies in the movie. Dylan has one good scene, which he steals by the Dylanesque way he reads the label of a can of "tomatoes.")

The ghosts of John and June, Waylon and Roger Miller, Mickey Newbury and Shel Silverstein, Audrey Williams, Hank, and Merle Kilgore accompany Kris as we stroll through the Row, me asking occasional questions but mostly just listening to his reminiscences and looking for places to recognize.

It was tough for him, given decades of change. "The Tally-Ho . . . I spent a lot of time in there," he said, pointing in the direction of the long-gone ramshackle joint where he tended bar between janitor jobs and songwriting stardom.

"I think I made $60 a week and all I could eat and drink," he said. "I'm sure I came out ahead on that deal." Robust laughter filled the Sunday silence.

Two of the three guys on this excursion long ago savored cold beers at the Tally-Ho. Only one tended bar and wrote songs for Johnny Cash at the picnic table beneath the big tree in back. Cash, it should be noted, turned "Sunday Mornin' Comin' Down" into "Sunday Morning Coming Down."

"I don't care what he did with it. All I can tell you is that when John did one of your songs, it became his. Forever."

Kristofferson ducked between buildings, pointing out a publishing house "where Mel Tillis wrote" and then the RCA building: "I remember the first day I was here, I was still in [army] uniform."

He and friends Marijohn Wilkins and others were in Cowboy Jack Clement's office. Singer Johnny Darrell had just cut Curly Putman's

"Green, Green Grass of Home," which Kris said "was one of the best songs ever written."

They were off to celebrate until their journey was interrupted by news that Porter Wagoner had just cut "Green, Green Grass."

"That's how I came to find out what it meant to be covered. [Darrell's] wasn't going to get any airplay. That became 'a Johnny Darrell.' Any time somebody wrote one, he got beat to covering it. 'With Pen in Hand.' 'Ruby Don't Take Your Love to Town.'"

Motivation changed because of the news that the great fancier of Nudie suits with the enormous physical and vocal gifts had cut a surefire hit with his "Green, Green Grass" version. But the end result of the excursion was the same: it was time to drink. The group went to a "professional club." Kristofferson scanned what was 16th Avenue, eyes lighting on a red house not far from the former Columbia Records building.

"That building there may have been it. I don't know about now, but back then you couldn't get liquor by the drink [in Nashville]. You had a professional club. . . . If they knew you, they ran a tab."

Barkeep Big Dot Swan came to know Kristofferson well and vice versa. "The reason she was called Big Dot is because there also was a Little Dot."

"Merle Kilgore was already there" on that day. "That had to be the place because right next to there, Merle worked with Audrey [Mrs. Hank] Williams." He pointed to another building.

Kris then crossed the quiet 16th Avenue and pulled at the doors of the Sony building, where he once was a janitor for Columbia, where Bob Dylan's career-swinging Nashville stuff was cut. Doors are locked. The guy who used to empty Dylan's ashtrays is left standing in the parking lot, looking in.

The movie star and great singer-songwriter then leaned up against the window panels, using his hands like binoculars to shade his eyes and peer inside an empty building. There were a couple of European sedans in the parking area, but no one was answering the door.

"Columbia A, the bigger [studio] upstairs, had Ray Price" and other big names. "B was a smaller studio. I cleaned them all."

Stepping back, he looked down this boulevard of broken dreams and glistening buildings.

"It's all gone. Used to be Decca Records up on the corner," he said.

Names and memories flowed: Bobby Bare, Funky Donnie Fritts, Billy Swan, being booed at the Isle of Wight along with Jimi Hendrix, the Who, Joan Baez, and Tiny Tim. Only Leonard Cohen drew hoorays at that fest—or hallelujahs perhaps.

"By the time I started workin', I never stopped workin'. If I wasn't making movies, I was on the road doing shows," Kristofferson said. Music Row no longer was his home. He'd seldom come back, making an exception for me.

That's when we stopped and sang "The Silver Tongued Devil" on the sidewalk outside the Curb building that had taken over the lot where the Tally-Ho had reigned.

Kris laughed after we finished. We sat down on a short retaining wall to rest and reflect while his son Johnny kept his camera rolling.

"Songwriters were the bottom of the food chain," Kris said. "They called us 'bugs.'"

"Everything I wanted to do, all these dreams came true. The audacity of coming here and throwing everything else away. I love Nashville. I got a feeling for it that it saved my life."

His time here "was more than five years, really, because you spent so many hours of the day awake, crammed as much experience as you could in those hours. Met exciting people.

"I'd be going to work late, and Marty Robbins picked me up in his truck."

Robbins, like so many of his heroes and running mates, is dead.

The worn boots shuffled back toward my car. Kris looked from his son to this writer and then back up the alley.

"I just wish the old stuff was still here."

Kris and I have spent many hours together since that day: over coffee in a hotel restaurant where he was promoting some movie about a horse or a long conversation before he would receive a lifetime achievement award (or some such) from the Americana Music Association.

At the latter, I was just familiar "cover" for this humble family man. If he sat down next to me and I scribbled into my notebook, no other journalists, no musicians, and no fans would bother him. And we talked about a lot of things, most meaningless though meaningful between friends.

An older fellow in a dapper suit didn't let our little deception stand, however.

It was another of my friends, a man who really never got his due as the inventor of the role of rock-'n'-roll guitarist: Scotty Moore, who, with bassist Bill Black and Elvis, conquered the world.

"Kristoffer. Kristoffer, how you doing?" Scotty asked as he approached.

Kris seemed startled and a bit blindsided. "Who is that?" he asked in a near whisper as Scotty drew nearer.

I felt proud that I was reintroducing two of my friends: Scotty Moore and Kris, whose janitorial work on the Row had included Scotty's studio back in the 1960s. They told stories, though Kris did seem a bit confused by this man and his familiarity.

In retrospect, though, I guess what I was witnessing was the early stages of the memory loss of this great American songwriter.

At first, the reports were that he was developing Alzheimer's. Then doctors said that it was Lyme disease from a tick bite that caused the lapses.

In any case, Kris's memory continued to decline, although he and I got along well, and he remembered me with hugs and smiles whenever we saw each other.

Even in the spring of 2020, in the thick of the COVID crisis, he was doing pretty well, according to his wife, who said that as soon as it was recommended that older people hole up at home, that's just what she and her 84-year-old husband did.

They had cut short what almost had become a never-ending tour. "He still gets joy singing in front of people and singing around our house," Lisa told me.

The concerts are done for good now, but he never let the audience suffer. Even as his memory faded, he didn't let his audience know it during waves of wild applause. Sure, he had to use a teleprompter to help him remember the words. But when they hit his brain, they triggered the vocal passion of the young man who wrote them.

His trips to Nashville have become less frequent; probably that last great stay here was when he and I went with his 16-year-old son for our walk on Music City Row (again, that's what he likes to call it).

Up until his retirement, triggered when COVID shut down his concert tours for good, he and Lisa did occasionally sneak into town for business, but they didn't want to see a lot of people. She and Kris know there's a standing offer for coffee or lunch with an old journalist, but I really doubt they'll ever be here to collect.

An example of the deterioration hit me hard one evening when I attended a Nashville Film Festival showing of *Bloodworth*, a very violent film of the B-level variety. The festival had chosen *Bloodworth* as its opening attraction back in 2011, I imagine because they thought Kristofferson would be a draw. And he was.

I contacted my friend, his publicist, Tamara Saviano, who had helped make sure Kris and I got together during his visits to Music City to see about doing an interview while he was in town.

She turned me down nicely, explaining that Kris wasn't going to be mixing much with folks during his visit here. While she made sure I had a ticket to the screening (and, indeed, I did get to hang out at the edge of the red carpet), she told me that being around people was getting harder on him, almost frightening.

He knew he was supposed to recognize the people, but sometimes, there were just so many. She told me that he'd be glad to say hello to me and was looking forward to it but that she was going to be escorting him out of the theater as soon as a post-screening panel discussion finished. If I could help get him to the door, that would be good.

For me, the highlight of that panel discussion came when some half-witted journalist for a niche cowboy magazine said that Kris pretty much was typecast on the basis of his songs and prior movies.

What he was saying was that the old man with the gruff voice and beard, a man who had put on some weight since I'd last seen him, was just playing himself in the movie.

I can't remember what I said, but I hollered out that this guy was ignorant and unprepared and that Kris had played a lot of different roles (or something like that). After all, he really has been a gifted actor for almost a half century. He has appeared in too many B-movies, but a guy's gotta pay the bills to take care of the family that is at life's center. But there's great stuff, too. Check out *Cisco Pike* sometime or "Pat and Billy."

The fat guy from the magazine looked at me and glared. Kris winked at me and gave me two thumbs up. In another setting, he would have put both index fingers into his mouth and whistled loudly, a joy-filled signal of approval.

When the post-screening discussion ended, Kris's fans and admirers descended to the front of the theater, and Tamara did her best to fend them off. But there was a dose of panic in the great man's eyes, as everyone wanted to get a piece of him.

The only role I played here was as sort of a pulling guard, trying to clear a hole in the attacking defensive line so that the quarterback could escape. All I did was step through the crowd, hug him, and then help block away the "attackers" as Tamara got him to the door next to the screen.

The last time I saw him up close and in person was that night. And the early fear at the "attacking" crowd had diminished to a twinkling smile as he got out the door.

I have seen him perform since that time, but while in years past I always made sure to get backstage after the show, I didn't do it. There were too many people who wanted to get their piece of him, and all he really wanted to do was pack up the teleprompter and get on the bus to the next town. His children, if they were on break from school, and Lisa (always) were in the bus with him.

It does make me melancholy. But really, he wants no one feeling sorry for him. He's still the smartest guy in the room, the guy who changed the verbiage of country music and made it okay to treat the serious topics of life, sex, drugs, war, and mental despair in country songs.

He may sometimes get confused, particularly in crowds, but don't forget that this was the guy who wrote "Sunday Morning Coming Down" and "Help Me Make It Through the Night" from his experiences. Those songs (and so many more) were taken to glory by just about every voice in country music.

He set a standard for country songwriting that unfortunately has been pushed aside by the guys who today sing about pickup trucks, beer, and loose women and make millions doing it before the song and sometimes the meteoric career end up in the tripe heap. But I'm getting grumpy here.

Regardless, as I think about him (I e-mail Lisa notes from time to time to make sure they are okay in their private paradise on the side of the volcano), I recall our first formal interview: the one in 2003 where he was publicizing a new album and talking to the journalist who remains a lifelong fan and a devoted friend.

In that conversation, we took on the major changes in our lives. I, too, had chased too many dawns and for decades lived like the narrator of "I May Smoke Too Much" from his *Spooky Lady's Sideshow* album:

> And I may smoke too much, drink too much
> Every blessed thing too much

Both of us may have lived that way for too long, we admitted.

"I followed William Blake's words for a long time: 'The road of excess leads to a palace of wisdom,'" he said.

But it took something else, wife Lisa, and their five kids to help this great man find his gilded palace of joy, the place where he could finally rest peacefully.

"I feel so lucky to be above the ground now," he told me those many years ago.

"Health's good. I get to go out and run four miles every day and work around my place. It's up in the mountains, on the slope of a volcano on Maui. It's a small town, nobody there. Just me and my family."

I stop now to think about a day in 2013 when news reports began circulating that the great Ray Price had died. We knew he had been battling pancreatic cancer, but he'd been living life as well as he could. He'd passed on surgical options and elected to stick with chemotherapy.

Price, perhaps the best singer in country music history (George Jones may argue) and a really nice fellow, had taken Kris's "For the Good Times" song and turned it into his signature tune, singing it in his "Ray Price Shuffle" style of honky-tonk music.

In 1970, it took Price back to the top of the country charts after many years away, mostly because the countrypolitan boom really didn't fit his unique phrasing. "For the Good Times" did. It was in the same chapter of Kristofferson's life that the late Janis Joplin's version of "Me and Bobby McGee" topped the pop charts.

Two slices of Kristofferson's musical autobiography that still grab the heart and soul today whenever you hear them.

While I did see Joplin in concert, I never met her. I did meet Ray and his wife, Janie, and enjoyed the music a lot.

Anyway, when word got out that he had died, I tried to get confirmation. None was available, but everybody was slipping into mourning, figuring the pancreatic cancer finally had won.

My staffers already were making phone calls to get reaction from other stars (standard obituary procedure), especially tough when on deadline and with unconfirmed reports.

I figured I'd better reach Kris, who I knew loved Ray, and let him know the rumor and try to prepare him in case it was true.

Lisa answered the phone. They'd just finished a seven-mile run from their hotel in Canada, where Kris was performing.

I told her the rumor but cautioned that it may not be true. I just wanted to prepare them.

She handed the phone to her husband.

"Tim, what can you tell me about Ray?" he asked, adding that he wanted to send flowers as soon as possible if there was going to be a funeral. "Call me back if you get an address for the funeral home. Thanks for calling. You are a good friend."

Finally, I got an open line at the Price home in Mount Pleasant, Texas. Janie answered. Yes, Ray was very sick, but the rumors weren't true.

Her husband was still fighting.

I caught Kris and Lisa back in their hotel room. I told them that I was sorry if I scared them but that Ray, while certainly not doing well, wasn't dead. No need to send flowers yet, I told them.

"Already sent them," said Kris. "Figured we'd just send them to the house rather than the funeral home.

"I'm glad you told us now, so he can enjoy the flowers while he's alive." He even laughed slightly. "I hope it's a nice arrangement."

In the last months of the pandemic, Lisa let it be known that her husband had retired and that he's loving his quiet in Hawaii and happy when singing his songs. The stresses of the road and the confusion simply was not worth it anymore.

She sent me a short video of Kris standing outside, admiring a rainbow. He moved a little bit and then added, "You can see the other end from here."

"Here comes that rainbow again," Lisa wrote, lifting the title of one of her husband's more optimistic songs.

> And the daylight grew heavy with thunder
> And the smell of the rain on the wind . . .
> Here comes that rainbow again

I look at that video sometimes.

We take our own chances and pay our own dues, the Silver Tongued Devil and I.

Little Jimmy Dickens

LITTLE JIMMY DICKENS STOPPED SHORT in the frozen-food aisle of the Kroger grocery and smiled up at me.

If he'd smiled down, about all he'd be able to see were his comfortable athletic shoes. The fancy cowboy boots and the rhinestone-studded costume, the traditional regalia worn by country's biggest (and littlest in his case) stars, were a couple miles away in his comfortable ranch home on West Concord Road in the lush Nashville suburb of Brentwood. I don't live in Brentwood. I'm more of a city boy, but I go out to that rich folks' village for my shopping and banking. And my pets' vet is out there.

Of course, so are some of my favorite music artists, thanks to Eddy Arnold, as chronicled earlier.

That's all beside the point of this little tale.

People in Brentwood always knew it was no big deal to see Little Jimmy negotiating the Kroger grocery in Brentwood. I don't think he made the transition when the Publix opened, even though it was just a short distance away.

In any case, he didn't shy away from the people who loved him—and we were plenty. This little guy with the big heart loved people.

Of course, it would be easy enough to miss him if you weren't watching where you were going. He was only 4-foot-11 and 150 pounds (and that's probably in cowboy boots and that big hat). You could run him over with your shopping cart if you weren't looking.

And just as he left his boots home in the house where he lived with wife, Mona, so did he leave his rhinestones. The flashy stage clothes (they say he was the guy who introduced that loud bit of glitz to live country performances) also are at his house, just across the street from an orphanage.

In Nashville, folks are known for leaving the stars alone when they are out in public. Sometimes, you might give a quick nod to Brad Paisley or Luke Bryan, but generally, you don't bother them. If you know Vince Gill, he might wave back at you as long as he has time. Garth Brooks may run up and hug you and call you by name—he has a politician's memory for names—but he's the exception.

People did not leave Little Jimmy alone. While he was not dressed the part when he was out doing pedestrian chores, he knew people would see him, seek him out, and offer him kindness when he was loading up his cart with frozen potatoes and the like. And he always was ready to respond to kindness in kind.

Send a big smile and a "Hello, Little Jim" his way, and he'd flash a big smile right back. And he also would call you out by name if he remembered it. And he tried to.

James Cecil Dickens died of cardiac arrest January 2, 2015, after suffering a stroke on Christmas Day. Just a few days before, he had celebrated his ninety-fourth birthday in the manner and location he always liked: on the stage of the Grand Ole Opry.

Actually, that December 20 show was a day after his birthday, but Jimmy, as always, lighted up the stage.

"I look forward from one weekend to another to get back out on the stage of the Grand Ole Opry and try to entertain people who have come from miles and miles and state to state to be entertained with country music," he said not that many days before the stroke, according to a press release from the Opry that announced his passing.

While this chapter isn't about his passing, that needs to be noted high because he was the oldest performer at the Opry.

"If they say only the good die young, well, evidently the greatest of all live to be 94 and sing two weeks before they pass on," said Vince Gill, one of the many younger stars who learned from and loved the old man.

Vince—who is requested to sing his mournful "Go Rest High on That Mountain" at about all country funerals ever since he began writing it as he sought solace after his troubled friend Keith Whitley died in 1989, finishing it after his brother died in 1993—was joined on that song by Carrie Underwood, who had trouble containing her emotions during Little Jim's service at the Grand Ole Opry House.

I was at the funeral in my role as Nashville correspondent for Reuters News Service, but I'd have been in the Opry House that day regardless. I really liked the little guy.

"We need to remember that smile, that personality, and that one-of-a-kind sense of humor," said Brad Paisley, perhaps Little Jimmy's most ardent admirer. The two worked together in Paisley's videos and in some awards show shticks over the years.

The joking around with Paisley fit Little Jim's personality.

The beautiful hockey wife and singer Carrie Underwood, another disciple of Jimmy's and also a Paisley pal and awards show cohost, told the audience at the funeral that before her first Opry performance, her mom told her to "watch out for Little Jimmy Dickens because he likes the pretty girls."

Crying, she testified that her hero kissed her hand every time he saw her.

Little Jimmy was just about the last (if not the very last) connection the Opry had to Hank Williams, the Shakespeare of country music whose tragic life, punctuated by back trouble, painkillers, alcohol, and willing women, would have been fine inspiration for one of the Bard's tragic plays.

Hank gave Little Jimmy his lasting nickname "Tater" (that's how his friends addressed him) after the little singer's early hit "Take an Old Cold Tater (and Wait)."

Some fans who attend the Opry to see the current stars, who more often wear work clothes and sing about beer and pickup trucks, may not have fully appreciated the depth of Tater and his career.

Inducted into the Country Music Hall of Fame in 1983, Tater was known for lighthearted fare, like "May the Bird of Paradise Fly Up Your Nose."

Other Tater classics included "Country Boy," "Out Behind the Barn," "A-Sleeping at the Foot of the Bed," and "I'm Little but I'm Loud."

His pal Hank Williams once decided to write a hit for Dickens and did it in 20 minutes on a plane flight that included the little fella, Minnie Pearl, and her husband, Henry Cannon.

That song was "Hey, Good Lookin'," and Hank quickly recorded it himself instead, telling his little sidekick, "That song's too good for you." They were pals, and country fans likely are pleased that Hank kept that one to himself. I always wondered how Little Jimmy inspired Hank to write anything about anybody who was good looking.

And Jimmy wasn't one to let the rock revolution completely sideline him, as he recorded rockabilly songs like "Salty Boogie," "Blackeyed Joe's," and "(I Got) A Hole in My Pocket." His penchant for loud, dueling guitars in his stellar show band would have made Lynyrd Skynyrd proud a generation later.

According to the Country Music Hall of Fame and Museum biography of Little Jimmy, his "pioneering twin-lead-guitar sound" included a collection of the hottest pickers in Nashville.

One of these, Howard Rhoton, in 1997 described his former boss's attack for the liner notes of *Country Boy*, the prestigious Bear Family boxed set of Tater's work.

"Jimmy wanted a specific tone from the guitars," Rhoton said. "Jimmy was keenly aware of what was going on all the time. He liked the single-string, hot-licks type of backup, while he was singing the up-tempo stuff. He was the only artist back in those days that you could play that way with."

Known for his hot licks and for his novelty songs, Jimmy did some serious stuff and was a fan favorite for his schmaltzy recitation "Raggedy Ann (You've Been Quite a Doll)."

Out at his house across Franklin Road from the orphanage, Jimmy was known as a good neighbor in the upper-class Brentwood Hills subdivision. And he was known for the Christmas display he put on the house and in the yard every year.

It was a joy for anyone but especially for country music fans, who could make an evening of it and drive by Tater's place before going out Franklin Road and finding their way to George Jones's ranch and Possum's holiday display. Jimmy stopped putting up his display after 2009, but I didn't learn about that until I drove out by his house one night and saw it was dark.

So I decided to go back, and on a cold and clear early December day in 2010, I went out to Jimmy's house to talk about Christmas (and the lack of it), growing old, Brad Paisley, whatever he wanted to talk about. Hell, we could have even spoken about the specials at the Kroger store we both frequented. I go into stores as much to see the people as to buy groceries, and I believe that to be the case with Tater as well.

On that day that I was out there for a story that ended up on the Brentwood Home Page community website, he opened the conversation to talk about the birds he was feeding on the West Concord Road property.

"I'm just kicking back and watching the birds," he said, quickly getting to the point, to his official announcement, confirmation really, that there was to be no Christmas display lighting up his one-acre lot and also the lives of fans who drove down there.

As his ninetieth birthday closed in (on December 19 of that year), he thought about it but decided not to put up the lights, which also delighted the neighborhood kids. He'd been doing it 20 years.

But he figured he was old enough to quit—he needed to, really. Unlike other folks of his economic status, Jimmy did his own decorating.

And he didn't think hiring someone to do it would do the trick. Setting up his display was a gift to the neighbors and fans, and he enjoyed doing it.

Until that ninetieth birthday snuck up on him.

"It's such a struggle to put them up by myself," he said with a melancholy sigh. "I just let it go this year."

There was a long pause, and he added, "I miss it. A lot. I been doing it for so long."

For the first time in his recent memory, he wasn't going to be home for Christmas, he said, noting that Mona, their two daughters, and their families were going to be gathering in East Tennessee's mountains rather than at the Dickenses' house, as was the tradition.

The family included "two granddaughters and a great-grandbaby, a girl. I'm surrounded by pretty girls."

I mentioned earlier that Carrie Underwood had been warned by her mom that Jimmy had a thirst for pretty young girls. That likely was the case when he was a hard-traveling honky-tonk hero.

Now, at almost 90, the "pretty girls" who claimed his heart were his family.

"We have a chalet up on the mountain in Gatlinburg that we're being given to use. I'm looking forward to it."

And it was to be more than a celebration of Santa's sleigh and Jesus' birth. Obviously, some attention would be paid to Grandpa's upcoming birthday, and Jimmy and Mona were going to be celebrating their fortieth anniversary of their Christmas Eve wedding.

"We'll just be with everybody," he said, eyes brightening at that thought.

Of course, his other family, the Grand Ole Opry, would mark his birthday in a few weeks. While he said he continued to do a few road gigs, mainly casinos with old friend Bill Anderson, his permanent home had been discovered in 1948 when "when Mr. [Roy] Acuff brought me to the Opry."

Acuff died in 1992, but Little Jimmy continued to thrive out there and was something of an ambassador not only of the Opry but also of Nashville and country music.

He admitted to joy at the fact that a young star like Paisley not only was his biggest admirer but also incorporated the little man into his shows and videos.

"I do a lot of interviews and things like that," he said of his role as "ambassador."

"I enjoy talking to people. I appreciate their interest. I worry when they don't call me."

Although he didn't say it that day, I'm sure he would worry if no one said, "Hello, Mr. Dickens" or "Hi, Little Jimmy" at the Kroger.

Otherwise, his passions were around the house where he had moved in 1970.

"There's always something to do around here daily," he said happily.

As noted earlier, wildlife ranks pretty highly on his list of passions. "We feed a lot of birds," he said, pointing to "at least a dozen" feeders within eyeshot.

"We have those little bitty wrens and whatever you call them. They're beautiful. Got a lot of redbirds, too."

He also tended to the pond filled with "big Japanese koi. They go to the bottom, though, this time of year."

Again, he thought about the lack of lights on his property. Just two generous wreaths and nothing else Yuletide could be seen from outside his beloved home.

"Oh, it's a lot of work. It takes me about a week to put them up," he said, adding that he didn't know how many lights he normally displayed.

"Golly, I have no idea. I just kept putting them up until I ran out," always on the day after Thanksgiving.

He looked around his yard and then over toward Franklin Road and the orphanage—the Tennessee Baptist Children's Home—on the other side.

"I like it when the kids in the neighborhood come by and look at them. And down at the Orphans Home, well, they bring the children by and see them lights," he said.

"That was worth it. They would just bring them buses by. That's the part I miss more than anything. The people in the neighborhood thanking me for putting them up and the kids enjoying them. That meant a lot to me."

There is a long pause and a twinkle. "I think I'll probably do them again next year."

Unfortunately, Little Jimmy never put the lights up again on the spacious home that he and Mona shared. There was no lack of holiday spirit.

He just got old and tired, and his health began to diminish. However, he kept on going out to the big auditorium for the Opry almost until his death.

"Until he died, he was the oldest member of the Opry cast," someone wrote after his death on January 2, 2015, days after his final show with the venerable radio broadcast.

And, as was his way, when his final Opry broadcast came to an end, he didn't holler out to the fans, "Good night."

His normal farewell was, "We appreciate you."

And for the better part of a century, country (and rockabilly) fans appreciated him right back.

I'm just so glad that there were many occasions when I encountered him offstage, not in stage gear, of course, his Nudie stuff in the closet at home.

Even so, he worked the crowd, whether at the Opry or in the frozen-food aisle. "I love people," said the little fellow who finally decided at age 90 that climbing up on a ladder and putting up Christmas lights was a mighty tall task.

Chet Atkins

"**O**NE OF THESE DAYS, YOU'RE GONNA CALL, and I won't be able to answer."

Chet Atkins, who was a dear friend and whose office nameplate rests next to a John Lennon "Give Peace a Chance" beer glass in my office, really wasn't joking.

Still, we both laughed every time he said that to me in the years before cancer killed him.

This great man, who died on June 30, 2001, liked me. And he liked poking fun at me and the friendship that pretty much began years before when I was the editor in charge of entertainment news at the old *Nashville Banner* newspaper.

I really liked Chet, too—a lot. He was perhaps the kindest and smartest man to ever orchestrate more than one revolution on Music Row.

In my role as features editor at the old *Nashville Banner*, I generally came to work at about 4:30 a.m. (sometimes 5 if the weather was bad). I had been moved from state editor (in charge of state and national political coverage and also overseeing the cops and news reports from across Tennessee) over to features editor because my bosses wanted a harder news edge on the stuff from the features department.

Well, there's more to it than that, but let me set the stage.

As a guy who handled stories about massive twin brothers who skinned their victims and burned the remains and mass shootings at schools as well as the editor with whom the governor, state legislature, and congressional delegation had to deal daily, I apparently was the likely candidate for the job of turning the soft features department into a news-gathering machine. At least, that's the way it was put to me at first.

It was a big change. Working with reporters like Charlie Appleton ("In a strange twist, the jack-o-lantern turned out to be the victim's head, with the eyeballs and ears missing" would be a perfect lede and story for him) and also working with reporters at the state capitol and Washington, D.C., as they uncovered scandals and reported on suicides by corrupt public officials was fun for me.

And it was nice, or at least flattering, when guys like the governor (Ned Ray McWherter) had enough respect for me that if he had a problem with a story my folks wrote, he didn't call my bosses. He called me at home.

So when I was moved to features boss, I wasn't really excited about it, even with the "newsy edge" to features explanation.

The publisher of the newspaper, Irby Simpkins, ambled into the newsroom the day after making the change, arriving early to talk to me before my staff arrived, and said to me, "You know why I made the change? I did it to [mess] with you, and as publisher I can do that."

He used those same words when he passed me over for managing editor a few years later.

Instead of worrying about Irby, I met with the features and entertainment staff, assuring them we'd have fun and we'd get more front-page play for our stories. I don't know if they had fun, but seldom a day went by from that day on that didn't have a features department story on the front page.

And many of them had to do with music. It seemed at first that we were the official publicity organ of a young, slim guy named Garth Brooks. It was the era of the hat acts: Alan Jackson, Clint Black, George Strait, a hatless Vince Gill, and Garth.

Garthmania was exceptional. When I would bring a story that my main music writer, Jay Orr, wrote about Garth and his sales, his concert crowds, his manipulative creating of the good-old-boy image, and more into the 6 a.m. news meeting, the other editors would know they'd been beaten for the lead story.

I should mention that in the old days, before corporate hatchet fears went into the choice of what went on the front page and even editorial pages, we'd begin each day with a news meeting.

Perhaps they still do in newsrooms out there, but, of course, the politically correct, demographic-targeting evil corporate slugs still exercise too much control.

The business, features, city, state, graphics, photography, and copy desks all had representatives at the 6 a.m. meeting, where we'd each present a list of what stories we had on our section fronts that day as well as anything else we had working.

"I have this one about Garth stopping to change a flat tire for a woman," I'd say.

"He's the biggest thing since Elvis," said Vice President and Senior Business Editor Bob Battle, quickly voting it to the front-page lineup. Bob knew because he had covered Elvis and had traveled with him—or something like that. He also had covered the Kennedy assassination, and he knew the inside scoop on a lot of things in Nashville.

He didn't live far from me, so many days, on my way home, I'd drive past the liquor store that now has George Jones's lawnmower incident (more later) painted on the side, and I'd see Bob coming out with his evening supply. He eventually switched from distilled spirits to white wine. "I just have a glass of white wine at night," he'd tell me.

I would joke him that it must have been bottomless, judging by the aroma. I loved the guy, an old-fashioned newspaperman. They're pretty much all dead now, well, except me, I guess—at least for now.

Bob also had the private phone numbers of just about everyone on Music Row back then, when a reporter could reach out to a star or some studio big shot in person instead of negotiating the corporate answering machine spiderweb after contacting the proper spokesperson who had to get approval from the front office.

Anyway, the fact was that most of my staff, including Jay Orr, came in a few hours after me. They generally would write their stories the day before and leave them for me. And Jay and Calvin Gilbert and later Michael Gray would get in by 9 or so to take over, producing any news stories for the home edition.

The problem was that my deadline for the state edition (we published across the state of Tennessee, with our focus between Knoxville and Jackson) was in the 7:30 a.m. area.

And that meant that if any big news happened in the music business overnight, I was pretty much on my own. I may call those fellows for contacts or information, but mostly, I had to take care of such breaking news on my own for that edition. It was, by the way, only fair, as those fellows had to spend afternoons and evenings at number 1 parties and star flagellations.

Sometimes, the story tip came to me in a faxed press release. Sometimes, it would come in the form of a note that already had made it onto the AP and UPI wires. Or, as I mentioned above, it might come in the form of a phone call from Bob Battle, who sat 50 feet from me.

He didn't want credit for being any sort of tipster; he just wanted to make sure the newspaper at which he'd spent his life looked good and beat *The Tennessean*, which didn't publish until the next morning.

I took a lot of pride in the fact that my guys—Jay, Calvin, Michael, and even media reporter Jim Molpus—were breaking stories that the morning newspaper had to limply chase for something fresh the next day.

As the guy in charge of entertainment news, one thing that happened was that I had access to the obituaries that came in overnight (back when newspapers printed pages filled with obituaries for free as a public service as opposed to today's money machine of paid death notices). I'd look at the obits to see any entertainment business ties. Bob did the same thing, looking for anyone who should be elevated to a story obituary. Tom Normand, the obit writer, also would bring me any interesting death news.

And sometimes, a voice from the music industry would simply call me (my number was listed in the newspaper back in those pre-digital days, when people actually spoke) with the information.

This is a roundabout way of explaining how I became friends with Chet.

I didn't know anyone on Music Row after spending my life to that point on news involving gunplay, DUI fatalities, cannibalism, rape, abducted and murdered teenagers, sex scandals, Bill Clinton and Al Gore, filibusters, and, before that, sports.

So when Bob or one of the callers or even an obit or a wire note reported to me that some musician (Roger Miller, Charlie Rich, Carl Perkins, or Floyd Cramer) had died, I at first didn't know where to turn.

And they weren't always household names or stars. Sometimes, they were key session players or producers, the folks behind the scenes who made the city what it was.

I knew they all should be covered, but coming from the world of news, sex scandals, and murder, I didn't necessarily know how important they were or how to cover their deaths.

I knew the music writers would be in on time to do the full-blown story for the home edition that had a noon deadline and cleared the composing room floor at 12:30.

But I knew that something needed to get reported for the first edition: the state edition.

All I knew is that I didn't know these people. I didn't know who to contact for reflections on their careers and their passings, their influence on music, or their big hits and misses.

That's when it struck me: the man who knew everybody on Music Row had to be Chet Atkins.

I didn't know Chet, but I'd seen him perform a few times, and he always struck me as a nice fellow. So whenever I got word a musician had died, I just called his direct number. It was far easier to get personal phone

Guitarist and music executive Chet Atkins, shown here on The Johnny Cash Show, *was at the forefront of trends, sometimes even bucking them, on Music Row. ABC/PHOTOFEST © ABC*

numbers back in those days. "Hello, Chet Atkins," was the response I got. No secretaries or publicists or soulless phone trees to navigate.

I had several of his albums, most given to me by late record store proprietor Louis Buckley. Louis had stores in Nashville and serviced jukeboxes in houses of ill repute and more until the clerk at his Church Street store was robbed and stabbed to death. Louis packed up all his albums and took them to empty storefronts in his hometown of Guthrie, Kentucky.

That's a long story, but Louis, whom I befriended in the 1980s when I lived in Clarksville (near Guthrie, which is only 45 miles from Nashville), would let me pick through his albums. Or sometimes, he'd pick them out for me.

"You really need to have this one," Louis said one day as we wandered through his storefronts filled with brand-new records—from 78s, like the one he gave me from Jelly Roll Morton, all the way through the early 1980s.

But the record he was holding out for me so insistently was *The Night Atlanta Burned*, ostensibly a Chet Atkins record, though it mixed all musical genres and consisted of a foursome of valuable acoustic instrumental wizards: Johnny Gimble on mandolin, Lisa Silver on violin and viola, Paul Yandell on rhythm guitar, and Chet on lead guitar.

It remains unlike just about any other album I have, and it certainly showcased just what Mr. Guitar could do to inspire the imagination and the heart.

I'll give you parts of the bio written by Tom Redmond that's published on Chet's Mr. Guitar website, since most of you know a lot about this great man already:

> Chester Burton Atkins, nicknamed by throngs of fans as "Mister Guitar," changed the world of guitar music, developing and elevating an innovative guitar playing style that has inspired scores of musicians including Mark Knopfler, George Harrison and Paul McCartney, Earl Klugh, Tommy Emmanuel, Doc Watson, Lenny Breau, Jerry Reed and many, many others. His style and sound are often duplicated but none can completely capture the sound of Chet. He possessed a true love of the guitar and played as a young man for hours until sleep would overtake him.
>
> A noted record producer as well, Chet Atkins worked his way from low playing radio gigs to success as a recording artist and also became one of the most prolific record producers in history. While on Music Row in Nashville, Chet discovered and signed many talented artists as Vice President of RCA and ushered in what was later to be known as the "Nashville Sound." Artists included Jim Reeves, Eddy Arnold, Dolly Parton, Jerry Reed, Waylon Jennings, Willie Nelson, Charley Pride and many others. Of course, fans loved not only his unique and captivating music but also his humble and down to earth demeanor. . . . He was an admirer of the music of Merle Travis, Les Paul and Django Reinhardt; they are influences that shaped him and fueled his creativity. Were he alive he might be uncomfortable with this heaping of praise, but as Lenny Breau once said, "There's only one Chet Atkins."

Chet's mark in American music is indelible. And, of course, as noted above, he influenced foreign players as well.

In fact, Mark Knopfler, front man for the great Brit group Dire Straits ("Money for Nothing," "Sultans of Swing," and "Brothers in Arms"), put his "chicks for free" rock star life aside to come to live in Nashville for a while, and he studied at the altar of Chet.

The pair (Knopfler doesn't have the overblown reputation of other Brit rock guitarists like Eric Clapton, Mick Taylor, and Ronnie Wood, but he is in their musical league) recorded both in Nashville and in England.

For the Mr. Guitar website, Redmond asked a number of pickers about Chet, and I think Knopfler's view of his friend is a perfect example of that great man's influence:

> I was at a friend's house and his dad had some records and he had some Chet Atkins stuff but you know we wanted to be rockers and besides, I

remember thinking that his guitar playing was from another planet, that I would never be able to play like that. I still think that actually. It just seemed impossible. I didn't know how it all happened. I really don't know how he was able to do all that. I listened to things like "Caravan" and stuff like that but I wouldn't have had any idea how you'd get to be that good on a guitar.

In 2005, Knopfler talked about Nashville pickers in general and his feeling for them in an interview with my friend, the historian and musician Peter Cooper, for *The Tennessean*.

Mark talks about a lot of great players in the piece, but it's obvious how much he loved and missed his old friend:

> The Everly Brothers, I heard them when I was 9 years old and they made a huge impression on me, just like they did on The Beatles. And it was Chet Atkins who was producing those Everly Brothers records. Looking back now, it's hard to believe I was able to spend so much time with Chet. Hard to believe I recorded with [session piano legend] Floyd Cramer, or that I recorded with Waylon, who I adored.

On the subject of Waylon, one of the best quotes about Chet's death came from the great outlaw, who helped turn standard Music Row production style (including Chet's) on its ear when he demanded and got control of his own sessions. He actually followed Bobby Bare in that "war," but Waylon gets most of the "Outlaw" credit, mainly, I suppose, because his music reached beyond country and into LP-friendly FM rock radio.

Still, he never lost regard for Chet, and when Mr. Guitar died in 2001, Waylon told obituary writer Peter Cooper, "Wrote him up good, Hoss. You can't write him as good as he was."

Although I had been out to his grave a few times to pay respects, because of change in newspaper jobs from the *Nashville Banner* to *The Tennessean*, where I began work as a night copy editor, I'd never really been able to pay my respects in print to Chet until February 20, 2004.

At that time, I was writing a column for a neighborhoods section of *The Tennessean*, so I decided to take a little walk from 1100 Broadway (the historic and now long-erased home of newspapers in Nashville) to the site of Chet Atkins's statue downtown. It was probably a mile, but I was on a mission.

Here's just a taste of what I had to say that day:

> After slipping between the posts of a chain-link fence at Fifth and Union, I rubbed the bronze guitar, sat on the accompanying stool and said goodbye, finally, to Chet Atkins.

The trek to see Chet at the Bank of America Plaza was spurred by thoughts of the passing of another old friend, the *Nashville Banner*, which folded six years ago today.

Because of the *Banner*'s closing, I'd really never been able to offer up a proper farewell to Chester, who succumbed to cancer in 2001, a year and a half after the statue was dedicated.

Thoughts about that old afternoon newspaper and how my job there enabled me to form a bond with a great guitarist and gentleman drew me to Fifth and Union.

My plans: say farewell from the stool that sculptor Russ Faxon installed next to the master to enable Nashville Cats to sit and pick with Chet.

The chain link of progress almost fenced me out, though . . . until Rick Quinn piped up.

A musician and construction worker, Rick was finishing his lunch break and reading the newspaper behind the statue.

"Come in and say something to Mr. Atkins if you want to," he said, instructing me how to slip through the blockade, erected to keep passers-by safe while the bank property is getting something of a facelift. "I talk to him all the time."

Several months ago, this newspaper gave me the chance to write a column again. So it seemed appropriate that six years after the *Banner* closed, I finally said goodbye to Mr. Guitar.

"Sit down on the stool and talk to him," said Rick, the construction worker. "I say, 'Good morning, Mr. Chet' every day when I get here at quarter to 6. It's cool."

In the middle of a city teeming with folks rushing back from lunch, I climbed up, sat down on the bronze stool and said "thanks" and "so long."

At Chet's funeral, a lot of great things by great people were said—no need to go over all of that here.

But it was another of my friends, Eddy Arnold, who put it best about his longtime friend: "We won't ever see the like, the talent, in one man. If you ever heard of any man—anywhere—who had it all, it was this man."

I'll leave the analysis of Chet's music, his Nashville Sound revolution, and his business acumen to the music scholars.

For me, well, I remember him every day.

One of the first things I see each morning when I descend into my office in the basement of my house is the Chet Atkins nameplate.

It's here because his widow, Leona, knew I was devastated by her husband's death.

I hadn't seen him in a while. The last time, if I remember correctly, he was driving a green convertible down Old Hickory Boulevard along the edge of Forest Hills at the extreme southern edge of Nashville.

He was wearing a yellow hat, I believe, and I marveled that it wasn't blowing off. I could have the make and color of the car wrong, as he was going a pretty good clip and I was going in the other direction.

I honked my horn and waved. He waved, too, though I'm sure it was out of general friendliness because he wouldn't have recognized me in the old Saab I drive. Or perhaps he didn't see me at all. He may have been waving his hand in tempo to some music in his head.

I think after that, he mostly stayed home with his bride, Leona, as the cancer put him in his death spiral.

Although we all knew he had a mortal battle with cancer going on, it still was a personal shock when he died.

I actually was out of town on a vacation when I went to a market only to see *The Tennessean* headlines shouting of his death, followed by a long farewell written by my friend Peter Cooper and freelance journalist Robert K. Oermann.

I felt ill, and my gut tightened. Like I say, I had known his death was coming up, but I wasn't mentally prepared for it.

I remembered the many times I'd called him for quotes and tips on whom to contact when someone in the music community died.

Sometimes, he was just traffic cop and did not give me his own quotes, getting me instead to people who knew the subject best.

I'd use the quotes in a breaking news obit or in a day-after reflection, a column about the musician and his or her impact. Often, I did both types of writing, always thanking Chet for his guidance.

"My wife and I were just laughing when the phone rang," said Chet to me one day after someone died, but I can't remember now who it was.

"I knew it would be you, Tim. We were just talking about you the other night and how you always called me when these people died," he said, or something to that effect.

He said that both he and Leona laughed about that but also that he appreciated me and my interest in him and, especially, in making sure his fellow musicians got their due.

Of course, I continued to call him as long as I was writing and as long as he was alive. The patter was pretty standard, often with a dash of wit along with the realization that, while it was a somber task, I was doing my best to tell what we thought were important stories.

I've already mentioned the nameplate in my office. It was hand carved by Chet (wood carving was a hobby), and it was on his Music Row desk.

A few days after his death, Leona dropped a small package off for me at the newspaper. It was wrapped in a few yards of tissue paper to protect what I regard as a priceless gift. Like I said earlier, that nameplate is in a place of honor in my office, and I look at it often while pondering life and death—and remembering Chet.

In her note, Leona said she knew how much I liked Chet and added just how much he enjoyed hearing from me. She'd been cleaning out his office and thought I'd give the nameplate a good home.

I wasn't a music journalist when I began the long friendship with Nashville's most fabulous guitarist and musical statesman. I was just a young, relatively cynical editor who needed direction on how to find my way around Music Row and whom to call for quotes or reflections after a musician died. I had figured out that if anyone knew where I should turn, surely it was Chet Atkins.

In general, journalists don't make those kinds of calls anymore. They go through spokespeople, lawyers, and corporate hacks and settle for an e-mail comment.

"I'm glad you aren't calling about me," Chet would always say to me before offering up a quote and telling me whom else I should contact.

"But you know, one of these days you're going to call, and I'm not going to be able to come to the phone."

I have to admit, all these years later, that if I'd been at work when Chet died, I probably would have called his number first—not for a quote but out of respect, as a farewell.

Heck, I still have that number: I don't clean out my old phone files. Maybe I'll call.

Mac Wiseman

I T WAS ONE OF THOSE DRAWLING, hot summer afternoons not far from the Christmas tree that never left Mac Wiseman's living room in all the years I'd been coming here.

"Charley Pride was sitting right there in that same chair as you. We sang 'Footprints in the Snow,'" said Mac, trying to adjust his body, damaged by a combination of infantile paralysis and old man's arthritis.

I stopped for a moment and nodded at my friend, his crippled legs covered by pressure hose and propped up so that his slippers balanced on the leg rest of the easy chair. He clutched a blanket across his lap.

I had been here a bunch over the years for work, play, and pleasure. I had sat in a lot of different chairs, including this one that he demanded I wheel closer to him so that we could converse while he religiously worked the phone on the nearby end table.

Sometimes, it's a fan calling to wish him well.

Sometimes, it's an order for one of his CDs or his book.

Sometimes, it's a legend, like Charley Pride, on the other end of that phone, checking on an old friend.

John Prine, perhaps? Kristofferson?

Of course, sometimes, Charley and Prine and maybe even Kris came out in person as well, paying homage to one of the true originals of country music, laughing and enjoying song and food at one of Mac's occasional chili dinners/guitar pulls.

I didn't know Charley Pride really. I liked him plenty and talked to him a bit a few years back when he and his country music champion, Faron Young, went into the Country Music Hall of Fame together back in 2000.

And four years before that, Faron had shot himself. He had emphysema and prostate cancer and wasn't very happy about either. I actually interviewed him once. I found him to be a nice guy. "Live fast, love hard, die young" was his musical advice—and his life.

He made it to age 64 before he ended that life in country-heartbreak fashion.

To many, it was surprising that Faron, who seemed like he should be a blue-collar countryfied redneck, held the commercial doors open so that Charley, a black, hard-core country singer, could step inside and climb the ladder of stardom.

Suicide is painless, Hawkeye's old song says, but that's not the subject today, even though Faron pushed me in that direction.

Instead, today, I'm visiting a dear friend, Mac Wiseman, one of the great men of country music, a founder of the CMA, an original member of Flatt and Scruggs and the Foggy Mountain Boys, and a star of radio and records in his own right. He is forever in my heart.

He made a lot of music before the arthritis in both shoulders froze him up, keeping him from playing. "I can't form the chords with my left hand," he said one afternoon. Frustrated? Perhaps. Bitter? Not really. He'd had a good run with his heart-filled voice and the flat-top guitar.

"He taught me all I know about guitar," joked my pal Kris Kristofferson late one weeknight when we gathered in the after-show cheese-and-wine room at the Country Music Hall of Fame and Museum.

I can't remember if Scruggs, Tom T. Hall, or Kris was being honored then—I used to get invited to those things before I was "bought out" by the local newspaper and no longer the entertainment editor, obviously in less demand by folks seeking publicity. The newspaper buyout, by the way, was an offer you couldn't refuse. But that's all on that, at least as far as this chapter goes. However, I probably should mention that Mac, fuming when I told him of my treatment at the newspaper, was investigating starting a bluegrass music magazine so that I could have something to do. He even had me over for a "business meeting." It didn't happen, but I was just proud he was thinking of me. He was one of the greatest human beings.

As Kris fingered a demonstration that his guitar style was serviceable (even though his words were immortal), he quipped about learning from Mac, who still could pick better than most alive at that point.

Kris said Mac was one of music's heroes. Mac returned the praise. He loved to play the great songwriter's signature song "Me and Bobby McGee," and the fact Mac recorded that song "was one of the highlights of my life," said Kris.

One of the highlights of my life was simply sitting by Mac, in that chair that had been occupied by the great Charley Pride. It was a hot summer day, and to get into the front door of the house, I had to step over a water dish and a dish of Friskies on the front porch and dodge a black cat without chasing it away. Wasn't Mac's cat, but the old man liked animals, probably because he could trust them better than most of the guys in the corporate suites of Music Row and other locales in the factory town.

Unlike most (or at least a good share of those who cross the threshold into Mac's comfortable and heart-lifting lair), I wasn't there for any picking, just sitting in a chair, maybe grinning, probably.

I'm not a musician, like my pals Peter Cooper and Thomm Jutz, two benevolent souls who, if anything, could be considered Mac's apostles. No, they didn't think the old man could walk on water, but they hung on his every word—and also provided him with many of their own, as you'll find out soon.

The two nice guys—Cooper is my close ally and personal and professional sounding board, and Jutz an underappreciated gentle guitar genius—helped Mac compose a collection of memories for an album called *I Sang the Song*.

For nine straight Sundays, Peter, who is too old to be a hipster but who lives in faraway East Nashville anyway, and Jutz, a German hillbilly who lives a short crow flight from Mac, convened at his almost rural house.

They sat, guitars on laps and pens on paper, and nursed memories from Mac. The trio of men then put the stories together in music and song. Mac sang on the album, but most of the songs were performed by guest stars like Prine and Jim Lauderdale. Alison Krauss, acoustic goddess, literally begged to be included.

"Peter and Thomm had done their research," said Mac. "They knew what stories they wanted to tell, and they'd sit here and ask questions, and we came up with the songs."

The album features 10 songs fashioned from those sittings, with the finale being "'Tis Sweet to Be Remembered," Mac's signature tune back when he was a troubadour with wanderlust in his heart.

Other than a few "intros" and "outros" between songs, this is the only song Mac actually performs on the album. And his companion is Krauss, one of the many musicians who worship at the altar of Mac.

"Alison heard about [the biographical album], and she said, 'Can I be on it?' That pleased me to death. . . . I sang it in the key of G, the same key I sang in 1951 when I was working with Molly O'Day," Mac said to me.

Wiseman worshippers and contributors included now full-grown mandolin prodigy Sierra Hull, fiddle genius Andrea Zonn (whom I love as a human being and who, when not recording in Nashville, travels the world as a leader in the band that backs "Sweet Baby James" Taylor as every night he sees fire and he sees rain), Shawn Camp, and often-sardonic folksinger John Prine ("Angel from Montgomery," "Illegal Smile," and "Sam Stone" fame). "Sam Stone" is an antiwar song with some of modern music's greatest lyrics: "There's a hole in daddy's arm where all the money goes, Jesus died for nothing I suppose." Prine sings the title tune on *I Sang the Song*, with Cooper—who said "they all did this because they love Mac"—providing tuneful harmony.

Mac bragged, with a dash of awe, about the seriousness with which the army of worshippers and coconspirators treated these sessions. "When Jim Lauderdale [who mixes his country leanings with Grateful Dead–infused spirit thanks to his friendship with late Dead lyricist Robert Hunter] was recording 'Barefoot Till After the Frost,' he called me to ask me how I would say something. He wanted to do it just right," said Mac.

"Well, I'm very impressed with the talent we got to appear on it. They all know my kind of music. I thought they did a tremendous job of interpreting it."

Mac said he wasn't sure if anyone else had ever done a similar project of telling his life story in song. The closest I can think of is John Lennon's Plastic Ono Band recording.

In any case, Mac was proud of his participation and the team that coaxed the tales from his mind onto note paper and guitar strings.

"I am very fortunate and thankful that I have a very good memory, going back to when I was four or five years old. But I can't remember what I had for breakfast."

Of the musical signposts through the decades, "I remember those things in detail. I tried to paint a picture of them I told to Thomm and Peter. . . . It wasn't no trouble at all. I just sat here and rambled right in my easy chair, and they came up with it."

Both of those men have told me that Mac didn't just sit there and recollect; he helped compose the songs as well. No, he no longer could capture music on the guitar because of the arthritis, but he sure knew how to keep track of the music being composed by the younger men.

Thomm and Peter later coaxed Mac to record a batch of songs whose lyrics his mother had written down from Great Depression radio broadcasts. *Songs from My Mother's Hand* is the magical result of that effort.

"In wintertime, when it was too cold to do anything outside, my mother would sit by the radio. She couldn't work outside, but she was there crocheting, quilting, and mending clothes," Mac told me during one of my many visits to his living room.

He said his mother always had a notebook nearby to capture lyrics from the broadcasts. It took many listening sessions for her to get each word right, but winters are cold and cruel in Crimora, Kentucky.

"I've got 13 books of her very legible handwriting that she copied off the radio. She used those composition books that we used in school."

I've held the notebooks filled with his mom's handwritten lyrics, and I love that album and the tired, tender voice. As I fingered through the collection of his mom's scribblings, I urged Mac and his two apostles to record another set. Such plans were afoot. Then, of course, he died.

As I sat there in Charley Pride's chair, I figured that Peter and Thomm surely plopped down in this chair more than once, at least when Charley wasn't around. Here they played their stringed instruments and matched melodies with the home owner.

Whenever I was at Mac's, it was the end of a journey that is strictly for that purpose: to see a friend. I called him frequently and have been invited to guitar pulls out here, but I didn't usually go because I didn't play an acoustic instrument and my voice fades to a gravel-coated whisper as the day wears on.

Usually, Mac just asked me to come see him. Or sometimes, I woke up and called to see if it was a good day to visit.

On this day, as I thought about Charley Pride sitting in the padded office chair I often scooted up to be close to Mac, I thought about others who have planted themselves in the living room of the comfortable little ranch house "out in L.A.," as Mac refers to the middle-class Nashville suburb of Lower Antioch.

I already mentioned Prine and his visits, Alison Krauss, "Whisperin'" Bill Anderson, Shawn Camp, Buddy Cannon, and radio great Keith Bilbrey. Other Music City singers and songwriters also have sat in this chair. They sought wisdom, came to raise cheer, or perhaps needed their own hearts lifted.

I guess I should talk about Prine a bit, as he won't be in this book much, though he may make another appearance or so. We'll see how it goes.

Prine, who fell to COVID, was something of a Mac apostle, and the two made a classic album, *Standard Songs for Average People*, a 2007 collection of their favorite country, bluegrass, and gospel songs.

"I Forgot to Remember to Forget," "Old Dogs, Children and Watermelon Wine," and "Old Rugged Cross" are just three of the songs on this album. I have two copies. One was given to me by Mac, the other by the late Al Bunetta, who ran Prine's O Boy Records and who relied on me and my wife for advice about adopting internationally after our own experiences.

That was back before Al Gore invented the internet, by the way. The 1995 adoption by Suzanne and me of our daughter Emily from a Romanian orphanage was documented in a sprawling feature essay I wrote that took up much of the front section of the late and lamented *Nashville Banner* newspaper, where I was number 2 in charge and also the columnist.

After that was published, we got calls from all over the country about the adoption process in the Third World that is (or was) Eastern Europe. Some folks followed through. Some were scared off by our honesty. Like I said, it was pre-internet, and a lot of hopeful grandmas clipped out the story to send to their sons and daughters who were having difficulty in the sperm-and-egg dance.

Dawn and Al Bunetta spoke with both of us at length, and they followed their hearts.

Their son, Juri, died in a car crash, but only after they'd given him a life he'd never have imagined in the orphanage in Riga, Latvia. They say he was a great kid. He was 19 when he died.

I'd guess Al Bunetta sat in this chair where Charley Pride sat. And I'd not be surprised if I was told Vince Gill, Garth Brooks, and Glen Campbell had sat out here, soaking in the wisdom of the amazing Mr. Wiseman. You could tell me Vassar Clements brought his old friend Jerry Garcia out here, and I'd not be surprised.

I'm absolutely sure Merle Haggard, one of Mac's best friends and a practitioner of the old-time flavors of country and roots music, sat here. My only encounter with Merle, other than seeing him onstage, was a conversation on the phone. But he was a good guy, and damn he could sing—and think. And, while they don't smoke marijuana in Muskogee, that Oklahoma town's greatest advocate rolled it like cigars.

As great as Merle was, he did not possess the great and flexible voice of a young Mac (listen to the vintage recordings), nor was Merle the best flat-top picker in the world. Oh, he was good. Lord knows mama tried.

Mac didn't brag about who came, and he treated everybody the same.

I'd like to say that Tom Petty, my favorite American bandleader, came out here when he was in Nashville because he was such a student of music. At an October 17, 1991, concert at the Starwood Amphitheatre, the outdoor concert shed that closed decades ago but that was within a couple of miles of Mac's house, Tom and the Heartbreakers snuck out of "Refugee" and "American Girl" long enough to do "Sixteen Tons." Tennessee Ernie Ford, who had nothing to do with Tennessee as far as I know, had turned that song into his signature tune. He had just died.

Tom, Howie, Mike, and the guys did the song as a serious tribute to Old Ern, who had died that day. Then they went backstage to smoke some really good weed. Nah, I don't know about that, but, after all, Tom once did proclaim, "Let me get to the point, let's roll another joint. . . . You don't know how it feels to be me"—or me.

Even so, I don't think Tom Petty or any of the Heartbreakers sat in this padded desk chair in the tidy suburban development within eyeshot—if the leaves were off the trees—of nearby Percy Priest Lake.

But I got there a lot. And it pleased me that I was using the same padded office chair Mr. Pride used during his recent visit to the comfortable home and garage I refer to as "Mac Wiseman International Headquarters and Mail-Order Service."

Janie Boyd, an amazing woman who abandoned her life in Virginia to move to Nashville and care for and love Mac, helped for years in the mail-order business that Mac ran from his garage.

There was no room in that "warehouse" garage for Mac's old Cadillac Fleetwood, so he just let it rot in the driveway until he convinced Peter to take it home (to mixed reviews from his wife and son but raising great joy among East Nashville mechanics).

Of course, one big difference between Charley Pride's visit and his roosting in this padded desk chair and my own is that I don't sing in public. Oh, I have the Petty, Beatles, and Kristofferson songbooks in my head, but I don't allow them to come out of my mouth unless I'm miles from civilization. The Stones and Dylan are there as well, Springsteen and Cash, too, and plenty of Mac.

I didn't sing even to a great friend like Mac because on this visit, he was thriving and enjoying life at age 90 and didn't deserve to be subjected to a singing voice that makes Kristofferson sound like Pavarotti. Instead, we chased the slanting sun by talking about old friends, the Country Music Hall of Fame, the CMA Awards, age, change, and the weather.

If one's mouth ever got dry, a bowl filled with Jolly Ranchers was always nearby.

"Yeah, Charley was right there. Came with Mel Tillis, just to visit," said Mac, whose own induction into the Hall of Fame, a body he helped establish all those years ago, came in 2014, much later than it should have and after Garth, Vince, and other acolytes had made the grade.

"I was very disappointed, to be honest with you, that I wasn't in the Hall of Fame earlier," he said, casting off a glowing smile (he always did) while discussing everything and nothing, two friends sharing company in the living room of his home in Lower Antioch, or L.A., as he referred to the fairly rural stretch in Metro Nashville-Davidson County.

Mac gazed across the living room, which even today is something of a museum.

You don't have to buy Mac Wiseman's memories. They are hanging on the walls, even the ceiling, of the living room. There he is with his quail-hunting dog, Spot, and with his quarter horse, Sugar Bob.

His adventures and his life spent as a country music troubadour are chronicled in other photos and paraphernalia. A guitar he could no longer play hung near the kitchen. So did a mandolin. I can imagine Ricky Skaggs sitting here trying out that instrument, but I doubt it ever happened.

I saw Peter Cooper take a shot at it once, and Mac tried to praise him. I thought it was good.

"You can see the lake from here," Mac said, nodding toward the backyard of his home on a cul-de-sac in a developed area of Nashville that was rural when he moved out here 15 or 20 years before.

He pointed to a poster on the wall that was for a show that included not just Mac but also Doc Watson, Bill Monroe, and Lester and Earl, a grouping of fellows who picked away at an arm of old-time country music until something called "bluegrass music" was born.

"That was the very first bluegrass festival, 1965, at Fincastle, Virginia, out on a horse farm near Roanoke," said this man who befriended everyone from Tubb to Haggard to a stone-sober Hank Williams, as I noted in one of the many stories I wrote about Mac, like the following incident I recorded for the *Nashville Ledger*:

> Hank was with us on a package show as we traveled from Minneapolis to Dallas. There was booze on that bus, but I never saw him take a drink, even when we were together on the "Hayride" down in Shreveport. I guess, Hank would just go off on a binge.

He allowed his one unspoken rule on package tours was that artists never cover a song recorded by one of the others on the bill. "I forgot and sang 'Six More Miles,' which was one of Hank's songs. When I walked off that stage, he said, 'I'll never sing that G.D. song again.' He wasn't mad. He liked the way I did it."

Guitar-playing country immortal Grady Martin, a kingpin of Nashville's A-Team of session players, was not shy about telling Mac where he stood in the flat-top hierarchy.

"One day I was standing in the parking lot of the Willie Nelson Theater in Branson [the country music mecca in Missouri], and Grady said, 'You know you're the best flat-top picker in the business, don't you?'"

The next morning, Haggard, who also was appearing in Branson, told his friend the same thing.

"After hearing it from those two experts, I was inclined to think maybe I was," says Mac.

Finally, the Hall of Fame agreed.

"I'm glad I got in."

Mac tapped his right leg. "Polio in this leg. Then I broke it twice, too." Those leg injuries came before Janie moved here and took over his care. In fact, if it weren't for her, this country music legend would have been just another crippled old man dying slowly in a nursing home.

She helped him thrive, fed him, talked to him, and loved him—mutual, obvious by the warmth of their eyes.

Mac enjoyed his role in various bands on the run during his career with Gibson in hand and his cares in the rearview mirror. He willed himself through the effects of his childhood polio and delighted thousands.

Then, after I began hanging out with him, he sat in his big chair, legs lifted, and shared his memories with me of guys like Charley Pride, Charlie Daniels, Merle Haggard.

He laughed when measuring his career against those of the young country stars. "Hell, I've been making my living in show business for 72 years. These new ones, well, they're lucky if their careers last six months after they release their first hit song."

He was far from angry. Life had been good to him, good enough that he celebrated Christmas year-round, as I noted earlier: Tree, decorations, and wrapped presents never vacated the living room. If you talked with him long enough, you could swear he may just be that famous jolly old elf.

Suddenly, he laughed.

"You know, I was managed for a while by Colonel Tom Parker [who guided the early careers of people like Eddy Arnold, Hank Snow, and that weird, pimply Presley kid from Memphis public housing]. Back then Davy Crockett was all the rage because of the Disney TV movies.

"Colonel Tom wanted me to dress like Davy Crockett in a coonskin cap and with leather fringe."

While Mac went so far as to sing the King of the Wild Frontier's theme song in performance, he wasn't about to resort to such gimmickry. His relationship with the colonel was done.

He shook his head when asked to define the music of his era.

"Real country music is like a slice of life. That's why it used to be so popular. It was about tragedy. Train wrecks, love affairs, drunken drivers."

Modern country is "so make-believe."

As the long conversation wound down, he said he'd outlived his contemporaries because "I rest well and eat properly. . . . I'm not in any hurry to go. I don't dread going. I just want to be ready when the bell rings."

I knew it was about time for that bell to ring in February 2019 when I sat by his bed at a nursing home and rehab center not far from his home.

His eyes still had that mischievous sparkle when he focused them on me as Janie pushed a chair up next to his bed for me to sit on. I don't think Charley Pride had used this one.

"Don't pay any attention to all the silly things I say, Tim," Mac said, his voice faint but firm, at least for a man who obviously was dying—no way out this time.

"I say such silly things because of all of this," he added, pointing to the intravenous contraptions as the oxygen tubes slipped from his nostrils.

Janie, his literal backbone, crossed the room at the rehab center where he'd been sent to die and told him, "Honey, you've got to keep those in your nose."

He let her adjust the tube with its prongs for each nostril, and then he looked back at me.

"Mac, when you get out of here, it's about time to begin planning your birthday party," I said. "Ninety-fourth, right?"

He nodded, his eyes focusing on me. His mind likely was conjuring images of his prior celebrations. I've been a part of them since 2015, when he turned 90.

We'd spoken many times, as I noted above, but I'll not easily forget the one where he invited me to that ninetieth bash.

I was someplace between Tupelo and Corinth, Mississippi, rolling on roads originally built by slaves through the cotton country at what I assume was an illegal speed when I answered the beeping phone.

"Tim, this is Mac. I want to make sure you come to my birthday party. It's going to be out there at the Texas Troubadour. I'll be 90. I'd sure like it if you could come."

We talked about a few other odds and ends, including what I was doing on U.S. 45 on a spring afternoon—I was picking my son, Joe, up from his one year in Starkville, home of a beautiful university (Mississippi State) and a good hamburger joint. Mugshots, that burger joint, was just across the parking lot from Oktibbeha County Jail, the place where the Man in Black and some pills came in contact with the sheriff and a jail cell. Johnny Cash may have thought it was better that Starkville was seen through speed-glazed eyes.

Speaking of Cash, his former daughter-in-law, Laura Cash (now White), was among the performers at the theater to salute Mac's ninetieth. I like her.

"I don't know what John Carter was thinking," said Joanne Cash, one of that young man's aunts whom I sat with. Johnny and June's son had a family with Laura before divorcing her.

I can't remember the rest in the large crowd, mostly Opry types, but I do remember Thomm Jutz on guitar and serving in sort of a producer's role and John Prine and others, lovers of the music and the man who was the guest of honor.

I got there a little late, bones and butt still worn from the Starkville run the day before.

Other birthdays have been held out in Lower Antioch, the guests mixing and mingling around the house, all taking their time to visit the guest of honor, propped up in the big chair.

So my reference to the importance of the upcoming ninety-fourth birthday did perk him up a little. Then he said it was time to rest. "Don't pay attention when I say silly things," he reminded me.

I just sat there at his bedside, waiting for him to rouse. I knew he wasn't going to make it to another birthday, but I figured talking about it seemed to cheer him up, so why not?

The problem was that when he came to, he looked at me, and in his head, I had transformed to his great friend John Prine.

Prine had visited Mac the week before, and I figured that I'd not correct him. I thought about singing a line or two of "Sam Stone," but my voice couldn't pass for Prine's. I also wish I could write songs like Prine. "Jesus Christ died for nothin', I suppose."

Mac's mind and eyes cleared, both shining, when he recognized it was me. Again, he cautioned me against holding his "silly" mutterings against him.

The next time I saw Mac, a few days later, IVs were unsuccessfully being used to bring him back from the brink of death.

Without really going into unnecessary detail, he spent the day hollering "Santa Claus . . . Santa Claus . . . Santa Claus" louder and louder. I figured it was because he wanted to get back to his home, where St. Nick and other Christmas decorations are on display year-round.

When Mac yelled for Tater (his late pal Little Jimmy Dickens) and his Uncle Henry, I figured this great musician, though technically alive, was celebrating seeing these people in the next world. I have to admit I was kind of happy for him that he was surrounded by his beloved in his final days.

Mac's casket paused—or really the workmen did—a moment before it was pushed into the mausoleum wall at about rush hour on a Wednesday, a few days after that visit.

Most of those who had jammed the funeral home down the hill in the historic Spring Hill Cemetery left after the service, which even brought a bubble of a tear, at least, to this old writer, who even in death considers Mac one of my best friends.

Malcolm Bell "Mac" Wiseman, or Dr. Mac Wiseman, according to a well-earned honorary degree, was celebrated in a manner he would have liked. Humor, music, a few slightly off-kilter comments, and tears (he may have not liked that) filled the chapel for a little over an hour.

Most of those who came for the celebration got there early enough to offer condolences to Janie, the loving woman who had saved his life as long as she could.

"I've got to see my baby one more time," said Janie after she hugged me and turned back to the open casket.

Mac's other relatives and close friends filtered through the viewing room. Keith Bilbrey, great radio voice, historian, and great friend of Mac, turned to me and said, "We've lost a great one, Tim. A great one. Thanks for what you do writing about these people." I love these people, Mac especially.

I stood a few feet behind Ricky Skaggs at the casket as he said quiet words, probably about Jesus, knowing Ricky. We exchanged warm greetings. He can be a good fellow. And Jesus is just all right with me.

I consider it an honor that I have had the opportunity to write about Mac and others of his generation, most of whom are dead. But Mac was special. As I noted earlier, I often called him just so I could feel better. Mac was like that. Also, he liked to talk with me—with everybody, I imagine.

Inside the chapel, the service began with Les Leverett, the classic photographer, who offered his thoughts on his long friendship with Mac. Les, by the way, bookended the service by offering the closing prayer an hour or so later.

Next up was Mac himself, a recording of his classic "These Hands," followed by prayer and scripture from Brother Kevin Rose.

Del McCoury, the gentleman of bluegrass music, performed "The Old Folks at Home," drawing a rousing ovation.

Usually, people don't applaud at funerals, but I've got to admit the stuff had me almost feeling like whistling along with the clapping.

The most touching, funny at times, and melancholy at times portion was the segment called "Personal Reflections" by Peter Cooper, whom I'm proud to call a truly loyal friend. There aren't many of those, by the way, but that's another story.

Peter sang Mac verses to carry along his tribute. He also provoked laughter and raised quiet tears all the way from the podium through the crowd. I know it was hard for him. He really loved the guy. I was proud of him as a friend.

Fiddler Laura White (formerly Cash, remember?) followed Peter with "Maiden's Prayer." If there is a nicer, gentler, more real, and amazingly talented woman in Nashville music circles, perhaps I'll meet her. Laura, by the way, went to the rehab center and performed solo concerts for Mac in his last, painful days of life. It is said he smiled. He smiled at me when I visited as well, but I couldn't play the fiddle or sing. I could just be a friend. That's all I've got to offer.

Ronnie Reno followed in the farewell with personal reflections, triggering laughs so hard that you would have thought Mac was in the room. But I guess he was, or at least that's what we are taught to believe. Mac did. A benevolent God, open to all humankind, was awaiting him.

Ricky Skaggs and the Whites performed "I Heard My Mother Call My Name in Prayer." Damn he's good. Probably won't like the "damn" there, but it's the damn truth.

The final song was performed by the greatest singer, the "voice with a heart," Mac singing lead on the Flatt and Scruggs number "Someday We'll Meet Again Sweetheart."

Afterward, I was going to leave and not follow the small procession of mostly relatives and, I imagine, fans up to the mausoleum, but that's the direction my old Saab ended up taking me for the final prayer and to join in a soft-voiced choir of mourners singing Mac's "'Tis Sweet to Be Remembered."

Stepping outside, I watched as they raised the casket up to its resting place in the wall. I watched as they sealed the wall behind it.

He was a friend. I loved him. And I decided I'd better get home before I started crying or cursing the skies.

Today, I call Janie once in a while out at the house in Lower Antioch. The pictures still are on the walls. Love still fills the house.

And the Christmas lights still sparkle year-round.

Dixie and Tom T. Hall

HAND CARVED IN DARK, Jamaican hardwood, the tall angel overseeing my writing every day has strands of bright red Mardi Gras
beads strung over her neck, at least in part because I figured
Tom T. and Dixie would have gotten a laugh out of it. I was smiling and
thinking of them when I strung the beads.

My son, Joe, tells me that it is wrong—that the beads and the angel
represent different things and that the saints of heaven are represented by
the angel. The only saints represented by the beads, even the ones shaped
like Tabasco peppers, are the ones who come marching in, accompanied
by the krewes of Indian chiefs and the naked women who swing out of
the bars and above the crowds wandering Bourbon Street. Those swings
that they ride with obvious pride are like the ones on Grandpa's tree when
you were young and innocent. There is nothing innocent about the naked
legs and breasts swinging above while trombones and garbage cans set the
night rhythmically afire. Oh yes, those saints.

Well, to me, Tom T. and Dixie always will be real saints of both the
festive and spiritual bents.

"My friends wouldn't mind it, Joe," I said, with a sort of laugh when
he fiddled with the red beads. Those friends' names are inscribed in a silver
Sharpie on the base of the angel. "To Tim from Dixie and Tom T. Hall,"
Tom T. wrote painstakingly while we sat in the small home behind his
mansion.

Tom T. gave the angel to me a couple of years ago when I was visiting
his house in Williamson County, just south of Nashville. He'd invited me
for coffee and, it turned out, to present me with this wonderful wooden
angel, a gift from his late wife and himself. I'm pretty sure Dixie bought

it while she and June Carter Cash shopped in Jamaica while the boys, pals Johnny Cash and Tom T., picked and lied at the Man in Black's vacation residence. Of course, they may have been enjoying beverages, as much as Tom T. liked beer, in song and in person.

I had been out to the Halls' Fox Hollow plenty of times before, but Dixie always had been there to greet me. This day, well, it was an angel from an angel.

The day of the visit described above was the first time I'd been to Fox Hollow since Dixie died on January 16, 2015. She had a long and painful battle with brain cancer, the stuff that even stole the humor that was in her soul and, of course, robbed so much of her husband's happiness. I had tried to support her with my love, but I had been told toward the end that I shouldn't call out there—too much death going on in Tom T.'s soul and, literally, inside the wonderful woman who completed his life. So I prayed (or my closest resemblance thereof).

Although I knew it was coming, Dixie's death angered me. I lost not only a friend but also, forever, her generous reassurance. Now I have an angel, at least a wooden one, depending on what you believe.

I realized on August 20, 2021, when a lonely Tom T. shot himself to death, that he gave me the angel, as he was leaving those who loved him and whom he loved mementos. I have friends, for example, who got guitars. They are musicians.

I got this magnificent angel.

I had been around Tom T. a few times after Dixie died, beginning with the day he gave me the Jamaican angel. While he was in reasonably good spirits, he had the eyes of the bassett hounds he and Dixie raised.

"Miss Dixie really loved you, Tim," said Tom T. as he pushed himself from a dinette chair and began scouting the flock of angels his wife had collected that were on the floor and shelves of the combination living quarters and music studio. The couple, due to their passion for bluegrass music, had transformed the little cottage, turning it into a place where great acoustic musicians could come and stay to make their mountain music. Dixie was one of the best composers of bluegrass songs, with something like 500 songs to her credit. She was pretty great as a bluegrass composer and greater still as a woman of style and grace.

Dixie even enlisted the writing skills of her husband after he "retired" from the world of being a country music star. He quit his famous "story-telling" country song production in 1986 and his performing around 1994. He had occasionally been coaxed down off the hill at Fox Hollow in years since but not often.

He enjoyed writing bluegrass with his wife because that music form carries sensibilities and volume that Tom T. could understand and even relish, he told me during one of my visits back when Dixie was Queen of Fox Hollow. Well, I guess she always will be Queen of Fox Hollow, finally joined by her king in death as in life, ever after, I suppose.

Anyway, I was talking about why Tom T. preferred the acoustic Appalachian sound. Remember how at the start of "Sweet Home Alabama," Ronnie Van Zant yells to the sound engineer, "Turn it up" (and he liked it so much that he kept it in the song)? Well, Tom T. would like to holler, "Turn it down."

"I got out of the business before the volume, quit because of the volume," he said sometime in the early 2010s. "They couldn't understand why we don't want to be The Rolling Stones."

The pseudo-rock of modern country, the stuff desired in redneck roadhouses and ignorant, hate-filled Confederate frat-boy saloons, wasn't necessarily to his liking, though he wouldn't say it. Not much of the modern world was to the liking of this great man, who spent his life on the hill, watching the sun going down.

"I don't watch TV news programs," he told me years ago. "I have no idea what's going on in the world. And I don't care. I'm too dumb to fight, too old to be an activist. I just like to stay out here and grow my veggies."

I never really believed that part, though, as he was a decades-long friend of the Reverend Will Campbell and former President Jimmy Carter, two great men who pledged their lives to activism and patriotism and the goodness of the human spirit. But I don't need to go back into that here. Just believe me when I say that Tom T. Hall was as patriotic and as much a humanist as those fellows. When he sang "I Like Beer," he probably included "Billy Beer"—the horrible swill peddled by Billy, President Carter's drunken, redneck brother, whom I'm glad I met one day. Funny, fat fellow shoulda stayed on the peanut farm, though, as he embarrassed Jimmy into lusting after rabbits or whatever.

On my first Fox Hollow visit after Miss Dixie died and before Tom T. rescued this Jamaican angel I look at every day, the Storyteller made us a pot of coffee. We sipped long and slowly, and as the morning wore on, he made some more, as much as we could drink.

As he fixed the coffee, I just looked around this tidy little bedroom/studio where Tom T. and Dixie allowed the great Appalachian-style musicians to stay for free (they paid only engineer's fees).

Bluegrass music does not sell in numbers big enough for the artists to stay next to Luke Bryan or Blake Shelton at the Omni, nor does it allow even the greatest among them to be famous enough that they can be spokespersons for white-linen nightclubs, beer, and Jockey shorts. It's unlikely you'll catch bluegrass artists on *The Voice* or *American Idol* or on what today passes for country radio.

"We are kind of patrons of bluegrass music," Tom T. admitted, quietly, of course, back in the summer of 2005, one of the many times I received the emotional lift that is the gift of visiting Fox Hollow.

As an example of the couple's bluegrass patronage, I remember a long-ago conversation I had with Dale Jett, a proud twig of The Carter Family tree who would come to Dixie and Tom T.'s studio to record, sleep, watch TV, and even cook meals (there's a full kitchen). Of course, he may not have had to cook at all, especially if Dixie was fashioning her famed fried chicken and biscuits to be eaten with her preserves.

My conversation (actually, there were a few because I really liked the guy) with Dale Jett came because I was doing a story on the combined Carter-Cash family and the branches that grew together thanks to that "Ring of Fire" love affair and marriage. I called out to the Carter Fold in Virginia, the headquarters of the first family of country music, to track down Dale. It may have been Dixie's suggestion, as a matter of fact.

Dale said, "It's real nice, what they do" (or something like that) as he described how he and his band Hello Stranger (you really ought to listen to this stuff; it's magnificent) would come to Franklin and stay in the tidy studio/home behind the Halls' antebellum-style mansion that crowns the hill in one of the loveliest spots in Middle Tennessee. If I recall it correctly, Carl Smith and Goldie Hill were neighbors before they moved south of Franklin, farther into the nowhere they sought.

The Halls were not Carter Family members, but they didn't fall far from that family tree. They were friends with the Carter family and with Johnny and June Carter Cash. So it really was almost a family affair when Dale and his outfit bunked in the little home behind the antiques-filled main house.

Dale is the grandson of A. P. and Sara Carter, two-thirds of The Carter Family that Ralph Peer first captured on record in Bristol. They, along with Jimmie Rodgers, recorded for Peer, who took the music to the world after the legendary "Bristol Sessions." It wasn't the birth of country music—this stuff long had been heard in the hills and hollows and the rail yards, slave-filled cotton fields, and sanatoriums and on the chain gangs in the South. But Peer did provide mountain music its first spotlighted exposure to the rest of the country.

I'm skipping through history here, but Dale was the son of Janette Carter. His aunt, Maybelle Carter, the other third of The Carter Family and the one who revolutionized guitar playing, "raised" Dixie after Iris Violet May Lawrence (Mrs. Hall's given name) came to the United States. Maybelle, whom I had the good fortune to meet at John and June's house and to see perform many times with her daughters and one granddaughter, is long gone, of course. But I mention her guitar playing above, and her instrument, considered one of the most important in history, is in a permanent display case at the Country Music Hall of Fame and Museum.

Her presence, benevolence, and loyalty established the circumstances that led to the eventual coupling of Dixie and Tom T.

The story began when Violet May Lawrence, a lovely young Englishwoman from the town of Sutton Coldfield (not far from Manchester, England), across the Atlantic Sea (that's just a little nod to fans of *Hair* who believe in Claude), met Tex Ritter, the singing movie cowboy with the barrel of a voice (listen to *High Noon*, for example), on a train in Europe.

Tex, father of the late actor John Ritter of such cerebral fare as *Three's Company*, convinced the young woman to promote his music in England. (John Ritter and Johnny Cash died on the same day, September 12, 2003. In many places, Ritter's death drew more coverage because of his friendly sitcom demeanor. Come and knock on my door, indeed.)

When Dixie began promoting Tex's music in England, she had no experience at that game, but she did well. She told *Bluegrass Unlimited* in 2013 that success was almost an accident. "I took some of his material over to EMI Records, and they wound up releasing 'Green Grow the Lilacs' and some other things. I didn't at all know what I was doing. I guess I found their address in the phone book, or I just asked until I found out."

And before long, she was in the United States, working for Starday Records and helping to promote David "Stringbean" Akeman, the Stanley Brothers, and others. Her best friend and mentor was Maybelle, also her roommate, since Dixie kept a room at the house of the legendary musician out in the Nashville suburb of Madison. The last I heard, Maybelle's granddaughter, Carlene Carter, who spent years running down her dream with her lover Howie Epstein and other members of Tom Petty and the Heartbreakers, was hoping to restore that old house. But I may have made that up, just thinking it should be true. Carlene is a great person, by the way.

Anyway, Dixie Dean—the name used by the young Englishwoman, promoter, and journalist—and Tom T. met at a 1965 BMI banquet in Nashville. She had come as Maybelle's "date," but the guy seated across the table from her was Tom Hall (yet to add the T., a subtle career booster, I suppose).

"It was the usual steak-and-potato thing," she told *Bluegrass Unlimited*.

They conversed a little bit, then "Tom said, 'Do you like potatoes?' And I said 'Yes, why?' And he said 'Is that why you're so fat?' And I was positively skinny."

It's said that Maybelle, who appreciated a good come-on, didn't think much of Tom's pickup line. But Dixie Dean thought it was "cute." She remembered that encounter when Tom offered to take her fishing when they bumped into each other at the annual Disc Jockey Convention, the predecessor of Fan Fair, which was the predecessor of the CMA Music Fest. (One of my favorite Nashville memories was sneaking into that all-industry event, then held at the Municipal Auditorium, to catch a private Loretta Lynn showcase; I believe it was in 1972. I escaped with an armload of crappy 45s being offered to the jocks by country wannabes.)

Anyway, when Tom Hall offered, Dixie took the bait, and the fishing trip was a go. "I jumped at the chance. I thought he was okay."

I looked around the little house and studio where Tom was serving me coffee. Dixie had moved out there to die because it was easier for her to get around, and Tom T. abandoned the big house to move back there.

I thought about the first time I visited this building. Well, the innards are all modern and sparkly, but back then, it was pretty raw, almost like a chicken coop.

That visit came at least 30 years ago when I had come out here to do a feature story to help Dixie and Tom T. promote the annual Christmas open house they held in their home, the benefits going to an animal rescue (I think it was called Animal Land) that she had founded down in Franklin as well as to the Humane Society and other animal welfare charities.

I called out there to see if I could visit and do a column for the *Nashville Banner*, where I was features and entertainment editor, to help promote this worthy "Christmas at Fox Hollow."

I admired her husband, but I have to say that her enthusiastic "Yes, come on out" won my heart, so I turned the rest of the day's operation over to my assistant, Jane Srygley, and drove on out to Fox Hollow.

That time, I didn't really know where I was going when I pulled in off the winding highway and onto the huge plot of farmland. Tom T., who knew I was coming to interview his wife, was riding a tractor across the level field that stretched into the distance at the foot of the hill that was crowned by the mansion. There was a dog on his lap, and others were following him. I think he may have been mowing, but I can't remember. The more I think about it, I'd guess he was probably just taking his dog out for a tractor ride.

Anyway, he directed me up the hill to the main house, where Dixie graciously met me. She gave me a tour of Fox Hollow, talking about some of its history, but mostly she wanted to talk about the topic that brought me out here. Animals were her passion—Tom T.'s as well.

By the end of the three or four hours spent there, she had taken me out into the back house—the building that later was refreshed and refurbished for the studio and musicians' quarters—where her jams and preserves lined the shelves. These jars of goodness were sold in specialty shops around the Nashville area, and the proceeds were given to animal causes. I think that if you went to the Christmas open house, in addition to paying admission for dog and cat charities, you also were urged to buy some of her stuff.

She gave me several jars (I can't remember which flavors), and she refused my offered donation.

I had been captivated by her on the phone, but once I met her in person, it took about two minutes for me to fall in love with Dixie Hall. Tom T., who had come up the hill for his lunch, helped me get the jars to my old Saab, then "directed traffic" to get me turned around headfirst downhill. Snow had fallen some, and he was worried that I might have difficulty on the slippery gravel.

They eventually quit doing that fund-raiser, but I continued to call Dixie over the years. If I called just to check in or to get some help, she would say, "Tim, you call anytime" (or words to that effect) in her British-hillbilly drawl.

For example, she was the first person I called when June Carter Cash died. I knew they were almost like sisters. I wanted to offer my condolences but didn't want to push her into talking about the death.

She wanted to talk, though, and we did. She said she was glad to talk to me about her friend.

So a couple years back, when I sat in the little house behind Fox Hollow, reassuring Tom T. that black is the way I always take my coffee, I enjoyed myself. But there also was pain, deep in my gut, as Dixie was the one who always made me feel welcome out there or even at a funeral. When I was at June's 2003 funeral up in Hendersonville, Dixie called me over as I passed through the narthex.

"This is Tim," she reminded her husband. "He's the one who has written such beautiful things. He's one of us."

Tom T. extended his hand. "Sure, I remember. Good to see you, Tim."

There were variations on that phrase whenever I checked in with Dixie.

"Tim, you are one of us," Dixie always would say when I apologized for calling "at a time like this" since she was one of the first people I'd call when someone died in the music community. I'd ask for a quote from

Tom T. (he was generally mournfully silent) and asked her who else I should call.

"Don't even apologize," she'd cut me off before going through her mental phone directory to come up with names and numbers.

"Tim you are one of us," she would repeat, what I consider perhaps the biggest compliment I've received in my Nashville career.

She meant that I was an artist, she told me, and that she could feel my words. I was, in her mind, a member of the showbiz family in Nashville. She grouped me right in there with guys who like watermelon wine, banjo pick *The Beverly Hillbillies*, or dress in black. Those were the "us" she was talking about. And "us" included an old newspaperman who found love at Fox Hollow.

Yep, I repeatedly was told by her that I was, in spirit at least, kin to her, to the Cashes, to the Carters, and to all the old-timers—including, of course, her husband, whose genius and soft artistic soul as well as his plainspoken honesty made him an American treasure.

I first was introduced to Tom T. via vinyl. I purchased his *In Search of a Song* album in 1971 when I was still living up north and doing some personal research into the most literate American songs. "I've always been a word man, it's better than a bird man" (or something like that), Jim "The Lizard King" Morrison said on "Curses, Invocations" on the *American Prayer* album. Even if you don't like The Doors, you'll probably like this spoken-word album, especially if your spirit feels at home on Desolation Row.

Anyway, I really didn't know who Tom T. Hall was when I picked that album out of the bin in the Ames, Iowa, record store that was pretty much downstairs from the apartment of a friend who was somehow involved in the Black Panthers and the Black Muslims. I can't remember much about those visits, especially how they ended, except the narrow stairs to his apartment on Welch Avenue came down pretty much next to the store that I think also sold sleds in the long, cold, lonely Iowa winter.

It was the cover of the album that drew me in. The singer stands next to a gentleman who is fishing in a stream. The liner notes by music journalist Bill Littleton were pretty sparse: "I went with Tom to write this liner note and, just by chance, took a small camera. The pictures tell more than words could, so, in support of the old saying that one picture is worth a thousand words, I hereby submit this as a sixteen-thousand and sixty-one word liner. Now listen to the record for eleven more pictures." The photos, mostly of the singer in various locations during a road trip to Kentucky, a cup of coffee, and a cigarette burning in an ashtray, pretty much convinced me that this was worth my $3. I already had been buying Kristofferson and Cash records, adding them to my Beatles/Stones/Dylan/Elvis/Cream/Who-heavy stash.

Unfortunately, generations of young people probably didn't know that the guy who liked little baby ducks, old pickup trucks, slow-movin' trains, and rain was even alive in the years after his performing retirement. And they probably didn't care. And basically, he didn't care if they didn't care.

Now, as far as I'm concerned, "I Remember the Day That Clayton Delaney Died" is an iconic highlight of country music. But for most of the younger folks, well, Florida Georgia Line is perhaps more relevant with such jewels as "Cruise," "Stay," and "Dirt," or perhaps they prefer clever stuff like Little Big Town's "Pontoon" and "Skinny Dipping."

I don't begrudge success, and these folks are delivering what people want. I mean, 20 years ago, I certainly could understand what people saw in Shania Twain—she didn't hide much of it—but it didn't make me consider "Man! I Feel Like a Woman" as high art. "That Don't Impress Me Much."

Anyway, all of this is to just my way of backing into a compliment or at least my own uneducated opinion that Tom T. Hall, who is best known probably by a rock version of his "I Like Beer" song as reconstructed for a stupid Super Bowl commercial (that I'm sure made him a lot of money), was one of America's greatest songwriters.

My favorite Tom T. song is one of simple loneliness and desperation: "It Sure Can Get Cold in Des Moines":

> I awoke in the evening from a traveler's sleep . . .
> My head and my eyes said "You should have slept more . . ."
> Outside it was 14 below

That's on *In Search of a Song*, and I could feel that song in my bones. As a guy who spent four winters of my life going to school in Ames about 30 miles north of Des Moines, this song not only rings true but also connects with the desolation in my soul. I won't go any further than to say I feel bad for the woman in the lounge and for the depressed singer who goes back to his room to write the song. It was 15 below by the time he got back up to his room. It probably was about that same temperature as I walked Welch to get back to my room in Storms Hall and use my always-sharp album-opening nail (on my left thumb) to slit the cellophane, shrink-wrap, or whatever you call the plastic protecting album jackets.

In weather like that, "Who's Gonna Feed Them Hogs?"

Of course, the volumes of great story songs, filled with wit and desolation, are plenty. *In Search of a Song* is just my first and favorite.

And then there are the "hits" that snuck on through to radio: "Old Dogs, Children and Watermelon Wine," "I Love," "Harper Valley P.T.A.," and "Faster Horses," among others.

I live in a town that relishes songwriters, many of whom are my friends. I know Willie Nelson a bit (nobody knows him real well). Kris Kristofferson is a close friend, though his great words are beginning to fade. Billy Joe Shaver lived in Texas and was known to shoot a guy in the face for apparently good reason, but he was really a soft and Bible-believin' man who wrote almost every bit of Waylon's great *Honky Tonk Heroes* album. (Troy Seals and Funky Donnie Fritts wrote the last song on that album, "We Had it All." Great song, but the album didn't need it. In fact, I think it weighs down Billy Joe's more heart-blistering, honky-tonk, beer-and-cigarettes imagery.) I mean, there's one in every crowd, for cryin' out loud; why was it always turnin' out to be me?

As far as other songwriters, I knew John Hartford a little bit before he died. Mickey Newbury and Guy Clark are special. I listen to Townes Van Zandt to cheer myself up. Don Schlitz may be the best songwriter around. I have had the treat of sitting in his office and hearing him play and sing from his songbook, which, most famously, includes "The Gambler."

Those fellows are just a few who changed the language of country music. "Crazy," sang Willie. "Help Me Make It Through the Night," sang Kris. And there may never be a better down-and-out song than Billy Joe's "Old Five and Dimers Like Me."

I told Kristofferson's wife, Lisa, that her husband was my Bob Dylan. That is spouse-pleasing hyperbole, but she knew what I was saying. Rita Coolidge, one of Kris's prior wives, said Kris was "country music's Hemingway."

I love the guy, and I can buy that comparison, but if Kris is the Hemingway of the genre, Tom T. Hall was country music's Mark Twain. Even in death, Tom T., who liked bourbon in the glass and grass (and maybe a dash of moonshine from the Reverend Will), knew how to touch your soul by borrowing from real life.

"Clayton Delaney" and "Des Moines" are two of the most powerful songs ever written. The trouble is, I guess, that most folks haven't heard them, too busy listening to modern country's poor man's REO Speedwagon sound, accompanied by exhaling smoke machines and frivolous fireworks and boob imagery.

Going out and experiencing life and then writing about it—like running into the sad woman in the bar during an Iowa winter—is pure journalism, sort of like covering a jumping-frog contest and making a piece of literature out of it.

One day, back when Dixie still was alive, I was out at Fox Hollow for a gathering that carried with it the possibility that I could interview this great man.

I think the Country Music Hall of Fame and Museum guys were out there at the house to talk about Tom T.'s pending residency at the Hall of Fame, where he was going to do three shows in the 400-seat Ford Theater.

Peter Cooper, then chief entertainment writer at the newspaper, said I should come on out. He, by the way, was given Tom T.'s well-worn "road guitar" by the man, his personal hero, who became his friend. Peter and his friend Eric Brace even gathered their pals in the singer-songwriter community to remake Tom T.'s immortal children's album *Songs of Fox Hollow*, retitling it *I Love: Tom T. Hall's Songs of Fox Hollow*.

It's a great album, with Cooper and Brace joined by the likes of Duane Eddy (my pal, thank God), Buddy Miller, Elizabeth Cook, my honky-tonk friend Jon Byrd, and my generous and kind compadre Bobby Bare.

They all got together to reproduce that album live, again at the Hall of Fame and Museum, and it was delightful. After that show, I was able to spend time with both Bare and Tom T.

But let's get back to the day I was at the home of the Halls with Country Music Hall of Fame hotshots. I hadn't planned on going. After all, Peter was there as a newspaperman in picker's clothing.

I changed my mind when Dixie called me with a special request. She said that there'd be Hall of Fame staffers and great musicians and that there was going to be a bit of picking and grinning as they worked out songs for Tom T's residency. Tom T. had told me he was going to "come out of retirement" for the three nights of concerts.

"Why don't you come out here, and while everybody's talking, you and Tom can go down to the barn to look at his paintings?" Dixie suggested, sort of luring me to call it a day at the office. "He really doesn't like just sitting around, talking about things like this. I'll ask him because he's never shown off his painting before."

She called me back to say he'd love to take me to his art studio, so while Peter listened to the Hall of Fame folks plan out the big program and the musicians picked and piddled while enjoying the smell of Dixie frying chicken, Tom T. drove me down the hill to a barn inside of which he did his oil painting. I had been hoping we'd ride on the tractor on which I'd seen him joyriding with his dog.

"I just wanted to show you these," he said to me, sipping coffee from a mug labeled "Retired" while waiting for feedback on his paintings of

Jimmy Martin, Bill Monroe, himself ("I had to do that as a part of my studies"), and his dog, Pal. My cat's name was Pal, I told him, and he assured me that was a great choice. Those paintings were joined by his own "impression" of Van Gogh's *Sunflowers*. Hall titled his version *Vincent*.

I'm no art critic, but I'd have been glad to hang one up in my living room.

The songs planned for the August 3, 2005, show—the first of three at the Hall of Fame—made up what was called *Tom T's Bio in Song*.

"They wanted me to do three or four concerts. I said 'I can do three,'" he told me. "That's my lucky number. I'll do three shows and get lucky."

The second show was to be titled *Songs I Wish I'd Written and Some I'm Glad I Did*. The final one was called *Tom T's Return to Roots*, a showcase for the bluegrass mastery that he and Dixie were brewing up in the studio and residence behind the house.

His love of the quieter musical form is showcased in his artwork. Not only are Monroe and Martin among his subjects, but he also did separate portraits of Earl Scruggs and Lester Flatt. "Look at this," he said, pushing the two paintings together, matching the backgrounds up to form one: "See, I can put Flatt and Scruggs back together." Laughter flashed in his eyes as he spoke of the iconic bluegrass music tandem bandleaders whose teamwork died in artistic differences.

"I never knew that the reason artists always say to have northern light is because that light never changes. It's there all year," he said, explaining the simple arc of the sun during the seasons that leaves the light from the north basically the same year-round. "That's why I have these windows."

Like the songs he had written, the art studio was as much about him as about his subjects. "I designed it after talking to artists. I call it my yard-sale studio since all the furniture is from yard sales. Miss Dixie loves yard sales, and I figured that was a good way to fix this place up."

His wife, by the way, talked him into this "comeback" at the Hall of Fame. "I'm doing it more for Miss Dixie than anything else," he said, nodding up toward his house, where the planning and picking and chicken frying was going on.

When we returned to the top of the hill and to the room in the main house where the musicians gathered, Miss Dixie asked me to stay for dinner—I couldn't that night, so later on, she sent me home with a breast and a thigh in a bag—and added that it took quite a bit of arm-twisting for her to coax Tom T. out of retirement for three nights.

Tom T. sat down next to me and grabbed his guitar, nodding toward the musicians and then offering them direction: "My ambition in this whole project is I do not want to take this grand opportunity to make an ass of myself. I have been very quiet and very gentlemanly for the last nine years." (That was the length of time since he'd retired to spend his life with Dixie and their dogs and the tractor.)

He also assured the gathered that they were picked to play because he liked to work with them. "We didn't pick you because of your talent," he said, laughing at himself as much as his gathered friends.

"When I got out of the business, I told them we play living room music. We don't want it cranked. And that's what we're going to play at the Hall of Fame."

He later told me he had nothing against the current group of country hitmakers other than the volume (as I noted earlier) and the fact that stars today "make too much money."

"I'm lucky to have lived here when the music changed from 'hillbilly music' to 'country music.'"

And in Hall's case, he used that music to tell tales of love, loss, depression, and joy, many chronicling his own experience. You can taste the cigarettes and whiskey when you listen.

"I was smart enough, or dumb enough, to write down things as I saw them," he said. "It's sort of stream-of-consciousness."

He added that the three-night stand would be his finale. "This is it. I'm not coming back. Once this is over, there's a very real chance no one will ever see me again.

"I want to get as much out of life as I can. I have already done the music. I want to maintain my integrity, my dignity, my quiet, my reserve.

"That's all euphemism for the fact I'm a loner. I enjoy my own company."

As I sit here alone in my basement office, I slip on the first Tom T. Hall album I bought back in 1971. It's in remarkable shape, even if I'm not.

"It Sure Can Get Cold in Des Moines" makes my soul shiver, as it brings back the melancholy of the cold and the loneliness as brutal prairie winds sweep across Iowa. It's my favorite Tom T. song, I admit to the only guy in the room. There is icy pain in my heart as I think about Miss Dixie and her kindness to animals and to one old journalist who loved her—and the fact I can't talk with her anymore. His musical vitality won't really allow me to say farewell to Tom T. It never will, I suppose.

Then I look at the Mardi Gras beads I placed on the angel from Dixie and Tom T., and the warmth returns. "I'm trying to clean out some of our stuff," Tom T. said when he carried the heavy wooden Jamaican angel to me, showed it to me, and then grabbed the Sharpie for the "autographs" of himself and his late wife.

"Dixie liked collecting angels," Tom T. said, nodding toward me. "She would want you to have this. She loved you."

He handed me the angel, and I thought about the wonderful woman who gave me those preserves so long ago.

"Tim, you are one of us," Miss Dixie said.

Tom T. walked with me through the freshly fallen snow, making sure I didn't slip as I got to the old Saab. I held the angel in both arms.

Waylon Jennings

WAYLON JENNINGS, DESPITE HIS rough-hewn and for a while (at least) cocaine-inflected image, was a kind and gentle soul. Oh, I didn't know him well. I will note our rare personal interactions later.

Here's a quick prelude. The best, most personal look I ever got into Waylon's soul was back in the early 1970s when I saw Willie Nelson, bandana around his still-lengthening hair and a smoke, obviously hand rolled, in his free hand as he pulled out of the driveway with the "Flying W" over the archway and just before the guard shack.

Willie took a left on Old Hickory Boulevard and then took a quick right, obviously heading for the nearby liquor store. I wanted to join him and Waylon that day but wasn't invited. By the looks, though, I probably could have dropped in. If I could do it over again, I'd probably follow Willie and see if I could be the last man standing around Waylon's pool on that summer day.

"There's one in every crowd, for cryin' out loud, why was it always turnin' out to be me?" is actually from the song "Honky Tonk Heroes," which is the title of my favorite Waylon album. And, since I've always been a word man, that line lingers in my head, and I'll be driving along and just spit it out as loudly as I can.

Of course, even in my head and giving myself the benefit of all doubts, there's no way that line, as sung by me, can possibly come within a hair of the goose pimple–raising voice of Waylon Jennings, who to many was the King of the Outlaws (even though Bobby Bare was the leader of the movement).

Waylon Jennings was a gentle soul with a rowdy image. In addition to possessing the lonesome, on'ry, and mean stare, he had country's most distinctive and powerful voice. RCA/PHOTOFEST © RCA

But beyond Waylon's masterful voice and fiercely independent character, there was a sweet man. Ask anyone who knew him well.

This story may be apocryphal, but I believe it.

Waylon, who lived in the previously mentioned walled estate just at the southern edge of Nashville near the intersection of Old Hickory Boulevard and Franklin Road, had taken on the task of watching after the widow of Hank Williams, Audrey.

She lived in a sprawling mansion next to a huge Baptist church about three miles away on Franklin Road. Hank never lived there, but their son did. It also later became the house where Tammy Wynette lived and died.

But that's not part of this story.

Audrey was sort of an institution in Nashville and was known for the parties she threw with the help of Hank's guitar player and Hank Jr.'s manager Merle Kilgore.

I don't know how it was that Waylon became Audrey's babysitter, but I kind of believe this story. He apparently dropped in regularly just to make sure the widow of every country singer's hero was doing okay.

Also, it needs to be noted here that Waylon had become something of a father figure to Hank Jr., taking him on the road with him, talking sense and nonsense. If anyone understood why Hank Jr. smoke, drank, and lived like the songs his daddy wrote, it was Waylon. Of course for Bocephus, it was, as he sang, "A Family Tradition."

The two men also sang "The Conversation" together, a fine guitar-driven rouser back in the height of the so-called Outlaw movement:

Waylon: Hank let's talk about your daddy. Tell me how your momma loved that man.

Hank: Well, just breakout a bottle hoss. I'll tell ya about the drifting cowboy band.

Waylon: We won't talk about the habits.

Hank: Just the music and the man, that's all.

I'm just trying to illustrate a bit of the closeness between Waylon—who really was a fine man—and the Williams family as I finish this story about one particular day when the elder singer dropped in to check on Audrey.

Remember, this may not be true, but I sure like the story, so I'll continue: Audrey answered the door in her bathrobe.

She let Waylon into the house, where he saw perhaps Hank's greatest songwriting acolyte—a long and lean fellow who would go on to make hit records and a lot of movies while carving out his own outlaw-like image on top of a privileged, finishing school–like upbringing—coming out of the master bedroom, pulling up his pants and buckling his belt.

"What [various expletives] are you doing?" asked Waylon, more than a bit irritated by the younger man.

"Well, Waylon, Hank did it," aw-shucked the younger man by way of explanation. If Hank done it that way, then it was plenty okay for the young singer-songwriter who wanted to be the next Hank Williams, he apparently reckoned.

I can easily imagine the disapproving glower on Waylon's face when he confronted the younger singer. He likely chased him out the door.

I'd encountered that disapproving look on Waylon's face more than once.

The first and most memorable time came a few decades ago when I did a regular column for the *Nashville Banner*, a fine afternoon newspaper that was killed when they sold it to the company that operates *The Tennessean*, which folded the *Banner* the next day.

When I was doing that column (I've done one similar at four different newspapers and in my blog), the basic modus operandi was that I'd leave the newspaper building (it used to be at 1100 Broadway, a downtown landmark, again sold to make room for shopping and condos) and walk out to the parking lot.

I'd climb in my old Saab and wander the streets and alleys of Music City, looking for a story about a common man. I've been known to park and just climb, uninvited, on a front porch or even over a farmer's barbed-wire fence when seeking out these American tales.

One day, I spotted a guy doing some auto detailing in a parking lot that adjoins the alley that divides 16th Avenue South and 17th Avenue South, bisecting what back then was legitimately known as "Music Row."

They still call it that, and city fathers have tried to emphasize that point by changing those street names to Music Square West and Music Square East, all in the name of tourism (there also are Music Square North and Music Square South, one-block streets that connect the two).

Those street names serve, I suppose, to tell tourists that this is the heart of the action, Nashville's version of Hollywood, even though so much of the music making has moved, particularly to nearby Berry Hill.

I would wander to different parts of Nashville, keeping my eyes open for something that seemed interesting. That led me, for example, to tell the story of a guy who sold turnips by the side of the road in Nashville or perhaps to a homeless woman, with "F-E-A-R" tattooed on her fingers, sitting on the sidewalk outside the Salvation Army.

I also stopped when I saw an older gentleman dressed as Santa Claus in the middle of the projects on one cold, pre-Christmas afternoon. It seems he went out to this crosswalk every afternoon to holler "Merry Christmas," scold the dealers, and make sure the schoolkids got across the street without being bothered by the toughs and their crack (the popular drug then). I stood with him while the throng of junior Super Flys swore at him and threatened him. What happened to them? Well, as Curtis Mayfield sang long ago, "Freddy's dead, that's what I said."

I stopped at the old barbershop run by Oprah Winfrey's dad as well as at the shop across what was renamed "Vernon Winfrey Avenue." The owner across the street didn't resent Vernon and his child. In fact, he told me about Oprah's visits to his shop when she was growing up in East Nashville.

Anyway, back to the guy doing the detailing. I don't recall his name anymore, but I do remember Waylon and his wife, Jessi Colter, climbing from their car as I spoke with the detail man about his showbiz customers.

I said hello to Waylon, who gave me that lonesome, on'ry, and mean glower. Maybe he'd have reacted better if I'd said, "Hi, Hoss." His wife, whom I got to know better later, was typically sweet.

"I've seen that look a million times," my friend Lisa Kristofferson told me once. "It's just Waylon being Waylon."

That's right, Hoss, and Waylon being Waylon produced what I consider a landmark country music/outlaws/rock album in *Honky Tonk Heroes*.

The album that really pushed country barriers into an amplified, driving musical world then presided over by The Rolling Stones is sort of a theme album about lovable losers and no-account boozers, with the songs written by Billy Joe Shaver, who I'm glad was my friend.

Don't cross him, or he'll shoot you in the face, I used to tell people. He was a very nice man, and *Honky Tonk Heroes* was his literary masterwork, as interpreted by Waylon.

The track "We Had It All" was written by my running buddy (until he died) Funky Donnie Fritts and his pal Troy Seals. I once went to the Exit/In, my musical hangout of choice a half century ago when it was a listening room, to see/hear Billy Joe—one of the great songwriters—sing that entire album front to back. I got there early enough to get two fingers of whiskey neat and a table in the front. At the table next to me was Waylon, his wife Jessi, and some other outlaws, cheering Billy Joe on.

Billy Ray Reynolds, mentioned earlier, who became a great friend but died recently, was among them, he told me later.

Anyway, that night, I said something to Waylon, whom I liked, and I think he liked me, but he gave me that on'ry look again.

"Well, was one in every crowd, for cryin' out loud, why was it always turnin' out to be me?" as Waylon sings on *Honky Tonk Heroes*.

My pal Peter Cooper, a historian and musician, argues with me that *Dreaming My Dreams* is the better Waylon album, and some late nights, I tend to agree. But more often than not, if I'm in a Waylon mood, *Honky Tonk*

Heroes is the album I pick. Almost a half century after its release, where does it go? The good Lord only knows. It seems like it was just the other day.

I also nearly made a big impression on Waylon one summer when I was speeding down Old Hickory Boulevard (my parents lived just off that road) when I went over a rise in the then two-lane blacktop road and saw a green Mustang convertible parked in the road in front of me, the two occupants talking and waving at Waylon's compound. I had the quick choice of either hitting them or leaving the road and flipping down a steep embankment on my right, rolling over and dying.

I chose the former, of course, and the young women's afternoon of sightseeing ended when my old Duster plowed into their Mustang. No one was hurt, and most of the damage was on my car and my psyche.

The young women, college swimmers, were kind enough and took the blame. But I had to go contact the insurance and the police.

I went to Waylon's door first, but no one answered. I had been pretty excited by the prospect of meeting him at the front door and asking to borrow his phone. "Sure, Hoss. Right this way," he'd say.

But no one was home, so I went across the street to Johnny Rodriguez's house, where I was allowed in to use the telephone.

"Waylon and I hung out," said Funky Donnie Fritts in a conversation we had for a 2007 story.

"We just hit it off. We were together a lot. We did some serious hanging out."

Keeping up with Waylon back then meant chasing the devil, fueled on cocaine. Donnie admitted doing that and thanked his religion and his wife that he made it out alive.

Waylon also cleaned up his life, but he didn't make it out alive, dying way too soon at 64.

Waylon had a number of maladies, but his body surely was not helped by his history of abuse.

But even though he was ill, he remained loyal.

In one of his last appearances, he made his way—thanks to the influence of his wife, Jessi Colter—to a fund-raising concert in January 2000 in Florence, Alabama, Fritts's hometown, to help pay some of Donnie's massive medical bills, including those for a kidney transplant.

Jennings was not healthy.

He was propped up by a cane, and as far as anyone knew, he wasn't going to perform—too weak and too feeble. He was just there to offer support and listen.

That was his plan, too.

But he couldn't be silenced.

He started out quietly enough, behaving himself when all sorts of Muscle Shoals (synonymous really with Florence) guys did their stuff and then when Billy Swan and Delbert McClinton performed. Waylon happily sat there and applauded (probably whistled, too). That's what most of the Outlaws did when cheering.

The big finale was supposed to be Kris Kristofferson. But the whole evening was made worthwhile when Waylon gimped onto the stage.

"Although I may be a cripple, I still know how to kick ass!" he barked good-naturedly before taking over the lead on Kris's "Help Me Make It Through the Night."

Waylon Jennings may well have had the best voice in the history of country music, and he certainly was the guy who opened the country doors to rock 'n' roll, which is fitting given his own roots with Buddy Holly and in Arizona bars.

I've offered up several other options of people to be considered as country's best singer in the pages of this book. My favorite singer really is Bobby Bare, but his favorite is Waylon Jennings. And since Bobby is my friend, I'll agree with him.

That's why Bobby first called RCA chief (and his own label boss) Chet Atkins after seeing this former member of Buddy Holly's band tearing up a Phoenix, Arizona, saloon stage.

Let's take a little sidetrack before I go on with Bare's recommendation that Chet sign Waylon.

Many folks who know the following story presume that Waylon was a Cricket since he played bass behind Buddy on his tragic, final tour.

Actually, Waylon wasn't a real Cricket, just a member of Buddy's band after the Crickets dissolved due to some internal drama. Buddy had asked his old friends, Waylon and rockabilly/swing cat Tommy Allsup, to back him up on the Winter Dance Party Tour, which began on January 23, 1959, in Milwaukee, Wisconsin.

Waylon later said the only reason Buddy was even on that tour—along with J. P. "Big Bopper" Richardson and Ritchie "La Bamba" Valens— was because he was flat broke.

There were problems with the buses from the start. And after a February 2 show in Clear Lake, Iowa, Buddy decided to charter a plane for himself, Waylon, and Allsup so that they could fly to Fargo, North Dakota, instead of taking that long, cold bus trip.

Richardson, who was fighting the flu, asked Waylon for his seat. And Valens won a coin flip with Allsup, winning his seat.

It's reported that when Waylon told Buddy he was going to take the bus, Buddy said something like, "Well, I hope your bus breaks down."

Waylon's retort: "I hope your ol' plane crashes."

Of course, it did crash that night, "The Day the Music Died," according to Don McLean, and Waylon blamed himself.

"God almighty, for years I thought that I caused it," Waylon told CMT in an interview that touched on that crash, which occurred just six miles from the Clear Lake airport.

I'm sure Waylon got as tired of talking about that as he later did when all interviewers wanted to peg him as the King of the Outlaws and all he wanted to do was pick and sing.

Anyway, back to Bare's phone call to Chet. There really aren't too many people in any business who would want to bring the boss's attention to someone who could compete for their job. In Bare's case, he was pitching his boss on a singer who had the same rough-hewn and world-weary voice and attitude as his own and a commanding stage presence to match.

Bobby actually was trying to get Chet to pay attention to and sign obvious commercial competition.

That he made that call says countless things about Waylon's talent—and about Bobby's self-assured humility.

Few folks could get away with singing Bare-style songs except Waylon (and vice versa).

This is as good a place as any to mention again that Waylon, who got the most publicity as the "leader" of the so-called Outlaw movement, really was only following in Bare's footsteps there as well.

Oh, I know he was, as I said earlier, the King of the Outlaws, at least in the public's perception.

But it really was his pal Bare who started that movement.

Bobby had stepped away from the RCA and Music Row record assembly line to record his classic collection of his pal Shel Silverstein's songs *Lullabys, Legends and Lies*. He was tired of always trying to match or one-up his classic "Detroit City" for the bosses. So Chet gave him the go-ahead.

That little revolt actually inspired Waylon to go to Chet and say, "Well, Bare did it. I want to, too." He was given his artistic freedom and came back with *Honky Tonk Heroes*.

There is no need to review the history of that Outlaw movement here, but it eventually became the marketing scheme for Music Row, at about the time Waylon sang, "Don't you think this Outlaw bit's done gotten out of hand?"

And there is my preferred version of that song, an obviously weary lament on a life typecast: "Don't you think this Outlaw [expletive rhymes with "bit"] has gotten out of hand?

"What started out to be a joke, you all don't understand.

"Was it singin' through my nose that got me busted by the man. This ain't it. This Outlaw bit" [or the rhyming expletive].

Of course, it sounds perfect in that rich snarl of a voice, as distinctive as any in any form of popular music. Still, Waylon, Willie, and the boys were pigeonholed from then on.

And Music Row execs and other chameleons were exchanging tailored Italian suits or rhinestones for blue jeans and work shirts and scuffed brown cowboy boots.

Waylon's voice had a range and natural snarl, authority that turned the almost pointless "MacArthur Park" into a Grammy-winning masterpiece. I mean, really, who cares if someone left the cake out in the rain—unless it's Waylon who's telling you about it? Richard Harris, the actor, previously had a hit from the Jimmy Webb song, but those of us who "were cool" pretty much ignored it.

You couldn't ignore Waylon's version.

Back when Waylon died in 2002, I had to participate in the coverage of his death. I was entertainment editor still, I believe, and the job of turning out the major obituary on Waylon had to fall to senior music writer Peter Cooper, who then was a journalist before assuming prestigious work at the Country Music Hall of Fame and Museum.

We had two editions of *The Tennessean* back then. The first one, the state edition, had to clear the copy desk by 8 p.m. or so in order to get it printed, baled, and loaded up into trucks for delivery outside Nashville.

Many of the stories in that edition were those that made only the city edition, which people in Nashville had gotten that morning and which had cleared the composing room floor around midnight the night before.

The news copy desk would take the stories that were only in the city edition that morning, change time elements, stack on new headlines, and fill up the early pages of the state edition. Early breaking news did make it on the section fronts of that edition, and everything pretty much was done over again for the city edition.

Peter and his music-writing sidekick Craig Havighurst, a lava-lamp enthusiast (you should have seen his desk or the look on his face when the lamp malfunctioned), began working toward the Waylon obit for the front page of the city edition.

Peter had a lot of the information on hand and already had begun crafting the obituary. After all, we knew that Waylon, who was only 64, had not been well.

In addition to pulling together the facts of Waylon's death (his life already was chronicled in prewritten information), Peter and Craig had the task of gathering reaction from the music industry.

Their goal was to craft the lead story that would greet Nashvillians when they walked to the curb to get their newspaper. (I know, no one walks to the curb now; it's mostly to the computer.)

It was a good lead paragraph, too, that greeted readers grabbed by the headline: "Waylon Jennings: 1937–2002" streamed above "Country maverick made music his way."

Then it read "Waylon Jennings, whose powerful, resonant growl was capable of spirited boisterousness or soulful balladry, died yesterday at his Chandler, Ariz., home after a long battle with diabetes. He was 64."

That story was a work in progress during the evening of February 13, 2002, the day of his death, so there would be a full accounting of his life by the morning of February 14.

I have recently read it over again and consider this obituary to read pretty much like poetry, maybe with a gruff Waylon edge on it. Mainly Peter (but Craig and I as well) had delivered a good product for our city-edition readers.

But, of course, most everyone knew that Waylon had died that day, and while work was ongoing for the front-page centerpiece of the final/city edition, it was decided that we needed to crank out a short story for the earlier state edition, something to let our readers out in the hinterlands know that we actually were aware that Waylon Jennings had died. Can you imagine Al Gore out in Carthage, Tennessee, picking up *The Tennessean* and finding out nothing about the death of the greatest Outlaw? I mean, it wasn't hanging chads, but it surely would have angered him into using words that would anger Tipper, his censorship-crazed wife at the time.

So while the other fellows toiled on the clock to create a masterpiece, I launched into a quick obituary, filling in musicians' reactions, for the state edition.

Most country musicians offer their reactions not straight to the writer but rather filtered through their press agents. So other than the facts of his death, I wasn't having a lot of luck making my calls. My old source, Chet Atkins, was gone, and I couldn't get through to many others.

That's when I called Ramblin' Jack Elliott, the beat-era legend, who then was living in San Francisco. I can't remember how in the world I knew Ramblin' Jack, who sort of was the court jester on Bob Dylan's Rolling Thunder Revue tour, but I knew him and had his number, and I knew he liked me for some reason.

I did know that Ramblin' Jack and Waylon had spent time together, likely singing through their noses together in Manhattan, where the great Outlaw was a huge nightclub draw on the scale of, say, Tony Bennett, Miles Davis, Liza Minnelli, or even Dylan.

Ramblin' Jack's contributions were pretty much folded into the main obituary story when Peter finished that for the city edition. And I can't find in the archives a copy of that first edition, the short statewide version of the story. They likely went to the expense of archiving only the "final," or city, edition.

The main thing I remember about my first-edition effort is when Ramblin' Jack said his friend Jennings didn't just sing a song. "He took every song, and he Waylonized it," he said more or less. Like I said, who else could make you care about a cake left out in the rain?

Of course, as I've noted, there were flaws. We all have them. Waylon and Jessi's son, Shooter, talked about reliving his dad's lifestyle in a story I wrote for the November 17, 2005, edition of *The Tennessean.*

I was talking to Shooter about portraying his father in the Oscar-winning John and June biopic *Walk the Line.*

Shooter's dad and Cash, best of friends, "enjoyed" their lives as roommates and running mates.

"What was really cool for me was experiencing the whole thing. It means a lot to be in it. Johnny did it, and my dad did it. It's just a historical piece," said Shooter, noting he was leaning back on a lounge chair on his lawn in Southern California as we spoke.

"Being in a scene where Johnny and Waylon had an apartment together. Beer bottles, cocaine, and pills all over the place . . . to kind of have that period of their life reconstructed before you like that made me realize how not far from my own life, how my own apartment looked like a few years ago.

"You see in the movie that these artists are just people. You don't think about their apartments being messy and their lives not together. But they are just people."

The number 1 comrade in "Waylonizing" everything, not just songs but life in general, was Billy Ray Reynolds. I had the opportunity to spend time with him for a story I did on old Music Row for the June 14, 2019, edition of the *Nashville Ledger.*

We also spoke frequently thereafter, right up until the week before he died on November 29, 2019.

He was "settled down" in his hometown of Mount Olive, Mississippi, after the years of self-inflicted damage from running with Waylon and his roommate Johnny Cash, Funky Donnie, Cowboy Jack Clement (who produced *Dreaming My Dreams,* the Waylon album that Peter Cooper argues is better than *Honky Tonk Heroes*), Harlan Howard, Kristofferson, Billy Joe Shaver, Roger Miller, and my friend, crazy radio deejay Captain Midnight (Roger Schutt), who apparently was quite a knifeman.

Billy Ray's happy retirement in his hometown was pretty much punctuated by trips to the dialysis clinic.

A guitarist for anyone who needed him but really a fixture in Waylon's band, Billy Ray still visited Nashville right up until the summer before he died, but it always left him feeling empty and sad.

"Music Row is gone," he said when we compared his alley-running days with Waylon and Willie and the boys to today's soulless corporate version on streets where Italian suits again are back in style.

Of course, Music Row is physically here and evolving, but the place of myth, of Hillbilly Central, of all-night pinball at Bobby Bare's office, is at the very least comatose.

My friend Bare, not really a carouser, would leave Waylon and Captain Midnight to their games and go home to sleep while they rolled quarters into that bingo-like gambling machine or took breaks to have knife-throwing contests.

"We ran the blocks day and night," said Billy Ray, 79. "I'd go home and get a nap, and I couldn't wait to get back to Music Row."

One night, while running the blocks with Blue Moon Boys drummer D. J. Fontana, he ran into everybody's hero, Elvis Presley, arriving at RCA Studio B, where he did most of his recording. He rode in a Cadillac Fleetwood. "He was just the most awesome sight. I thought he was like a Saudi prince in this suit, with a sash over it. It was real eccentric."

Fontana had spent years as Elvis's drummer, so he wasn't awed. Billy Ray was basically breathless.

I'll have to add that I really liked Billy Ray. And I told him that there was a time in my life, in the early to mid-1970s, when I wandered those alleys. I didn't meet Elvis, though, but I did get to meet the Jordanaires and some Memphis Mafia fellows outside RCA.

"We actually figured the beginning of Music Row was Lower Broadway: Demon's Den, Linebaugh's, Ernest Tubb Record Shop, Wagon Wheel, Tootsie's," Billy Ray added. "Tootsie would close up at 3 a.m., and we'd go to Willie's house in Ridgetop and jam until 8 or 9 a.m. We'd go wake Eddie Cochran up at 3 a.m. It was a different world"—a special fraternity.

"I'm not a drinker. I get drunker on a Coke than most people would get out of a jug of alcohol. I was running with Waylon and Johnny Darrell and Faron and George. The Tally-Ho was one of the nastiest places in the world. It was a dump. The floor was crumbling. The chairs were broken. We all would be playing our songs," Billy Ray said.

"Anywhere they could find a pinball machine, they'd play 24 hours a day. Tompall [Glaser] would be drinking. Waylon would do whatever he did.

"It wasn't hard to stay occupied. We were all crazy and having a ball. It was a great life, always looking for the next thing. . . .

"I knew all these people, and I loved them dearly," he said as we spoke about everyone from the Outlaws to the music execs to the Opry stars who found pleasure, business, and cocktails on Music Row.

"Back then, you could go into any session you wanted to go, not invited." Who knew when a guy would be asked to add a guitar line or a rhyme?

"Back when we were touring, Waylon would tell me, 'Go out and do three or four songs and call me up.' We had a great band."

Billy Ray, a fine entertainer, would get things going, occasionally glancing offstage, waiting for Waylon's appearance. "Then I'd see him over in the wings, and I'd introduce him: I'd say 'Now, ladies and gentlemen, meet the greatest singer in the world,' and Waylon would come out."

Billy Ray grew solemn for a moment, recalling that after Waylon died in 2002—the funeral conducted by my friend the Reverend Will Campbell and sparsely attended by Outlaws and Highwaymen—he physically helped carry the great singer to his grave site.

Before saying good-bye to his friend and mentor, Billy Ray quietly repeated that same stage introduction across the lonesome Texas field, hoping that God, not just the wind, was listening.

"Now, ladies and gentlemen, meet the greatest singer in the world."

Grandpa Jones

THE OLD-TIME PICKER AND GRINNER who gave me the directions to his wooded oasis when I called that morning had told me to call his house when I got to the small grocery nearby.

I can't remember the market now, and it's probably changed over the years, since Grandpa Jones has been dead since 1998.

From what I know of Grandpa—and I spoke with him several times over the years but visited him only once at his home, really a rustic and sprawling gentleman's home, constructed in part from the logs of a 200-year-old barn—he likely passed away in the peace he sought throughout his life.

Grandpa didn't die in blood-soaked terror like his best pal.

It was the friend he drove to work at the Opry and for *Hee Haw* tapings, his partner in this wonderful spread of land that belies the urban mess of Nashville a few miles to the south. David "Stringbean" Akeman and his wife, Estell, who lived over the rise from Grandpa and Ramona, lived in peace. But they didn't die that way.

Stringbean and his wife, who had moved out to the property in Ridgetop, where they shared massive acreage with the Joneses, died 22 years before my visit. I had met old String only once, when I "crashed" a gathering of *Hee Haw* performers outside Nashville's Channel 5, where it was taped. I had seen him at the Opry plenty. Stringbean was not wearing his stage costume as far as I can remember, and I probably would remember, considering he always wore the long nightshirt and short jeans that he belted at his knees. He was a helluva banjo picker, but he also was an entertainer—and a gentle soul.

"Me and him hunted a lot together," Grandpa told me of his friend, who lived pretty simply, though he and his wife did have a color TV. "We were going grouse hunting that morning.

"I went over to pick him up. That's when I found 'em."

The Akemans were slaughtered by two greedy thugs who thought the simple fact that Stringbean believed in "cash only" meant that he and Estell had untold wealth stashed in their home. It was not (and may still not be) unusual for musicians to deal in cash, by the way. It's the nature of the business. Stringbean didn't believe in banks. But he wasn't wealthy either.

The killers, who ignored Estell's pleas for life after they had shot her husband, got away with a chainsaw and some firearms, including a rifle Grandpa had given to his pal.

As a side note, one of the killers (they were redneck cousins) died in prison. The other one was paroled a few years back, much to the protestations of the old-time music community.

My now late pal, Country Music Hall of Fame bluegrass and country hero Mac Wiseman, spoke about his opposition to that parole in a story in *The Tennessean*: "I fully believe the Good Lord forgives us for our mistakes," he said, adding that the parole board, however, "don't have the authority, spiritually or otherwise, to forgive that man, I don't think."

Grandpa and Stringbean were planning a day's pastoral pleasure on the 140 or so acres that contained both the men's homes, hunting, talking, and maybe a little hee-hawing as they wandered with their rifles in pursuit of the grouse. I read someplace that #6 buckshot is preferred for grouse. I don't know since I don't hunt. I have been known to grouse, though.

Of course, to country gents like Grandpa and Stringbean, a part of the reason for acreage is the ease of harvesting wildlife. Grandpa told me it relaxed him. When I talked with Grandpa on the day I spent at his oasis, I purposely did not get into the Stringbean murders. Finding the bodies of his best friend, his comic sideman, as well as that man's wife still reflected hollow in the eyes of the Grand Ole Opry star and roots and gospel music legend.

"It was just up there, over the rise" or "up the hollow." I can't remember which phrase he used as he pointed from the front yard of his house, across the stream that roared through its stone-hewn banks, and off into the horizon, toward the spot he found Stringbean and Estell.

Where Grandpa still could see his dead friend in his mind's eye as he looked into the distance I could see a few daffodils. Dogwood blossoms punctuated the forest that was just then filling out.

I said a while back that when Grandpa died, it was probably in relative peace, at least as compared to his buddy's heartless slaughter.

Peace? Well, there was no gunplay involved. But there was a mortal struggle, and he didn't give up without a fight, that's for sure. In fact, he lingered. He suffered two successive strokes moments after a January 3, 1998, Opry performance and died more than a month later on February 19.

This great showman, who on the spring day of my visit was really looking forward to things cranking up in the summer, when Opry crowds grow and when musicians are generally busier, died doing what he loved: playing on the *Grand Ole Opry* radio show.

That was back in the era of the Opryland theme park—a delight that died because developers wanted an ugly mall where gang members could have a place to hang out instead. The old-time country stars like Grandpa performed on the stages at the park.

And they also just hung out there if the weather was nice. When the so-called King of Country Music, Roy Acuff, was ailing before his November 23, 1992, death, I wandered out to the park.

Actually, I was there with a purpose. I'd called Charlie Collins, Acuff's guitarist and a gentle soul I'd met previously, to see if he wanted to talk about his ailing boss.

I got to sit down in Acuff's dressing room, the one closest to the Opry stage, where Charlie played a bit of guitar for me.

He then led me out onto the stage, where I stood in the six-foot circle of wood that had been cut from the Ryman stage when the Opry moved to the suburbs.

Charlie stood next to me, pointing out into the empty Opry House, and explained how much his boss loved it here, how he loved looking out into the thousands of faces filling his view. The love, of course, was mutual, a type of deep affection that probably no longer exists between the newer generations of Opry performers and the fans.

"Who is or was Roy Acuff?" the fans of current Opry stars Kelsea Ballerini and Dustin Lynch would likely ask if the name ever came up in conversation.

Today, this guy whose trademark was flashing around a yo-yo and singing "Wabash Cannonball" while peddling Martha White self-rising flour or whatever is basically forgotten. "The King of Country Music?" they might ask. Isn't that Luke Bryan?

I've interviewed Luke before and like him, but, of course, he's more the king of great marketing with an engaging smile and the ability to sing frat boy–friendly tunes.

But Roy Acuff *was* the Grand Ole Opry. He even lived in a house on the Opryland grounds. And other than the fact that he seemed to go over-board when singing the praises of Richard Milhous Nixon, who escaped

Watergate scrutiny for a day by coming to the new Opry House and playing the piano, he seemed like a nice guy. He probably believed Nixon's "I'm not a crook!" and "Peace with honor" mantras.

On the day I spent with Charlie Collins, he was very worried about his boss. And he also wandered around the park grounds with me. We sat down together on a bench, only to be joined by Johnny "Act Naturally" Russell and the fully glittered Porter Wagoner.

I can't remember if the latter, the man from West Plains, Missouri, was performing that day, as back in park days they did offer short Opry-style concerts in the arena during the day. It got tourists out of the heat and got them up close with their heroes. Since he was in full Nudie regalia, including the rhinestone cowboy boots, I'm sure he was on deck that day.

Porter was a good guy who helped me tell stories about himself as well as his friends, like Tater Dickens and George Jones.

Johnny Russell became more of a friend, especially after I helped him secure a meeting with Ringo Starr (the former Beatle was in Nashville for a show at the Arena), who had made "Act Naturally" a rock hit for the Fabs. "Act Naturally" had appeared in different places in The Beatles canon, as back in the early days, British and American releases didn't match up. It was on the flip side of "Yesterday," however.

Ringo and I chatted about the old Buck Owens and the Buckaroos signature tune on one of the occasions I was lucky enough to speak to a Beatle.

And, in one of our conversations, Johnny, who cowrote the song with Voni Morrison, told me he'd really like to meet Ringo.

Johnny was not really very well. But working with his family, I helped the two men get together before the big concert by the All-Starr Band. It should be noted that Ringo's version was one of his key contributions to The Beatles' touring sets, and he also recorded a duet with Buck Owens, whom I was never lucky enough to meet, though I did talk to him on the telephone. Oh, and I've seen the All-Starr Band a few times, and every time, this song brings the aging crowd to its feet.

Of course, that's a lot about the Opry, but Grandpa was one of the most beloved performers, and though the old radio show is a lot more glitzy and digital today, it isn't really the heart of country music as it was back in the twentieth century.

Anyway, when I pulled up to Grandpa's house, after checking in, as instructed, from the phone in one of those little half booths fastened to the side of the market where he told me to stop, he was waiting in the yard. And he was smiling broadly.

We went into the home, where he introduced me to his wife, Ramona, a kind woman. They offered me some refreshment (I think I chose water over buttermilk), and we sat down in the front room of the house. Grandpa, I've been told, loved his buttermilk, as, I'm sure, did Ramona.

Grandpa Jones was in a reflective mood as he talked about all the country stars who had gone before him.

"When I started [at the Opry], [Cowboy] Copas, Minnie [Pearl], all of 'em were there," he said. "Me and Bill Carlisle and Bill Monroe are about all that's left. Brother Oswald's the oldest now."

"Bashful Brother Oswald," resonator guitar master and Acuff sideman Beecher Ray Kirby, died in 2002. He, like Stringbean, was a colorful, almost vaudevillian sort of character with a batch of wisdom. He had been the last living member of Acuff's original Smoky Boys when the "King of Country Music" died.

Jumpin' Bill Carlisle, who in bittersweet irony spent his final years performing propped up by a walker but still driving crowds crazy, died in 2003. He never gave the crowd less than his very best.

Monroe, the true "Father of Bluegrass Music," died in 1996 and has not been replaced. I met him only once when I stopped at a market for some smokes and a Coke after spending the afternoon with Patsy Cline's widower, Charlie Dick, who became a friend. "Big Mon" was riding in a black (I think) limo, and he had his driver stop at the market. Can't remember what he bought, only that a nice-looking middle-aged woman sat close to Monroe in the backseat.

Of course, all these greats were alive back when I went to see Grandpa, and on that spring day in 1995, he seemed to brighten when he talked about his own popularity and longevity at the Opry.

"Heck, sometimes you wonder why they still got me out there. I'm sure glad they do. I love to work."

He told me he was going to learn a few new songs before the summer season arrived, although he nodded with a smile that it wasn't a priority. After all, there were new audiences every night.

And besides that, I pointed out, they want to hear Grandpa Jones do the songs that are familiar to him and to the crowd. "Mountain Dew," "Jonah and the Whale," and my favorite, "Ole Rattler":

> Rattler was a good old dog as blind as he could be
> But every night at suppertime I believe that dog could see . . .

Grandpa admitted that a lot of his popularity was from his recurring appearances on *Hee Haw*, the country variety show, a cornpone version of the popular TV satire show *Rowan & Martin's Laugh-In*.

The most popular of his skits on that country-fried blackout show had the cast asking him, "Hey, Grandpa, what's for supper?"

His response changed each week. For example, "Here's what's on the menu tonight: tender ham hocks cooked with wild greens, and a dish o' 'taters and a dish of brown beans, and blackberry wine, a glass for each plate, an' apple pie for dessert, I can't hardly wait."

Or, "Junior Samples is a-comin' to eat, so I cooked 200 biscuits and four hams of meat, half a bushel of beans, an' fried apples and stuff, an' three gallons of coffee, I hope that's enough." (TV.com has seasons' worth of his menus if you are interested in what he was having for supper on those episodes.)

The wonderful and still beautiful Gunilla Hutton, one of the "Hee Haw Honeys," and I were talking about that show a few years ago as she drove across Southern California. The subject of Grandpa inevitably came up.

"He was the sweetest person in the world," she said. "He couldn't have been further from show business. He and Ramona, they were these salt-of-the-earth people. He was sly. He was funny. He'd get one of those cute little giggles. We all adored him. You just had to hug Grandpa when you saw him."

On our visit, though, Grandpa and I didn't talk that much about *Hee Haw*, but he did mention his joy that younger fans were discovering down-home country music thanks to that show.

"I want to show you something," he said as he led me from the living room of the cabin. I told Ramona that I may not be coming back into the house before heading down to Nashville, so I wished her well.

But he stopped shy of going right outside. Instead, he raised his flannel-covered arm toward the den window.

"See that sprig out there? That's from a maple tree by the lake where that poet, Thoreau, wrote Walden Pond."

He'd purchased the tiny maple from folks who were attempting to save Thoreau's lair from developers. And he was proud of it.

A poet himself, Grandpa led me out to that tiny maple jutting from the edge of a daffodil bed.

"I just love trees," he said, looking from that sprig and toward the dogwoods and budding maples. "Love these woods."

He told me we could walk a mile from where we stood and still be on his land. And he liked it fine.

Sure, as a lifelong traveling troubadour, countless miles spent in the backseats of cars or tour buses, he had seen and experienced all the joys that are offered in the bright lights of the big cities.

He pulled a little bit on his bushy white mustache and allowed as how he really liked spring, the season of rebirth, the lead-in to the time when he would be busiest with his banjo and when he could hear the laughter and applause long after his contemporaries had gone.

"Come with me, but watch your step," he said as he turned away from the house and to a narrow walkway along the rock-lined stream, a roaring channel of water on this spring day.

He led the way to a comfortable shed a ways behind the house, and he unlocked the door. "This is where I answer letters from my fans. And where I sign autographs." He reached for an eight-by-ten black-and-white glossy print that he addressed to me.

"I keep pretty busy out here," he said as I toured the shed. He led me back toward my car, first cautioning again that I needed to watch my step.

Blackie the cat watched from near the daffodils as Grandpa led me back to my car. He knelt and hugged Chris, the German shepherd that he said is "spoiled rotten." Contentment and warmth decorated the faces of both the old man in the flannel shirt and the big dog.

He offered me a hug, which I gratefully accepted, then he looked again from me to the woods over in the general direction of his best friend's killing field.

I didn't know if that's what he was thinking about. I hoped not. I didn't really want to leave this great man in a mournful mood.

"I just love trees," he said again, adding that he has written poems about trees. "Love this time of year."

He and the big dog were hugging in the shadow of a towering birch when I drove away, rattling past the creek and away from the great banjo player's own Walden, a place where he still discovered peace even though his best friend had been murdered just over the rise.

I stopped at that nearby market for a Diet Coke and eased on back toward Nashville.

"Come on back, now, y'hear," he had told me. "Anytime."

Stonewall Jackson

O N A CHILLY NOVEMBER DAY, I finally gave in to my curiosity:
I turned the old Saab off the busy Brentwood, Tennessee, thoroughfare and rolled up the hill that overlooks Waterloo.

I'd been driving the busy road—Church Street—for decades, watching
the countryside that once was where I sought soul salvation among trees,
rock walls, streams, lakes, and farmland transform into clusters of what are
popularly dubbed "McMansions." I don't like the term, mainly because
it seems to denigrate the work of the Golden Arches, where my dad first
took me for 12-cent hamburgers on the Grand Rapids, Michigan, Beltway
60 or so years ago.

I can't remember what the fries and chocolate malt cost. I think the
sign read "Over 15 Million Sold." I don't think they keep track and publish that "sold" information on their marquee in this gentler era. I suppose
18 trillion have been sold, but none tasted as good as those I ate in the
backseat of my dad's white Oldsmobile convertible while we sat in the
parking lot.

But let's get to the point. For five decades or so, I'd drive this road
through what first was Brentwood's black community—that's what it was
before Eddy Arnold led the hillbillies out here to roost—and watch the
phases and changes of the then small core of the Nashville suburb.

This is not a knock on Eddy, who was a great man and a friend of mine
whom I still miss when I drive by the small office building I used to visit
regularly—when he was alive, of course. His grandson, Shannon Pollard,
a good guy, makes music and develops and sells real estate from that office
today. His grandfather made an obvious impression.

Eddy's role in the development of Brentwood is pretty simple (if you like things simplified). The country stars needed places to build their homes long ago. Like black people, Yankee water heater salesmen, and carnies, the hillbillies weren't wanted among the "Old Nashville" wealthy in Belle Meade. But they had money. So Eddy, who was a fine land speculator, pretty much dragged them out to Brentwood.

That's changed dramatically over the years, as the "new" Brentwood, pretty much founded by the classiest country singer ever to wear a tuxedo and cufflinks, became a burgeoning bedroom community for Nashville.

New industry would come to town, their employees needing places to live—and they didn't want to live in Nashville. There may have been some prejudice involved, but that's another story.

Even after Eddy died, I continued my drives through Brentwood. My parents, since deceased, lived in Nashville but near that suburban giant, so my wanderings through that town became frequent.

And that meant occasionally taking Church Street east out of the custom-stucco heart of Brentwood, where I'd see development. Apartments, fancy houses, funeral parlors, and even a Montessori school—everything kept changing, everything except the 29-acre Walden-like paradise that filled the hollow.

There is a house on the top of a hillside that overlooks that valley whose floor is covered by a lake.

For a long time, I didn't know who lived in that modest ranch house, but I envied them, especially their location, location, location.

I finally figured it out one day when I saw a bus bearing country star Stonewall Jackson's name pull off that main road and park next to a raggedy old house across the lake from the tidy rancher on the hill.

"Stonewall Jackson lives here," I told myself, not really surprised since I had guessed that to be a strong likelihood given the "Lake Waterloo" sign near the edge of that gentle body of water.

After all, the hard-core country star sang, "Everybody has to meet his Waterloo" in his breakthrough number 1 hit back in 1959.

I continued to drive past this house, sometimes just because it was a quieter pathway out of Brentwood and toward my home and sometimes because I was keeping mental track of the elimination of the old black community that once was the heart of the city. I think it was a glistening new hotel that took out the last few clapboard houses, where black children had played in the yard.

Occasionally when I passed Lake Waterloo, I'd see men in a rowboat— generally docked or anchored nearest the road side of the lake—fishing.

I could easily recognize one of the men, the great Opry star and kind man Little Jimmy Dickens. Tater did not cast a giant shadow.

Others in that boat at times included Jerry Reed, who I'd been lucky enough to meet and write about, as well as Jim Ed Brown and Charlie Louvin. Stonewall Jr. (aka "Turp," who lived in the stone house across the lake from his folks) likely was out there, too.

I'd never seen Stonewall himself. I had seen him only from a distance as he stood on the Grand Ole Opry stage, but I generally reckoned the taller man whom I frequently saw with those visiting anglers was the guy who sang, "Everybody has to meet his Waterloo."

Simply put, the song that name-checks Napoleon, the mean little man who met his fate at Waterloo, basically means we all must meet our fate someday.

Anyway, when I finally tired of my hesitancy to trespass, I drove up to that rancher in my old Saab because I wanted to get to know this great old man of the Opry (he had become a central figure in a fight to keep the senior citizens' contingent of Opry performers employed) while I still could.

I parked in what seemed like a precarious spot, a long plunge downhill a possibility, but pulled on the parking brake and walked to the front door.

A woman answered the door. It turns out she was Mrs. Stonewall, which is what I assumed from the smile and the afternoon housecoat.

I told her who I was and gave her a quick summary of my reason for just dropping in on a very cold early winter's day.

I could smell the wood burning inside. Or maybe it was from the house over the hill, Jim Ed Brown's. It didn't matter: it smelled good on an uncommonly cold Brentwood day.

She asked me to stay at the front door while she went to get Stonewall, who, she said, would be glad to talk with me.

It was a few minutes, and though it was cold, it was sunny, and I turned around to survey what really was an oasis from the urbanization of Brentwood. I saw some activity near the tour bus outside the house across the lake but couldn't really tell what was going on.

Finally, this man in an old-fashioned undershirt (the kind that has been maligned with the "wife-beater" tag in recent year) and dark trousers came to the door.

His hair, a little longer and thicker than I'd expected, was disheveled. He obviously had been napping. I can't remember, but it may have been "too early for company" after one of the midweek Opry programs that featured the veterans, the answer to the fight Stonewall had waged and won (at least until all the veterans died off, something I'm sure the corporate folks were counting on when they made their compromise).

I went through my spiel—who I was and what I was doing at his house, and assuring him I was relatively harmless—and he smiled and opened wide the storm and the main doors, motioning me into his home.

He asked me to sit down and wondered if I wanted a cup of coffee. Since I didn't know how long I'd be staying, I turned him down. Maybe an hour or two later, I had some water.

"I just love it here," he told me of the 29 acres along Cloverland (the name given to Church Street as it rolled into the country long before it, like almost any road in the Nashville area, became choked with development).

He'd owned the land for a half century. And it easily could have been sold long ago as a lakefront development containing eight or nine houses.

But he was 81 on that visit. He didn't need money. He and his wife, Juanita ("Marty Stuart calls her "Mama Doll"), had a comfortable house. He could drive down to the bottom of the hill to go fishing. And peace could be found by standing on the front porch.

"I want to leave it to my family, and they can make a park here," he told me as I sat there in his living room, where his dogs, Waffles and George, were sprawled out in front of the fireplace.

"I don't know what kind of dogs they are," said Stonewall, as Waffles (or was it George?) came over to rub against my leg.

The dogs occasionally would bark at the traffic passing on Cloverland, particularly as the afternoon grew long and rush hour inched near.

"When we first moved out here, there were 12 cars a day along that road. I liked it better then. I'd get off the road and come here, and it was quiet. Course, it's not really that noisy now," said old Stonewall.

One regular visitor was Marty Stuart (mentioned above). "He's like a second son to us."

As the day drew on, it was obvious that Stonewall was wearing out and that his dinnertime was approaching.

I wanted to take a photograph of him, perhaps out on the porch, with the lake and the land in the background.

"I don't look good right now," he said. "Can you come back tomorrow to take the picture? I'd feel better about it if I looked right."

I agreed, but I began to worry as that next day began with snow, the kind that in the South just makes roads slick. I wasn't sure I could make it down the hills and hollows and then up the hill to his house.

But I'd promised, so I was going to give it a try.

It was worth it. After the treacherous drive, I climbed up onto the porch and knocked on the storm door.

This time, I was greeted by a tall man in full country music regalia, black with rhinestones, head to toe.

"This is better for the picture," he said. And since the sun was about right and the snow had pretty much begun to melt, I figured he was right.

He stepped out onto the porch and looked out across his land.

He motioned across the lake. "That's a 1976 Eagle bus," he said. "I don't go out in the bus anymore. Fly nowadays."

There still was an audience for his music. And there still were fans, at that time, who came out to his property to get their pictures taken by the lake and, if they were lucky, with the fellow who had been an Opry member for 55 years at that point.

"I like people. They can come here, as long as they don't fish."

He told me that he wanted the land to become Stonewall Jackson Park, a place where families could have fun, picnic, and play in the old Eagle bus. Heck, eventually, he might even allow a little fishing in the bass-stocked lake.

For a moment, he stopped to talk about his (at the time) recently deceased friend George Jones, cowriter of Stonewall's 1958 prisoner's lament "Life to Go."

"I wrote most of it, but George finished it. I gave him the writer's credit."

He laughed at himself and looked back into the house. "Sometimes a guy ought to ask his wife before giving things away like that."

Of course, while he was no George Jones, he had plenty of success. "With the Lord's help, I had 14 number 1 singles."

He admitted that getting up earlier to put on his show clothes for me was unusual for him.

"I really don't get going much until around 2 or so," he said as he led me back into the house.

He also said he was in good shape because "I'm a God man. When they was havin' all those parties, I sent the band, and I went back to the motel and watched television."

I left his place. As mentioned, the snow was gone. He had told me to come back out when there was a real snow. "It's really pretty then," he said.

He also told me to come back anytime.

Of course, I didn't. I don't like to bother people or take advantage of them or steal away some of their valuable time.

But I think about him every time I drive past Lake Waterloo and wonder if the bass are biting.

And then I always remember, with a smile, that when he told me about the song George Jones had cowritten, Stonewall tipped his head to the ceiling and sang it:

> I've got a sad sad story friend that I don't like to tell.
> I had a home and family when they locked me in this cell.
> I've been in here eighteen years a long long time I know.
> But time don't mean a thing to me cause I've got life to go.
> Well I went one night where the lights were bright just to see
>   what I could see,
> I met up with the old friend who just thought the world of me.
> Well he brought me drinks and he took me to every honky-
>   tonk in town
> Then words were said and now he's dead I just had to bring
>   him down . . .

Waffles and George barked accompaniment, and the old man smiled in his nicely creased black, rhinestone-studded stage outfit.

Charlie Daniels

A MIGHTY BIG ARM PULLED ME into a semi–bear hug on that sticky and, at that point, disappointing night of May 12, 1976, in Clarksville, Tennessee.

"What's the matter, son? They giving you trouble gettin' in? Why that little guy keep throwin' you out?"

I turned to look squarely into the eyes of the long-haired country boy since I immediately recognized Charlie Daniels.

I introduced myself to him, and he said, "Hi, Tim, nice to meet you. My name's Charlie. I'm playing here in a little while."

Of course, as a music fan, I knew this was Charlie Daniels, lead fiddler and voice and writer for the then smoking-hot Charlie Daniels Band, one of the main warm-up acts for the night's festivities.

I explained to this obviously gentle soul in denim jeans and a cowboy shirt and his trademark Buckaroo Block hat that I was a newspaper reporter and that I was supposed to be inside the arena, covering the almost festival of a concert.

The large man with the huge, white hat loosened the hug a little bit but kept his arm draped around both of my shoulders. "You a newspaperman?" he asked, digging his tongue way down deep into his left cheek. I assume he was working a pinch of snuff or some chewing tobacco. "They need to let you in there."

I told him I was from the local paper in Clarksville, and he nodded. "Maybe they don't care about small-town newspaper guys, but I do. I'll take care of it."

I told him I'd requested credentials from Sound Seventy, the promoter, and had been told to show up at the will call, which was at the ticket booth inside the door, right in front of where we stood, his arm still across my shoulders.

Next to that ticket booth, to the right and just inside the door of the Winfield Dunn Center, was the "Governors' Club," a potato-chips and cheap-liquor-and-Coke room for boosters of Austin Peay State University's sports programs on game days.

I had been in there in my role as a sportswriter who enjoyed smuggled bourbon dollops in Coke at halftime—or pregame for that matter. The city was dry, so you got your liquor where you could, unless you wanted to drive out to Pal's Package Store, the back room of which eventually became the "Little Ole Opry," but that's another story. I saw Faron, Little Jimmy, Jan Howard, and others there.

On this night, I watched through the door's glass to see Nashville newspeople I recognized darting in and out of the Governors' Club, "backstage" for this event, gathering quotes for the 10 p.m. news or the newspapers down in that city, an hour away.

This was a big cultural event, it seemed, but the local media hadn't been invited to the party. I mean, the *Clarksville Leaf-Chronicle* (founded in 1808) was the oldest newspaper in the state. This was happening a mile from our newsroom. But it seemed like Nashville promoters didn't care about us.

I was out of luck and too broke to buy a physical ticket (they used to sell these rectangular pieces of cardboard as "tickets" to events). I had been pretty unhappy until the guy whose belly was pushing hard on the lower snaps of his cowboy-style shirt came to my rescue.

"You come on with me, old son," the big fellow said after a couple of "that ain't rights" and "they should let you ins" and I think a bit of Skoal spit onto the dusty ground. It could have been regular chewing tobacco and not snuff since, before he became a star, this fellow worked the tobacco fields near his hometown of Wilmington, North Carolina, at least until he left the fields to play bluegrass music with the Misty Mountain Boys.

That was before he hit Nashville with his guitar and charmed the men with whom he did session work, guys like Bob Dylan on the genre-bending-and-lifting *Nashville Skyline* (and other Dylan Music Row sessions) and Ringo on his gorgeous take on country music, *Beaucoups of Blues*.

Cash, Bare, Harold Bradley, Scotty Moore, and Chet. They all loved this big guy with the guitar and fiddle expertise. Most of those guys are dead now. So is Charlie, of course. And when he did die on July 6, 2020, Barc said, "Charlie's been like a brother to me since the early '70s. He's one of the greatest, kindest people I'd ever met in my life. Not only Charlie—but he surrounded himself with incredible people that I love, especially his wife Hazel. We did a duet of a song Charlie wrote called 'Willie Jones,' and it was one of the most fun studio sessions I've been in. I've always loved playing Volunteer Jams through the years—I will miss my dear friend."

But let me take you back again to the young newspaperman and the young fiddler in the custom cowboy hat who were leaning against each other on that hot Clarksville night nearly a half century ago.

While we exchanged very small talk, I did catch a whiff of pot in the air but couldn't at first tell who was responsible. I could tell it wasn't my new friend, even though his best song bragged, "I get stoned in the morning and get drunk in the afternoon."

But, ooh that smell? I decided that the likely origin was Willie Nelson's bus, which we were standing near and from which I could hear laughter.

Waylon, Cash, Junior, June, Shaver, Tompall, and members of the Flying Burrito Brothers climbed in for short socializing. Jack Greene and Jeannie Seely, whose "If It Ain't Love" showcased a classic country duet partnership, also were somewhere around in the fleet of buses parked behind the Winfield Dunn Center that night. I'll bet my future pal Bobby Bare was there, too, and Captain Midnight and Billy Ray Reynolds, too, I'm sure.

I did interview Willie a few times later in my career, and he's one of the kindest men I've ever met. He's also no doubt a national treasure. Once, he was on his bus rolling across Texas when we spoke, and that same aroma seemed to slip through the phone lines. Just my imagination, I suppose. But I couldn't stop giggling at his jokes. I've always really liked Willie Nelson, which really was why I was at that show.

I'd been buying Willie Nelson records for a few years, beginning with *Shotgun Willie*, which I bought at a Cats store in Nashville on the same day I bought Alice Cooper's *Muscle of Love*. The perky-breasted cashier in the Vanderbilt T-shirt asked me, "Who is this Shotgun Willie?" I told her, among other things, he was bitin' on a bullet and pullin' out all of his hair.

Yeah, some people say I'm no good, crazy as a loon. Regardless of that, this story is about Charlie Daniels and the night he saved my life (or at least rescued a young newspaperman).

By the time I was hugged by Charlie, I'd already missed Poco because of the security guard. I thought the little weasel worked for the promoter, but he may have been a self-important Willie roadie. I never found out. I did hear Poco's "Keep on Tryin'" and, I think, "Crazy Eyes" during the four times I entered the Winfield Dunn Center—only to be thrown out by the weasel. I'd been told at each door that the will call was at another entrance, I walked all the way around the arena at least two times. The

same little guy found me each time and yelled profanities. Eventually, I was
frustrated, and the little guy found out he shouldn't get in a profanity duel
with me, but he still wouldn't let me in. Actually, I'm sure he was more
determined than ever to keep me out.

The Flying Burrito Brothers, three years after the death of their founding spirit Gram Parsons, were going on next. Their lineup at that time
included Eagles founder Bernie Leadon, Gene Parsons, Al Perkins, and
more members of the incestuous Southern California rock scene, and I was
anxious to hear them. Bernie, of course, went on to help found the Eagles
and in more recent years has called a rural stretch outside Nashville home.
Good fellow. He and Henley wrote "Witchy Woman," which I consider
the Eagles' best song.

A friend of mine, Jeff Bibb, a successful Clarksville businessman, was
a student at Austin Peay back then, and he also was a member of the Pi
Kappa Alpha fraternity, aka the "Pikes." He and another Pike and good
guy from Clarksville, Lawson Mabry, filled me in recently as I was trying
to refresh my decades-old memories of that night.

Jeff said his official archives listed the performers as Waylon Jennings,
Bobbie Nelson, Charlie Daniels, Faron Young, Hank Cochran, Jack
Greene, Jeannie Seely, Tracy Nelson, Guy Clark, Billy Joe Shaver, and
Tompall Glaser. Others, like Cash, as I noted, simply dropped in, and
Willie was the headliner.

Jeff remembers the Burritos, featuring Chris Hillman, only playing
warm-up, but that was a long time ago, and Jeff admits to having a "scrambled brain" that he attributes to age. Lawson says he "hazily" remembers the
evening. Lawson, however, does remember a nightlong after-party at the
Pike House that was attended by Willie, the Burritos, and Faron Young.

"The best part was loading a passed-out Faron Young into the backseat
of his turquoise Lincoln Continental Mark III at 4 in the morning so Willie
could drive them back to Ridgetop."

I was old, pushing 25, and not invited to the frat party. In fact, after
the concert ended, I'd go back to the newspaper to write a feature story
about it.

As a sportswriter back then, I worked most nights, so concerts were
generally missed. But then a night off (summers were quieter, and most
sports were during the daytime) coincided with an announced concert by
Willie Nelson and friends at the then almost new gym that was home to
the Austin Peay State University Governors basketball team. They called
it "The House That Fly Built" because playground hero James "Fly" Williams of Brownsville (the "tough" section of Brooklyn, New York) had

played for Austin Peay a couple of years before. It seemed odd that a guy who was the hero in the toughest, most crime-ridden section of New York (the 73rd Precinct keeps busy in Brownsville) would be so popular in a sleepy southern city.

Fly packed them in at the old "Little Red Barn" gym, so a new arena, the Winfield Dunn Center, was built. Unfortunately, by then, Fly, who never saw a schoolbook he liked or could read, had moved on to the Spirits of St. Louis of the old American Basketball Association. He washed out. We kept in touch over the years.

For a good bit of time, he was living in deserted buildings with a short, stubby kid he took with him to college at Austin Peay (not sure how the "clean" basketball program worked that out). He had no phone, of course, but I had his mom's number. She was a very nice woman. If I wanted to talk to Fly or get an update on his life, I'd call her. She'd tell me to call back the next day while she tracked her son down. Then when I called back, she'd give me the number in a phone booth in Brooklyn and what time I needed to call. As odd as that sounds, it worked, and I became friends with Fly, at least between his jail stints.

The last I heard, he was back at Attica after being busted as a heroin kingpin by night while working for the park district as a coach and mentor by day—something like that. I'll tell you, I really liked Fly. Nice guy, really. And damn, he could play ball. He didn't have many teeth, though.

Maybe I'll get around to telling about that sometime, but today is supposed to be about Charlie Daniels, a man who my pal Kris Kristofferson might call a "walking contradiction, partly truth and partly fiction." Charlie was back then the "long-haired country boy" who played his fiddle rough and glorified the pot-smoking, authority-thumbing, religion-doubting heart of what was called "southern rock."

Others in the field included Barefoot Jerry (who never made it real big, but I liked them), the Marshall Tucker Band, 38 Special, Molly Hatchet, and the Allman Brothers (who really surpassed the southern rock label with their jazz/Dead-influenced lyrics and meanderings but actually lost their heart in 1971 when Duane, Derek's lead Domino, died while taking on a flatbed truck with his motorcycle down in Macon, Georgia). Bell-bottom blues will make you cry.

And then, of course, was Lynyrd Skynyrd, whose three-lead-guitar explosion and "what's yer name" hollerings made them the kings of the genre until half the band was lost in a 1977 plane crash—free bird, indeed. A random note here: Skynyrd was scheduled to play the Winfield Dunn Center on October 27, 1977. I was going to go cover that one. The crash that killed their soul and turned the survivors and stragglers into a tribute band occurred in Mississippi on October 20, 1977.

The plane they were in was carrying them from a show in Greenville, South Carolina, to Baton Rouge and a show at Louisiana State University.

It ran out of fuel and crashed in the woods near Gillsburg, Mississippi. Ronnie Van Zant, the bandleader and lead vocalist (other than Charlie, the most important man in southern rock), died. Others who died in that field included guitarist and vocalist Steve Gaines, his older sister and backing vocalist Cassie Gaines, assistant road manager Dean Kilpatrick, and pilot Walter McCreary. All 20 who survived were seriously injured, and the ironically titled "Street Survivors" tour was concluded.

But in many quarters, the Charlie Daniels Band defined southern rock. Well, hell, they actually did define it in "The South's Gonna Do It Again":

> Get loud, well you can get loud and be proud . . .
> Be proud you're a rebel 'cause the South's gonna do it again

In the song, he name-checks southern rock royalty before singing, "and all the good people down in Tennessee are diggin' Barefoot Jerry and CDB."

I probably ought to note that Tom Petty and the Heartbreakers, who turned out to be America's best rock band in my mind, began in Gainesville, Florida, with some of that same swamp flavor and easily could have been better than any on that list. But they moved to Los Angeles, where Petty and songwriting partner Mike Campbell found their souls on Mulholland while still mixing in Tom's drawl and a bit of the southern guitar sound. The baseball cap he wore in Gainesville, with the Confederate battle flag on the front, I think was tossed out somewhere along Interstate 10, thankfully.

I actually think about Charlie fondly, quite often, over the years, even as he traversed the large gap between preaching about booze and pot and honky-tonks and celebrating the devil's fiddle playing to his later-in-life proselytizing about God, white folks, and soldiers.

Instead of the "Simple Man" of song and the tornado-like fury of "Devil Went Down to Georgia," he became an outspoken Christian (not that there's anything wrong with that) as well as a spokesman for right-wing causes:

> Johnny said, "Devil, just come on back . . .
> I done told you once you son of a bitch
> I'm the best that's ever been . . ."

The truth is that sometimes, when I listen to that song, I cheer against Johnny. When Charlie died, that last line of the verse above was printed 3,211 times by obituary writers. "He's always told us he was 'the best that's ever been,' and he was," the newscasters would say, winking at their witty originality.

Best there's ever been? Charlie was a true original.

I don't know what sparked the change in the heavyset fellow who began his musical life as a free-swinging ace Nashville session player. Some say it's because he fell off a horse, but I don't know that.

Charlie's version of "I'll Fly Away" was a favorite of evangelist Billy Graham, and they were friends.

At his funeral on July 10, 2020, one of the speakers joked that he wasn't sure who would have given Charlie his first handshake on passing through St. Pete's gate: Ronnie Van Zant or Billy Graham. Apparently, Graham's son, Franklin, who was in attendance, said both of those dear friends would have "bull-rushed to get to Charlie first" (or something like that).

Great writer and cultural historian Frye Gaillard spends a good bit of time discussing Charlie in his excellent *Watermelon Wine: Remembering the Golden Years of Country Music.*

Frye perfectly paints the picture of the man whom southern rock fans nearly deified while chugging quart bottles of cheap swill to wash down the hedgerow hemp.

In the book, Charlie and Frye are talking about the song that paints the most accurate picture of southern rock both on the stage and in the stands: "long-haired country boy."

That song pretty much established Charlie's early, rabid fan base: white people, rednecks, really, who cheered at the idea of getting stoned in the morning and drunk in the afternoon. The finale, "If you don't like the way I'm livin', you just leave this long-haired country boy alone," always resulted in drunken hysteria.

"Yeah, that's kind of my philosophy of life," Charlie says to Frye. "I ain't got no image to protect or none of that bullshit. We don't wear no rhinestone Nudie suits, we don't have to worry about nobody knowing that we drink or smoke dope. I don't give a fuck, you know? The kind of people we appeal to don't give a damn. I ain't worried about the Baptists banning us because they don't come to see us anyway. We're kind of a hard-livin' bunch of people. I think that reflects in our music. We just are what we are."

Later on, an ordained Baptist minister, perhaps the most revered Christian evangelist of the twentieth century, Billy Graham, became a big fan and chum. And Charlie was a long way from being the stoned, drunk, long-haired country philosopher at those Crusades. Hell, when it came to the laying-on-of-the-hands part, I'll bet Charlie was cheering as loudly as anyone in those giant stadiums where ringmaster Graham worked.

Regardless of his philosophical and religious meanderings during his career, I personally always found Charlie just as direct and honest as he was in the exchange with Frye.

He was likable and always on a first-name basis and proud of his band's heritage. He loved God and soldiers. He also adopted right-wing posings and filled social media with hate-filled rants, many directed at Barack Obama, our first black president, which, of course, reinforced the perception that Charlie was a racist.

Actually, I'm not sure if he was. And I believe he felt Black Lives Matter as a concept. He may have had difficulty dealing with it and brown-skinned people as a reality.

A great friend of mine, the musician, historian, and writer Peter Cooper, and I were talking about our mutual fondness for Charlie as well as our disgust at the racist rants.

"Charlie may have called Obama a Muslim and said other horrible things about him and about black people in general," said Peter. "But if he and Obama sat down over iced tea, they would have become best friends."

Charlie just liked people, even if he was uncomfortable with "concepts" of brown and black people.

Still, he always was a charming guy, always willing to answer my questions. If I was doing a story about some great session—say, the stuff with Dylan, Ringo, Cash, or whomever—I called him.

When I wanted to do a story about the summer that Beatle Paul McCartney spent out in Mount Juliet while he was preparing for a Wings Over America tour, I called Charlie. He'd at least tell me whom I should be talking to.

Paul and Linda were staying at Curly Putman's 133-acre farm in Wilson County in 1974. That's Charlie Daniels country. To kill time here, other than hitting the drive-in movies and riding motorcycles through the countryside to buy watermelon, Paul and company huddled with my friend Ernie Winfrey, the late recording engineer, at the Sound Shop (since torn down, unfortunately) on Demonbreun Street back when Music Row really existed. They recorded "Sally G.," "Junior's Farm" (Putman's nickname was Junior), and a few more. Chet Atkins even got involved.

Charlie wasn't involved in Paul's sessions, but he did talk to me about them and about having McCartney in the neighborhood.

He was all over Ringo's record.

The Beatles drummer and showman was in Nashville in the summer of 1970, just two months after the best band ever formally announced their divorce, the beginning of the "sue you, sue me blues," as later described by George Harrison.

In a story I wrote for the *Nashville Scene* weekly newspaper, Charlie told me that Ringo did not act like the rock star from Abbey Road when he set up shop at Music City Recorders on 19th Avenue South.

Charlie's guitar helped establish the pure country feel of *Beaucoups of Blues* during those summer 1970 sessions.

Charlie told me that Ringo was at ease in the "pretty typical Nashville sessions. You know, three songs in three hours. It was go in, sit down and work. 'Here's the songs, here's the chords, let's get it done.' It was not a Beatles-type leisurely session. It was work."

Of course, it hadn't been too many years since The Beatles—with their musical godfather George Martin—knocked out albums in the same assembly-line fashion (in the years when they were Fab) before leaving the screaming masses and angry dictators' wives and setting on an experimental music course that again changed rock music. Oh, yeah, George Martin was their chief coconspirator then as well.

Charlie's affiliation with various Fabs sprung from his work with Dylan that led to him being invited to New York City for a jam session with Dylan and his pal George Harrison.

During those sessions, finally released in 2020 on *Bob Dylan 1970*, George asked Charlie who provided the great steel on Ringo's record. Charlie got on the phone and got Pete "Mr. Talking Steel" Drake and George together in London, where Ringo did much of the drumming on the Harrison must-have triple-LP *All Things Must Pass*.

Charlie remembered that the steel wizard was pretty much responsible for getting Ringo to town to record the album that Pete produced, mixing in the sidemen, who included the then anonymous "long-haired country boy" with other Dylan sessions veterans.

The big man always maintained that Ringo's country record was important, even if it got a lukewarm reception on Abbey Road, where they were more enamored with Lennon's *Plastic Ono Band*, McCartney's self-titled solo album, and Harrison's *All Things* masterwork as well as the "far out" work of other Abbey Road studio clients like Pink Floyd, Deep Purple, and Fela Kuti in 1970.

"In retrospect, I don't think it was the explosive album [Apple executives] wanted it to be," Charlie told me. "I'm sure they wanted it to be a multimillion seller. But it was not in The Beatles tradition, like what George and the other guys had done." Instead, it was a full-frontal country album. And as such, he said, it helped "legitimize country music in the rock world."

Without going any further, I think it's pretty clear that Charlie, a pot-smoking guitar wizard who enjoyed working with Dylan, The Beatles, and Leonard Cohen (among many others), changed dramatically philosophically and politically over the years.

And his conservative views about religion and politics and behavior seemed far out of line with the philosophy of the long-haired country boy who had been a major admirer of Martin Luther King Jr. and who was a great friend of President Jimmy Carter, even mounting what was in essence one of his Volunteer Jams during the inaugural activities.

The same man who loved King and likely drank Billy Beer down on the Plains, Georgia, peanut farm and southern White House also published several letters that, if not racist, were at least tinged with it, directed at President Barack Obama.

Here's a sample, a letter to Obama attributed to Charlie and published in 2010 by the conservative site Newsbusters.org:

"Am I accusing you of being a Muslim? No I'm not.

"But the jury is still out a little bit on that subject in my mind, because many times your sympathies seem to lean in that direction. You need to watch who you bow to Mr. President. . . .

"Am I calling you a failure, Mr. President? With all due respect that's exactly what I'm doing."

And there's no doubt where he stood on President Donald Trump: "I do like President Trump. But I do not . . . I have never endorsed political candidates. I don't do that. I agree with them a lot of times and I write things about them, but it's not really an endorsement; it's not a . . . just the way I feel about things," he told McCall.com for the *Morning Call* feature in 2018.

As far as tearing down Confederate statues, "Well, I think it's kind of silly, you know? Why should they be torn down?

"If tearing them down did any good, I'd be all for it. But I don't see where it does any good. . . . What is it accomplishing? I mean, who is it really helping?

"I mean, Robert E. Lee was an honorable man. He fought the losing side in the War Between the States, but he was an honorable man. He thought he was doing the right thing."

In the weeks leading to Charlie's death, the destruction of Confederate statues and the Black Lives Matter movement, both ignited by the suffocation murder of George Floyd by a Minneapolis cop, probably didn't make sense to him.

Yet, when he died, almost everyone mourned. It was a national news item. Flags were lowered to half-staff in Tennessee. None of the news commentators mentioned that darker side of Charlie's legacy.

He was a "complicated man." Every time I say that phrase, it brings Isaac Hayes's "Theme from Shaft" into my mind. Private eye John Shaft was, in the Gordon Parks movie, a "complicated man" in the song and in the classic 1971 film that brought white people into theaters to see the heroics of a black man.

Thinking of Charlie and John Shaft in the same mental musical measure makes me smile.

And I was smiling the last time I spoke with Charlie. It was the beginning of the COVID pandemic, and I explored the damage it would have on the concert scene, like The Rolling Stones and James Taylor cancellations in Nashville and how hard-touring artists like the Charlie Daniels Band were going to deal with the inevitable.

Nashville is a musicians' town, and for a story in the *Nashville Ledger*, I talked with all levels of pickers, from the Americana folks who are reliant on tip jars and house concerts all the way up to legendary fiddler/violinist Andrea Zonn, a friend who is a key part of Sweet Baby James's touring outfit. Andrea, by the way, said after Charlie died that playing the fiddle part in "Devil" at the big fellow's Country Music Hall of Fame induction was one of her life highlights. She, like so many of us, loved Charlie.

When I spoke to Charlie at the outbreak of COVID, he said that his band was ready to thrill the devil out of concert fans but not if it offered any danger to himself or his audience.

"We're kind of rolling with the punches," he said from his Wilson County home, where he was holed up with his wife and son, rigidly following the social distancing idea.

"I don't like being off work. I want to get to work. I want to play some music for people, man. It's not feasible. Even if it was permissible, I wouldn't do it.

"That has to do with patriotism and responsibility."

At that point, he was canceling dates and rescheduling them for the fall.

Livestreaming was being utilized by the Americana troubadour set, but Charlie said he wasn't going to do that because he's not crazy as a loon and doesn't want to get his six-piece band, crew, and technical folks together in one confined space.

"I've been on this earth for 83 years," he points out. "I've seen a lot of things come and go. I've been through polio when they didn't want a bunch of kids playing, but I've never seen anything that's anything like this, anything so contagious as fast as this. . . . It's a terrifying thing for everybody."

Before I finish up my recollections of this man, I probably ought to mention that I covered two of his late-career Volunteer Jam redneck music extravaganzas for CMT.com. He began these multi-genre celebrations in 1974. The rednecks prevailed onstage, but Rodney Crowell, Billy Joel, Amy Grant, B.B. King, James Brown, John Prine, and even Roy Acuff participated during the jam's long history.

The last one I covered was in 2016. As an old man with long hair and a Stones *Exile on Main Street* or a Lennon "Give Peace a Chance" T-shirt, I didn't really fit in with the crowd that filled Nashville's hockey arena.

The crowd was more like the slack-jawed, beer-guzzling, very white, mostly males with short-haired crowd you'd see at a Trump campaign rally for college students or younger voters. Of course, there were plenty of obese old rednecks pushing hard against their CDB and Confederate flag T-shirts as well.

And Charlie played right to his people. "For all of you people who call me a redneck and a hillbilly, I got two words: 'Thank you.'"

It's kind of a standard line for Daniels. I'd heard it before on various occasions. Hell, someone even brought it up from the grave for his star-studded series of eulogies and tears.

Generally (but not so much at the funeral), that redneck braggadocio line is met by hoots and hollers, and, unfortunately, Rebel yells and the waving by audience members of the Stars and Bars. Course, some of the Charlie Daniels fans had that flag tattooed on their forearms or butts, I imagine. Probably their brains.

One highlight of the last Volunteer Jam I went to simply had Charlie sitting on a stool at center stage and picking out a melodic and acoustic introduction into his take on the hymn "How Great Thou Art." His solo voice sailed into the nosebleeds at the hockey arena, and the song soni-cally escalated, with a keyboard accompaniment swelling it into a full-on, Bible-thumping and heart-pumping southern gospel version of what many would consider their favorite hymn.

There was not the slightest bit of irony—given the swirling night of music that led up to and included Daniels' jam-packed set—that just before that bit of Christian exaltation, Daniels had blessed the crowd with one of his most recognized songs: "Long-Haired Country Boy": getting stoned in the morning and drunk in the afternoon and praising Jesus in the evening, as the five-hour show crawled toward a midnight finale.

He was, indeed, a complicated man.

I'll miss our conversations, for they were many over the years. And I have to add that I'm very pleased with the ending of the final interview about COVID in the spring of 2020, a couple months before he died.

I thanked him for his time. He said it was his pleasure. Normal stuff. "Always good to talk to you, Tim" sort of stuff.

For some reason, I was moved to tell him, "I want to thank you for all of your kindness to me over the years."

When he died, I remembered that and figured it had been a good way to end the conversation that began 44 years before outside Austin Peay's Winfield Dunn Center.

"I don't like that they threw you out, son," he said to the long-haired newspaperman who became his friend on that long-ago night. "Not at all."

He said hello to Waylon as he walked past and then said, "You stick with me, son."

This giant of a man wrapped his arm even tighter across both my shoulders and walked to the door, where the same little guy was checking in artists and ready to throw me out again.

"I'm Charlie Daniels," he told the mean little weasel. "This is Tim. He's with me."

Arm over my shoulders, he led me through both sets of doors and walked me to a seat very near the stage. "You can get good pictures here, I think, Tim."

The little guy had followed us all the way, anger in his eyes. Likely, he was ready to throw me out as soon as Charlie left to go backstage and warm up.

The long-haired country boy with the big heart, though, looked at the little security boy and put his hand on my shoulder. "You leave this young man alone."

Jimmy Otey

M Y ORIGINAL PLAN HAD BEEN to ride on the Metro Nashville bus while drumming great Jimmy Otey piloted his route through West Nashville. But his illness, which eventually proved mortal, changed that plan.

The chemical engineer had taken the job as a Nashville bus driver to help make ends meet between drumming gigs. He had stepped off the corporate ladder to avoid a promotion that would take him to what he called "that dreaded Kansas City."

"There's nothing in Kansas City, 'specially for a black person," he explained to me on more than one occasion as we chatted. "Some of the backwardest people in the world live in Kansas City. They're like the hillbillies in Missouri and East Tennessee." (Apologies here to the Missouri and East Tennessee hillbillies.)

We talked frequently on the phone about me either catching the bus down at the terminal near the state capitol or catching it farther down the line and riding back with him if I didn't want to spend the whole day on a bus.

"Or you could pick me up at the end of a run and drive me home," he suggested, noting that sometimes he walked home.

The problem was that health woes eventually sidelined him before we could figure out a plan. Then he disappeared, not answering his phones (he had three of them).

I didn't know that he'd pretty much died, or at least got close enough to where the angels were tuning up the chorus during his extended, mostly comatose stint in the hospital.

Post-coma Jimmy was trying to heal up and get back to drumming when I arrived at his house in Nashville's Bordeaux area, a thriving settlement of middle-class black people. Now, as the city grows and neighborhoods lose their identities, Bordeaux's soul is sure to fall victim to integration. For the most part, Nashville's soul has been squashed by white "immigrants" from California and Michigan who only care about clear highways and celebrate when Whataburger announces a new location.

Anyway, since my skin tone wasn't common on Jimmy's street, one of his sons who lived with him, Keith Otey, semi-sprinted out to my old Saab and led me to the side door, beneath the carport, and into Jimmy's house. Keith seemed like a good guy. He was found dead in his room about a week after my visit.

Jimmy smiled me into the room after Keith let me through the door. Then we began hours' worth of joy and reminiscence.

"I met The Beatles in Liverpool," said Jimmy as matter-of-factly as if he was talking about the Smiths or Joneses next door after I found a seat just a few feet from where he comfortably enjoyed the afternoon on his large sofa.

Frail and pale—but his spirit and good humor flourished.

He kept a blanket over his legs part of the time to fight off the February chill. Briefly, as we spent the day together, he even put that blanket over his shoulders and asked if I was warm enough.

When Keith was leading me to the den his dad occupied, I'd passed a Harley and a Mercedes in the carport. There also was one of those big Winnebago-like houses on wheels parked next to the house. Another car, I think it was a red Cadillac, had a drum kit in the backseat. I suppose Jimmy had kept it there just in case someone wanted to gig while he was wandering the R&B side of Music City.

"That's a Bounder," Jimmy told me of the big vehicle he'd used as a landmark ("drive past the big bus, and I'm the first house on the left"). I still use old-fashioned directions rather than some sort of directional device to get places.

"I've had at least two or three of the 40-footers. I love to camp," he said of his bus infatuation. "I go everywhere."

For decades, his wife, Jeanette, was his road-trip companion. Her death and his illnesses had forced him off the nation's blue highways.

Weak and weeks since his coma, he was planning on getting behind the wheel of the Bounder "when I get my strength back."

"I may go camping again," he said. "I've been all over the world, all over the United States playing my drums." He also played soprano, tenor and alto sax, bass guitar, "and a little piano, but I'm not as versed on it as the others."

His health had been deteriorating, and he was razor thin, his head bald from his treatments.

On that first day I dropped in on him, he did not look like the robust man I'd seen working the drums at the weekly R&B night at Carol Ann's Home Cooking Café, a soul-food joint in the shadow of Interstate 40 and near the projects out on Murfreesboro Road in South Nashville. Those jams, staged by R&B bandleader Jimmy Church, bring all sorts of "retired" music stars out for chicken, beer, sweet cocktails, and a love for swapping tunes and backbeat.

"I can still play, I just don't feel like playing now," the great drummer told me as we sat in his den.

He shook his head softly and rhythmically, focusing his bright eyes on me rather than the constant stream of game shows that played silently on the wall-sized television across from his sofa.

Jimmy had been diagnosed with congestive heart failure a few years before this visit, so he watched his health but stayed active behind his drum kit when wanted, certainly behind the big wheel of the Metro Transit Authority bus. I guess they call the bus system "WeGo" now, but I'll stick with MTA. Sometimes branding and marketing get outlandish.

A December 2018 heart attack convinced Jimmy to drive himself to the hospital barely in time. One red light, and he might've been dead on arrival—if he'd made it to the emergency room at all.

He lost 40-plus pounds while hospitalized for the heart attack and treatment of the congestive heart failure and weak kidneys.

Battered but undefeated, he was taking regular dialysis and was closely monitored by doctors. But that didn't stop him from having fun with his new friend, me.

He was planning a return to the drum kit after he regained some weight and health.

"I haven't played in quite a while. I haven't felt like it," said Jimmy, who dropped from 173 to 130 or so during his December 1–24, 2018, hospitalization that included time in an induced coma.

"As thin as I am, I don't want to go out there and have people to say: 'Look at Jimmy, he looks bad.'

"I'm pretty self-conscious about the way I look. If I can get back to 170—I like that weight, and I think I look good at that weight. . . . One day, God willing, I'll play again."

He never got back to playing weight before he died on September 5, 2019, a few months after our friendship was formed in the low-lit room with the Harley leaning on a brick wall outside. I ought to note that one other thing he'd hoped to get strong enough to do was ride that motor-cycle again. A longtime Harley man, he loved the feel of the road beneath him as he straddled the roaring machine, the wind blowing his face. But he needed strength to wrestle that machine. And he never regained that.

We'd actually had many conversations leading up to this visit back when we'd been trying to arrange how or when I'd ride the bus with him.

And we spoke often afterward, a few times out at the house in Bor-deaux, once at a funeral for Jimmy Church's wife, and again when I offered my condolences for his son's death. But most often, our visits were on the telephone as I checked in on a friend.

Joy flavored his words whenever we spoke, either on the telephone or in this comfortable den, decorated by the big TV and some floral prints on the walls.

The only taste of showbiz that could be seen in that room was a black-and-white picture of him with Bill Cosby (from back when people thought Cos was a "Fat Albert" great guy rather than a sexual predator), who had employed Jimmy as bandleader on his Johnny Carson–style talk show out in Los Angeles. "Hey-hey-hey!"

Other than the Cosby photo, there really weren't many photos or pieces of memorabilia around Jimmy's pleasant ranch house, which was purchased by showbiz spoils this great man stashed away to buy a place to raise his family.

When the drums were put away, he liked life quiet and gentlemanly.

I asked him if I could see pictures of him with some of the big stars (other than Cosby), and he did fish out a few old Polaroids of him with other musicians, but the images were either too dark or blurry.

Of course, I really didn't need pictures, I told him. The joy was in being around this man, this drum legend.

Jimmy was a fixture on the Nashville R&B scene when it thrived back in the 1960s and 1970s, even gigging at night while by day immersed in the chemical engineering career he began with bachelor's and master's degrees from the University of Michigan.

He wasn't around Jefferson Street—the old R&B nightclub district that was demolished for an interstate highway and urban renewal, further destruction of the city's soul—drinking quarts, smoking joints, chasing women, or joking around by day like so many of his friends. He was soberly doing his chemical engineer's magic at a Nashville ink plant before going home for dinner with his family.

After dinner, drum kit in his car, he'd go wherever he'd been hired to play music with some of Nashville's best musicians.

"I was always private about my life," he said, even separating his family life from his showbiz life and keeping his daytime profession secret when he was banging on the drum all night.

"They [his best friends Jimi Hendrix, Billy Cox, Jimmy Church, Bobby Hebb, and Johnny Jones] knew I was doing some kind of job during the day, but I didn't talk much about it."

Hendrix, by the way, had a devoted friend in Jimmy. "He was a really nice guy, always had his guitar with him, ready to play, as he walked down Jefferson Street. Some of the guys didn't like his playing, but I did. It was different. Jimi was different."

Hendrix, who shared a one-hanging-bulb apartment with Cox right on Jefferson Street, could be seen toting his guitar in a paper sack.

Chemical engineer Jimmy Otey made a good living using his master's education at an ink plant. But he said he needed to continue gigging on nights and weekends because "once you get married and start having babies, you gotta feed them, take care of them"—buy a nice house, not an urban apartment like so many of his nighttime colleagues, a place for the Oteys to live a solid upper-middle-class existence.

His move away from the ink plant and to Hollywood and seven years of touring and playing in the upper echelon of showbiz was done with both mercenary motive and his precious family in mind: it made him more available to the stars, and he could get top-paying jobs. He could hand deliver that money to his wife and kids.

"I would make three times the money out there than I could make in Nashville."

Making about $1,000 a week, "I wasn't out there for the glory and want to be seen. I wasn't the star. I was in it to make my family nest egg.

"I didn't have no vices—women, drugs, drinkin', or nothing—so I saved that money for when I could get back home."

And, he pointed out, when he was on the road, as part of a traveling band, he had a per diem for food and "didn't have to pay a dime" for his hotel. "Sent my money all home."

"Even when I was living at Sunset and Western, right across the street from the 20th Century Fox movie studios in Los Angeles, back when I was working with Little Richard, I insisted that they fly me back to Nashville during breaks," he told me.

"I had a young family back here. I didn't want to be one of those musicians that started off with a family but lost it because I was gone all the time.

"It was in my contract with Little Richard that he pay for my flights back to Nashville. I was getting paid [on salary], but sometimes we'd be just laying around in L.A., waiting for our next gig, for a couple of weeks. Little Richard flew me home."

Richard also loved Vegas, and again, if he and his band were there, sometimes for a month at a time, Jimmy's deal had the rock singer bank-rolling flights back to Nashville every weekend.

"I didn't want to get used to being gone, and I didn't want my family to get used to me being gone."

Jimmy didn't really have the strength to get his drums out during the time we hung out. They were broken down and stashed away, but he'd gladly put them back together and play again, he insisted. He was sure that day was coming. He just had to regain that weight and stamina.

He didn't, of course.

Even if he had gone back to work, he was always going to leave one of his drums idle: a snare given to him by his friend Ringo Starr, one of the four pals he hung out with in Liverpool. That drum was stored away for safekeeping, to be brought out only when he wanted a reminder of his good times with The Beatles.

Drummers and music collectors had tried to talk him into selling it, but Ringo had autographed it and given it to Jimmy out of respect. "It was a gift," Jimmy explained, "from Ringo, a friend."

Jimmy was never going to part with it. I should have checked with his family after he died, but I assume it is in good hands.

That drum from Ringo came in the day or so after Jimmy was in the northern England shipbuilding city of Liverpool, playing drums for Little Richard in the Cavern Club.

Any Beatles fan knows about that dank little club where Brian Epstein fell in love with John Lennon and his mates and honed them for world conquest.

Jimmy knew the Cavern's history, but it really was nothing special—just another night, just another joint, until he met John, Paul, George, and Ringo.

He said he first noticed the Cavern's former house band as the young men edged close to the edge of the stage, soaking in the American music, which they swiped, translated into Scouse, and used as the musical under-pinning for composing their songs.

Jimmy told me the four young fellows were having great fun watching as Little Richard and his band, driven by this magnificent stick man, roared through "Tutti Frutti," "Good Golly Miss Molly," and other rollicking rockers that helped The Beatles shape their early repertoire.

It was just another night at work for Jimmy, who had built a reputation as one of America's best drummers, alternating between stints with Little

Richard and James Brown and playing occasional gigs with Aretha Franklin, his friend Taj Mahal, and just about any singer or bandleader seeking a man who had mastered the sticks as a young teenager.

He told me those four "nice guys" introduced him to five other "nice, young guys" who called themselves The Rolling Stones due to their fondness for American blues music, which was reflected especially well in their recorded music through the early 1970s (or at least as long as Brian Jones was alive).

While Jimmy praised The Beatles, especially for the lads' songwriting, this great drummer only smiled when talking about the guy he truly loved who provided the backbeat:

"I'm not putting Ringo down, but he wasn't no helluva drummer," he told me for a story that ran on February 8, 2019, in the *Nashville Ledger*. "He got famous because he was in The Beatles. And he had that look. If you look in the pictures, the other three could have passed for brothers or cousins, but Ringo, who had that big nose and everything, stood out. It was that look that made Ringo."

Jimmy and Ringo were "talking shop" when the latter demonstrated some of his snare drum style to the drummer from Nashville.

"He said, 'You like that sound, man? I'll give it to you.'" That's the drum Jimmy kept for the rest of his life after Ringo autographed it for him.

That gift was made the day after the Cavern show, when The Beatles and Little Richard's band all climbed aboard an open-topped tour bus and traveled around the British countryside waiting for the sun.

Ringo was the friendliest of the four, Jimmy said, adding that George Harrison and Paul McCartney also were friendly but that "the one who got killed" [John Lennon] stayed off by himself: "Guys like that always got something going in their heads, probably writing songs."

Jimmy leaned back on the couch and talked about some of his other pals in the rock business. He called Janis Joplin "a good friend."

That ill-fated blues belter, who made Kris Kristofferson's "Me and Bobby McGee" into one of popular music's iconic songs, was one of Jimmy's best friends when out in California. Iron Butterfly, pal and mutual admirer Carlos Santana, Cream (Eric Clapton, Jack Bruce, and Ginger Baker), and Jefferson Airplane "were the kind of guys I was running with," he said.

He also enjoyed friendships with Waylon and Willie and the boys since they all intersected in the clubs and studios of Music City.

Jimmy turned from music to his bus-driving days.

"The driving part is all right. It's the public you have to deal with." Most of that public was good, responding to the way he treated them, he said.

If people didn't have money but needed to get to a job, he'd let them ride. In return, "on birthdays, around Thanksgiving, and the holidays, they'd be bringing me pies, cakes, and plates of food. I made friends with people." Probably not the types of fares MTA approved of (and certainly WeGo would balk), but I'd have to say Jimmy was among the sweetest, kindest souls I met in the music world.

It wasn't friendliness that Jimmy saw a couple years before his death when a big man packing a sidearm got on the bus and insisted on standing threateningly over the driver, Jimmy told me for the story in the *Nashville Ledger*.

"He was looking real weird. . . . He never did say anything. I hit the panic button and called the police."

After police toted that man off, Jimmy finished his route. "I got back to the bus company and said, 'I'm too old for this,' and I retired."

"I wanna show you something," he said as he left me in his den, nursing a glass of ice water and watching Alex Trebek on the television.

I thought he was going to get some photos or other publicity materials. Instead, he returned with a wide fedora on his head. "I'm known for always wearing hats when I play," he said. "How's this look?"

Looked fine to me, though perhaps it was a bit oversized now that his face was so thin and his head so shiny and bald. Still, while wearing that hat, he couldn't keep from smiling. I'm sure he figured that when the hat did fit, he'd get out his kit.

He excused himself again to go put that hat away, for safekeeping, I assume: keep it clean for the first night he felt like playing the drums again.

I guess it never was worn again.

George Jones

I CAN'T REMEMBER WHICH CAME FIRST: the golden eagle heist or the
Lexus wreck, the latter when George Jones fell off the wagon and over
a bridge abutment and scared everyone that finally he'd finally offered
his accidental but seemingly inevitable farewell toast to life.

All I know is that friendship—at least to the point where we watched
Bonanza together while his little dog played in the family room and I drank
"white lightning" while George chain-chewed Chiclets and tossed out
precious memories—flourished in his latter days.

To be clear, while "White Lightning" was an early Jones hit and white
lightning—the generic term for moonshine—got Possum in trouble on
more than one occurrence, the stuff I was drinking was a new product on
the market that he was using me to sample: George Jones White Lightning
Tennessee Spring Water. This was on the early end of the bottled-water
craze. And it sure tasted good after a hot day of touring his "yard" before
we settled into the overstuffed chairs in his TV room to talk and watch
Bonanza. Or perhaps it was *Gunsmoke*. Probably both, as we enjoyed the
late afternoon together.

If I'm thinking right, his wife, Nancy, also offered me a George Jones–
brand country sausage and biscuit. It went great with the white lightning.
It probably would have been better with the real thing, not the water, but
George was doing his best to stay "on the wagon." And so was I, at least
most of the time, then as now.

He was a loving and laughing guy who enjoyed telling stories that
made him the goat. No, not the "Greatest Of All Time" (GOAT) as used
today too frequently. Well, in that silly ESPN-language sense, he was the
GOAT when it came to country singers. He was what Tom Brady is to

football, Aaron Judge (showing my personal prejudice here) is to baseball, and Michael Jordan is to basketball (though I prefer Magic Johnson,
myself). Sports arguments aside, in George's field of trade, there never has
been one better—or at least he is the GOAT if you concede that no one
could surpass Hank Williams, making country's short-lived Shakespeare
ineligible for this ranking system.

By the way, Thumper Jones and Hank met when the tragic country
poet came to a radio station in Beaumont, Texas, where young George
was a staff guitarist. According to some reports, George was so stunned by
standing by his hero that he—and his guitar—froze.

George enjoyed being the butt of his own jokes, aka the "fall guy,"
"target," or "goat." He knew he had made a drunken fool of himself at
times in his life, and he didn't mind talking about that—or about his wife,
Nancy, or Hoss, Little Joe, and Matt Dillon for that matter.

As our day turned toward dusk, we even talked about more get-
togethers—he insisted on taking me out to a steak dinner in the near
future—and he invited me to come to the house anytime. A couple of
mid-grade, contemporary/temporary country hitmakers came to pay their
respects to their hero while I sat there with George, and he appreciated
their company. He also shook off any praise.

And, since these folks had dropped in to genuflect or whatever, he
made it clear that the day belonged to me. Troubled at times in his life,
sure. But it truly was a nice guy they laid in the ground at Woodlawn
Cemetery in South Nashville a few days after his death on April 26, 2013.
His monument is within easy eyeshot of the grave of Johnny Paycheck,
the "Take This Job and Shove It" (and so much more) honky-tonk hero
who died pretty much a pauper. George and Nancy had him buried in a
chunk of the graveyard they had purchased. There's room for more of his
friends there, too.

After George died, I had to convince an international wire service I was
working with that he mattered, that he was important around the world.
They took the obit, and it became the hottest news item of the day if I
remember correctly (and I don't always).

I also covered the funeral, again for Reuters. I think they got such great
feedback that they were just hoping more country stars would die so that
I could write obits and funeral stories. I do have to admit that, while I'm
sad, I do love a good funeral, and I've been to a lot of them, from Jones
to June to Cash to Scruggs to Porter to my really great friend and booster
Mac Wiseman.

I almost teared up when Alan Jackson sang "He Stopped Lovin' Her
Today" as George Jones's casket was being gathered up. The man they

called "Possum"—he did look like one, after all—was preparing for his final exit from the Grand Ole Opry House. I should make a quick side trip here because I doubt that I'll be writing much about Alan Jackson, who is the truest country voice of recent generations. Sorry Garth, but at least you've got friends in low places. Alan, who joined you in the "hat act invasion" of Nashville, is a naturally gifted, classic country singer, and Jones was his hero.

In 1999, George made a big-hit comeback with "Choices," a sort of lamentation and celebration of a flawed, proud life. The CMA, which puts on one of the biggest, self-serving award shows of them all, usually allows the stars with the big hits to play their full songs on the three-hour telecast.

But this was the time of Garth, A.J., Brooks & Dunn, Reba, Buddy Jewell (really?), and others. Old George Jones was not a part of the demographic they courted. So he was told he could sing just a few seconds of that song written by Billy Yates.

George balked at the abbreviated offer and took it as the insult it really was, so he stayed home. A.J., who, of course, was at the peak of his career, was on tap to sing his hit "Pop a Top," his version of an old Nat Stuckey hit. Alan, who can sing true, blue country, also enjoys novelty songs.

For example, I remember one of my music writers telling the then chart-topping young Alan on the phone one day that he never should have followed his string "Gone Country," "Song for the Life," and "I Don't Even Know Your Name" with "Tall, Tall Trees," which was, it turns out, written by Jones with my long-ago 2 a.m. coffee partner Roger Miller.

"I think George had forgotten he'd written it," A.J. writes on liner notes to his *Greatest Hits* album.

Anyway, back to the 1999 show and the "Choices" snub by the CMA— and A.J.'s most uplifting protest. Both the band and Alan began with their scheduled number, "Pop a Top," before they quickly shifted gears into "Choices," which was an uplifting middle finger pointed directly at the CMA, which had ignored and insulted Jackson's hero. George couldn't sing it. Alan Jackson could.

During my many years editing CMA awards coverage by my staff, it was my favorite moment, and it made Alan Jackson a sort of personal hero, to me, I'm sure to George, and to countless fans across the country.

Now, so many years later, I sit here, listening to some of George's early recordings, and smile.

What a nice man. Oh sure, he was wild when he was drunk, when he earned the "No-Show Jones" moniker for finding himself in the bottom of a bottle rather than at center stage at the Cass County Fair in Fargo, North Dakota, or the "Mon" County Fair in Morgantown, West Virginia.

George Jones, in his youth, had the perfect country hitmaker voice. Age and excess during his "No Show Jones" days robbed some vocal clarity, but "Choices" earned him a Grammy for the best male country vocal performance in 2000. *PBS/PHOTOFEST © PBS*

But when he was on, well, he was the best there ever was—or at least as good as there ever was. In fact, I like his late stuff, like "Choices," as much as "The Race Is On" or other stuff from his early years. "White Lightning," the song, not the water or the liquor, may be a favorite.

Whether early in his career or at the time of his "Choices" resurrection, Jones was fabulous. Perhaps that's because by nature, I like things a bit world-worn and rugged—or even ragged. Jones was all of that, with a sweet voice.

I'm not sure which was first, as I noted above, but let's start with the golden eagle theft.

George and Nancy Jones used to open the gates of their 15-acre estate in Franklin, Tennessee, for every Christmas season. It was a good old-fashioned fairyland, with the lights and the figures. And if Santa wasn't too far into the nog, you might even get to see George Jones.

It was an open-house, no-security type of thing, a relic of times past before people became so mean.

Then came the morning the phone rang at the newspaper where I worked, *The Tennessean.* I was the entertainment editor and generally the first person in the office in the features department other than a columnist who made her substantial living by writing about frugality.

Back to the phone call. It was Nancy Jones calling. This elegant woman was upset. It seems that the golden eagle statues, probably of brass or bronze rather than gold, that topped the two pillars of the entry gate had been stolen.

It's not that the Joneses couldn't afford more golden eagles—or silver ones or platinum ones. It's just that it was a violation of their sanctity, a slap in the face of the generosity that every year had them open their place to strangers.

Their goal, of course, was to dazzle the children of Franklin, that elegant southern city a few miles south of Nashville. Of course, no children were involved in the eagle heist.

Nancy, whom I didn't know, was calling for me because, she said, she was familiar with my writing, first in the old *Nashville Banner* and then in the morning paper. She wanted to know if I could help her get the eagles back.

I wrote a little note to put in the celebrity/gossip column written by journalist Brad Schmitt. And I got the word out to other media.

There's nothing really dramatic about the end of the story. I called Nancy back each day to see if the eagles had landed and filed updates for Brad. And finally, the eagles returned. All was right out there at the estate.

But, if I remember correctly, that incident led to the Joneses ceasing their Christmastime "open house," their garden of lights and attractions that delighted kids and just old-time fans who were able to get close to the icon.

I doubt if you can drive onto the property of any star, country or otherwise, these days. The theft of the eagles revealed that trust was no longer warranted.

Nancy never forgot my role in getting those birds back to their elegant roosts.

I'm not sure that the eagle theft (both Nancy and George called to thank me profusely for my help in getting them back to their concrete roosts) was my first real contact with this couple.

It may have been a less fun incident.

I was home on a Saturday night when I got a call from *The Tennessean* city editor or copy desk chief (it may have been my old pal Jerry Manley as a matter of fact) that the police scanner was going crazy because of George Jones.

Today, no newspapers, no newsrooms, and no one I know of has a police scanner anymore. Most communication between reporters and sources is all done by e-mail, Twitter, Instagram. The same is true of communication from editors to reporters. There are no reporters working today with their ears perked up as they sit by the police scanner for jabber about murders, wrecks, fires, and Klan rallies (thank God those days are gone, but I once had to send a reporter out to one that was getting out of hand).

In the old days (and I am old), if you heard on the scanner that a fire had engulfed a home and that five people may be inside, you'd plop a fresh reporter's notebook into your butt pocket, make sure your pen had ink in it, and rush out the door—and grab a camera in case the photographer couldn't make it.

When I was the night editor at the old *Nashville Banner*, my job included manning that scanner. My police reporter, Jose Lambiet—who would have to leave his job and his position as my iced-tea-and-vodka-swilling sidekick because he got drafted by the Belgian army—had a portable scanner that also served as his "telephone" to the radio on my desk.

"Ten-four, Ten-four, good buddy!" I'd holler to my Belgian pal after he told me he was at the scene of a fatal stabbing in East Nashville (back before the white people took it over, evicting the black residents). Jose (pronounced Joe-zay) would come back to the newsroom with the notebook full of quotes and write a story that I'd edit and leave for the morning crew.

When was the last time you saw a story about a single murder in your newspaper? Or a fire? For a few years, I worked for a wire service part-time, and my job was to keep them informed about possible stories in Tennessee.

One morning, a crazy guy had gunned down six people in a house in Memphis. Sad news, but an important news story, right? Nope, they said, didn't rise to the standards for national or international news. That's how far we've come (gone?) in the media business.

I got off on a tangent there about news coverage, but that's because I spent most of my life, proudly, as a print journalist. That business is an embarrassment now. Focus is online, print is scarce, and it's $30 a month for the print product, 99 cents for online. I haven't found it worth 99 cents in recent years.

I dropped my print subscription, too. But that was more personal. I called the editor and a reporter/friend at the newspaper to let him know that my father had died. Downtown Kiwanis was saluting him as the last World War II veteran to be a member of that prestigious business club. He also was the voluntary head of large charitable organizations to help the homeless, vets, or, especially, homeless vets and was on the Salvation Army board.

I figured that he, a former CEO of a water-heater manufacturing firm, a decorated World War II vet, and a community-oriented fellow warranted a short story obit. Nah, gotta go through advertising and buy it, I was told. We figured out that it was going to cost at a minimum of $1,000 to say what we wanted to say. So we donated the money to one of the homeless vets' organizations instead.

Okay, enough on that for now.

The night, I was called at home and told that the scanner was going crazy because of George Jones; the news was bad.

It appeared from the reports that George Jones, the lovable but troubled genius, may have died; that was the rumor—not far off as it turned out.

He had for sure crashed his Lexus through a bridge rail not far from his home in Franklin. For two hours, rescuers had toiled working to free him from the wreckage, and he was in critical condition at Vanderbilt University Medical Center, my editor friend Jerry Manley told me.

I also was told that they had tried to get ace music writer Jay Orr on the phone, figuring he'd be the one to do the story, especially if Jones was dead.

Jay, whose knowledge and wisdom now has him deep into a career as a top-echelon exec at the Country Music Hall of Fame and Museum, was the one who should have been called by the city desk.

He had a company cell phone (people didn't have their own back then) for just such occasions. But he wasn't answering it. I knew this was a top-of-the-front-page Sunday morning story, and I too wanted Jay, truly a great music journalist, to write it.

So I tried him a couple of times at his home and on the cell. He didn't answer.

I jumped in my old Saab and tore downtown, the adrenaline of a story in my veins but also sad because from all reports, I was going to be writing an obituary for a guy I really liked.

Throwing my last cigarette down at the guard-shack entrance to the newspaper building—the no-smoking silliness had taken over the world by then—I got on the elevator to the third floor.

I asked Jerry what he knew so far, and he told me. Nothing much was new since I'd left home 10 minutes before.

"Damn, I need Jay," I said to myself. I called the cops, the hospital, and whoever I could think of to tell me what was going on.

In between each of those calls, I tried Jay. No answer.

Finally, he picked up. He was at a restaurant, celebrating the birthday of one of his sons, so he was playing possum, so to speak, when the phone rang.

"I'm not coming in," said Jay. "You can pretend like you didn't reach me."

Being a reasonable boss and a guy fond of my staff and their families and celebrations, I agreed and simply asked Jay for phone numbers I could call. I thought his night was best spent with his kids and wife.

My first choice was to call the in-progress Grand Ole Opry, which I did, and I was patched through (I'm sure by a publicist) to backstage, where I asked if I could talk with some of the stars about Jones's wreck.

I remember Little Jimmy telling me how much he was "praying for Mr. Jones" as he did his best to do his job of lifting fans' spirits with his short jokes and guitar dynamism.

Porter Wagoner, whom I knew pretty well, at first thanked me for thinking of the Opry when it came time to get reactions.

"I appreciate what you and your staff do for real country music," he said before going into a brief and melancholy riff on his feelings for George Jones.

I can't remember who else I got. It was a long time ago.

But laced with quotes, I wrote that Jones was in critical condition at Vanderbilt University Medical Center.

He was on a ventilator and suffered injuries, including a collapsed lung and bleeding in his chest. Docs were worried about any other internal injuries, including a ruptured liver. Some might say that, given his lifestyle, he was fortunate to have a liver at all.

Of course, after that night, the story was turned over to Jay and to the cops reporters, and as I'd expected, George had fallen off the wagon, was drinking and using his cell phone, and lost control of his luxury car.

He survived, thrived, even.

This was one reason I could spend a day at his house. The fine day ended when it came time for George and Nancy to go out to eat. They asked me along, but I knew that it was just a courtesy and that they already had plans with some of those low-level country singers they'd been entertaining that day.

George hugged me as I stood up to begin the long walk through his stately home to my old car parked in the roundabout out front.

He walked with me, even held my car door open for me. Afterward, I said my good-byes and prepared to leave the grounds.

"Nice car," he said.

"Not a Lexus," I said, and we both laughed.

As I prepared to drive off, there was a gentle tap at my driver's-side window.

It was George Jones, of course, so I rolled the window down.

"Tim, give me a call, and we'll go out for a steak sometime," he said. "I'll buy."

I wasn't even sure if he meant it, but it sure made me feel good.

I'm sorry I never got that steak. But I relish the fact that this great man, a hell-raiser who had reinvented himself for the better, welcomed me into his house.

And we broke biscuits over White Lightning (the name on the bottle label).

Billy Cox and Jimi Hendrix

BILLY COX SAT IN HIS GARAGE STUDIO, where he makes music and remembers Jimi Hendrix, a pal who shared a brief span of his own rich life in rock 'n' roll, blues, and gospel.

"I believe he's in heaven, looking down on us," Billy said, love and admiration mixing in his voice, as he relaxed in his comfortable North Nashville home.

Oh, there's an undeniable dash of loneliness, too. It was a half century since his best friend and army chum, Jimi Hendrix, died. Clearly, he still missed him.

While the great and incendiary rock guitarist doesn't define Billy's life, this gentle bassist always has been comfortable with the association.

For one thing, he lugs his bass out as a main attraction on the Experience Hendrix tour circuit, which features a large cast of music luminaries who pay tribute to the "Purple Haze" composer and singer and guitarist while showing off their own chops.

The festival-like salute to Hendrix began in 1995 and annually draws some of the biggest names in the guitar and rock world. For example, the 2019 tour included Billy, of course, along with Buddy Guy, Jonny Lang, Taj Mahal, Joe Satriani, Dweezil Zappa, and more.

The COVID pandemic halted the 2020 tour, but Billy will be out there as long as he's wanted and able.

Billy, a fiercely independent soul, knows he'll forever be associated with his pal. In fact, the first time I met Billy, it was in the convention center room of what back in the 1970s was Clarksville, Tennessee's, biggest hotel.

If I recall correctly (a leap of faith at best more than four decades later), the show by Billy, who was "gussied up" in Jimi-style clothing and hairdo, didn't do well at the box office. It wasn't that there wasn't interest, because hard-core fans fought through an ice storm to get there. Clarksville is a hilly city, and unless you are really dying to see someone, you stayed in. Most chose that option.

I don't recall much about the show other than that it was sort of "in the round," and Billy not only played but also did his best to meet whoever came to see him.

I was doing a little story for the newspaper in Clarksville, so I spent time with him, and I remember he was a little disappointed with the crowd size.

You see, he expected he'd do pretty well at the hotel, as Clarksville was the stomping grounds of him and his skinny pal from Seattle both during their army days at Fort Campbell—the vast army post that straddles the Tennessee–Kentucky line at Clarksville's edge—and then after they got out.

After leaving the army, the young men moved into a house on East Franklin Street in the black section of town back in those days when racism was not nearly as evil and prevalent as it has been in recent years. The young men played at the American Legion Hall, the Elks Club, and Trane Union Hall (Trane, a manufacturer of air conditioners, was Clarksville's biggest industrial employer). I would guess that the former 101st Airborne paratroopers played for anyone who paid them.

Their regular place of employment, though, was the Pink Poodle on College Street, within walking distance of where they lived in Clarksville. They played that club even in later years after the two moved to Nashville.

Collins Music Store on Commerce Street in Clarksville reportedly leased Jimi a $90 guitar for $20 a month, and the receipt for that transaction was on display at that store until a 1999 tornado destroyed downtown Clarksville. I borrowed that receipt for a newspaper story 40 years ago. Somehow, that receipt got into the hands of a beer joint owner on Franklin Street, and the last time I saw it was in 2012 or so. That bar has since closed.

While Billy is forever associated with Hendrix (and he still misses the guy), he has had a lot of other success in the music business.

Among his personal highlights was a stint as bassist with the early Charlie Daniels Band.

In 2017, Billy, who sometimes calls himself the "Last Gypsy" (for reasons I'll explain later), wrote a Facebook entry about his fellowship with the long-haired country boy.

"In 2009, Charlie Daniels and I were inducted into the Musicians Hall of Fame.

"It had been some time since Charlie and I had seen each other, so we had a lot of catching up to do. At the reception, a reporter nearby came over to us and said, 'You guys are having such a good time; it looks like you know each other. Do you?'

"To her amazement, Charlie answered, 'Sure do, Billy use to play in my band, one of the best bass players that I know.'

"It was in the early '70s that I played with Charlie. All the cats in the band were great guys, and we had lots of good times and I have many fun memories of touring with them. I also played on *Whiskey*, one of Charlie's early albums. You cannot meet a better person, and at that time, Charlie helped me to remember that you could still play music and also have fun."

Of course, Billy was coming off a pretty depressing time in which his pal Jimi had died.

His list of musical bosses is extensive, and this isn't all of them. He played behind the great J. J. Cale onstage and recording. Cale, if I remember correctly, lived in a campground while trying to break into the music business in Nashville. I had the opportunity to get to know him a bit later in his life, and he was perhaps the most down-to-earth musical genius who ever lived in a campground. If I remember correctly, by then he was living in a shack in Death Valley with his dog and maybe a wife.

In addition to playing together in the King Kasuals show band and otherwise, Billy and Jimi played in Nashville's legendary Jimmy Church Band, a glorious show band of the type that the Blues Brothers were patterned after. Jimmy Church, a great man who named his bass-playing son Jimi, would have no time for a Jake and Elwood amateur hour in his band, though.

Billy also played bass with Little Milton, Lou Rawls, Freddie King, Sam Cooke, Jackie Wilson, Slim Harpo, Wilson Pickett, and Gene Chandler.

"I also played on most of the major Excello gospel albums in the 1960s," he said of time spent with the R&B, blues, and gospel label owned by Ernie Young.

Working at Nashville's Excello label would mean that Billy could have played behind other artists like Lightnin' Slim, Roscoe Shelton, Lazy Lester, Marion James, Arthur Gunter, and others. That label also put out a spoken-word sermon by the Reverend Dr. Martin Luther King Jr. I don't think he needed a bass line.

While Billy is self-assured (with good reason), he was beyond flattered many years ago when Texas guitar great Stevie Ray Vaughan introduced him to a Nashville audience by saying simply, "Y'all know Mr. Bass."

In the years before they died, Jimi Hendrix Experience members Noel Redding and Mitch Mitchell visited Nashville, spending time with Billy as well as with Elvis's original guitarist, Scotty Moore.

Redding (bass) and Mitchell (drums) were two-thirds of the Jimi Hendrix Experience in its "Purple Haze" and "All Along the Watchtower" prime. Redding found it hard to work with Jimi, so he left, and Jimi called his old friend Billy Cox to take over in the Experience. Other reports say that Jimi fired Noel—and he knew just who to call in as a replacement. Either way, Billy was ready.

Billy and Mitch backed Jimi on what many consider the iconic guitar player's best album, the very bluesy *Cry of Love*, released after drugs and inhaled vomit killed the great musician. Some say it was in an apartment owned by Beatle Ringo Starr. Actually, some time before his death, Hendrix had moved from Ringo's apartment at 34 Montagu Square in Marylebone, London. Ringo, who I know as an even-tempered fellow, had gotten disgusted by Jimi's vandalism, particularly when Hendrix whitewashed the walls while on an acid trip.

There were other Hendrix albums and concerts with the Billy, Mitch, and Jimi grouping. In fact, it seems that recordings from that era keep emerging from a limitless well. Elvis and Jimi have got to be the two dead musicians releasing the most "new" material, although John Lennon is catching up.

After the Experience, Billy played bass while drummer Buddy Miles backed Hendrix toward the end, including on the iconic *Band of Gypsys*.

Billy has played bass for his church in recent years. And, though he certainly doesn't need the work, he'll occasionally go out and play with friends at clubs.

"It's a privilege to be around good people," said Billy one day when we discussed the wonderful 2020, expanded 50-year *Band of Gypsys* repackaging and release.

"I enjoy my friends," he said. "I've had a great life. And I've enjoyed myself. And I've met some great and some smart people on this journey."

Scotty Moore was my dear friend who invented rock-'n'-roll guitar as sideman and manager to Elvis. Heck, until Scotty died, Billy might just get on his Harley and ride up U.S. 41A, the treacherous Clarksville Highway, and off into the countryside in search of a reason to play.

"When [Scotty] was alive, I'd ride my Harley up there to Blueberry Hill to say 'Hi,'" said Billy, who enjoyed the winding roads and hills encountered en route to Scotty's house on the street named for a Fats Domino classic.

A satisfied mind played across Billy's face as he talked about Scotty, who "was forced" to invent the role of lead rock guitarist, something that influenced Hendrix, of course, but also Keith Richards, Ronnie Wood, Eric Clapton, George Harrison, Jimmy Page, and even Eddie Van Halen, who seemed to inject a bit more playfulness into the music than his forebears. Go ahead and jump.

"There are only two types of guitarists," Cox said in an interview I did for July 17, 2006, editions of *The Tennessean*. "Those who admit they were influenced by Jimi Hendrix and those who don't admit it."

Still, long after Jimi was gone, Billy was hanging out with Scotty, whom Jimi no doubt emulated. Sometimes, at least until Scotty's health robbed him of the ability to play, music would erupt during those visits. It has been said, at least by me, that two members of The Rolling Stones, Scotty's drinking buddies Keith Richards and Ronnie Wood, also paid visits to the Joelton house on Blueberry Hill, which contained a full studio, most of which Scotty carted into the country after business woes in Nashville.

Scotty used to tell me how much he enjoyed the company of Billy and another regular "drop-in," rockabilly king Carl Perkins. I regret I never made one of those sessions. Scotty actually became one of my close friends in the years after Carl, whose "Blue Suede Shoes" was appropriated in the sales charts by his pal Elvis's version, died on January 19, 1998. I knew Carl only slightly, but his death stung, tore at my rock-'n'-roll youth.

Because music writer Jay Orr wasn't in the *Nashville Banner* office when Carl died, it was my honor to write his obituary as well.

Scotty also spoke fondly of Fats, who used to sing to me over the telephone if I contacted him in his home in the Lower Ninth Ward of New Orleans before Hurricane Katrina nearly took his life. He lived out his days in comfort in a higher and drier part of the city but would visit his offices in the Lower Ninth regularly. "This is Fats," he'd say when answering his phone, sometimes breaking into song if he was at the piano.

Of course, this book is about Nashville's musicians, so Fats doesn't really fit in here other than the fact I considered him a friend whom I could call for a musical interlude or just because I could.

Back to Billy and Scotty Moore briefly. The relationship between the men goes back decades to when Scotty had his own studio, Music City Recorders, on Nashville's Music Row. One of his janitors, it ought to be noted, was a former army helicopter pilot and Rhodes scholar who basically threw it away for a song. Well, to be fair, that janitor, Kris Kristofferson, threw it all away for a lot of songs and changed the vocabulary of country music.

In his post-Experience and Band of Gypsys days, Billy, who had settled in Nashville right out of the army and who made it his lifelong home, spent a good bit of time at Scotty's studio. Scotty would easily admit that he was a much better producer and engineer than businessman to explain why he no longer was running a commercial studio, even as most of the studio equipment was parked behind the glass-walled studio off his living room.

And there's even a member of The Beatles involved in this tale, as Scotty engineered Ringo Starr's critically acclaimed country album *Beaucoups of Blues* at the studio on Music Row.

"I worked a lot at Music City Recorders," said Billy. "Me and Scotty and D.J. We made tapes."

Drummer D. J. Fontana joined Elvis, Scotty, and Bill—the Blue Moon Boys—early on as the Hillbilly Cat and his pals conquered the world.

"Jimi was a friend," Billy told me when we talked about the *Band of Gypsys* golden anniversary. "Buddy [Miles] was a friend, too. I miss them both deeply."

Of course, Hendrix's death was one of the "big three" when he died on September 18, 1970. Other baby-boomer icons, Janis Joplin (October 4, 1970) and Jim Morrison (July 3, 1971), joined Hendrix in displaying in very short order that while rock 'n' roll may never die, it sure can be deadly.

Miles lived on and was musically successful for decades before succumbing at age 60 to congestive heart failure on February 26, 2008, at his home in Austin, Texas.

His *New York Times* obituary, published two days later, goes through his early work with the Ink Spots, the Delfonics, and Wilson Pickett before describing his work with Hendrix and Billy:

> Mr. Miles played with a brisk, assertive, deeply funky attack that made him an apt partner for Hendrix. With his luxuriant Afro and his American-flag shirts, he was a prime mover in the psychedelic blues-rock of the late 1960s, not only with Hendrix but also as a founder, drummer and occasional lead singer for the Electric Flag. During the 1980s, he was widely heard as the lead voice of the California Raisins in television commercials.

He played pretty much right up until his death, and he and his old bass-playing genius of a friend stayed in touch.

"Even after the years went by, Buddy spent the night here [at Billy's comfortable home] three times," staying there for lengthy spells among kindred souls in Music City.

I've been fortunate in my life to have spent a fair amount of time around Billy, a born-again son of a preacher from Wheeling, West Virginia.

When he spoke freely about his friendship with Hendrix and his personal commitment to Jesus, it was almost like the two were there with us in the converted-garage studio.

"I'm a collector of rare junk," he said shortly after I entered that garage for a story published in the July 17, 2006, editions of *The Tennessean* in Nashville.

He motioned his arms around the converted garage, walls lined with mementos, knickknacks, and other "things from my life."

He pointed to the Coca-Cola memorabilia—stuff that TV junk-hunters Frank Fritz and Mike Wolfe would drool over—and noted that most of it was collected during his ramblings around the world with Jimi after he replaced Noel in the Jimi Hendrix Experience.

"[Jimi would] be sleeping in the hotel. He was lazy. Me and Mitch [drummer Mitch Mitchell] liked to get up and go antique shopping, go to the flea markets."

There are many stories of Jimi and Billy, who lived above Joyce's House of Glamour, next to the Del Morocco on Jefferson Street, during the heyday of the Nashville R&B scene of the early 1960s.

There were clubs up and down that street for probably 20 blocks, and Jefferson Street was as alive with black music and art as was Harlem.

When the federal government put in Interstate 40 in the early 1970s, it went right through the club district. Among the literal victims were Joyce's House of Glamour and the Del Morocco. Among the figurative victims was the club district that had been sliced in half, as was the middle-class black neighborhood built up near Jefferson Street that treks past historically black Fisk University and Meharry Medical Center all the way to Tennessee State University.

Alums of the latter historically black state university include Olympic legend Wilma Rudolph, who won three gold medals in track at the 1960 games (where she befriended, for life, a young Louisville boxer named Cassius Clay); Dallas Cowboys defensive legend Ed "Too Tall" Jones; and "Jefferson Street Joe" Gilliam.

Joe, obviously nicknamed in the era of Broadway Joe Namath, starred at Tennessee State and went on to play for the Pittsburgh Steelers. He was a gentle enough man with a weakness for drugs that finally killed him. He died of a cocaine overdose on Christmas Day 2000, just a few days shy of his fiftieth birthday.

In my life, I was fortunate enough to befriend Wilma, the cousin of my dear friend, Montgomery County, Tennessee, barbecue hero "Ole Steve" Pettus.

"Ole Steve" taught me the tricks of barbecuing pork shoulder during long nights spent with him and his brother, Euless, at the ramshackle barbecue stand in a wooded field outside Clarksville. I became a good friend of the Pettus family and was invited to attend their family reunions in the summertime. All the cousins, including Cousin Wilma, toiled over casseroles, greens, pies, and the works in the house while "Ole Steve" took care of the steaks on the grill.

I also got to know "Jefferson Street Joe" and "Too Tall" slightly because of my stint as a sportswriter and sports editor at the paper in Clarksville.

Billy and his pal, the young Jimmy Hendrix ("Jimi" came later), just liked to make music, a love that drew them to Nashville. And it shouldn't have surprised anyone that the two young musicians were a bit "out there" by Jefferson Street standards.

"We had to be different after we'd been jumping out of airplanes for a living," Billy told me when we spoke about the two men's time spent as paratroopers at Fort Campbell.

"I think back now to how I did that," Billy said of his paratrooping days. "Man," he laughed while recalling making a living by jumping out of planes. By the way, the 101st Airborne (Air Assault) at Fort Campbell changed their way of delivering troops to battle during the Vietnam War, switching from parachutes to Blackhawk and Huey helicopters. The soldiers would rappel out, precariously, or simply jump while arriving for a firefight.

Billy said he first met Jimi when he followed his ears after hearing unusual sounds being produced by someone practicing guitar at Service Club No. 1, a recreation hall on the army post. Other soldiers found the music "weird." Cox soon began jamming with the guitarist and soul mate.

After their army days, as noted, they played around Clarksville for a while and moved to Indianapolis briefly and then back to Clarksville before rolling down U.S. 41A to Nashville.

Others from the old Nashville R&B scene remember Jimi as a kind fellow, introverted and hemp glazed, who would never be seen walking down Jefferson Street without his guitar, generally without a case, sometimes in a paper bag.

Eventually, Jimi's unique guitar playing coaxed him to leave Nashville, settling briefly in New York City, where he impressed Chas Chandler of the Animals ("House of the Rising Sun," "We Gotta Get Out of This Place"), one of the British Invasion groups most influenced by American R&B.

"Jimi called me from New York and told me, 'There's a guy who says he's going to take me over to England and make me a rock star, and I want you to come," Billy told me.

"I said, 'Man, I'm renting my amp, and I got three strings on my bass, and I got the fourth string tied in a square knot.'

"He said, 'Okay, I'll make it [to the big time]. And then I'll send for you.' And that's what he did."

Jimi was the toast of Swinging London, and the Jimi Hendrix Experience occupied the same stratosphere as The Beatles and The Rolling Stones.

He appreciated where he was in London rock royalty, and three days after The Beatles released *Sergeant Pepper's Lonely Hearts Club Band*, Jimi busted out his own version of the title song in a club show attended by Paul McCartney and George Harrison. Listen to it sometime: it's certainly a thrill. It's included in the Jimi Hendrix Experience boxed set and likely other sources.

It has been reported that the very physical play of Hendrix knocked his guitar out of tune during that show and that he asked another friend, a guitar player of some note named Eric Clapton, to come up from the audience and tune it for him. According to different legends, Clapton either took on the task for his friend or turned him down.

The Experience was unlike anything—it still is for that matter—but when either he kicked him out or Noel Redding left on his own (likely), Jimi turned to more bluesy material.

He called Nashville and offered the job to Billy. "I said, 'Jimi, why you calling me? You could get the best bass player in the world.'

"He said, 'I am.' . . . We thought a lot alike."

Billy said he had a music publishing company and other things "in the works" in Nashville, but he could not resist the promised call from his old friend.

"I put my belongings in a matchbox and jumped on the plane."

Even as a starring member of a legendary touring outfit, including his dawn stint on the Woodstock stage, where he watched his pal shred the National Anthem without rehearsal (and without the band having any idea of how to chime in), Billy has always called Nashville home.

He'd just returned from a European tour when he got a phone call at his house telling him Hendrix had died in London, a casualty of rock excess. "It was a Wednesday. I was supposed to meet him in New York for some recording on Friday.

"I didn't believe it. I still don't believe it. In fact I believe he's up in a cloud now. . . . Most geniuses don't live that long. They come and bring us some newity, I guess that's a new word, newity. It's their own style and flavor. And then they are gone.

"John Coltrane, Charlie Parker, they don't live to be 70. That's their destiny. Jimi Hendrix was no exception. He gave us 108 different songs we can take and enjoy. Good, good music."

He continues playing that music, sometimes for Experience Hendrix, the traveling road show of the Jimi Hendrix estate.

That and his self-described workaholic mentality help him maintain a good lifestyle, including enjoying his Harley in his "semiretirement years." He's a member of the Steel Horsemen motorcycle club. "We all have Harleys. That's the only way to get in."

(It ought to be noted here that Jimmy Otey, another of my friends visited in this book, was, by Billy's description, "my road dog. Everything I know about riding a Harley safely I learned from him.")

"Nashville is the last frontier," Billy said. "We still have a semblance of education here; we have churches here. You can even walk across Broadway here. You try doing that in New York . . . Nashville is a small city. Of all the places I've lived, this is the best."

It's also where he and Hendrix met trumpet player and showman Jimmy "Buzzard" Stuart.

"He was a musician extraordinaire. He heard us at the New Era [another storied Nashville R&B joint], and he wanted to help us. He taught us musical theory and helped us with the blues.

"He was an unsung hero of the old R&B scene." Stuart was married to Marion James, Nashville's Queen of the Blues.

Marion, who died in 2015, kept a picture of Jimi on prominent display in the living room two blocks from the site of the old Del Morocco. She also pushed, unsuccessfully, for a Jimi statue to be erected in a park next to the broad width of Interstate 40 that consumed the club and much of the neighborhood.

"He was all right," she told me during an afternoon at her house in 2012. "I hired him to play for me some."

She agreed with the general consensus that Jimi was a low-key, good fellow who perhaps laid a little bit too hard on the dope. More on my time with Marion later.

Johnny Jones may have been the guy responsible for Jimi's trip to stardom.

The truth is that back in those days, Johnny, whose body exterminators discovered on their regular trip to his apartment complex in 2009, was the one who many folks thought would become the big guitar star to come out of Nashville.

"Anytime I get the chance to play my guitar, it's more than money. It's therapy for me. I need to get time with my guitar every day," he told me in 2005 when I spent an hour or two with him at Rod's Market, within eyeshot of my friend Afro Doctor's barbershop and across the parking lot from the Elks Lodge.

I mention the Afro Doc primarily because I liked him a lot and he was a pal of Waylon and Willie and the boys. Whenever I got the chance and I was in the neighborhood near the Elks Lodge, I would drop in on the Afro Doc. A man whose heart belonged to his community, he'd ask me to climb up in his extra barber chair, where we'd talk about Jefferson Street, urban violence (he had to prove his own physical toughness on occasion), and the reason he enjoyed Waylon's company. And vice versa.

The Elks Lodge, though, formerly was the Club Baron, and it was where the storied guitar duel between Jimi and Johnny Jones took place. A generation of North Nashvillians will tell you they were there for the battling axes, but, of course, few of them were.

Johnny remembered Jimi coming into the bar with his pal Larry Lee, who went on to play with Hendrix at Woodstock and also became Al Green's guitar player. Jones was at the bar, having a drink during intermission. Confident in Hendrix's abilities, Lee issued the challenge to Johnny.

"I was louder than he was, and I was getting all the applause," Johnny said, noting that Jimi played well on his "little amp" in a losing cause when the duel played out after that intermission.

"I was wearing them out. I had that low-down Delta blues feel. Jimi needed that, and he got it from me. You gotta come from way down below the Mason–Dixon line to have that.

"Once he got it from me, he left. It was nice to know him and know I had something he could use."

At the time of our day together—I did call him often—Johnny still was active, playing his guitar around town, out of love if nothing else.

"It's the only thing that's stayed with me the last 50 years. I've changed wives four or five times. I've changed cars. I've changed everything. Everything except my guitar."

Another fixture on the R&B scene was Frank Howard & the Commanders. Frank, Charlie Fite, and Herschel Carter made up a harmonizing doo-wop group known as much for their flying splits as for their voices.

Frank, now a banker (aka "repo man") in Nashville and a close friend of mine, knew Jimi and Billy well.

"That was my boy, there," he says of Hendrix. "He played behind us for years at the Del Morocco. If Johnny Jones was missing for any reason, Jimi would sit in. . . . When he started playing here, he just was playing a few chords."

Frank, an admirer and friend of Billy's, said the latter should get much more credit for his role in Nashville music since he used his bass skills to lay down the foot-moving "bottom" on countless recordings during the R&B era.

"Billy wrote a couple of songs for me in the '60s: 'I'm So Glad' and 'I Feel Sorry for You,'" Frank said, adding that the apartment Billy and Jimi shared, above the beauty college, was pretty stark and lighted by a single light bulb dangling from the ceiling.

Billy's proud of the strange brew he and his former GI pal produced in that apartment and on the Nashville stages, all the way from Jefferson Street to the "white" club, the Jolly Roger, in Printer's Alley.

"Every now and then, a spirit slips through the portals of time into this reality and blows our mind," he said of Hendrix.

And Billy Cox, through his bass playing and his own substance-free view on life, laid down the bass lines.

Roy Clark

E VEN THOUGH HE CHANGED COUNTRY MUSIC, Roy Clark was a
humble fellow. And he didn't have much hair. But he could smile
and charm.

I spoke to him a few times during our careers—me as a journalist, him
as a legend—generally on the telephone. He'd talk about Branson, Missouri, which he helped settle as a hillbilly show oasis. Or we'd talk about
Hee Haw and Buck Owens and Grandpa Jones or about guitar pickers. Of
course, he was an expert resource.

I can't really put a date on the last time we spoke. Obviously, it was
before November 15, 2018, because that's when he died at age 85. He was
82 when I interviewed him.

An editor (and beloved personal friend) Calvin Gilbert called me from
the CMT.com skyscraper in downtown Nashville and wondered if I'd
have time to get to a publicist's office on 17th Avenue South (Music
Square West I believe is the tourism name) for a brief interview of Roy
Clark. Calvin had wanted to do it himself, but his editor's job had him
locked in the skyscraper, chewing on M&M's or putting peanuts in his
RC Cola.

Roy's health wasn't great, Calvin told me.

And CMT.com didn't want to pass up the opportunity to catch an
interview, albeit fleeting, with this legendary showman before it was too
late.

When I first was led down the stairs to the lower level of the publicist's
office, a friendly guy in a cowboy hat, fiddling with the cane between his
legs, looked up and smiled.

We were able to exchange only "Hi" or "Hello" nods before a publicist pulled him away and put him in a separate room (actually two rooms) where interviews were to be conducted. One room was for TV camera crews, the other one for writers who don't need special lighting and makeup. Well, I gotta admit, I could use some makeup.

I have tried to find the exact date or even the archived copy of what happened on what was a very happy day for me, but somehow it's vanished.

That's okay. I have a spare copy and some raw notes stored away in my computer. I kept it because I had hoped that when he died, Reuters News Service, for which I did some freelance work, would want an obituary.

They passed, probably content to go with the obituary handled by publicists and professional hyperbolists.

I actually was led into the interview room while Roy was across the hall, doing a spot for local TV news.

Then he ducked into the darker, classroom-like chamber where I'd been waiting. Oh, I'd done my homework. I didn't really know what I'd ask that hadn't already been reported, though.

"You ready for me?" he asked.

The guitar player who helped change country music forever leaned heavily on his cane—doctor's orders after back surgeries—as he slowly made it across the room and plopped into a sturdy enough desk chair.

After pushing back slightly on the brim of his cowboy hat, he reintroduced himself to me (as if he needed to). Then he made sure he knew my name as well.

I flatter myself by saying that he remembered talking with me before about his shows up in Branson. I'm sure he didn't, nor would I expect it. Hell, I had a hard time remembering it myself, and it was me asking the questions.

Many would call Roy Clark the top entertainer ever in country music, and he had the hardware from the CMA and the Academy of Country Music (ACM) to prove it, going way back into the early 1970s.

Although a stalwart of Nashville music, the Virginia native had long called Tulsa home. Of course, there was something of a music scene in Tulsa long ago, as both J. J. Cale and Leon Russell made some noise there. Heck, look it up, and it says that David Gates from Bread came from Tulsa. Yep, the genius behind "Baby I'm a Want You" was from Tulsa.

But Roy chose it not necessarily because of its music scene. He chose it because he was a barnstorming musician, and living in Tulsa put him smack-dab in the middle of the United States.

"It puts me in a one-day reach of the rest of the country," he said.

Unlike most such gatherings, when publicists summon real members of the Fourth Estate as well as entertainment writers, there was no stated reason for Roy's visit. He wasn't peddling a new record or TV spot.

He simply was coming to town on business and figured he might as well do a few interviews while he was at it. He liked Nashville, and, considering his health, who knew when he'd make it back here? I think the latter, really, is what fueled his scheme to sit for interviews.

"We planned this like you would plan a concert," said the affable fellow who helped spread the gospel of country music from *Hee Haw* and Kornfield Kounty into the living rooms of America.

Despite all of the well-deserved accolades for the Country Music Hall of Fame member, when people of a certain age think of Roy Clark, they think of *Hee Haw*.

Roy, of course, hosted this sort of cornpone *Laugh-In* with Bakersfield guitar legend Buck Owens.

This is a good enough place to mention the role of Charlie McCoy since he was *Hee Haw*'s music director for most of its run, and he recruited the band from the best of the Nashville Cats.

"It was like the Grand Ole Opry was years before that. It became a tradition" for families to gather around the TV set back when a big screen was 25 inches and a speaker three inches. It was time for *Hee Haw* to chase away the week's gloom, despair, and agony, Charlie told me for a story I did for the *Nashville Ledger*.

Charlie added that the popularity of the show became such that if America's biggest stars didn't have conflicts and were asked to do *Hee Haw*, "they'd say 'absolutely.' It was more promotion for them."

"Every day you walked in the studio, you were surrounded by legends," Charlie says. "There was Roy and Buck. Grandpa Jones. Minnie Pearl. Roy Acuff."

And then there was the regular supporting cast of folks like Archie Campbell, Junior Samples, David "Stringbean" Akeman, and so many more, including the eye-pleasing, scantily clad Hee Haw Honeys, now busty relics of less politically correct popular entertainment.

Sam Lovullo, *Hee Haw* producer and longtime crony of Roy's, occasionally dropped into my conversation with his pal on the day in the publicist's office. He wasn't intruding. But he wanted to fill in the blanks and also debunk the myth that Roy and Buck didn't get along.

Buck left the show late in the run, but Roy stayed until the end, and, while Owens had his strengths, Sam said Roy was "special."

"He was a triple threat. He could sing, do comedy, and do music with his friends," said Lovullo.

The success, of course, neither began nor ended with *Hee Haw*. In the years before, Roy already was blazing his trail toward stardom on stages across the country and on radio and television. And it wasn't just country. He appeared on a show fronted by Hank Williams, but he also fronted rockabilly queen Wanda Jackson's band live and on recordings and sampled Las Vegas success by opening for her in 1960 at the Golden Nugget Hotel.

His guitar stylings made him much in demand: his first album after signing with Capitol Records in 1960 was aptly titled *The Lightning Fingers of Roy Clark*.

By all measures, he already was a success when *Hee Haw* launched Roy into middle America's mainstream consciousness. His irrepressible charm as a storyteller and his genius as a guitarist and banjo player landed him on *The Tonight Show* (as both guest host and as performer), *The Beverly Hillbillies* (he was "Cousin Roy" for several appearances), *The Flip Wilson Show*, and even *Love, American Style*. There even were some movies.

With his personality, guitar talent, and passel of awards—CMA's Entertainer of the Year in 1973, ACM Entertainer of the Year in 1972 and 1973, and an armload of other awards, including three CMA Instrumentalist of the Year nods—Roy was a gentle soul who was welcome in every living room in America and in every big showroom from Las Vegas to Atlantic City.

He also was the first country performer to open his own venue in the heady early days of Branson's boom toward becoming a live music oasis.

"I was there first," Roy told me in a serious and proud tone. "And then I started having Mickey Gilley, Mel Tillis, and Jim Stafford up there performing at my theater. They finally said 'Wait, we're working for Roy, we should have our own theaters.' And they did."

Laughter, a standard part of our interview, punctuated that tale before he talked about his reason for leaving Branson a quarter century before.

Roy pulled out of Branson because of its cost and his international popularity.

"I was on the road so much, but the theater in Branson still had to be fed." If he wasn't there, he had to pay someone else to play.

While the fine fellow in the cowboy hat talked about just about any subject raised during the conversation, the biggest emotion was reserved for *Hee Haw*.

"To put it [his feelings about that landmark show] into one word is awfully hard to do," he said, fingering the brim of his hat. "Most of it is love."

He said when it started, none of the cast knew what was going on or what they needed to do. There'd been nothing like this, with quick comedy sketches at a frenetic pace, pretty women and music, and simple country corn all thrown together.

"We'd meet in the men's room—which was our dressing room—and ask each other, 'What are we doing?'" Finally, they asked for a rough cut of the show so they could understand it.

"Then we saw that it was a little 'iffin' and 'offin' [he says those words in the rhythm in which they were repeated in the show]. Then it was 'Howdee' and play a tune. We saw that [rough cut], and we said, 'Okay we're ready.'"

As an international, hard-touring performer, he said the production schedule in Nashville gave him welcome respite. "I used to rejuvenate in *Hee Haw*," he said.

Oh, one thing we talked about was his long string of hits, especially the song his pal Mickey Mantle asked him to sing at his funeral: "Yesterday, When I Was Young":

> Yesterday when I was young
> The taste of life was sweet as rain upon my tongue

A fan of both Mantle and this great guitarist, I could almost hear that melancholy look back at life as Roy stood, pushing himself up with his cane, to shuffle over to the next TV interview. I walked with him until he got to that door.

He straightened out his cowboy hat, polished up his smile, and went into the TV-lit room.

George Hamilton IV

GEORGE HAMILTON IV GAVE HIGH MARKS to the movie *The Iron Lady*, a 2011 biopic about Margaret Thatcher that he'd seen with his wife, Tink, the night before.

I'd called him not for a movie review—though I wasn't surprised he liked it, considering his mutual affection with people and things British. I called because he'd asked me to the evening before. We were having one of our semi-regular chats when he had to cut it short when he was reminded by his wife that showtime was approaching.

"We need to get going," he had said apologetically since he had made the call in the first place. "I hear it's a long movie."

The film already had won acclaim, especially for actress Meryl Streep, who won her third Oscar for her portrayal of Thatcher.

George, given his heritage as a country revolutionary of the most kind type, was an Anglophile—understandable in that even in the early twenty-first century, he could fill arenas in England with his gentlemanly folkish country songs while the United States belonged to Brooks & Dunn, Tim McGraw, Kenny Chesney, Toby Keith, Faith Hill, and Lonestar.

George and I were talking about the movie just because we occasionally enjoyed conversation. He also was a partaker in what now seems an ancient form of communication: the handwritten letter.

Going back to my days as a columnist and editor at the old *Nashville Banner* and then at *The Tennessean*, if George saw something he liked or that interested him in the entertainment pages or in music news in general, he'd drop me a letter.

For example, I think it was a story about the court battle regarding late country singer Jim Reeves's estate, including the home in East Nashville, that spurred the first letter from George back when I was at the *Nashville Banner.*

In fact, I may still have been state editor (I handled government news and news outside Metro Nashville as well as relative oddities, like court cases involving dead celebrities) when I got the letter from George. It was a note about his old friend Jim and how he and some others went out to search for the airplane after it crashed in Brentwood, just outside the Nashville city limits.

Jim was at the controls of the rented plane, and his piano player and business partner, Dean Manuel, also died in the crash.

The two had been flying back to Nashville on July 31, 1964, from a business meeting in Batesville, Arkansas, where they had secured a real estate deal.

They were almost home when Jim flew the plane into a violent storm over Brentwood, and the country star reportedly was trying to rely on the course of Franklin Road (U.S. 31), just below him, when the plane stalled and crashed.

George's note was a simple enough courtesy. He wasn't complaining about the coverage. He just wanted to offer his services if I needed any information.

He wrote that Jim was a great and good friend and that if ever I wanted to go to the actual crash site, he'd show me.

The plane wreckage actually wasn't far from where I've lived in Nashville for a few decades. It's pretty developed now, but it took 42 hours for searchers to find it back in 1964. The plane pretty much was buried, part by part, in the ground.

"Ernest [Tubb], Marty [Robbins] and I were among those out there searching for it," George wrote (or words to that effect).

We never did hook up to make the trek out there, but he told me where it was, and I pretty much located the site, though what when Jim crashed was a green and pristine section of Davidson County at the Williamson County line now is upscale residential for the most part (not my part, I should note).

George was a friendly and, in his own country, mostly "forgotten" fellow, which really didn't bother him that much. He'd had his time at the top.

He and I talked fairly often about his popularity in England, something that I'm sure went long past his dying day. I'm sure they still love him over there.

George IV was a pioneer in popularizing country music of the traditional variety in the United Kingdom.

In a lengthy series of conversations with George IV, this truly gentle man talked about that international superstardom and how he had blazed the trail and kept it open for country musicians willing to hop the Atlantic.

Those interviews really were just conversations, rambling widely, in part for a story package I wrote for the *Nashville Ledger* about the British appetite for Nashville music. He also was soft and easy as he talked about his relative anonymity in Nashville, where he could go to the movies undisturbed but where his main musical appearances were as a beloved member of the Grand Ole Opry.

George IV began his career as a pop heartthrob, sharing the stages with Sam Cooke, Buddy Holly, Chuck Berry, Jerry Lee Lewis, and even Louis Armstrong, before he converted to ear-friendly, heartwarming country music and its gospel offshoots.

His approach and his ego are displayed in the liner notes of his 1968 *The Gentle Country Sound of George Hamilton IV*.

My friend Peter Cooper used those comments to successfully cast a warming shadow on George IV in the obituary that was published in *The Tennessean* on September 18, 2014, a day after George's death.

Peter noted that in the liner notes, George IV wrote of a "quiet, beautiful musical revolution in the world of country music."

"This revolutionary grew up in the city of Winston-Salem, North Carolina, went to college for four years, doesn't dig saloons and is happily married," George wrote in those liner notes. "Do I have to sing honky-tonk songs about slippin' around and wear a rhinestone-studded cowboy suit to be real?"

I figure this is as good a place as any to further emphasize the character of the man, whose deep Christian faith led him to become a fierce supporter of racial equality. Against the norm—and that certainly is one thing you could say about George IV—is the fact that he was the rare country music star who actively supported progressive politicians, integration, and other socially conscious causes in the turbulent 1960s. I'm not saying he was the only one who thought that way. He was just about the only one who willfully entered the fray as an advocate for social reform, taking a big risk of alienating the good ol' boys in his fan base.

In 1968, he and wife Tink attended Democratic presidential candidate Robert F. Kennedy's speech at Vanderbilt University's Memorial Gym.

The candidate was delayed by weather as he flew into Nashville. According to accounts in *The Tennessean*, the speech was scheduled for 7:30 p.m., and students began arriving an hour before. Kennedy, though, arrived a couple of hours late.

"Almost no one left during the delay, however, partly because singer George Hamilton IV entertained them magnificently," according to an account written by Frye Gaillard for *The Tennessean*.

George IV considered "opening" for Kennedy to be a highlight of his musical career.

And that career traveled from grand venues to small churches and at least one old-fashioned hardware store where I caught him one morning on a broadcast with his pal John D. Loudermilk.

"I'm an intellectual," said John D. on that morning in 2013 when he needlessly "apologized" for his guitar playing for an audience of about 90 gathered in a hardware store.

"I changed my strings last night and trimmed my fingernails the night before."

I was in that audience in Handy Hardware in Franklin, 20 or so miles south of Nashville, to attend a livestreaming radio broadcast staged regularly by George V (the IV's musical son). I'd chosen this particular broadcast to highlight because the special guests that day were Loudermilk and George IV.

"I consider John D. a gift from God," said George IV, who was sitting to John D.'s left.

The two men had been waging the country music wars, virtually side by side, for more than 55 years. George IV's first record, "A Rose & a Baby Ruth," was a million-selling hit in 1957. It also was writer Loudermilk's first song to make it to the top of the charts and the first of several of his songs—think "Abilene," "Break My Mind," and "Fort Worth, Dallas and Houston," for example—recorded by Hamilton.

That gray spring day, George IV was relaxed in the down-home atmosphere that was thousands of miles from the turf where he still was among country's greatest stars.

In fact, he told me after his segment on the air was done (I sat with the two buddies in the hardware store office) that the very next morning, he was jetting to England for a troubadour-style, man-with-guitar tour in theaters across the United Kingdom.

"The British fans seem to like traditional country," he told me in a separate interview for the February 3, 2012, editions of the *Nashville Ledger*. "Certain artists have received a warmer response there than here back home."

As noted briefly above, I was exploring the phenomenon of George IV and other classic stylists' continuing popularity in England while they could go to a hardware store (not always one where they performed) or a pharmacy and go unnoticed here.

George, who had been dubbed the "International Ambassador of Country Music," was generally given credit for establishing the business model, nurturing that British fan base with charm, grace, and good music and at the same time building enduring box office success.

In Nashville, the flavor and cleavage of the day relegate older artists to the status of a regular on the *Grand Ole Opry* radio show (a status that makes them proud, by the way). Of course, George IV and others also followed the snowbird flight path and continued to deliver "Abilene," "Early Morning Rain," and more classic stuff to blue-haired Florida retirees.

Perhaps the greatest musician Nashville ever produced, Charlie McCoy, and his wife still spend their winters in Florida, packing them in at retirement villages and the like, just like George did up until his death at age 77.

But George's most rabid fans were the folks in Jolly Old England, where he played arenas and theaters and even wandered from church to church, where this Christian gentleman played for freewill offerings. And for love.

George IV, with pastors serving as emcees, would "do about 20 minutes of hit records and then ease into country gospel for them."

As he noted, these shows "aren't a financial windfall," but expenses were low, acoustics great, and the spiritual rewards fulfilling.

"I want to make sure that I point out that I was by no means the first to go over there," the dapper gentleman said when I talked with him about his regular success in the United Kingdom.

"My advice to an artist just getting started here is to make sure they don't overlook that market," he told me. "There is a huge market, particularly in the British Isles: England, Scotland, Ireland, and Wales.

"The artists who have taken the trouble to go over there and tour have all done really well."

While generally given credit for mapping out this strategy, George IV was quick to point to his predecessors, in particular Slim Whitman, the great yodeler and infomercial star hardly known in the United States but a massive success in England.

"The first person I know to become an international star by playing in England was Slim Whitman," Hamilton said.

"He was playing the London Palladium in the mid-1950s and packing it. And he did a lot of concert tours in the mid-'50s, and he's remained popular over there until recent times," George IV told me. Look elsewhere in this book for more on Slim, who, like George, was a self-deprecating man of immense talent, drive, and the type of simple, endearing charm not existent anymore.

"He was the pioneer. . . . He preceded all of us," George said of Slim.

When Bobby Bare (r) got his star in the Music City Walk of Fame in 2022, Tim Ghianni (l) was among the first to congratulate him. The Walk is a block from where Shel Silverstein and Bare volunteered to help Tim "rescue" road bricks in 1972. PHOTO COURTESY SHANNON BARE

Countrypolitan king Eddy Arnold gets a lift from Cowboy Jack Clement, who worked at Sun Studio in Memphis to help capture the sounds of Elvis, Carl Perkins, Johnny Cash, and Jerry Lee Lewis. Later Nashville clients included Arnold, U2, and Charley Pride. PHOTO COURTESY SHANNON POLLARD

Kris Kristofferson (l), arguably one of country's greatest songwriters, visits with his friend Tim Ghianni, backstage in 2007 after the singer performed at the Country Music Hall of Fame and Museum. © 2022 JOHN PARTIPILO PHOTOGRAPHY

Kris Kristofferson (l) and the author sing in "harmony" at the site of the long-demolished Tally-Ho Tavern on Music Row in 2003. The song is Kristofferson's classic "The Silver Tongued Devil and I," set in that tavern. PHOTO BY JOHNNY KRISTOFFERSON

Kris and Lisa Kristofferson relax during a family gathering at Donner Pass in Spring 2022. PHOTO BY KRIS KRISTOFFERSON JR.

George Hamilton IV (r) began his career as a teenage heartthrob, but he became one of the most beloved members of The Grand Ole Opry, where he spent time backstage with folks like Little Jimmy Dickens. PHOTO BY GEORGE HAMILTON V

Little Jimmy Dickens was the heart and soul of The Grand Ole Opry. Here, acclaimed photographer Bill Steber captures him outside the Ryman Auditorium, former home of The Opry. © BILL STEBER PHOTOGRAPHY

Mac Wiseman, one of the original Foggy Mountain Boys, and two friends, Peter Cooper and Thomm Jutz, wrote a theme-album biography, I Sang the Song. One song is about his boyhood church, shown in the picture over his chair. © 2022 JOHN PARTIPILO PHOTOGRAPHY

Music historian/singer-songwriter Peter Cooper, left, and singer-songwriter/guitar guru Thomm Jutz, right, worked with their hero Mac Wiseman, co-producing two late-life albums: I Sang the Song and Songs from My Mother's Hand, a collection Mac learned from his mother's handwritten songbook. PHOTO COURTESY SANDY KNOX

Tom T. Hall kept himself busy in the years after the love of his life, Miss Dixie, died. A favorite pursuit was firing up a cigar and a tractor and working the land at Fox Hollow, south of Nashville. PHOTO COURTESY MELISSA LAWRENCE BUCK

Dixie Hall's passions included bluegrass music and dogs. Here the heart of Fox Hollow gets loving from a puppy belonging to visiting bluegrass musicians Heather and Tony Mabe. PHOTO COURTESY REBEKAH SPEER

Grandpa Jones (r), a star long before Hee Haw *launched him into the national spotlight, visits backstage at the Opry with Jim McReynolds, tenor of the duo Jim and Jesse (his brother).* © *BILL STEBER PHOTOGRAPHY*

Stonewall Jackson put on his old-school, country star regalia for this picture on his front porch above Lake Waterloo, named for his 1959 crossover hit. PHOTO BY TIM GHIANNI

Charlie Daniels, with American Quarter Horse Association mare Ms. Passeos Country and her twin American Paint Horse foals, enjoys a quiet moment on his Lebanon, Tennessee, ranch with his wife, Hazel. PHOTO COURTESY THURMAN MULLINS

Jimmy Otey was a star drummer for everyone from James Brown to Little Richard. It didn't matter where he was working, his goal was to get home to Nashville every weekend to be with his family. PHOTO BY TIM GHIANNI

After years as a drummer for James Brown, Little Richard, and the like, Jimmy Otey settled into a career as a Nashville city bus driver. He liked the people and was glad to spend nights in his own bed. COURTESY NASHVILLE'S WEGO PUBLIC TRANSIT

Billy Cox is a key part of Experience Hendrix, a roving festival salute to Billy's Army chum and long-ago Nashville roommate, Jimi Hendrix. Billy played bass in the later stage of The Jimi Hendrix Experience and then Band of Gypsys. *PHOTO BY STEVEN C. PESANT, AUTHENTICHENDRIX / COURTESY BOB MERLIS, EXPERIENCE HENDRIX L.L.C.*

A guitar-wielding king of massive showrooms, Roy Clark (l) was propelled into American living rooms as a folksy cohost with Buck Owens on Hee Haw. GAYLORD/PHOTOFEST © GAYLORD PRODS.

North Carolina native George Hamilton IV performs in Wilkesboro, NC, in 2012 when honored by his home state's Wilkes Heritage Museum's Blue Ridge Music Hall of Fame as "Nationally Known Artist" for that year. PHOTO BY MONTY COMBS/COURTESY WILKES HERITAGE MUSEUM

Beloved overseas, George Hamilton IV was always "home" at The Grand Ole Opry with his country music colleagues like Dolly Parton. PHOTO BY GEORGE HAMILTON V

Charlie McCoy reacts emotionally when speaking at his induction ceremony into the West Virginia Music Hall of Fame in 2008. The versatile singer and musician is a native of Oak Hill, West Virginia. Michael Lipton, director of the Hall in Charleston, supplied this photo. PHOTO BY MIKE KELLER/ COURTESY WEST VIRGINIA MUSIC HALL OF FAME

Rodney Crowell, left, and John Carter Cash, right, helped in the celebration when harmonica ace and wildly versatile musician Charlie McCoy was inducted into the Musicians Hall of Fame & Museum in 2007. COURTESY MUSICIANS HALL OF FAME & MUSEUM AT HISTORIC NASHVILLE MUNICIPAL AUDITORIUM

Marion James at the piano in the Elks Lodge on Jefferson Street, formerly the Club Baron, site of a famous guitar showdown between Jimi Hendrix and Johnny Jones. PHOTO BY TOD ELLSWORTH

Team Scruggs: Earl played banjo while Louise handled business. The Scruggs family at the Country Music Hall of Fame and Museum in 2004. Sitting, Earl and Louise; Standing, Gary, left, and Randy, right. COURTESY OF THE COUNTRY MUSIC HALL OF FAME® AND MUSEUM

Jimmy Church, shown performing at a Music City Roots broadcast, is Nashville's R&B "god-father." The Jimmy Church Band continues to thrive decades after breaking in with Jimi Hendrix, Billy Cox, Frank Howard, Roscoe Shelton, and others. COURTESY OF THE COUNTRY MUSIC HALL OF FAME® AND MUSEUM

Deed and Duane Eddy flank filmmaker Ken Burns backstage at the 2013 Americana Music Honors & Awards. COURTESY AMERICANA MUSIC ASSOCIATION

Duane Eddy, whose twanging guitar helped create rock 'n' roll, performs at the 2013 Americana Music Honors & Awards, where he was honored for lifetime achievement as an instrumentalist. COURTESY AMERICANA MUSIC ASSOCIATION

Carl Smith and Goldie Hill sit surrounded by their family for a fortieth anniversary photo in 1997. Back row, from left: son, Carl Jr.; his wife, Pam; daughter, Lori Lynn; Dean Smith's wife, Tammy; and Dean. PHOTO COURTESY DEAN SMITH

Harold Bradley with BR549's Smilin' Jay McDowell (left), at his ninety-second birthday party held at the Musicians Hall of Fame & Museum. Harold played guitar on more sessions than anyone. Bass-playing Smilin' Jay is the multimedia archivist at the Hall. COURTESY MUSICIANS HALL OF FAME & MUSEUM AT HISTORIC NASHVILLE MUNICIPAL AUDITORIUM

Harold Bradley was in the first class of inductees into the Musicians Hall of Fame & Museum in 2007. COURTESY MUSICIANS HALL OF FAME & MUSEUM AT HISTORIC NASHVILLE MUNICIPAL AUDITORIUM

Tyrone "Super T" Smith spends a part of each show flying about the stage in a Superman-style costume. His Tyrone Smith/Super T Revue's fans included President George W. Bush, who learned the Super T Booty Green dance at a White House party. PHOTO COURTESY BILLY CANNON

Bobby Hebb, whose disposition is showcased in his song "Sunny," performs in a May 1998 recording/interview session in Medford, Massachusetts, produced and directed by his friend, Joe Viglione. © JOE VIGLIONE

Frank Howard, long-ago leader of Frank Howard & The Commanders, performs at a Music City Roots broadcast in Nashville. He's been key in helping resurrect the city's R&B scene. COURTESY OF THE COUNTRY MUSIC HALL OF FAME® AND MUSEUM

Scotty Moore, left, and D. J. Fontana, right, were in the first class inducted into the Musicians Hall of Fame & Museum in 2007. Others depicted: Vince Gill and Jerry Phillips, son of Sun Records producer Sam Phillips, who helped Elvis, guitarist Scotty, and bassist Bill Black "invent" rock 'n' roll in 1954. Drummer D. J. joined in 1955. COURTESY MUSICIANS HALL OF FAME & MUSEUM AT HISTORIC NASHVILLE MUNICIPAL AUDITORIUM

Keith Richards appreciated his long friendship with Scotty Moore. "Everyone else wanted to be Elvis. I wanted to be Scotty," the Rolling Stones co-founder, guitarist, and lyricist said, recalling the first time he heard "Heartbreak Hotel." Scotty made the mold for rock guitarists. © J. BOUQUET, DECEMBER 3, 2005. BACKSTAGE, MEMPHIS, TN, BIGGER BANG TOUR

Keith Richards (l) and Ronnie Wood (r) both idolized Scotty Moore and they were loyal to their hero and close friend, the man who invented the role of rock 'n' roll lead guitarist. The two Rolling Stones and Elvis's original guitarist also robustly shared a love for drinking. © J. BOUQUET, DECEMBER 3, 2005. BACKSTAGE, MEMPHIS, TN, BIGGER BANG TOUR

Billy Joe Shaver was a hard-living "Outlaw" and a near-angelic follower of The Word. The honky-tonk poet always softened when he was around dogs. PHOTO BY JIM McGUIRE / COURTESY LOGAN ROGERS, LIGHTNING ROD RECORDS

Donnie Fritts, left, holds court with record producer and musician Norbert Putnam; musician, producer, and studio owner Johnny Johnson; and Dan Del Fiorentino, NAMM music historian, during a July 12, 2015, gathering at Putnam's house in Muscle Shoals, Alabama. PHOTO BY ERIC GLASNAPP/NAMM

Funky Donnie Fritts (l) — also known as "The Alabama Leaning Man" — and Kris Kristofferson outside Muscle Shoals (Alabama) Sound Studio during Fritts's 1974 Prone to Lean recording sessions. Kristofferson co-produced the album with Jerry Wexler and contributed harmony. PHOTO BY DICK COOPER/ COURTESY MICKEY J. LOLLAR, CURATOR, ALABAMA MUSIC HALL OF FAME

He liked to shine the spotlight elsewhere, but George became a successful staple of British theaters ever since his first "accidental" visit.

Back in 1967, his manager, Wesley Rose, of Acuff-Rose, booked him for a tour of military bases in Germany.

"In those days, in the 1960s, a lot of Nashville artists went over to play the bases. There was a huge military presence in Germany and in Europe during the days of the Cold War and Iron Curtain and all that," George said.

"There was a lot of tension between the Soviets and the USA."

Most of the Opry family made trips to Cold War outposts, and Hamilton, with his polished good looks, pop-music chops, and mellow voice, was an instant hit with the GIs, their families, and the many German citizens who were "sneaked" into the enlisted men's and officer's clubs and other concert locales, he told me.

"There are a lot of real loyal country fans in Germany, Spain, and Italy. These civilians managed to get themselves invited as guests to these shows because they were real country fans, and it was their opportunity to see Nashville artists."

In November 1967, Rose suggested that before coming back to Music City, George take a side trip to England, visit the London office, and "check out the scene."

"He said, 'Country music is very popular there.'"

Sure, it was a time when The Beatles dazzled brains and ears with "Sgt. Pepper's Lonely Hearts Club Band" and "A Day in the Life" and Roger Miller sang "England Swings" (like a pendulum do), yet there was plenty of love to go around for old George IV, who again credited not only Whitman but other predecessors as well.

George IV talks about the success of that first visit and his subsequent love affair with the Brits before clearing his throat and turning a bit solemn.

Jim Reeves, the friend whose body he sought with Ernest Tubb and Marty Robbins, "had preceded me there, and he was very popular in the British Isles. While I was there, they got me on a country music BBC live radio show in front of an audience. It was sort of the British version of the Opry."

On the "BBC Playhouse Theatre on the Thames," he rolled out a few of his hits, and "I was pleasantly surprised to find out they were popular there."

Because he was following fellows like Whitman and Reeves, Hamilton's smooth, folk-oriented ballads were easily accepted by the Brits.

"After one of the radio interviews I did with the BBC, these guys took me to a little pub for a pub lunch. I was sitting at a table with a group of

BBC presenters, programmers, and some guys from the record company there in England.

"The topic of conversation was that this fellow Mervyn Conn [legendary promoter] had announced that he was going to promote the first International Festival of Country Music at Wembley Arena.

"These radio and record company types were all laughing and giggling about Mr. Conn's proposed festival. The line of conversation was that 'he won't be able to draw enough to fill his living room.'"

Hamilton didn't laugh. "I remember thinking to myself, 'That sounds like a great idea.'"

Conn came to Nashville to entice top talent with the plea that the festival would be a stepping-stone to Europe. He couldn't pay, though he did provide air transport, room and board, and expenses for the artists who participated in the inaugural fest on Easter weekend 1969.

Hamilton was joined by Charlie Walker, Bill Anderson, Roy Acuff and His Smoky Mountain Boys, the Glaser Brothers, and others.

"We all came back to Nashville, very enthusiastic about the possibilities of country music in England, Ireland, and Europe," Hamilton said in the story I did for the *Nashville Ledger*. "The festival jump-started country music on that side of the Atlantic. As we had hoped, the festival lighted a fire under the scene."

George IV credited the 1970 Wembley Fest, broadcast by BBC, with taking him one more huge step to British stardom.

A BBC producer was intrigued by George IV's music and, just as much, his style.

"I looked quite unlike the cowboy, and the producer said, 'I think I can use that guy.' He had been thinking of doing a country music series in London, and he was looking for a host that might bridge the gap between England and Nashville, who might be palatable to the great British public, who weren't used to country music."

Again, there is a certain debt to Reeves, who had been known in the United Kingdom for his gentleman's threads and demeanor, a style echoed by George IV.

"I just happened to be wearing a pinstriped, three-piece suit with a roman number IV on my breast pocket," said Hamilton, remembering his big break.

Seen as accessible to British hearts because of his gentlemanly appearance and his polished performance style, he was asked to host a UK country music series, turning him into a household name. "It was ridiculous the amount of exposure I was getting," Hamilton said.

He said part of the attraction that he, Reeves, Whitman, and other guys enjoyed in England sprung from their classic singing, but it indeed was backed up by sartorial style. This wasn't just a country music thing: remember, The Beatles' first success came after Brian Epstein put them in suits rather than leathers and Levis. The music was the same, but perception changed.

"Most of the [Nashville singers] who have done well there have been people who sing traditional country music or who have the Don Williams approach, the smooth ballads and story songs."

Pretty much up until his death, George IV made regular visits to England and even found fans as far east as the former Iron Curtain countries.

The previously mentioned church tours, the guitar-toting troubadour performing for stained-glass-illuminated fans, were among his favorites.

George V picked up that tradition when his dad died. I don't know if he still does it, but I'd guess his own talent and the residual goodwill left by his pop have had him receiving raves in the crowded sanctuaries.

George IV told me in my *Nashville Ledger* story that a good number of current country stars are making a mistake by focusing on staying home, cashing in on huge arena crowds, singing, and laughing all the way to the bank rather than worrying about European logistics. It was a mistake that Elvis made. It didn't interrupt his too-short career, but he missed out on the chance to be received by even more of the adoring crowds that kept him going even when drug bloated and weary.

George IV said the youngsters should not just bank the massive proceeds from the arenas and stadiums because that degree of fame and box office fleecing is fleeting (unless you are The Rolling Stones).

"But there always comes a day in an artist's career when the hits stop coming and there aren't records on the charts. If they had taken the trouble to court that market over there and make themselves known, they then would have had a whole second career internationally.

"It's a big world out there, and there are more country music fans than one would think."

Slim Whitman

SLIM WHITMAN, WHO CAST A G-RATED, mustachioed yodel over Nashville music, was a little surprised when George Hamilton IV told him I wanted to give him a call at Woodpecker Paradise, the ranch he and his wife shared outside Jacksonville, Florida.

And the surprise remained in this wonderful man's voice when I made that promised call (and subsequent ones).

You see, I wouldn't have talked to him at all if it hadn't been for George IV's insistence. But the fact is, it simply was George being George, a humble fellow wanting to know that proper credit was given to the person who deserved it.

I was just getting started on a story I'd successfully pitched to the *Nashville Ledger* in early 2012. I knew that George IV, a guy I liked a lot, was a huge star in England even though he was relegated largely to Opry cast status back here in the United States. He remained proud of that Opry star status, but Americans really didn't know what they were missing.

My story focused on how George IV, the "International Ambassador of Country Music," and others of his vintage still packed them in over in the United Kingdom and elsewhere, while, for the most part, American artists avoided Europe to pack folks into the massive arenas and parade around in their underwear or mechanics' clothes in the sheds of the United States.

Heck, Elvis was one of the notable American artists who never played Europe, home of much of his devoted following, many of whom make the transatlantic pilgrimage to light candles, buy Elvis curios, eat deep-fried peanut butter and banana sandwiches, and otherwise enjoy Dead Elvis Days in Memphis every August. It was, of course, August 16, 1977, that the King of Rock 'n' Roll, my first real hero, suffered a drug-induced heart attack.

George IV told me his story of European adoration in a self-deprecating fashion, and we became friends. He'd already written me a few letters of appreciation and friendship whenever I wrote about old country musicians, be they his contemporaries or predecessors.

It wasn't that long into his description of his British conquest when he stopped and asked me to promise him something before he continued.

He insisted on one thing that I had to promise to do if I was going to tell his story about country innocents abroad: "You really need to talk to Slim Whitman. He started it."

George IV told me that Slim opened up three-quarters of the planet to country music when he began playing shows in England in the 1950s.

"He was Elvis" in the United Kingdom, according to George, who was among the first to follow Slim to Europe.

"I'd love to talk with him," I told George IV, who became a longtime friend right up until his own death on September 17, 2014.

The promise to interview Slim was joyfully granted, and I asked George IV, "You have Slim's number?" or something similar.

"Well, he doesn't talk much these days, but let me call him and ask. If he says it's okay, I'll call you back and give you his number."

Within an hour, I was talking to the extremely gentle man. In my dusty old Rolodex, I still have the square blue sticky note on which I'd scribbled Slim's number. There are the numbers of a lot of dead guys in that Rolodex, so it's not really that useful, but I hate to throw it away.

I figured Slim was likely an obscurity to modern consumers of hip-thrusting, tattooed-thigh, breast-pounding-and-proffering country music, but I couldn't pass up the opportunity to talk to this pop-culture legend.

Slim long ago had set the trend for selling records on late-night TV infomercials. He was almost a caricature of a cowboy, with his swashbuckling mustache and bright smile and that black and white western suit.

He was the pioneer in a trend, reaching audiences that country radio had forgotten or discarded.

Waylon Jennings was one who recognized the importance of such infomercial marketing. "Radio doesn't have any room for us," he said of his generation of artists, who now, of course, are mostly gone. "Our people watch television."

Waylon's comments about radio versus TV advertising came when a label exec told the Old Dogs supergroup—Waymore, Bobby Bare, Jerry Reed, and Mel Tillis, accompanied by every A-Teamer you could name—that they needed to rush a cut from their self-titled recording to radio. All of those guys agreed with Waylon. And hell, I know my dear friend Bobby Bare knows that's where the fans are. Of course, the fans are dying off about as fast as the artists. I doubt that the till-death-do-us-part type of fan loyalty will still exist when Florida Georgia Line or John Rich and their like turn 85.

I can just imagine Waylon's lonesome, on'ry, and mean stare when informing publicists that the Old Dogs belonged on TV infomercials. What Waylon wanted he generally got. The record was promoted on TV, like Slim had been doing for years.

In years since, of course, TV marketing has become major, especially for vintage artists and their CDs. There even are those half-hour "variety shows" that feature old footage of artists along with the constant beckoning to buy the CDs. They generally don't talk about downloads on those commercials, which are aimed for folks of my vintage or even older.

As for Slim, the infomercials gave Americans a hint of what folks in Europe had known for decades about this man and his role in taking country music worldwide, even as he got little recognition in the United States or even in Nashville, where he generally recorded.

Johnny Carson, who for baby boomers was America's late-night TV host and the mentor for Leno and Letterman (who, in turn, raised the bar for Kimmel, Colbert, and Fallon), apparently loved those infomercials. (There were guys before Johnny, such as Jack Paar and Steve Allen, but Johnny turned late night into that overused marketing phrase "must-see TV.")

The guy who followed Ed McMahon's "Heeeeere's Johnny!" onto the NBC stage was the architect of the late-night talk show, concocting a formula pretty much used to this day: monologue focusing on timely issues, a band, guests, the occasional comic sketch, and maybe an entertaining sidekick or bandleader.

Johnny and his troupe the "Mighty Carson Art Players" performed silly and satirical sketches loaded with double entendre and dosed with cornpone, the same sort of stuff later perfected and turned cornier still by *Hee Haw*.

Right alongside Carnac the Magnificent, Art Fern, Aunt Blabby, and other Carson characters, there was the yodeling cowboy singer parody. At least that's the way I remember it.

And that's where I "met" Slim Whitman, who eventually followed the Carson satire publicity right onto the couch on *The Tonight Show* set in Burbank, California. During that 1981 visit, he told Johnny that when it came to the commercial selling the vinyl album or eight-track tape of his hits, "some people laugh at it, but they buy it."

The following year, the "Rose Marie" singer played Letterman, where he told the host that the commercial was the only reason anyone would care to book him onto a variety/talk show.

Like I said above, Slim was pretty surprised anyone was really interested in talking to him by the time my friend George IV connected us on his eighty-ninth birthday on January 20, 2012.

The mustachioed and self-described "country-and-western crooner and yodeler" was largely forgotten. His flash of American fame, courtesy of the TV commercials, was past. And that didn't bother him much.

Slim Whitman was known for late-night infomercials, but the yodeling showman was credited by George Hamilton IV, International Ambassador of Country Music, for opening Europe for country stars. PHOTOFEST

Ranch life was good, and Ottis Dewey Whitman Jr. was, after all, a Florida boy, having been one of six children of Ottis Sr. and his wife, Lucy, and growing up in the Oak Park neighborhood of Tampa, Florida.

Until George IV connected us, I didn't even guess that Slim Whitman—the guy with the tenor falsetto, black mustache and sideburns, and bright smile whose "Indian Love Call" made Martians' heads explode in Tim Burton's 1996 *Mars Attacks!*—was still alive, let alone willing to talk with an aging journalist.

Slim, it's said, took the fact that his voice repels Martians in stride. Heck, I'd guess he laughed right along. According to an Associated Press obituary, he once told an interviewer, "Yes. I'm the one who killed the blasted Martians."

His movie soundtrack career continued when Rob Zombie used Slim's "I Remember You" in the film *House of 1,000 Corpses*, which he directed.

Slim's "It's a Sin to Tell a Lie" was used in Zombie's 2019 film *3 from Hell.*

Zombie told film writer Brad Gullickson in a 2019 interview for the Film School Rejects blog that Slim was important to the latter film.

"I wanted to use Slim Whitman. I wanted to find a few ways that I could throw back to *House of 1,000 Corpses* because visually I knew it wouldn't really do that, and tone-wise it wouldn't do that, but having a big, show-stopping moment in the middle of the film to a Slim Whitman song was, I thought, the best way to reference their beginnings, just referencing that scene in *Corpses* with the long hold before Otis kills the cop and the Slim Whitman song plays right before it. That was my throwback moment."

The first time I called him (and there were other calls), Slim told me he was planning on coming back up to Nashville to record again with another old friend of mine, Harold Bradley, a producer and guitarist who had played more recording sessions than anyone in history. At least that's what Harold always told me. He had no reason to lie about. And, besides that, I loved Harold.

Slim, who had sold more than 120 million records worldwide, was living in quiet anonymity, far removed from pop culture's "what have you done for me lately" spotlight—and not missing it at all.

He also didn't miss the road much, and he liked being around the home he had shared with his wife, Alma Geraldine "Jerry," a songwriter, performer, embroiderer, and daughter of a preacher. She died in 2009. Their union produced good music in addition to a son and a daughter, two grandchildren, and two great-grandchildren, making Woodpecker Paradise ranch a lively place.

As I already have noted, George IV—the International Ambassador of Country Music and perhaps the nicest guy in the entertainment business—was the guy who presented me the gift of getting to know Slim.

Slim was a happy family man. Even at his advanced age, he'd have been able to fill up ballrooms in England, but, like he said, "my legs give me trouble."

So he spent his time enjoying life on his 40-acre ranch.

One guy who sang Slim's praises louder than that man himself was George IV.

While Slim figured he'd been written off by Nashville because he didn't have any number 1s to show in the United States, he had been a constant draw in England, which he first toured in 1956.

"My last tour over there was 2002, before my wife [Alma Geraldine] died [in 2009]."

So, while perhaps "success" (other than as a novelty of sorts) eluded him in the United States, he was selling enough copies of "Rose Marie," "Indian Love Call," and more to be a regular at the top of the charts in the United Kingdom.

He said there was a simple reason for his fame in the United States versus in the land of Big Ben. The music industry "ignores me because I didn't ever have a number 1 record here in the U.S. . . . Nashville didn't think I'd done anything."

George IV knew better. "He was the pioneer [in England]. . . . He preceded all of us. Sadly, he has been totally overlooked by the CMA and the Country Music Hall of Fame.

"He has every right to be in the Hall of Fame: he was selling millions of records in the '50s," George said, noting that Whitman defined the meaning of "international star" for country musicians in the United Kingdom and beyond.

But it wasn't my last encounter with Slim. I called a few more times just to talk. I do that for some reason with vintage artists—until their phones are no longer in service. And Slim was singing "Secret Love" or "Rose Marie" on the other side of the Pearly Gates.

"My son said, 'You'll live to be 100.' I said, 'If I live to be 100, you'll have to do the yodeling,'" he told me on the day of our birthday conversation, January 24, 2012.

"Today I got a thing from Africa, a Happy Birthday. It's all over the world," he said of his stardom. "It wasn't just England. We toured everywhere, Australia, New Zealand. I had a six-week tour of Africa. All that started with England," where his accomplishments included an extended stay at the London Palladium and at times in the 1960s topping The Beatles on the UK charts.

"I feel good," he said back in 2012, although he admitted that "sitting by the television night and day with my legs straight down, and you aren't supposed to do it," contributed to health woes that kept him from making it back up to Nashville to work on more music with Harold Bradley.

"Held me back from some things I needed to do," said Slim. "I needed to go back to Nashville and finish another album."

He said the cowboy songs album he'd done with Harold was done and ready if anyone wanted to release it.

"It was kind of a tribute album," he said. "Gene Autry was a favorite of the wife and a favorite of mine. So I started out with 'Back in the Saddle Again.' It was a little different than Gene Autry because I did some twists he didn't do."

He talked as much about Harold Bradley as he did himself. "When I went to Nashville in 1949, he was my leader. And he was my leader this time. That shows how long we were friends. He's been all over the world with me."

Harold, who had a variety of illnesses as he grew older, couldn't travel to Slim's funeral on July 29, 2013, in Florida.

But, via video, he delivered the eulogy.

Here is a sample: "Slim and I were best friends, and Slim and I had a lot in common. . . . The music bonded us together in a greatly personal and enduring relationship. I really just love Slim. I thought he was very honest and straightforward with his opinions. His word was his bond. And he would always do whatever he said he would do, and, if necessary, he would do more."

He said the two men, both former baseball players and navy vets of World War II, quickly became close after their introduction.

"I first met Slim in Nashville in 1949, and we became lifelong friends. . . . Slim was like all the superstars that I've worked with but very humble. He was a one-of-a-kind singer. I watched him step up to the mic and start to sing real softly, and I watched the crowd just go absolutely silent. He had a God-given gift as a singer."

According to Slim, Harold was bandleader on tour (and on Carson's and Letterman's shows) and on 90 percent of his records, which were recorded mostly in Nashville, where Slim lived for a bit early in his career.

That second batch of tunes never was finished, but when I called Harold, he noted there were 10 to 12 fine songs ready for release from those sessions as well. Of course, no one released the cowboy songs.

During our very long birthday conversation, Slim and I talked about other things, the chart reign of "Rose Marie," and his other signature songs. He showed a complete lack of bitterness at being ignored by Nashville.

He kept turning the interview back to his life—and his wife.

"If it hadn't been for her, I'd have probably been a bum. I met her when she came down with her dad, and she went to the same high school I did. . . . At first she wasn't paying attention to anybody. She was a good-looking girl. She was only 13. All of the sudden, we started looking at each other.

"They wouldn't let us go out unless there was somebody with us. I said one day, 'You think you'll ever get married?' She said, 'Let's go for it.'

"I loved to fish, and girls was second. I borrowed 10 bucks from my mother to get the license. She said I never paid her back."

After they were wed, Slim looked at his new bride. "I said, 'Okay, now what are we gonna do?' She said, 'I guess we'll go fishing.'"

We talked more about top hits and folks he has known and influenced, like The Beatles. "They were there in the Palladium when I played. McCartney plays left-handed guitar. Learned that from me."

Beatles guitarist George Harrison also is said to have been influenced by Slim's records, which his father played on the record machine in their Liverpool home.

"The first person I ever saw playing a guitar was Slim Whitman, either a photo of him in a magazine or live on television. Guitars were definitely coming in," George has been quoted as saying.

Slim also talked about the Americans who followed him to England and Europe: Bobby Bare, George IV, and Johnny Cash, all folks he relished in knowing.

And then there was the good friend who wanted to go to England but who was trapped by his manager and never made the trip. Both had the same manager, Colonel Tom Parker, early in their careers. Slim moved on. Elvis never really did.

"I want to tell you a bitty thing about Elvis. Elvis had just started. And I was in Memphis, and I had a show, and I was a headliner, and they brought Elvis over, and so I watched Elvis.

"I watched him and listened to him, and when he was singing, the girls in the crowd didn't do much. But when he wiggled, they hollered."

Then he laughed about spending time traveling with his own family and with the young man with the swiveling hips.

"The wife met him. My daughter, too. We was on the same bus together.

"One night, I was singing 'Indian Love Call,' and I heard somebody singing behind the curtain. It was Elvis, singing 'Indian Love Call' while I was singing. I said, 'Don't do that no more.'"

Elvis agreed that he wouldn't do it. Besides that, it was tough on the voice to sing along with Slim, who admitted patterning his singing style after Eddy Arnold but sped up the tempo to claim it as his own.

As for Elvis, "We were friends till the end. I knew what was going on, but we were friends. We all got tears in our eyes when he died in 1977."

Slim was tremendously talented and humble. And he had simple aspirations for the rest of his life.

"I don't think you've ever heard anything bad about me, and I'd like to keep it that way," Slim told the Associated Press. "I'd like my son [Bryon] to remember me as a good dad. I'd like the people to remember me as having a good voice and a clean suit."

Slim was getting a little weary in that first long discussion, so I decided to let him go, at least until the next call to Woodpecker Paradise.

"I didn't drink, smoke, take drugs, or anything," he said when I asked him what the secrets to a long and happy career and life were. "And I never used a word you couldn't sing in church.

"I've always been a nice guy."

I always hated to hang up. But at least I did so with a smile.

Charlie McCoy

B EST KNOWN PERHAPS FOR PERFECTING THE HARMONICA—which cost him 50 cents and a cereal box top back when such consumer rewards were the norm—Charlie McCoy is the best overall musician in Nashville.

He's also one of the gentlest and least ego-driven musicians you will encounter—if you are lucky—and one of the music scene's nicest human beings.

He won't say it, but perhaps he learned his lessons of humility from his mother, who sacrificed in order to fund her little boy's cereal box dream, the gateway to his success (even though he preferred, at first at least, the guitar).

That humility—professionalism and warmth combined—is in his voice when he talks about his decades in Nashville, where he has worked on sessions with the top names in all genres of music, from Dylan to Elvis to Johnny Cash to Ringo Starr to Chet to Eddy Arnold and Waylon.

You see, most of those fellows—almost everyone Charlie has spoken to me about during years of calling him for information about Nashville's musical history and his own contributions—not only provided paychecks but also allowed Charlie to have fun.

"It was a great time, working with him," said Charlie by way of example years ago when I was doing a cover story for the *Nashville Scene* about Ringo Starr's summer of 1970 *Beaucoups of Blues* album recording session at my late pal Scotty Moore's Music City Recorders.

Scotty, of course, was the man who invented the role of rock-'n'-roll lead guitarist when he worked for (and for a short time even managed) the kid with the strange name from the Memphis projects. I figure this is as good a place as any to fit in a note about Elvis, a primary inspiration for musicians from Music Row to Liverpool.

Hell, Charlie even went to Hollywood to work on the soundtracks for Elvis's "films."

Ringo, who I've been fortunate enough to interview a few times in relation to his ties to Nashville, to preview a concert, or both, told me that he liked the way Charlie and the Nashville Cats worked in the recording studio.

Ringo, who was here not long after his formerly Fab bandmates began workng through their divorce proceedings, had been immersed in the endless experimentation, tape loops, symphony orchestras, and distortions that had become a part of The Beatles' stock-in-trade in their later years. He found that doing it the Nashville way, hit-and-run, like George Martin's early Beatles sessions, was invigorating.

"We'd find five songs in the morning, and then we'd record five songs at night," said Ringo. The "we" in this case was producer and steel guru Pete Drake and Starr, who shuffled through song contenders to start their day and finished those cuts by the next sunrise.

Charlie—who I've never known to say anything bad about a musician, especially one who is working at his art—played organ, vibes, and harmonica on the sessions.

He not only enjoyed the songs that ended up on the album, a classic country "must" for Beatles fans (and actually for fans of old-school country with a Scouse accent), but also loved the fun that came as the workdays drew to their conclusions.

Charlie said, "At the end of everything, after we had finished up the recording, Ringo went behind the drums and played, and everybody jumped in. We just jumped in the groove. He played much better than I had the impression he played from just hearing The Beatles' records."

Charlie told my friend the musician, historian, and author Peter Cooper (in a June 7, 2006, story in *The Tennessean*) that his need for the harmonica was whetted when "I saw an ad in a comic book: a harmonica for 50 cents and a box top."

And, as noted a little earlier with the mention of his love for guitar playing, while the mention of Charlie's name is virtually synonymous with "harmonica maestro," he put a plethora of instruments to work in the studios of Music Row.

For example, he played guitar on such classics as Bob Dylan's "Desolation Row" and Bobby Bare's "Detroit City." He has said that Dylan, with whom Charlie had a long working relationship, basically was withdrawn during those sessions, with one of the few requests he got from Mr. Zimmerman being to pick up a guitar for a run-through of "Desolation Row."

"Hey, why don't you get that extra guitar over there and play along?" Dylan asked when Charlie dropped in to visit his old friend the producer Bob Johnston at a New York studio while in the Big Apple to catch the 1964 World's Fair.

Six months later, Johnston contacted Charlie about Dylan's plans to come to Nashville.

The then young singer/songwriter's appearance in Tennessee spurred interest in Nashville and created opportunities for younger musicians, as top session players were already booked solid, McCoy said.

"After [Johnston] brought Dylan here, the floodgates were opened," McCoy said in an interview. "There suddenly was a need for more studios and more musicians."

Charlie played trumpet on Dylan's "Rainy Day Women #12 & 35" ("everybody must get stoned") when working on *Blonde on Blonde*, one of the rock poet's trifecta-plus of landmark albums that were recorded in Nashville and for which Charlie pretty much was always on the scene.

I'll probably get back to that, but I ought to add that he also played bass on the Dylan Nashville albums, Charlie Rich's "Mohair Sam," Jeannie Seely's "Don't Touch Me," and "Songs from a Room" by Leonard Cohen.

Oh, and then there's the little matter of playing mallets on Lynn Anderson's "Rose Garden" and on Ronnie Milsap's "Almost Like a Song" and "Smoky Mountain Rain."

And, oh yeah, he played organ for Elvis, tuba for Roy Clark, and sax on Roy Orbison's "Pretty Woman."

Then, of course, is the harmonica, which is his ticket to worldwide acclaim. You can hear him on such recordings as Tom T. Hall's "Old Dogs, Children and Watermelon Wine" and George Jones's "He Stopped Loving Her Today," two landmark Nashville recordings.

And that's not even talking about Bare's "500 Miles from Home" or Waylon Jennings's "Only Daddy That'll Walk the Line."

That's just a tiny sample of the stuff that Charlie recorded on as he worked an average of 400 sessions a year during Nashville's prime.

Charlie recorded on many major recordings for Elvis, Kris Kristofferson, Joan Baez, Merle Haggard, Brenda Lee, Tammy Wynette, Charley Pride, Tanya Tucker, Kitty Wells, Leon Russell, Nancy Sinatra, Paul Simon—well, just about everybody.

And that's not even mentioning his time as a member of breakthrough Nashville bands Area Code 615 and Barefoot Jerry and on some great solo stuff.

According to the Country Music Hall of Fame and Museum, where Charlie is rightly enshrined, he came to Nashville from Oak Hill, West

Virginia, his hometown and where he was when he sent off four bits and a box top in 1960.

It was the era of rock 'n' roll, and that's the style of music the young man tried out first, recording as a singer and guitarist for the Cadence and Monument labels.

I don't need to go through the whole biography other than to mention that early on, RCA's Chet Atkins heard the young man's harmonica playing on a demo tape and signed him up for a 1961 Ann-Margret session that produced "I Just Don't Understand," a hit for the buxom actress and close "friend" of Elvis.

What really opened up the session world for Charlie was his work on Roy Orbison's Monument version of "Candy Man," which featured great harmonica work.

"It got Roy another hit and me a career, and for a 20-year-old to make $49 for three hours' work back then, it was a dream," Charlie is quoted in the Hall of Fame biography.

He became so significant in Nashville music that when it was time for Sam Lovullo to choose a music director for his *Laugh-In*-style cornpone show *Hee Haw*, there really was only one person to choose.

I'll revisit *Hee Haw* some in a bit.

Kenny Buttrey, the great drummer who pounded down the walls between rock 'n' roll and country music, was one of Charlie's favorites in the studio, in performance (with Barefoot Jerry and Area Code 615), and as a friend.

Charlie easily could take credit for being the guy who made Dylan and subsequent rock artists comfortable in the Nashville sessions.

But when Kenny, whom I spoke with some on the phone as he was in the final stages of his fight with lung cancer, died, Charlie, as is typical for this kind genius, gave the credit to Kenny for breaking the Nashville skyline wide open to the world of rock 'n' roll.

"He was the best drummer I'd ever heard," Charlie said of the first time he met Buttrey, who died in September 2004 of his disease.

"His track record stands for itself,'" Charlie told me. "But it was people like him that allowed us to bring the Bob Dylans and the like to town.

"At that time, as great as they were, those alternative acts knew the A-Team here mainly by their reputation of being strictly country."

That wasn't necessarily true, but it took someone with a rock-'n'-roll attitude to coax Bob and Neil Young and the others down here.

"Kenny was exactly the guy," said Charlie.

Since this may be the only mention of Kenny in this book, I should note that when he died, I was called by the legendary Los Angeles–based drummer Jim Keltner.

Jim, who had played with members of The Beatles, The Rolling Stones, Randy Newman, and more, said that Kenny was one of his primary influences and that, since he knew I was working on his friend's obituary, he wanted to put in a good word or two.

"[Kenny] was a great musician in that everything he ever played made such great sense. He wasn't known for flashy chops. . . . He just had the ability to self-arrange what he played, such a way that made tremendous sense for a song."

I wish I'd gotten to know him better.

Charlie, of course, enjoyed meeting the stars and playing for them.

Sometimes, he even liked them an awful lot.

While Dylan was reserved "even when we were face-to-face," according to Charlie, Elvis was quite the opposite.

"He was so nice. The studio was his safe place. The fans couldn't get in. He was there with people he respects and he likes, and doing what he likes to do. You could feel that."

In June 2019, I wrote a cover story for the *Nashville Ledger* about the fiftieth anniversary of *Hee Haw*. I was fortunate to talk with a lot of the original performers.

They still showed enthusiasm for the old country variety show.

And the guy who really loved recalling that show was its music director, Charlie McCoy.

"It wasn't all cornball country music," said Charlie, swearing by the show's importance in the history of Nashville and country music.

Charlie was *Hee Haw*'s music director for most of its 585-episode run, recruiting the band from the army of his superb cohorts among the Nashville Cats. He joined those same cats by night in session work for Dylan, Elvis, Waylon, Simon and Garfunkel—just about any giants worshipping and wowing in the studios of what was a vibrant Music Row.

Remember, Music Row aces worked four sessions in a day, so even with part of his day dedicated to *Hee Haw*, there still was time for the multi-instrumentalist in the studios.

"It was key," Charlie told me when talking about *Hee Haw*'s contribution to the national and international status of Nashville and country music.

"It came along at a great time, and I think it was one of the best things that happened to country music." And Nashville.

"The thing that impressed me most was they would go from the most cornball comedy to the hit music of the day, with a great set, great sound. It was presented like it was special," Charlie said in that story I wrote.

"Yeah, we had our pickin' and our grinnin' when we are all layin' around on hay bales," he admitted with a laugh.

Such informality ended when it was time for the musical aces to set up for special guests like Brother Ray Charles, Dolly Parton, Sammy Davis Jr., John Denver, George Strait, Roy Rogers, and even Big Bird.

That show, with Charlie as musical boss, got off to a hot start when Charley Pride and Loretta Lynn guested on June 15, 1969, the first episode.

"I cannot tell you how many people say to me—I play for a lot of seniors—'We couldn't wait for *Hee Haw* to come on Saturdays,' especially out in rural America, where there wasn't a lot going on," said Charlie, who spends his winters in Florida, where he entertains on the retirement-home circuit.

He told me that all sorts of nationally known artists lined up to play on *Hee Haw*, as they were reaching an audience they didn't reach in Las Vegas, Los Angeles, or New York.

If they were asked, "they'd say 'absolutely.' It was more promotion for them."

Besides the big-name guests, the cameras focused closely on the great music and musicians and personalities who regularly populated Kornfield Kounty.

"Every day you walked in the studio, you were surrounded by legends," Charlie said. "There was Roy [Clark] and Buck [Owens]. Grandpa Jones. Minnie Pearl. Roy Acuff." And then guests like Richard Petty, Amy Grant, and the San Diego Chicken dropped by to visit.

On the subject of legends: "When we got down to around season 20, Sam [producer Sam Lovullo] got this idea for the Million Dollar Band: Chet [Atkins], Boots ["Yakety Sax" Randolph], Floyd [Cramer], Danny Davis, Johnny Gimble, Jethro Burns [of Homer and Jethro, aka the "Thinking Man's Hillbillies"], Roy Clark, and me," Charlie said, pausing to see if he'd forgotten members of the supergroup.

"That was one of the coolest segments we did down there," he said. "It was done five or six times, over a three- or four-year period."

It was Charlie who called me when Johnston—mentioned above in relation to the Dylan sessions he produced—died in 2015 at age 83.

Charlie laughed about the scene in the studio when "Rainy Day Women" was recorded.

He said that Dylan was searching for a Salvation Army Band kind of feel and that Johnston just wanted the whole studio to have fun.

"All that noise you hear on it, it was happening as he recorded. He wanted us to have a party. We were shouting and screaming the whole time," said McCoy, who played the trumpet, yelped, or did whatever while Dylan recorded what may be his happiest song as well.

Kind of a good image to end a chapter on the happiest and best musician in Nashville.

Marion James

ARION JAMES'S FINAL RIDE down Jefferson Street—the then decrepit pathway through the heart of Nashville's once-glorious and neon-lit R&B scene—was inside a coffin that was visible through the picture windows making up the sides of a black, horse-drawn carriage.

Marion—a friend who died December 30, 2015, after years of declining health—including a long stint in a wheelchair and too many hospital nights—was 81. I should add here that three years before, when I asked her age for a spread I was writing for *Living Blues* magazine (the University of Mississippi's much-heralded magazine that pays proper respect to the blues, which has its heart in the Mississippi Delta), she stubbornly declined with a wink. "I've got some years behind me, but I can't afford to tell you the exact age. All I can say is I've been out there in this musical world practically all my life."

Many of the characters from that world were in cars trailing the horse-drawn hearse.

The elegant funeral carriage offered stark contrast to the decay of the street where she reigned for decades. That rot was defined in the tombstone eyes of the score or so of young men who stretched their necks from across the street to see what was going on. No doubt the flashing lights escorting the funeral procession increased their paranoia because it was like seeing a police car. They laughed and jostled, eyeing the hearse carriage and the flood of cars that had rolled into the parking lot of Jefferson Street Missionary Baptist Church. Not all mourners were part of the procession, and several cars that arrived before the hearse were shooed away from the curb in front of the narthex doorway. Smith Brothers Funeral Directors staff members were simply protecting Marion's space.

That church-front curb was where the carriage would be parked after its rolling procession from the funeral home on Monroe Street to the church that is nestled near Tennessee State University and right by the Elks Lodge. That lodge long ago was the Club Baron, where Johnny Jones said he outdueled Jimi Hendrix one night. Most I've spoken to about that famous duel agree.

Jimi (then Jimmy) was a gentle, often stoned young man whom everyone on Jefferson Street loved, a guy who—with his bass-playing best friend Billy Cox—could be summoned to back just about any band on the strip, which on this funeral day is a desolate trail for the final performance of the Queen of the Blues.

"I had him play behind me for a while," Marion had told me on more than one occasion when we talked about Hendrix.

The skinny, soft-spoken guy who went on to conquer the world before kissing the sky would be honored to play behind her: she was Nashville's Queen of the Blues, a fixture on the R&B scene who had fierce determination to keep the blues alive in her hometown. Foxy lady, indeed.

While she dazzled crowds on the old Chitlin' Circuit and liked to talk about her success in and love of Italy—"I seen so many things that I read about when I was in high school. It's history and I got to see some of it"—she was best known in her later years for organizing and hosting the annual Musicians Reunion. She was the chief cook and the hostess of the gathering that brought together R&B and blues musicians from "back in the day."

In addition to fried chicken and greens and musical jamming among the attendees, the reunions were held to raise money for the Musicians' Aid Society. She founded and oversaw that charity for more than three decades.

The basic purpose was to tend to the needs of those whose names once appeared in neon over the long-forgotten, abandoned glory that was Jefferson Street back when she and one of her husbands, trumpet player James "Buzzard" Stuart, welcomed touring musicians and those down on their luck to crash at their house on 34th Avenue North, tucked behind Tennessee State University.

"Buzzard attracted them," she explained for the story I did for *Living Blues*. I also covered the funeral for the magazine, though I would have gone anyway. I always like to be there when musicians I cherish are saluted in prayer and song, in this case a mixture of the gospel music of Marion's youth and the smooth R&B and more raw blues of her mature years. My friend the fine bluesman James "Nick" Nixon—then crippled up and in his latter days himself—put together the musical program.

Marion told me that Buzzard made it well known that their house was a place of refuge. "Most of all the musicians that came to Nashville would stop at our house.

"Some would get stranded here, maybe not get paid by a club owner, and couldn't get home, so they would stay in our house until they got a job" and made enough money for the bus or midnight train.

"Little Johnny Taylor ["Part Time Love"] stayed at my house. He was from out in California, but he stayed there. Gene Allison, this was his home, right here in Nashville."

Allison, who rose to glory with "You Can Make It if You Try," which allowed him to buy his own 24-hour "soul food restaurant," Gene's Drive-In, was a hometown boy (born in nearby Pegram, Tennessee). But he sure loved to drop in at Buzzard's 24-hour open house for musicians, wayward travelers, and locals.

"He used to come over to my house all the time, and him and Little Johnny Taylor would get in the kitchen and cook up the best meal you ever seen," Marion said of Gene.

No one was required to pay, but they would scrape up enough to help with the overhead. "The rest of the musicians would nickel up. Oh, we had good times back then. We sure did."

Marion's biggest smiles during my many hours spent with her came when she talked about those celebratory, music-filled days at the house she and Buzzard shared.

Buzzard, who long preceded her in death, was a beloved and talented star of the Nashville R&B scene back then. But he missed his hometown of Little Rock, Arkansas, and finally decided to move back there. He asked his wife, Marion, to join him.

Love wasn't enough to get Marion to move to that state she reviled as rough, rural, and backwoods.

"I didn't want nothing to do with Arkansas," she told me. "You ever see how they live over there?"

She let Buzzard go home, and she later married James Majors. She never had children, but talking to her over the years, it was clear that the men and women who brought Jefferson Street to life were her family, extended and otherwise. Jimi Hendrix was a favorite son, for example.

Her Musicians' Aid Society was evidence of her care for her mostly forgotten contemporaries, the folks who shared stages with her on endless North Nashville nights.

"It's just a little organization that helps them," she explained. "I never have raised a great figure amount of money, but what I've raised, I've always tried to share with them, to give them some kind of little cash, so it might help pay for medicine or buy them a meal. Maybe they need $50 for a light bill, a copay on their insurance: ain't no such thing as getting medical stock-free these days."

The Musicians Reunion, which benefited her charity, was a Labor Day tradition, and all the great musicians, from Johnny Jones to Jimmy Church to Frank Howard to Billy Cox, were a part of it during its long run. For that day annually, the glory that had been the Jefferson Street scene was briefly resuscitated.

For example, the old song-and-dance men, like my dear friend Frank Howard and his comrades Herschel Carter and Charlie Fite, would regroup. Their harmonies as Frank Howard & the Commanders still wove nicely right up until Charlie died in May 2016. But they no longer were as thin and limber (Herschel did remain thin) to do their trademark flying splits to punctuate a song's denouement. But they still could sing "I'm So Glad." More on Frank later in the book.

Marion could not get enough of these aging musicians, and she was the most prominent supporter. For years, I was entertainment editor at the *Nashville Banner* and then at *The Tennessean*. Every year, as Labor Day approached, I could count on a call from Marion. Sometimes, hand-scribbled information on lined school paper—listing the who, what, and where of the event—would be dropped off at the newspaper reception desk. Perhaps it would spark a story for me or my staff members. More often, it was listed as one of the great entertainment adventures of the holiday weekend in Nashville. And she would call to thank me.

Even when she was ill—before the deadly stroke killed her in the hospital—Marion would come out and sing if given the opportunity.

One time, she even escaped her nursing home to appear on a special edition of the generally Americana and cowboy-oriented radio program *Music City Roots*, which was celebrating the city's R&B heritage.

Other greats from the era—from the 1950s to the 1970s, when R&B and Jefferson Street created a pre-hillbilly Music City USA—played on that radio show.

I wasn't there at the "Roots" broadcast. But my friend, the music historian Michael Gray—who helped reignite the city's R&B soul with a two-year exhibit celebrating it at the Country Music Hall of Fame and Museum, where he is an editor—said it literally "blew me away." That's the way Michael talks when his hip R&B passion is discussed.

"I remember wondering if Marion still had it," said Michael, who had orchestrated that edition of the Nashville roots music variety program in

Nashville's "Queen of the Blues" Marion James, loved to tell stories about her long life along Jefferson Street, hotbed of Music City's old R&B scene. © 2022 JOHN PARTIPILO PHOTOGRAPHY

addition to being the fiercest white advocate for the Jefferson Street sound in Nashville.

Michael was among those who hoisted the wheelchair, with Marion in it, onto the stage for that live broadcast. "She killed it. She was great. I was so happy for her," he told me when I was collecting memories for her obituary, again for *Living Blues*.

"She was a great live performer," said Michael of the woman whose showstopper generally was her version of the B.B. King classic "Rock Me Baby":

> Rock me baby, rock me all night long
> Rock me baby, like my back ain't got no bones

Even in her eighties, health failing and most of her great musical friends gone, this woman in a wheelchair, generally wearing a floral-print house-coat, could convince a listener that, yes, she indeed could fulfill the lascivious promise of that song.

About three years before her death, I spent the good part of a day at Marion's house on Scovel Street in a tidy neighborhood of worn cottages and bright floral yards in North Nashville.

Purple phlox lined both sides of the sidewalk to her house. I was there for the *Living Blues* piece.

In the years since that visit (about a decade now), so much of that neighborhood has been gentrified, like too much of Nashville, with speculators and landlords steamrolling the lives of the people who made those neighborhoods. Demolishing homes and markets and apartment houses— whole neighborhoods really—continues to make room for the mostly white "immigrants" from Los Angeles, New York, Milwaukee, and elsewhere who have transformed Nashville from a honeysuckle-flavored, warm place to live into the neon-lit "It City," where no one knows your name.

I'd actually been to Marion's house a few times before, usually in the late morning. I'd knock. Wait. Knock again. I'd walk away disappointed, figuring she was dodging me. Those visits had been unannounced. I was just in the neighborhood and figured I'd drop in on the Queen of the Blues. Such impromptu stops at other houses, barbecue joints, barbershops, mom-and-pop markets, saloons, and the like supplied me with so many newspaper stories and beloved friends over the years.

I didn't find out until I visited her home by appointment for that story that she sometimes slept until 2 p.m. after staying up until almost dawn writing songs in a little section of her house that she reserved for such toil.

"I writes by mood," she said. "Matter of fact, when I writes, I writes at 3 or 4 in the morning because ideas come to me better. . . .

"I can write a song better late at night because somehow or other, that's when the ideas come, when everything is quiet and you can think better.

"Most of the stuff comes to me a cappella first, then I go to the piano and try to put what little music I can to it."

She pointed to a framed portrait of Jimi Hendrix in her living room, tidy but for an overabundance of pillows and stuffed animals, mostly tigers.

"Jimi used to play right back there," she said, nodding toward the noise of what is Interstate 40, whose constant steam of commuters and cross-country truckers made so much noise that they even drowned out the coughing drone of her window air conditioners.

That interstate, visible from her backyard, pretty much doomed the club district that had flourished for decades. Instead of a long series of blocks, with a club or restaurant centering each block or even on every corner, the construction of the interstate sliced right through the neighborhood. For as long as it took for the highway to be built, historically black North Nashville—with its rich blues, medical, literary, gastronomic, and educational heritage—was sliced in half.

Historically black universities Tennessee State (home of the wonderful Wilma Rudolph and the gold medal–winning Tiger Belles as well as of football stars "Jefferson Street Joe" Gilliam and Ed "Too Tall" Jones) and Fisk were separated by the highway. Meharry Medical Center is tucked behind Fisk (depending on the direction from which you approach).

With their neighborhood divided by blasting and demolition, shoppers no longer could go from one end of Jefferson Street as it crosses the Cumberland River to the other end at the Tennessee State campus entry. Families who were a block away from each other for decades suddenly were separated by miles of construction detours. The social interruption continued even after the interstate was finished, as its path eats up about six blocks in the middle of what once was the neighborhood.

One of the most important night clubs in the district, the Del Morocco, was torn down to make room for the highway. Next to it, a beauty college also was demolished in addition to houses and the like.

The Del was the club Marion was talking about when she nodded toward the back of her house and talked about Jimi playing there. A person could literally walk two blocks, through what were expansive, green yards, like hers, to the Del Morocco back in the 1960s.

The importance of the Del is relative, as there were plenty of other clubs up and down the stretch. But it was where Jimi and army chum Cox were part of the house band, playing behind the great traveling R&B performers as well as the homegrown talent, like the legendary Jimmy Church Band—and, as already noted, Marion James.

Hendrix and Cox, as highlighted elsewhere in this book, also lived next to the club in the attic of the beauty college.

"He was all right, a nice guy," said Marion, turning toward the portrait on an end table. "I hired him to play for me some."

When she died, her dream of having a statue of Hendrix erected next to the interstate, under which so many drifters, dopers, and prostitutes hole up in the shadows on hot days and winter nights, had not been realized.

On that day in her living room, she gazed over the stuffed tigers (I supposed for the Tennessee State Tigers athletic programs, but I didn't ask) to me as I sat on the couch and scribbled furiously in more than one reporter's notebook to capture her memories.

Her thoughts for a moment turned to the fact that, for most people, Music City is perceived as the capital of country music. Oh, it is that. But it is so much more to anyone who takes a look at the history of the R&B scene.

"It's not fair that only one kind of music gets the recognition and another doesn't," she said.

They were making R&B music over on Jefferson Street already on December 11, 1946, when a brilliant young fellow named Hiram Williams—better known as "Hank" unless he was posing as "Luke the

Drifter"—recorded "Never Again (Will I Knock on Your Door)" and other cuts at Nashville's Castle Recording Company's Studio D. His first efforts were lukewarm, but within months, he moved to MGM, and in June 1947, "Move It on Over" launched the young man to stardom and, of course, a very early grave.

Williams actually owed a good bit of his songwriting and singing to black musical styles. He and other great singers turned Nashville into the center for recording country music. A few blocks away from Music Row's hillbillies, landmark music was being made by black performers on Jefferson Street.

Ray Charles, Little Richard, Lou Rawls, Gorgeous George (who swiped Hendrix for his band), and the greats of R&B and soul made the city one of the primary stops on the so-called Chitlin' Circuit.

Other members of the musical elite—Johnny Bragg ("Walkin' in the Rain"), Bobby Hebb ("Sunny") and his brother Harold (he sang with Bragg and the Marigolds after beginning with his brother), Earl Gaines ("It's Love Baby (24 Hours a Day)"), Roscoe Shelton ("Strain on My Heart"), Frank Howard & the Commanders ("Just Like Him"), and Robert Knight ("Everlasting Love")—were local guys.

"I played quite a few clubs up and down there," Marion said of the cracked and worn street that in recent decades gave way to empty storefronts, chicken shacks, and crack and smack retailers. "Club Stealaway, Del Morocco."

"Matter of fact, I worked at Price's Dinner Club below TSU [Tennessee State University] as a waitress, and then when he got ready to open this club in the back of the restaurant and dinner club, I am the one who named that room 'The Green Door.'

"He had quite a few artists come through there."

She said it was a place where many of the great touring artists—Ray Charles, Lou Rawls, Ike and Tina Turner, Little Richard, and Gorgeous George—would visit when in town to play at any of the throng of clubs along Jefferson Street.

"I remember Fats Domino coming through there," said Marion, who was a waitress at the restaurant when not performing along the strip of clubs. "He was a visitor. He was playing someplace else here in Nashville. He had a convertible Cadillac.

"It was pink and blue. I won't forget that," she told me for the feature I wrote for *Living Blues*.

I'd have to add here that I became pretty well acquainted with Fats late in life—he'd answer his phone simply "Fats" or "This's Fats" in his office in the Lower Ninth Ward of New Orleans. Sometimes, he'd serenade me while sitting at his piano. He always had great things to say about Nashville and the musicians here. He was one of the gentlest of music pioneers, and he was saluted by them all—even Elvis thought Fats was number 1.

That's an aside, but Fats and others came to Nashville and pretty much knocked down some of the racial divides. Even in segregated Nashville, white citizens were flocking to Jefferson Street for music from show bands, sultry singers, fiery guitar players, and gospel-flavored R&B harmonies. And that's not to mention the world-class dining, drinking, and dancing.

East, toward where the street crosses the Cumberland River, was Sulphur Dell ballpark, the baseball field where the Nashville Stars of the Negro leagues, shared time with the Nashville Vols (the white team) and the Nashville Black Cubs.

Nashville baseball historian Skip Nipper writes in his book *Baseball in Nashville* that Henry Aaron's professional debut took place at that park. Just signed as a shortstop with the Indianapolis Clowns, the 18-year-old's illustrious career was birthed in a 1952 exhibition against the Philadelphia Stars at Sulphur Dell. Today, promoters are pushing for Major League Baseball to come to Nashville and use the "Stars" nickname. For the moment, the Nashville Sounds AAA affiliate team plays in a ballpark roughly at the Sulphur Dell site.

Jefferson Street's importance as a historic thoroughfare through what in actuality was Nashville's "black downtown" diminished and decayed for decades. In recent years, new homes of "urban pioneers" and costly condos have replaced the old cottages, the storefronts, the restaurants, and, of course, the nightclubs on that street and in surrounding neighborhoods.

Marion mused that maybe one day, Jefferson Street would be reborn as a hub of black entertainment and culture. But the way things are going, they are crucifying the street. It seems likely that most of the traces of what made her street a mecca for black musicians and mixed-race crowds of adoring fans will be gone soon.

Marion sat in a chair, across the room filled with stuffed tigers and the Hendrix portrait, until her dog started barking. She stood up and went to retrieve him from his spot in the backyard to bring him into the house. It was late afternoon, and the dog likely would be up late, standing sentry, while Marion wrote the blues.

Earl and Louise Scruggs

WHEN I WANDERED SLOWLY through the sprawling, modernistic home that hardly looked like the kind of place the world's greatest banjo picker would spend his life, I had to duck to get through the room filled with dark suits.

Earl Scruggs's suits were hanging everywhere, seemingly as high as the ceiling. Earl's Suit Warehouse: a suit hoarder's paradise where suits were kept clean and pressed, ready for the great picker's performances.

I'm basically color-blind, but I believe every one of the suits in this massive cache was dark gray, perfect for a funeral—he had worn one of them himself a few months before my visit. That's when he was celebrated and laid to rest. And I'd seen him wearing one over corn bread and beans (I think) at Vittles, a now defunct meat 'n' three in Brentwood, just south of Nashville.

I pondered buying one of the suits, but I knew Earl Scruggs was shorter and thicker than me. And, as the old saying born around campfires in the Smokies goes, "The last thing a guy needs to add to his closet is a dead man's suit."

I made up that old saying that day as I was passing up the suit room and moving on into the rest of the house paid for by genius banjo playing.

I also don't know how in the world he played that instrument better than all the rest. To me, the banjo is an instrument about as mysterious as Ravi Shankar's sitar. I've seen both Earl and Ravi a few times in concert and met them both, similarly self-deprecating personas. I met and interviewed Ravi's daughter, the amazing Norah Jones, back in the early years of this century. She was at a Willie Nelson tribute concert (I think Keith Richards was on the bill, although I went to a fistful of Willie and friends types of shows). I also met Elton John's songwriting partner Bernie Taupin that night. Nice guy, but Norah was more my taste, even if trying to get her to talk about herself was as hard as it is to get gold from a silver mine.

Briefly, Norah, who had her big commercial success in the first decade of the century, didn't have much to say about her dad. "I don't like talking about him because he doesn't have anything to do with me or my music," she told *Rolling Stone* in 2004.

I did also meet Earl's kids over the years. They were glad to talk about their dad.

None of the kids were there for the estate sale. And I really hadn't planned to buy anything.

I have a weakness for recorded material—going back to the early Elvis 45s I bought from a kid whose dad ran a bar and who sold me the used records from the jukebox for a nickel each—so I did succumb when I began scouting through Earl's album collection.

I picked out a couple that looked interesting, and my "is it worth it when you need to buy gas" reservations were washed away at least in part because of the small bit of education I received from a great bass player as I was holding the records.

You see, the guy standing next to me, also fingering through the albums on the shelves and those on the floor of the music room—dominated by a 1980s-era Fisher stereo system with dual cassette players/recorder, a turntable, and CD player—was Mike Bub, one of Nashville's and the world's best bassists.

"That's the Bible for everything banjo," Mike told me as he reached over and "borrowed" my still-unpurchased copy of *Foggy Mountain Banjo* by Flatt and Scruggs.

He slid the actual disc from the sleeve and inspected it carefully.

"This one's never been played. Or, at least, it looks almost new," he said, using his well-tuned musician's hands to delicately slip it back into its sleeve and jacket.

He reached for my other choice, *Nashville Airplane*, and he smiled.

"This is the one that finally split up Flatt and Scruggs," Mike said as he got his eyes down in the grooves. "It's got all those Dylan songs on it. I don't think Lester [Flatt] wanted to play that type of music. I think that's the last album they ever made together."

Mike—who already had stacked up a batch of albums down by the cashier on the other end of the seemingly football-field-length house but who had come back for more—said my shuffling through the stacks and shelves had led me to great rewards.

"If you're gonna buy two, that's the two you want," he said. He also was going to buy Louise's safe, legendary repository for so many great bookings and sly cash deals.

Those records cost me $5 each. I was lucky I had $10 in my pocket. I hadn't planned on stopping here, let alone buying anything. I'd planned on getting $10 of gas at the Shell station on my way home.

I'm not an estate-sale type of guy, as in general I don't need someone else's junk, but I couldn't pass up at least visiting the sale at the Scruggs estate, at least in part because I really liked the guy. I loved his wife more. I knew many pickers (some dead) who were his sidemen and friends. And for years, I'd driven twice daily past the estate on Nashville's broad Franklin Road. Not far from my house (yet a world removed), I'd be on my way home when I'd see Earl and Louise nursing that big blue Cadillac through the automatic gates. If the car wasn't blue, I apologize. Like I said, I'm color-blind.

Louise often was behind the wheel. After she died on February 2, 2006, Earl stayed at the house and pretty much followed the routine, and I'd see the lonely picker pulling the Cadillac out of the gate. I'm not sure, but I think one of his sons, Gary perhaps, moved in with him after his wife died.

Earl died on March 28, 2012, and by then, I was working part-time for Reuters News Service, for which I wrote the obituary.

Earl's son, Gary—who I'd also bothered when his mother died—told me his dad's health had been on a decline for a long time.

"He's 88, and it's a slow process," said Gary, who played bass guitar with his dad during the Grateful Dead–flavored era.

Anyway, as I noted a couple of paragraphs prior, I'd often see Earl and Louise leave their tree-lined estate, exiting their automatic gate, and turning, most times, south toward the Nashville suburb of Brentwood, where food specials at the restaurants lasted until about 5 p.m. My old friend Eddy Arnold and his wife Sally often could be spotted at these restaurants. I did spot the Scruggses a couple of times at the O'Charley's where Waylon's face decorated the back wall, but I didn't disturb them. And at Vittles, too.

You just don't disturb the world's greatest banjo picker—or the wife who had been so kind to me on many occasions.

And, by the way, you certainly didn't bother Waylon, who lived with Jessi and Shooter just across Old Hickory Boulevard from the O'Charley's. He was a good old boy, never meaning no harm. But he also liked his family time.

One time as my family sat at the restaurant, Louise looked up and recognized me at a table maybe 10 yards from their own, so I got up and dropped by, just to shake hands and say "Hi." But usually, Earl and the

Earl Scruggs, the great banjo stylist, told the author "I don't have a worry in the world when I start playing music." © Bill Steber Photography

woman, who was, in a very good way, his backbone, were looking into each other's eyes and talking seriously, not to be disturbed.

Louise took care of business for Earl, who could focus more on his banjo magic.

I probably ought to note that not long after I made that June 2016 estate-sale farewell tour of the home of Earl and Louise Scruggs, the newcomers, likely some of the way too many folks who move to Nashville every day, cleaned up the landscaping some and put up a less stately wooden gate at the front of the property. The large statue that prior owner Tammy Wynette long ago had installed in front of the house was sold during the estate sale. I watched the picker/antique dealer from Leiper's Fork winch it out of the ground.

"I don't think this is a sculpture, I'd call it a monument," said the picker/dealer Justin Ebert, who said he was naming the sculpture *Mother and Child* because of the two abstract heads atop the piece.

Justin wouldn't tell me what he paid but admitted it cost him more than the pickup truck hauling his flatbed trailer.

He said he probably was going to return the next morning to wrestle free the remainder of the statue (the base and so on) because the big sculpture already occupied most of his hauling space and, I assume, weight maximums.

He said that on first blush, he figured the statue weighed 1,000 pounds. As the day wore on, he had upped that estimate times three. Who knows how much it would have weighed to him the next day?

The statue in some ways reminded me of the Picasso in Chicago's Daley Plaza, which you've doubtless seen if you've ever wandered the Loop or watched the grand finale chase scene in *The Blues Brothers* (the original one, with Dan Aykroyd and John Belushi, as Elwood and Joliet Jake).

The statue in the Scruggs compound didn't look like anything Louise would have picked out as something she'd like to view when looking out the living room windows. Like I said, it was Tammy who had it installed there when she and her then husband, George "White Lightning" Jones, lived in the modernistic mansion at 4121 Franklin Road.

It's from this place that a DUI-grounded George drove his riding lawnmower to the nearest liquor store. He made choices since the day that he was born, remember? I sure loved George later in life, when he was mostly sober. Me, too.

The liquor store George supposedly visited that day is in Berry Hill, a mile or so north of the house he and Tammy shared. There is a mural of a tractor-riding possum on the north side of the building. I, personally, am tired of all these urban murals and am looking forward to the occasion when I actually see a plain brick wall on the side of some hipster's joint. The real world doesn't need to be disguised by so-called art. Go to New York and paint a subway car or something.

This really was—and I'm sure still is with the Californians who bought it—a splendid house, and the Scruggs had moved here because Earl finally had more than his Gibson banjo and the clothes on his back. There was cash in Louise's safe by then. I surmise that the house had become available because Tammy had tired of standing by her man. Or perhaps it was during those times when George couldn't stand up, let alone stand by his woman.

This house was the payoff for Earl's brilliance and his labor. And it became the Scruggs house thanks to Louise.

It was Louise's management skills—she honed those talents as manager for her husband and his longtime guitarist partner Lester Flatt and the Foggy Mountain Boys and kept on handling Earl right up through the times he played with the Grateful Dead and the Byrds—that really made them rich. Well, the genius with the banjo could make some of the world's most identifiable music pretty much right up until he died, but he didn't have to worry about collecting his pay and royalties when his wife was around. Louise took care of that.

By the time Earl let his hair grow long and his sideburns rival those on a B-grade Vegas Elvis impersonator, he and Lester were going their separate ways over Dylanesque differences that Mike Bub, the bassist, mentioned earlier. Lester wasn't interested in a long, strange trip. The backroads of the Shenandoah Valley and Highway 61 were plenty for him.

Lester enlisted child prodigy Marty Stuart into the band and stayed with the fabulous old-timey stuff while Earl jumped ahead. Sure, Jerry Garcia loved to pick with him, but Earl maintained his roots by playing at bluegrass festivals. And he liked to drop in on one of his old sidemen at the Station Inn, the low-slung blockhouse that for decades has been the Nashville headquarters for bluegrass and roots music.

"Dropping in" is a time-honored Station Inn tradition. In their prime (which is to say all the way up until they died), Earl, Mac Wiseman, Vassar Clements, Lester, Jimmy Martin, and Uncle Josh Graves sometimes were the center-stage featured act here.

Other times, they dusted the popcorn salt or the grease from the famous superthin "homemade" Station Inn pizza from their hands and climbed onstage, raising unrehearsed joyful noise inside the blockhouse monument to what is great about country music. I hope that by the time you are reading this, the Station Inn still is there, a musical dandelion of sorts that seems out of place among the glisten of skyscrapers, coffee shops, and boutiques that have overtaken Nashville's old railroad gulch.

J. T. Gray, who was a friend of mine, was the longtime owner, and he had been determined to keep the blockhouse as an iconic and historic club. He died in 2021, and, as of this writing, it looks like the old club will emerge intact on the other side of the COVID plague.

Today, Nashville is overwhelmed by upscale urban settlers, developers, and bicoastal snobs, and that's the flavor of the surrounding skyline.

But for decades, before Silicon Valley and auto corporations decided there was gold in them there hills, the Station Inn proudly stood, about the only life among the rotting buildings and empty lots of the Gulch. You may have seen John Cowan, Peter Rowan, Ricky Skaggs, or Uncle Josh inside the club. You were at least as likely to see a homeless guy urinating on the sidewalk outside. And you wanted to park as closely to the club as possible, beneath the dim lights rather than out on the unlighted nearby gravel lot. Some things are improved by progress, of course. It's okay to clean up an area. I'm just worried that they'll take a wrecking ball to the building that really is from a time out of mind, a joint that really wasn't made for these days.

When Bill Monroe—who at one point was Earl's and Lester's boss— was in town, he'd get antsy and drive down there, stealing the stage from whatever performer was working that night. Can't argue with Big Mon, man.

I first became a friend of Uncle Josh because Vassar, whom I called frequently just to chat, had enlisted my aid in publicizing a Station Inn fundraiser for the great Flatt and Scruggs Dobro player after he had his legs amputated. You can read more about Uncle Josh elsewhere in this book.

Let's get back into the estate sale, where my wanderings kept leading me back to the room where, eventually, Earl's record collection was scattered all over the floor.

Near that room was a relatively small space that had served as Louise's office.

I bothered her here quite often, though she didn't treat it as a bother.

She liked me, yet I did not waste her time. If I had a question about some great picker who had died or if I needed to talk to Earl about something, I'd just call her. If Earl was in the living room nearby, perhaps staring out at Tammy Wynette's hideous lawn sculpture, Louise would pass him the phone. Other times, he called me back. Sometimes, she'd simply ask him the question I had and then repeat his answer back into the phone. I'd hear him echoing agreement in the background.

Today, you have to go through management, handlers, and sycophants to get to any artist. I just had to go through Earl's wife by calling their home phone.

On the day of the estate sale—which I ended up writing a column about for the *Nashville Ledger*'s weekly business publication—I stood alone in Louise's office, looking at her electric typewriter and a well-used Canon calculator.

This room, to me, represented the kindness and generosity of the Scruggses. It was from this small room that Louise embarked on a daylong pursuit of Bob Dylan, specifically for me.

As you'll read elsewhere in this book, that chase for Bob began almost immediately on the morning I came in predawn to work with chief music writer Peter Cooper (he's now a full-time musician and historian and no longer a Gannett journalist) as we gathered reactions to the death of Johnny Cash.

The third wheel in *The Tennessean* entertainment news crew then was celebrity columnist Brad Schmitt, who went to sit in for me in an interview with country deejay Gerry House. I'd scheduled the sit-down to occur during the *House Patrol* (I think?) broadcast, but my "superiors" wanted me to work the phones getting "reax," the old newspaper term for reactions to the news. "You know all these old guys" or some such was the explanation.

Peter had the history down, exhaustively, in a story that ought to be a collector's item. My job was to speak with musicians while Peter filled in his gaps with quotes and info I pitched at him.

In addition to Earl (and the hoped-for Bob Dylan), I called Bobby Bare. (Actually, I spoke with his wife, Jeannie, who tracked him down while he was fishing in Kentucky—it was early in the cell phone era, so I think she tracked him down on the landline at a bait shop or breakfast joint.) I also called Cash's Tennessee Two and Three bassist Marshall Grant—a friend of mine who had worked hard with June to get John to sober up—as well as Tom T. and Dixie Hall. I tried Kristofferson, Willie, Little Jimmy—anyone I could think of. Ramblin' Jack Elliott may have had something to do with it, too.

I really wanted to talk with Dylan, a close friend of both Cash and Earl. The three were not shy about swapping musical influences or about crediting each other. And Dylan has always been secretive and less than forthcoming with the media.

So I called Louise, who had a warm relationship with Bob. She answered the phone in this same office while Earl relaxed in the comfortable adjoining living room.

I told her I wanted to get a quote from Earl—and I really wanted one from Dylan. (Look on the internet, and you can find footage of Dylan, along with Earl and sons Gary and Randy, performing "East Virginia Blues" and "Nashville Skyline Rag.")

"Tim, I'll start working on this now," she said, adding that she shared my belief that if anybody could track down the press-shy Dylan for me, she was the one.

"I'll get Bobby for you," she vowed, calling back repeatedly during the 18-hour day to report that she couldn't find him but that she'd keep trying. We stayed in close phone contact for several hours until Louise finally gave up. The chameleon-like folk-rock minstrel did not want to be found, probably lost in the rain in Juárez with his face masked by white pancake.

Louise loved "Bobby" and told me, as the day came to an end, that whenever she got in touch with him, she'd make sure he called me.

He never did, though. If you are reading this, Bobby, I'd like to talk to you about your 115th Dream. Lines from that song lined the wall of the hallway outside my college dorm room.

I'm sure the newcomers to the house on Franklin Road have refreshed the inside of the house some, but the outside remains unchanged as far as I can tell when I drive by and look in, thinking about the couple in the blue Cadillac I saw so often traversing that gate. I'm not sure, but judging by my imperfect geography, I believe that if you walked to the back of Earl's property, you'd come onto the estate previously occupied by Minnie Pearl and her gracious husband, Henry Cannon. I may be wrong. I may be crazy. Well, "Howdee," as the lady said.

For all I know, the new home owners may have put one of those "lawn jockeys" in the spot where Tammy Wynette had installed the Picasso-lite sculpture.

These new occupants at first had a "California South" sign out on the front gate. It's gone now, but it made me believe they were from Los Angeles. I imagined them touring the place with the long hallways and spacious sitting rooms, looking out the sliding-glass door to see the "cement pond," as Jed Clampett would say, and found this home a good substitute for the ones found in the hills of Beverly. That's, of course, where Buddy Ebsen (Jed Clampett) settled with Granny and the rest after a hunting misfire exposed a bubbling crude—oil, that is.

"C'mon listen to a story 'bout a man named Jed," the lyrics went as Flatt and Scruggs played guitar and banjo. Lester and Earl also made appearances on that hillbilly Pygmalion piece of country corn. I believe, though I can't remember, that they probably performed out by the cement pond. Maybe Jethro or Ellie Mae looked on. She sure was a good-looking hillbilly. Swimmin' pools, movie stars.

Back to the closet of suits. Earl had picked from the dozens of looka-likes before performing at a couple of performances I'd seen him dazzle with his three-finger roll at the Country Music Hall of Fame and Museum.

And he and Lester Flatt and the Foggy Mountain Boys could have been spotted wearing suits similar to these back when they rolled across the country by cars or by bus. Look at old pictures of traveling musicians, and you'll see they "dressed" for performances. Now they either are undressed and tattooed or wear mechanics' clothes. I think I got that disdain for musicians in mechanics' clothes from either Mac Wiseman, Uncle Josh, Harold Bradley, Little Jimmy Dickens, or Porter Wagoner, all old-time showmen who knew how to dress for the occasion. I miss all five of those fellows.

Louise, as noted earlier, booked those performances. She probably picked out her husband's suits, too.

When she died, she rightly was saluted in obituaries around the country, particularly in music towns.

I actually wrote the first obituary for *The Tennessean*. Peter, who remains my most loyal friend, and gossip columnist Brad Schmitt had chosen that day to accept jobs elsewhere in Nashville. Newspaper brass didn't like that, so they spent a couple hours with the boys, neatly "bribing" them to stay, with figurative fists filled with cash.

But it was during those hush-hush front-office negotiations that word came to the newsroom that Louise had died. As entertainment editor, I didn't hesitate to jump into obit-writing form.

I called Gary Scruggs and a few other people and got a modest obituary story in for the first edition. If I remember correctly, I covered the basics, mainly to get something out there for our "state" readers, for whom the press deadline was very early. The state edition closed for news stories around 8 p.m., and the city edition closed around midnight for the front pages of news and sports.

I wrote how Louise had invaded what her husband had bragged was a "man's world" when she and the Scruggs Talent Agency Inc. got to work turning Earl (and Lester at first) into superstars.

One of her biggest notions was that what her husband played should not be considered strictly bluegrass music, and in 1959, she got Earl to play the first Newport Folk Festival. She thought, by the way, that the term "bluegrass music" hurt the potential for radio play.

Newport was Earl's swan dive right into the heart of the "folkie" boom of the day.

Her persistence paid off with two classic albums, *Flatt & Scruggs Live at Carnegie Hall* and *Flatt & Scruggs Recorded Live at Vanderbilt University*, records and performances that further reached the souls of nontraditional bluegrass fans while still being must-have LPs for the old guard.

On the first-edition version of the obit, written while Peter was in heated contract negotiations, I gave Peter a co-byline, figuring that would make the Scruggses happiest, as the family was fond of Peter. I am, too. He would have done the same for me (probably did sometime).

He came back to the newsroom, still a *Tennessean* employee, pockets bulging with cash (nah), and wrote a longer version of the obit for the "home edition" of the paper. I'll lift a little bit here:

Louise Scruggs, who blazed trails as Nashville's first female music manager, who helped bring bluegrass music into the folk music boom of the 1950s and '60s and who helped create the notion of bluegrass as a successful business venture, died yesterday at Baptist Hospital in Nashville.

Mrs. Scruggs, wife of banjo legend and Country Music Hall of Famer Earl Scruggs, had been suffering from respiratory problems. She was 78 years old.

"One of the loudest sounds ever in country music just silently left," said country artist Dwight Yoakam. "She truly is one of the legendary icons behind the scenes of country music. She didn't take the curtain calls, but a lot of us would never have heard Flatt and Scruggs if it hadn't been for Louise Scruggs."

Earl was typically brief yet poetic. "I didn't get where I went just on talent. What talent I had would never have peaked without her. She helped shape music up as a business instead of just people out picking and grinning."

Louise was the one with the vision to get Lester and Earl booked at folk festivals, expanding their brand. And while I've already mentioned "The Ballad of Jed Clampett" and the duo's appearances on *The Beverly Hillbillies*, I have not mentioned *Bonnie and Clyde*.

Louise had negotiated for "Foggy Mountain Breakdown" to be used in full and in parts as the film's soundtrack. That 1967 film, part of the so-called New Hollywood aimed for antiauthoritarian baby-boomer audiences, was a smash. And it still stacks up well with stuff like *Easy Rider*, *Five Easy Pieces*, *M★A★S★H*, *Butch Cassidy and the Sundance Kid*, *The Graduate*, and others from that era that showed and talked about things counter to what was popular among Nixon's Silent Majority. And let's not forget *Shaft*, whom Isaac Hayes described in the soundtrack as "the black private dick that's a sex machine to all the chicks."

By the time Earl died, I was working part-time as a correspondent for Reuters News Service. I'd been exiled by *The Tennessean* in 2007 and, then, as now, I used my computer and the occasional compilation of random words to feed my family.

A very small piece of that obituary from Reuters:

Scruggs' style of banjo playing set him apart. Rather than flailing at the banjo strings, as most of his contemporaries did, he delicately hit the strings with three right fingers, coaxing the instrument to produce precise melodies.

His style influenced the likes of The Grateful Dead's Jerry Garcia and others who took up the banjo because of the playing of Scruggs.

I also called my good friend Mac Wiseman, written about elsewhere in this book. Mac, crippled up from his childhood bout with polio that made worse the maladies of age, was saddened.

He also apologized in advance for missing the funeral. "I will miss my friend," said Mac, an original flattop guitarist with the Foggy Mountain Boys, as he sat in his recliner out in Lower Antioch, at the time a less populated section of Metro Nashville.

Pretty much confined to his recliner and wheelchair, Mac, who was 86 at the time, said he would try to compensate for missing the funeral by relishing the memories.

"I'm not getting around too well," he said. "I'll remember him as he was when we were together."

I also covered the funeral that was held at Nashville's Ryman Auditorium, the longtime home of the Grand Ole Opry, before it moved to the suburbs. The Opry still performs there in the winter, and it is a regular venue for memorial services for traditional musicians who have passed on.

The former church was filled with flowers and stars, the centerpiece of it all being the man in the silver-colored casket.

Prominent there was Scruggs's Gibson Mastertone, which was propped up below a screen where archival footage was played.

"I can't even begin to explain the depth and sound of that instrument sitting out there," Vince Gill had said moments before he teamed with Ricky Skaggs and Patty Loveless for "Go Rest High on That Mountain."

Vince began writing what has become a classic country funeral salute after his friend, troubled country music superstar Keith Whitley's meteor, over-fueled by alcohol, burned out in 1989, He finished writing it after his brother, Bob, died in 1993.

Now, it's not really a country music funeral if Vince isn't there to sing that song.

A litany of scripture and testimony from the music world filled the Ryman for Earl's funeral. And there's really no need to list the stars. All the royalty of acoustic and bluegrass music attended, and most performed.

Their sentiments were summarized in one sentence spoken by Emmylou Harris, the goddess of American music: "I was thinking how lucky we all are to have lived at the same time as Earl Scruggs."

"Music is a part of my life," Earl once told me as we talked about a TV special he was going to do with Ricky Skaggs and Doc Watson, adding, "I don't have a worry in the world when I start playing music. I am right at home."

Willie Nelson

I owe Willie Nelson an apology—or maybe a phone call.

He doesn't know it, but for a while (several months if not longer) back in the early 2000s, the great American, both a working-class and a honky-tonk hero, provided me with a quick bit of relaxation, an opportunity to exhale.

And he didn't know it.

I know that my mentioning of Willie, relaxation, and exhaling in one sentence has you thinking the obvious about my relationship with Willie, the roll-me-up-and-smoke-me-when-I-die fellow. I do admire the philosophy and am sure there will be folks lining up to partake when that day arrives.

My personal contacts, my relaxation with Willie, was back in the days when artists didn't use their publicists or managers as their shields. Oh, I don't mind that they do, as they pay these folks well, and most of them are pretty good.

Johnny Cash's longtime manager Lou Robin was the prototype, as he worked out of his Creative Artists Agency offices in Hollywood or his Malibu beach house (I think) to make sure the Man in Black was treated fairly. I had fights with Lou at times. He got mad when I called him early at home on a deadline story about Cash. ("Don't you know how early it is here in California? Call me at the office in a couple hours," he ranted before giving me the answer I needed on deadline.)

Sure, we had disputes. But he told me, in a phone call after Cash died, that I was the only journalist who called him to offer personal condolences as opposed to simple "professional courtesy." I knew the men were friends, and I knew Lou would be devastated. He let his deep melancholy loose in that phone call.

That's all beside the point, I suppose. I'll have to say I'm not sure who Willie's publicist was back then, perhaps Elaine Schock, as kind and as human a professional as you can find. When I lost my job at *The Tennessean* because I was too old (explained elsewhere in this book), Elaine tried to direct work that she couldn't fit into her busy schedule my way.

Anyway, somehow, back in the early 2000s (and it may have been in 2003) when I was doing a story on Willie's release of the demos he had recorded for Ray Price's publishing company in the early to mid-1960s, I got his personal phone number. (Quick note: Patsy Cline's "Crazy" is perhaps the best-known hit to come from this batch, and I have come to love Willie's heartbreaking demo better than Patsy's.)

Or I may have gotten the phone number earlier. And I can't remember for sure who gave it to me. It could have been his publicist, but it just as easily could have been Ray Price, Kristofferson, or Billy Joe Shaver.

Anyway, one day I called that cell number at an appointed hour to interview Willie about that album of great old song-plugging demos. Since I was the entertainment editor of *The Tennessean*, I think I was given a 25-minute window that Willie and I stretched out past an hour. I know I liked him a lot, and, it seemed, he was having fun talking with me. I don't know who he "blew off" to extend our conversation, but I appreciate it.

Well, I guess I should mention it quickly. When I first called Willie for that story, I asked the man I referred to as "Mr. Nelson" when he answered the phone how I should address him.

"Willie sounds right to me," he said.

I'll talk about that interview and other encounters with him (my first meeting with him was in 1976) later in this story.

But first I've got to admit that when I did get off the phone with Willie after that long conversation and interview, I felt red-eyed mellow.

"I really like Willie," I told Craig Havighurst, one of the entertainment writers, who was the only member of my staff in the office at that hour. I think he was over there at his desk, perhaps eight feet from my own, and he was trying to get his lava lamp to work while waiting for Ralph Stanley to call. Or something like that.

Craig also had the opportunity, if he desired (and I'm not sure if he did), to listen to my half of the long and laugh-filled conversation with Willie.

"We share the same worldview," I told Craig after my Willie-induced refreshment.

And that's true enough. I'm not talking about smoking weed when I say we shared the same values, although that's certainly fine with me. But I'm just talking about his general kindness and his willingness to share the glory with those who worked with him on the album. And then there was the simple emotion displayed when talking about individual songs and incidents.

The call was scheduled to help promote the *Demo Sessions CD*, but Willie was not—is not—all about Willie. He likes to downplay his own importance.

Willie, I'll note here, played a role in my sanity that he doesn't know.

I'll have to say that I did not like my job at *The Tennessean*. It wasn't that I wasn't having fun talking to Waylon and Willie and the boys, but there were some mighty Gannett corporate folks who second-guessed everything and everyone.

In any case, while I loved my staff, I usually was the first person to come in each morning to the entertainment department, which I governed with a silk glove.

I felt vulnerable when I showed up and my troops were "working from home" or simply recovering from a vodka overdose. It wasn't that I was under constant attack, but I just felt uncomfortable. And I didn't trust the instincts of my superiors, including a fellow who, while identifying himself as the editor of the newspaper, did a nationally televised campaign commercial proclaiming his undying love for Al Gore and telling people to vote for him in 2000. Real newspaper people don't even put campaign signs in their yards, let alone endorse someone on television.

Al, who had been a reporter for *The Tennessean* in his Vanderbilt days and beyond, was a good friend of the editor, and they were much alike. I did get to know and love Al's mom, Pauline, and even his dad, Senator Al Sr.

Other editors also were barking at my heels on a regular basis, some-times wondering where the vodka guy was or even calling into question the ability of my top music reporter, Peter Cooper, to produce meaningful copy at home (he could, and his mini-dachshund, Russell, usually tucked inside his shirt, helped him). And the vodka guy, well, he always made it in eventually and worked very hard for the newspaper that probably sprung his nasty habit in the first place.

So on really stressful days when some superior was barking about some-thing, I'd occasionally do one simple thing: I'd dig out that private phone number I'd been given. And I'd call Willie.

The first time I called on one of these unofficial long-distance visits, I was surprised by the "This is Willie" recorded intro on the answering machine. I listened, and I felt better. There is something comforting in his voice both as a performer and as a recorded phone answerer.

I didn't do it often, but once in a while, under similar stressful situations and before my staff got in, I'd turn away from the torment and tell myself, "I'm going to call Willie."

And usually all I got was the answering machine, which was enough. But occasionally, he would answer, and we'd chat about the weather, about Tootsie's Orchid Lounge, about Darrell Royal, about Waylon—about who I was and why in the hell I was bothering him. Actually, he was very warm. I really like Willie Nelson a lot to this day because of his welcoming demeanor in those times when I was slowly being pushed to the curb by corporate journalism.

"I'm just checking in on you to see how you're doing," I'd say to him (or something like that). While I didn't often leave a message on his machine, I did sometimes, telling him not to bother calling back and to have a good day. And "Thanks!"

I already had begun a habit of calling older performers just to let them know someone still cared about them, so I figured Willie could be on that list.

And, even if all I got was his voice-mail greeting, I always felt better.

A couple of times, I got a quote or two that I would pass on to the celebrity columnist or one of the music writers if it might help their stories.

Once, when music writer Craig Havighurst—the "Man of Constant Sorrow" lava lamp fellow mentioned above—was tasked by big shots to come up with a country stars "reax" story about the Dixie Chicks' disavowal of George W. Bush the night before in a London concert, he stopped cursing long enough to ask me if I had any ideas as to whom he should call.

Willie is as great an American as there is, after all. So I called Willie and asked if he'd mind talking to Craig for five minutes or so about the Chicks. He didn't mind, so I just switched the call over to Craig.

After a while, I quit calling. I mean, the contact with this great man was reassuring to my soul, but I didn't want to be a pest. I kept calling other old veterans, but I figured Willie probably liked to be left alone.

I will say that one thing I did find out during these short conversations is that Willie is a nice man.

The first time I met him in person was back on May 12, 1976, when I volunteered to cover a Willie Nelson and Friends show at the Winfield Dunn Center (Austin Peay State University's basketball gym) in Clarksville, Tennessee. I talk a bit more about this in my chapter about Charlie Daniels, who was among the redheaded stranger's guests that night.

Willie Nelson leads his band through "Whiskey River" in a May 1976 concert in Clarksville, Tennessee. Charlie Daniels helped sneak the author into this show, where he shot this stage-front photo. PHOTO BY TIM GHIANNI

I was a sportswriter at the local newspaper—the *Clarksville Leaf-Chronicle*—and when the concert was announced, I asked the features editor (or whatever his title) if I could cover it on my own time.

It wasn't that there was an overwhelming tug-of-war with other staffers, most of whom didn't care a thing about country music or heard of Willie Nelson. Those reporters all grew up to have respectable corporate jobs. Here I am writing about a musician and relishing the fact that my good friend Bobby Bare, whom I call frequently, has told me he picks up the phone only if it's "from you or Willie or Peter Cooper."

Anyway, back to that concert nearly a half century ago. I had been a fan for a few years, buying my first Willie album, *Shotgun Willie*, in 1973 at a Cats store in Nashville. I'd actually gone to the store just to browse, a time-honored but now-extinct form of recreation practiced mainly by men. Women were welcome, of course, especially from my point of view.

My intentions going in were to browse the new stock, but I had two albums in my mind: *Shotgun Willie* by this "outlaw" from Texas and Alice Cooper's *Muscle of Love*. I always liked Alice both in his stage shows and offstage, where he was a friendly guy and frustrated golfer. I followed him for a round during an old pro-am they used to hold at Percy Warner Park golf course in Nashville.

The Pro-Celebrity Golf Tournament was part of a big weekend of fun in Nashville, all built around a concert that featured Boots Randolph, Floyd Cramer, and Chet Atkins. Others would participate, guys like Mickey Newbury, Danny Davis and the Nashville Brass, and Jimmy Dean. Some performers even came in from both coasts to participate in the tourney and the concert, both of which raised money for Vanderbilt Children's Hospital.

Enough about that other than that I chose to walk the round with Alice rather than Mickey Mantle and Whitey Ford because the two great Yankees, whom I did get a chance to talk to personally, had obviously enjoyed prematch "teeing up," especially the Mick. And besides that, about all of the journalists there were, like me, sportswriters. They came from a wide radius around Nashville, and all of them wanted to be with the two great Yankees.

It was sort of like an Arnie's Army of besotted (in both definitions: look 'em up) newspaper and TV sports guys, and I knew that, as much as I didn't mind that number 7 was a bit drunk, I'd get no more personal time with either him or Whitey. The Yanks would be staging a drunken joke fest for the sports journalists. That was their shtick.

So I stood back while they all staggered off onto the first fairway at Percy Warner Park's 18-hole course. I waited for Alice, who basically was teeing off with some wealthy businessmen I didn't know. I figured I'd walk along with Alice and/or his cart and talk about golf, big snakes, and killing Santa in the finale of his Christmas show. He also gave me a can of beer from the cooler he carted along.

Enough on that. Let's go back into the Cats records store. When I checked out with my two purchases, a nice-enough-looking young woman, obviously a Vanderbilt student, was the cashier.

"This is good," she said while fiddling with my *Muscle of Love* (the album, to be clear). She looked at the second LP I was purchasing and looked stunned. "Who is this Shotgun Willie?" she asked, almost incensed that I'd overlooked Emerson, Lake & Palmer's *Brain Salad Surgery* or Status Quo's *Hello* for what appeared to be a country album. As noted earlier, I told her he's a guy who sits around in his underwear, bitin' on a bullet and pullin' out all of his hair. I'd learned that much from FM radio.

When I got home to play *Shotgun Willie*, I quickly was hooked on Willie and bought his next few records—*Phases and Stages*, *Red Headed Stranger*, and *The Sound in Your Mind*—by the time of his appearance at the Winfield Dunn Center. I'd gone into the sale bins to pick up *Yesterday's Wine* and *Willie Nelson and Family*. And, of course, I bought *Wanted: The Outlaws*, the greatly flawed, weak-sounding, patched-together label-greed album that also featured Waylon Jennings, his wife Jessi Colter, and Tompall Glaser.

By the way, during the course of my career, I interviewed to some extent (or at least met) these people (except for Tompall). For years, I tried to get the overlooked "Outlaw" for an interview, and he declined through his wife. He was in the phone book and lived, I think, over near the Tennessee State Fairgrounds in South Nashville. I always thought his part in what Waylon termed the "Outlaw Bit" was underrecognized, almost as much as the Glaser Brothers harmonies have been forgotten. Finally, in late 2012, Tompall actually got on the phone himself. I had called his wife the day before and said I'd really like to talk with him. I'd always been pleasant and respectful to her during previous calls, so she kind of caved.

She said she'd see if she could talk him into it and for me to "call back tomorrow." The next day, he got on the phone and said something like, "Thanks for thinking about me, Tim, but I had my time. It was a long time ago." He seemed like a nice fellow, dead within a year I think.

Tompall, by the way, was on the bill for that 1976 Clarksville concert. And just about everyone in the Outlaw periphery showed up to take part or hang out.

I'd only requested one press pass. Back then, before the world got digitally castrated, reporters generally took care of what we called the "art" (photography) to accompany our stories. Since I'd shot dozens of basketball games in the Winfield Dunn Center, I knew my f-stop and shutter speed (no one cares about those things anymore in this automatic world) to shoot with available light. You do not want to shoot a concert or a ball game with a flash, a bush-league mistake for young reporters who shoot mostly pictures of wrecks and back-of-the-head city council meetings rather than people. Now, most don't even use cameras, as iPhones are almost idiot-proof, even if I have trouble with my own.

My Charlie Daniels chapter goes into my adventures getting into the arena, but I did get in, and I was able to scoot my way all the way to the front of the stage, right below Willie, to shoot my art. Willie kept on looking at me as I fired away.

From the moment he romped out with "Whiskey River" to the time he closed (and I can't remember, but it may have been by singing "Good-Hearted Woman" with fellow Outlaws, or perhaps he closed with "Blue Eyes Crying in the Rain"), this was a wonderful show. I guess I've seen Willie at least a dozen times since. He's kind of like the Grateful Dead: sometimes great, sometimes just okay, but always what you expected.

Willie's Family Band is as good a group of musicians as you can find, and Willie, then a young man, was pretty rambunctious as he moved around the stage.

But he kept staring down at me from center stage. Suddenly, he began to move forward, signaling me to come toward him at the front edge of the stage. He crouched down to my level and extended his hand toward my face. I reached out, and we did one of those double-fisted "brother" handshakes, and he was talking to me.

The problem was that both of us were in front of one of the speakers; Mickey Raphael, Paul English, Bobbie Nelson, and the rest were still wailing; and I could not hear what he was saying. So, while we clasped hands and Willie spoke, I just nodded, smiled, and said "Yes, this is a great show" or "I enjoy a whiskey river myself" or some such—maybe "Nice hair" or "Great red kerchief, man."

For all I know, he had been telling me to stop bothering him with my 50-mm Nikon lens. Or perhaps he was inviting me to the party he was going to at the Pikes' frat house that night. Maybe he was asking me if I knew where he could get some pot or where the nearest gas station was.

Some of those Austin Peay State University Pikes have told me that Willie and Faron Young drank almost until dawn at that party. I personally doubt that alcohol was all that was involved, but the good brothers of that frat house won't go into details, as they now are mostly retired and respected Clarksville businessmen. I do know that at least that night, some of them did drown in a whiskey river. And a couple of them went out for a quick ride around the college with Willie.

I ran into Willie a few more times, mainly at industry things or at an after-party, like the one he held at Merchants' restaurant in Nashville after one of his star-studded tribute concerts at the Ryman Auditorium.

I don't usually go to such after-gatherings, but Keith Richards had been on the bill, and I'm a sucker for The Stones. He didn't come to the party. Willie arrived late, likely because he went to his bus (or maybe Keith's hotel room) to "relax" for a while after the concert. But he was his normal charming self.

He told me once that he considered Keith a good friend. "Keith is kinda like my canary in the mine. If he's still alive this morning, I know I'm gonna live at least another day."

I remember one time when Willie was being interviewed by Dan Miller, the most popular TV news anchor ever to hit Nashville (he held that crown until he died). Dan had a show called *Miller & Company* (I think it was on Sunday nights after the local news).

It really was a good one-on-one interview program; Dan was skilled and relaxed and made his subjects relax as well. It was on that show that I first saw Kris Kristofferson use Winston Churchill's "Black Dogs of Depression" to describe his own mental state, which I share.

But this episode featured Willie, who (like Kris) has a home in Hawaii. Just weeks before, he'd been in the news when he suffered a collapsed lung while swimming with his family in that Pacific paradise. That was in 1981, and marijuana wasn't talked about much. Willie's rep at CBS Records, Woody Bowles, told reporters at the time that the singer's dangerous health condition likely was caused by his grueling schedule of 200 to 250 dates per year. Of course, he wasn't fooling anyone.

On the interview show, Dan Miller and Willie were talking about the latter's well-publicized formidable consumption of marijuana.

Dan asked how Willie knew when he had smoked too much pot.

The response: "Well, I guess you know after you've smoked so much your lungs collapse" (or something in that vein).

Anyway, I like Willie a lot, and he has helped me. For example, I once did a story on Ray Charles and his impact on Nashville with his *Modern Sounds in Country and Western Music* compilations.

Ray was dead. But there was going to be a display about the importance of that recording and Ray himself at the Country Music Hall of Fame and Museum.

I called around Nashville and elsewhere for input on the story to preview that exhibit. As I may have noted elsewhere, I was the guy who tried best to publicize things at the Hall of Fame.

The lead on my March 6, 2006, story for *The Tennessean* was this: "One could argue that the most influential man in country music's worldwide success was a blind, black R&B pianist from Georgia."

And my very best quote came from one of my calls to Willie. "When Ray did 'I Can't Stop Loving You,' that was probably the time when country music was heard by more people than ever before.

"He kicked country music forward 50 years. Before him, a lot of people had probably never heard of songs by Don Gibson or Hank Williams."

In addition to the 22-month display that was set to open at the Hall of Fame, Willie and I talked about why Brother Ray (Willie's chess and pot partner) should be inducted into that country music shrine.

"He's got to be there," said Willie. "He belongs there as much as anybody else. He's done as much as any of us to progress country music and let it be heard around the world and give it the respect it deserves."

He and I spoke on another occasion about his long friendship with Ray, and again, the chess rivalry brought humor into the conversation.

Willie said Ray used notched pieces and a textured board. "I learned how to play chess with the lights on. So Ray had a tendency to leave the lights off when we played.

"Oh, he knew what he was doing. Ray always did."

By the way, Merle Haggard echoed Willie's assessment of the great Brother Ray in a brief conversation (I lament never having the opportunity to spend much time with Merle, who was a nice man): "Ray Charles was the man that crossed all boundaries and brought it all together."

I have to tell you that the exhibit's grand opening at the Hall of Fame was a stellar affair. The problem was that Neil Young was screening a concert movie he'd made at the Ryman Auditorium at the same time.

Because I spent so much time on the Ray story, I decided I should be at the Hall of Fame. I unfortunately passed on what would have been my only opportunity ever to meet Neil Young. It's a cold bowl of chili when love lets you down.

But back to Willie. Over the years, if a country music figure died, I'd call Willie (or really his publicist Elaine Schock) to see if he wanted to make a comment. I had stopped using that private line and don't know if he still has it. I knew Elaine would turn me down, but I had to make the call just in case.

Willie doesn't talk about death. I found that out long ago. Still, I didn't want to pass him by when writing about Cash, Faron, Waylon, or Ray Price.

Willie told Elaine he'd be glad to do an interview with me about Ray Charles.

The interview took place as Willie and the rest rode the bus rolling across Texas, bound, I believe, for a free concert for wounded Iraqi War veterans in San Antonio.

Willie answered me on the first ring. There's almost always a mix of melancholy and mirth in this great man's voice, and this was no exception.

"He was one of the best friends I ever had," Willie said of Ray. "He's still here. He always is."

Like I say, I really like the guy—a lot. I doubt if he really remembers me despite our meetings and interviews.

Willie told me that he always thought the recordings issued on *Crazy: The Demo Sessions* were worthwhile back when he wrote them. "Now, 40 years later, here they are," he said in that interview published in *The Tennessean* in March 2003.

"I play 'em for everybody," he said. "I always did like them. I couldn't figure out why they didn't just put them out then. Now, 40 years later, here they are."

While we talked about that album, we also discussed our shared worldview, and I told Willie that while he has rambled like a Texas blue norther from song plugger to Outlaw to American icon, he never really has changed. He seemed to appreciate that assessment.

The *Demo Sessions* album springs from a time when Willie was alone, bruised, battered, dazed, and confused.

"I would hope the despair comes through," he said of the sparse feel.

"It's like all things in my life," he said. "Back in those days, I can't remember a time when I didn't have mixed emotions. I was going through domestic problems and financial problems.

"I can't remember when I wasn't. It was kinda my life in general.

"I was going through a divorce. For the first 40 or 50 years of my life, that's what I was doing. I was getting married, and I was getting divorced.

"I don't know if I was getting married too much or getting divorced too much."

I remember his laughter as he went into his next line, something I'm sure he'd used before:

"You know what I say when people ask why are divorces so expensive? I tell 'em: 'it's because they're worth it.'"

Some of the songs on the *Demo Sessions* album became hits for others. Others stayed in the Willie Nelson archives, a wondrous treasury of music that's still likely not fully tapped. He'll be like Elvis, Sinatra, and John Lennon, putting out new music long past the time he's been rolled up and smoked.

The latest reports have him giving up smoking pot because of all the damage from it and from the three packs of Chesterfields he used to smoke daily. He reportedly is using other forms of the herb, and, of course, he has his own cannabis company, Willie's Reserve, whose products he likes to test for potential consumers.

Back in 2003, I asked about the latest reports of him whacking away at his weed consumption.

"I haven't cut back a lot. I know a guy who heard that if he didn't quit smoking, it'd kill him. He quit smoking and got run over by a truck the next day."

As I was writing this, I thought of a basically anonymous musician, a dreamer like those who come to Nashville every day, thinking they might be the next big thing. In his case, he'd come from relative success in Louisiana honky-tonks to take his shot in Nashville.

Tony Fardella, a thin, older man who was pedal steel–playing bandleader for Tony Farr and his Farr-Outs, told me long ago about Willie's kindness to him, a basically unknown journeyman.

"Willie is the kind of guy that if he knows you, he knows you.

"There's nothin' phony about Willie Nelson. I ain't seen Willie in a long time, but I betcha if he saw me, he'd remember me."

As I sit here, I think again back to the day I interviewed Willie as he and his band bounced in the bus across Texas to the wounded veterans concert in San Antone.

There was a lot of laughter on the bus, and, no matter what I said, Willie was obviously in sky-high spirits.

At the conclusion of the conversation, I told him I'd like to ride on the bus with him for a few days. It wouldn't cost him anything, and I wouldn't report on or partake in any of his band's activities, I said.

All I wanted was to breathe the air, I told him. I'd even bring my own potato chips, Twinkies, and candy bars.

"We'll see if we can work that out someday," said the redheaded stranger.

Nothing ever came of that. Maybe it's finally time to see if that top-secret phone number still works.

Jimmy Church

ESCAPING THE WARTS-AND-ALL SECTION of South Nashville, I ducked into the low-slung building, letting the aroma of fried fish and the throttling sound of soul music slap my face, warming me on a bitter winter night.

I was greeted by Jimmy Church, the legendary R&B bandleader, who offered up a quick hug before turning back to his job.

"Everybody comes out on Tuesday night for grown folks night," is Jimmy's summation of what happens at Carol Ann's Home Cooking Café.

Here, on Tuesday nights, perhaps three or four miles southeast of the tourist mecca that is Lower Broadway—where second-rate country music and too much beer have conventioneers and rednecks mingling with bachelorettes whose skimpy dresses seem designed to go over their heads, whether or not by intention—Jimmy for years has volunteered his time to keep one of Music City's rhythmic flavors thriving.

Weekly, at least until the COVID-induced shutdown of restaurants and nightclubs, Church—one of the most bighearted and unassuming musicians who has kept R&B alive in Nashville—instructs the guy at the soundboard, sets a running order for the many blues players and soul stars who show up to jam, and emcees the evening.

If you are lucky, sometime during the four hours in which the warmth and charm of the man is reflected in the 50 to 100 folks in the crowd (many of them will get up to perform, others simply to dance), Jimmy takes the stage himself.

On those fortunate Tuesdays, he'd sing and direct the Jimmy Church Band—with its lead guitarist, his son, Jimi (named both for the old R&B

bandleader and for one of his late friends and employees, Jimi Hendrix)—through its paces.

That band has long been a delight across the country, going back to the days when Hendrix and his bass-playing pal, Billy Cox, helped provide the backing for the lively showman.

On this Tuesday night at 407 Murfreesboro Road, Jimmy switches on his microphone and announces that the next performer will be James "Nick" Nixon.

Nick, a blues guitar warhorse whose health concerns have affected his energy and stamina, never looked like a musician on the decline as he worked the stage, even almost to the end. He died on February 28, 2018, and I still miss his music, especially his devotion to sharing the blues in Nashville Metro Schools classrooms.

Carol Ann's has been an anomaly, a bastion of urban music that's a "no-hip-hop zone," where the flat-billed ball caps of youth were replaced by fedoras, fezzes, and feathers on customers who wear their shimmering best to experience the music of underappreciated R&B legends.

Older, mostly black R&B fans, who were young in the 1960s when this music reigned over what now is a derelict section of Nashville on Jefferson Street, enjoyed their plates of fish and chicken, greens and beans, and piled-high pie. Over at the bar, the blender worked all evening, as fruity cocktails were served up, along with beer, to the crowd.

"It's all because of Jimmy," said owner Carol Ann Jenkins, who cornered me when I asked for a Diet Coke before sauntering down to the room where the music is nonstop. (She died in 2016, but passed the R&B baton to her daughter.) During my time spent with her—and I was fortunate to be her guest at the bar on a couple of occasions—she gave Jimmy all the credit.

He did deserve most of it, as he's the guy who drew in the other musicians. But she gave them a place to celebrate. I liked her a lot—busty, bright smile, teasing eyes, and pride.

While Jimmy verbally teased the crowd into something that (for their ages, at least), resembled a frenzy, Nick took the main microphone.

He scanned the room, where some danced, many chatted, and others washed down the "best catfish in Tennessee" with frozen fruit-and-liquor concoctions, cold drafts, or sweet iced tea. Actually, in Nashville and in the South in general, if you order iced tea, it's always sweetened. They'll make you some unsweetened if you ask nicely.

The activity didn't disturb venerable bluesman and trained opera singer Nick, who took the throttle off the driving tale of "Mustang Sally," leaned into the microphone, and began a monologue about men, women, and mustangs—mostly women, of course.

Surrounding him beneath the banner reading "Carol Ann's All Star Band," an assortment of R&B players laid hypnotic musical texture beneath Nixon's ready rap.

The fans who were jammed into the showroom watched and listened to the bantering man at center stage and his cluster of compadres: guitarists, drummers, keyboardists, horn men, and harmonists. They made their livings in the city's best show bands, studios, and R&B outfits but eagerly volunteered for duty the third night of every week at Carol Ann's Home Cooking Café.

In R&B show band fashion nurtured by everyone from James Brown to John Belushi, the musicians helped Nixon, a young 72, add as much drama as possible to the slow-and-steady storytelling before exploding in unison.

"Ride, Sally, ride," semi-screamed Nixon, triggering a climax of claps and orgasmic gasps, before he led the band, full throttle, back into the lyrics made famous by "The Wicked" Wilson Pickett: "I bought you a brand-new Mustang, a 1965. Huh!"

Jimmy worked the room, asking those in the crowd from Robert Knight (of "Everlasting Love" fame) to Clifford Curry ("She Shot a Hole in My Soul") if they wanted to take the stage for the night's R&B jam.

Frank Howard, written about elsewhere in this book, agreed that he and his "new" group, the Valentines, would do a couple of songs, probably "My Girl" at the very least. Frank, as noted elsewhere, rose to prominence as the front man of Frank Howard & the Commanders.

They did have a bit of a resurgence until Charlie Fite died, also in 2016, so Frank teamed up with another old-school Nashville R&B group, the Valentines. Herschel Carter, the other Commander who told me he was born again and had shed his body-and-soul–consuming wicked ways, also sometimes performs.

Jimmy Church, though, is the real star of the night, even if he doesn't perform, as he makes sure others do get up there to entertain while also wandering around, making sure the "regulars," folks who come weekly from as far away as Tullahoma and Pulaski, an hour or two away, enjoy themselves.

The Jimmy Church Band has been ripping it up since the 1960s with the likes of Cox, Larry Lee, Johnny Jones, Hendrix, Marion James, Curry, Knight, Earl Gaines, Roscoe Shelton, Harold Hebb, and Johnny Bragg (the Nashville contingent of R&B stars) as well as touring the country, on the Chitlin' Circuit or otherwise.

On the Circuit, he regarded the immortal Jackie Wilson as his mentor.

"When I was young, I favored Jackie, so he used to have me riding in his limo with him."

Jimmy, still not one to ever duck the ladies' attentions, said, "We'd get places, and there'd be all these girls, and he'd tell them that I was Jackie Wilson."

He also learned lessons from others. He admitted that he learned a lot about playing bass from Billy Cox. From Cox's crony, the often-stoned fellow with the blistering guitar, Jimi (then "Jimmy" Hendrix), Church said he learned how *not* to perform.

"Without [guitarist] Larry Lee in that band, we wouldn't have sounded like nothing. Hendrix was doing all that kind of stuff," said Church, whose hard-charging, choreographed shows all these years later show a dedication to discipline.

"People wanted to hear music, but Jimi kept doing that [stuff], so Larry kept playing a big old chord to make the band sound like a band."

The free-flying and free-falling Hendrix learned some of his charismatic skills by simply paying close attention during his Jefferson Street show band experience with Church.

Even though there was no room for guitar haze, purple or otherwise, in his choreographed shows, Jimmy Church loved the guy who left Nashville to unseat Eric Clapton as the best guitarist of the 1960s.

"Jimi was a good cat. He was real humble. He stayed high. I didn't know nothing about no drugs."

"We played Clarksville [where Hendrix and Billy Cox first teamed up as 101st Airborne paratroopers] one time, and Hendrix broke the speaker. He kept playing. He was into the fuzz tone before it first came out."

When Church formed his own show band—with a full complement of musicians and the bountiful sights and sounds provided by a cadre of female singers—he was determined to provide high-caliber, ear-pleasing music, dosed with showmanship and discipline. This is a show band with drum-punctuated, horn-exploding purpose.

"I'm still in the mix now because of it," Jimmy Church said during a conversation a few years ago (we speak often).

"You got to have a showman. You gotta sing it just like the record goes. People want to hear the song just like they heard it on the record they bought."

Too many artists, he lamented, strayed from the original versions of the songs they were covering and disappointed the audience.

"You do it like it goes," he said. "You don't add nothing. You show up on time and do your job, and people will come to see you."

Doing it like the original—in this case, Wilson Pickett—is what Nick Nixon is doing when performing "Mustang Sally," with Church's band, including young Jimi, backing him.

Michael Gray, a regular customer on Tuesdays, is a Nashville R&B scholar and an editor at the Country Music Hall of Fame and Museum, short miles from Carol Ann's.

Michael, who curated a long-running exhibit called *Night Train to Nashville*, celebrating the R&B history of the city, called on Jimmy for the musical presentations during the two-year run of the exhibit in the early 2000s.

"For decades he has been leading one of the tightest bands in the country," Michael says. "The Hall of Fame has been fortunate—on many levels—to have the Jimmy Church Band anchor many of our Night Train to Nashville festivities. Many of the veteran artists that we have wanted to showcase no longer have their own backing bands, but every one of those singers knows and respects Jimmy and feels comfortable sitting in with his group."

Oh, versatility is key for Jimmy. While there still are calls for him to play on the convention circuit, he also is heavily booked into big weddings and family celebrations.

If the bride and her father want to dance to "Midnight Hour" and have it stay true to Wilson Pickett, Jimmy Church and his team are ready.

One YouTube video shows Church's band playing a 2002 bar mitzvah at Nashville's West End Synagogue, slipping from a lively "Havah Nagilah" to the Louis Armstrong "What a Wonderful World."

"We do Beyoncé, Pink, all the stuff those kids want to hear, from the Supremes to the Pointer Sisters all the way to Rihanna," he said, noting that even at his age, he wants to be able to give the audience what it wants.

"Always know you gotta give people a show," he said.

He long ago learned that by staying true to the Top 40 covers and giving people a show, he was breaking racial and cultural barriers, particularly when he was young and his outfit was making its first appearances on the endless fraternity dance party circuit of the South.

"What really helped me was what happened when white kids saw our show. I was so scared. Going to Ole Miss to play for these white kids. They'd never had a black band before."

With the girls dancing, the horns blaring, and the tuxedo-clad bandleader smiling and singing, the Jimmy Church Band was pretty well launched onto the mostly white college circuit that night.

"The kids were extremely nice. That got us a lot of work. People would ask, 'Who was that black band?'"

Even today, his audience remains "99 percent white," but times and venues have changed.

"Ninety-eight percent of our gigs are weddings," Church said. "We play the old version. I get gigs on top of gigs because we play 'Mustang Sally' like 'Mustang Sally' goes."

Nick Nixon finished that song with Jimmy's band and slowly collapsed into a chair. He was spent. But the crowd went wild.

The Jimmy Church Band, this time led by young Jimi, went into a long R&B instrumental jam while the emcee worked the room, thanking folks for coming and coaxing others to get up on the stage.

Perry Baggs with
Jason & the Scorchers

Perry Baggs—or "Baggz," depending on the day's concoction and perhaps his mood—was the best rock drummer to ever plop down at the chair next to my desk and talk about Jesus, my Hawaiian shirts, his love of Van Halen, or, if you pushed him, his role in what was the best rock band ever to come out of Nashville.

Heck, Jason & the Scorchers really were among the top rock bands in the world, though they never received the level of fame they deserved. For proof, dial up YouTube and check out the boys' version of Dylan's "Absolutely Sweet Marie."

My favorite version is from Denmark's Roskilde Festival in 1985. Oh, there are other versions online of the Scorchers doing this Dylan song and others of them doing other stuff in their frenetic, Ramones–meet–Little Jimmy Dickens style.

Anyway, also on the bill with Jason Ringenberg, Perry, and the boys at the music festival back on June 28–30, 1985, were those same Ramones—the masters of the stripped-lyric, three-minute, hard-rock, shock-treatment recordings—and other royalty of that era (and others).

The Cure, the Clash, Leonard Cohen, Paul Young, and Billy Bragg are just a few who shared the stage with the fellows from Nashville, who definitely belonged there. Sure, the Clash and Cohen, in particular, had lengthy stays at the heights that Jason and the boys reached only briefly. They deserved a lengthier stay.

The Scorchers, with that frenetic energy (or perhaps madness), inspired my good friend, musician and historian Peter Cooper, to tell me that if The Rolling Stones were playing the Exit/In and the Scorchers were playing the End (basically across the street in Nashville), he'd go see Jason and the boys. I'd go see The Stones, of course, but I may run across the street for a while.

There is one great similarity. Neither of those groups has their original and best drummer. In 2021, Charlie Watts died, finishing his six decades of handling The Stones' sticks in his jazzy-carnal style. Perry, the Scorchers' iconic drummer, has been dead since 2012, and health forced him to lay down his sticks even earlier.

If you look through the archives, you'll find that for a brief while during the year of that Danish festival, the Scorchers were heralded in many quarters as likely contenders for the "World's Greatest Rock-'n'-Roll Band" moniker that was bestowed (probably by Mick and Keith) on The Rolling Stones sometime back in the *Beggars Banquet* and *Let It Bleed* days. The comparisons between those two bands are plenty, actually. The Scorchers created "cowpunk," a sort of Little Jimmy Dickens or even Hank Williams–meets–the Ramones music form (with brilliant dashes of Jagger-style angry swagger). And Perry and Jason Ringenberg, the leader of the band who has aged into children's music as Farmer Jason, wrote some fine, drawling songs. Heck, and with little effort, they could turn songs like "Absolutely Sweet Marie" into their own.

Mick and Keith, similarly, infused their music with tones and tunes of the South, from New Orleans to Memphis to Nashville to Muscle Shoals.

I can happily imagine Jason & the Scorchers doing one of my favorite Stones country songs, "Sweet Virginia," and kicking "the shit right off their shoes" and those of their audience.

Peter is one of the few people I love and trust—Perry Baggs has something to do with that, too—and he and I have had front man discussions in the past. While I maintain that Mick Jagger is the all-time best front man in rock music (The Beatles were a better band, and John Lennon is my favorite visionary and singer-songwriter, but the Fabs didn't have a single front man, you may recall), Peter would take Jason over Mick any day.

I really can't argue too hard when I see the Scorchers on video or the few times I saw them in person. Perhaps their most storied concert was at Cat's Records, near Vanderbilt, early in their career. It is one of those Nashville rock history hallmarks, and not everyone who says they were there possibly could have been. It was a great show: Jason whirling around stage in his buckskins and cowboy hat, guitar wizard Warner Hodges spinning around in circles and missing neither a note nor a puff on his cigarette in a truly dizzy and dizzying performance (a genius that he shrugs off as "it's like arm-wrestling an alligator, that's all it is"), Jeff Johnson holding down the low end on bass while maintaining a Bill Wyman–like stoicism

Newspaper librarian Perry Baggs provided the backbeat for Jason & the Scorchers, the best rock 'n' roll band to come out of Nashville: Jason Ringenberg, left; Perry, middle; Jeff Johnson, right; and Warner Hodges, front and center; circa 1986. EMI/PHOTOFEST © EMI

(for the most part), and Perry attacking the snare with the precision of Buddy Rich on amphetamines.

Perry was to Jason, Warner, and Jeff what Charlie was to Mick, Keith, and Ronnie Wood (or Mick Taylor or Brian Jones on guitar and for decades Bill Wyman on bass). It's hard to imagine this gentleman with the leprechaun's smirk as the steadying force in a musical outfit, but he really was. Perry had the backbeat; you can't lose it.

"He was THAT guy," says Warner. "He was crazy talented."

Perry died in June 2012, his body found in his house. He was only 50, but the toll taken by diabetes and kidney disease (he was on dialysis) was too vicious for his frail, battered body. Add to that the other factor that, when they were young, the Scorchers lived like rock stars. It couldn't have helped his longevity that the newspaper to which he had been loyal and hardworking let him go—a "voluntary buyout" is how they euphemistically phrase it. Still, he had been ill for a while. Life isn't easy for a former almost rock star with diabetes and failing kidneys. It ain't easy being green.

In fact, as Warner recalls, his pal left the band around 2002, simply because he had to. His body couldn't take the demands of rock stardom after 20 years as part of the mad chemistry that was Jason & the Scorchers.

"Rock shows were getting longer, and it was harder for him," says Warner, among my very favorite Nashville musicians.

Not only was Perry on dialysis, but his health was shot in general from rock star concoctions and cocktails and worse: "He had the worst type of diabetes, and Perry really didn't have the intelligence to learn how to deal with it. It whipped his ass," says Warner.

Warner then talks a bit about how he and Perry became such great friends.

"We ended up together at Cohn High School," says Warner of their Nashville schooldays. "But I met Perry before he went to Cohn.

"There was a little music store in the Charlotte Park area. I came in one day, Perry was 12 and I was 14, and he was sitting on an amplifier."

Perry quickly had a guitar in his hands, and before the two even had a decent conversation, Perry was playing and singing "More Than a Feeling," the old Boston song. "I didn't really like Boston," says Warner of the band, which easily could be considered the opposite end of the rock spectrum from the Scorchers. "But he could play it, and he could sing it.

"He was a guitar player and keyboardist. I never knew Perry could play drums until he came when I had this high school band. We were piddling around in the basement, and Perry was there, and he said, 'I could play drums.'"

It wasn't long before Jeff Johnson and Warner created a band called the Electric Boys. Perry was their drummer.

Then Jason coaxed bassist Johnson into a band he was forming. "Jeff brought me into that," says Warner of the Scorchers. "And then I brought Perry in. He was the natural choice to play drums."

"We knew the day he came in on the first song," recalls Warner of the speed with which the band was formed and found a groove. "There was a chemistry, an electricity that happened between the four of us that we all knew immediately. He was a very talented person."

"You know when it's right, know when it's wrong," he says of that chemistry. "It was a magic that happened. It literally was the sum of the four of us rather than the individuals. It was a glorious noise that happened when the four of us were headed in the same direction."

There was a dream among the boys. "We said, 'One day we'll tour the world, one day we'll be on TV.' One day, well, we were doing it."

They picked up a record deal. "All of this was over a couple of months period," says Warner. "Everything was moving really quick."

Before long, the Scorchers were opening for folks like R.E.M. and Bob Dylan. Perry used to like to talk about sharing tight sleeping quarters with R.E.M. front man Michael Stipe, who apparently was taken by that elfin grin. As for Dylan, I remember Perry describing using a urinal next to the Bard from the North Country. A hard rain's gonna fall indeed.

Oh, the Scorchers never had the wealth of the big stars as they tentatively clung to their "Next Big Thing" rung on the rock ladder for a couple years without ever grasping the top rung. That's not a knock on them at all. They had the goods to be world conquerors. Just take a look at the hitmakers of the 1980s for an illustration that there are dozens of bands that almost made it to the "toppermost of the poppermost," the place the young Beatles vowed was their aim. The Beatles did become toppermost. But there are a lot more bands they inspired, like the Scorchers, who suffered because of fickle fans, lifestyle choices, stubborn defiance of trends, or bad decisions by them and by the corporate world.

I will never understand why the Dave Matthews Band, whose base is roughly in the same region as the Scorchers, hit the stratosphere while Nashville's best rock band did not. I guess the world likes long, experimental musical jams. And some great bands have made it work. All I need to add here is that Matthews's band from Charlottesville, Virginia, is not the Grateful Dead, and even Jerry Garcia ran out of steam sometimes before finally checking out.

To be fair, I am very prejudiced about the Scorchers not just because I like their music. Well, actually the biggest reason I am a fan is not because Perry was a brilliant drummer. It's because he was a great and energetic librarian.

No, not the librarian that is mousy and retiring in popular fiction and in movies like *It's a Wonderful Life* (remember meek and skittish Mary Bailey when "never-born George" meets her at the Pottersville Library?).

And while there was no Clarence the angel involved in this story, there was something angelic (deceptively so, I'd wager) about librarian Perry Baggs.

You see Perry was librarian (archivist?) at *The Tennessean*, where I worked for 10 years (the best of which had Peter as chief music writer and Brad Schmitt, who never really calls me by my name, as gossip columnist).

I'd seen Perry around the building at 1100 Broadway in downtown Nashville (the historic newspaper building that has since been demolished to make way for Nashville's new trademark of ugly, soulless, overpriced urban construction). Before my *Tennessean* years, I spent 10 years at the *Nashville Banner*, which was downstairs from the larger morning newspaper. When the *Banner* closed because of greed, I was lucky enough to be hired by *The Tennessean*.

I had a terminally ill mother in Nashville, and my wife and I were in the middle of a second adoption of a child from a Romanian orphanage when the *Nashville Banner* closed, so I didn't want to move to another city, though I had choices. I would make the same decision today given the circumstances. Even though my stubborn nature and resistance to corporate mantras made me a front-office outcast, I love the "real" Nashville. It was a great town in which to bring up Romanian orphans.

Anyway, I knew who Perry was when I made the move upstairs. I got to know this rock-'n'-roll librarian's sweet nature and precise knowledge of the job early on.

Indeed, on one of the first nights I worked at *The Tennessean* (my first job there was on the night copy desk), we all stopped what we were doing to watch Perry and his Scorchers pals on, I believe, *The Conan O'Brien Show*, back when it aired right after Leno's *Tonight Show* on NBC.

I was one of those to congratulate him a couple days later when he got back to his normal work, cutting and pasting old stories, filing photographs, organizing news clippings, and running photos on demand to the city desk, the copy desk, the features desk, wherever. He just smiled softly, his eyes beaming (they always did), and offered a mild "thanks." Then he started using invisible drumsticks to pound the air in the newspaper library. "It's like this, Tim," he laughed.

Many months after that tour on the copy desk, I was promoted to entertainment editor, and Perry immediately seemed drawn to the chair by my desk.

He liked to talk about music and faith—he was deeply devout, a gospel music-hearted, born-again guy who didn't mind talking about Christ, though he didn't force it on me. Jesus is just all right with me, of course.

Like I noted above, Perry liked the Hawaiian shirts I often wore. He even got himself one that, like my most outrageous, went almost to his knees. I applauded his fashion sense as his high-pitched giggle escalated.

He also liked to laugh if I quoted Dylan, Kristofferson, Lennon, Jagger, or George Jones.

The latter's songs, by the way, probably had more influence on Perry's and Jason's songwriting than the string of rock stars listed, though I will repeat that the Scorchers' take on Dylan's "Absolutely Sweet Marie" is my favorite Dylan cover.

And he didn't mind it a bit if I started to talk about "Runnin' with the Devil," "Jump," or "Panama," the last my favorite Van Halen song.

Perry was particularly fond of the 1974–1985 Van Halen lineup of lead vocalist David Lee Roth, guitar-scorching bandleader Eddie Van Halen, bassist Michael Anthony, and, of course, drummer Alex Van Halen. While he wasn't necessarily a fan of the Sammy Hagar version of the great American hard-rock band, he was pretty delighted when I interviewed Sammy and described to him that conversation.

I really enjoyed Sammy's company more than his stage persona. Although I kind of appreciated the first Farm Aid, where he was introduced as the new front man after Diamond Dave got crazy from the heat. Sammy, in turn, introduced his "I Can't Drive 55" to the farmers and pot smokers of Illinois by proclaiming, "Here's a song for all you tractor-pulling mother f—— out there!" Wholesome, God-fearing folks at the Nashville Network collectively blushed during the live feed, and there were on-air apologies afterward. I mean, Ralph Emery never used that language—at least not on the air.

Perry also liked to talk about Jason & the Scorchers and his dreams that maybe he'd be able to get out and play with them again one day. His health had made the road too hard, as noted above. The Scorchers disbanded and periodically reunited, and for a time, Perry stayed involved.

Then the band had to move on without him, although he did continue to be close and even sang harmony (he had a great voice) with later incarnations of the Scorchers. Check out their last album, *Halcyon Days*, from 2010 and listen to the harmonies.

But they really never were the same—kind of like the Who without Keith Moon or The Stones without Charlie Watts. Hell, Zeppelin folded its tents when Jon Bonham died. Can you imagine The Beatles without Ringo? Genesis without Phil Collins? (Actually, I can imagine a world without Genesis *and* Phil Collins.)

"Perry was an original Scorcher," says Warner, adding that the band was most special when that drummer was behind them.

"We all learned how to play together. When we started playing together, Perry was 14, and Jeff and I were 17. We learned to play rock music together." That tight threesome was perfect, of course, behind Jason, who was learning how to be a rock star and front man of the first order.

The Scorchers traveled on and did some great work, settling on fine Swedish drummer Pontus Snibb—"He's a real monster back there," says Warner. But their biggest fan spent his days filing clips and photos for a newspaper whose corporate honchos didn't appreciate who he really was.

"Tim," he'd say, as I walked past the library, "I think I've got it now. This will be it. I'm going to wear chaps, the whole cowboy outfit. I've got [he'd list other local rockers], and we're going to try it out at the Exit/In [mythic Nashville rock showplace]."

I can't remember our conversations about that musical effort or others verbatim, of course. I was talking to a friend, not interviewing one. I do remember him reaching for his hips, like a gunfighter grabbing his two six-shooters, and drawing, pointing his fingers at me. "Pow. Pow," he said, then blowing at the index fingertips.

And laughing. Man, could he laugh.

I've spoken earlier about my friend Peter Cooper, whom I hired to be a music writer on the entertainment team.

Peter presented himself as sort of an aw-shucks country boy with great artistic knowledge and aspirations when he came in for the interview.

He'd been an education reporter for a newspaper in Spartanburg, South Carolina, a town best known for the Marshall Tucker Band but really a place where good music in general is brewed.

His clips that I reviewed were largely related to education reporting, though I think (this was about two decades ago) he included some of the music journalism he did as a freelancer. I may have even read the 3,000-word salute to Jason & the Scorchers that he wrote for someone, a glowing and gritty tale that quickly earned him a sort of kinship with the band.

That story, he has told me, is the one that earned him a backstage invite the first time he met Jason at a gig in Columbia, South Carolina. It was backstage where he witnessed the wise and witty Perry delivering a less-than-friendly sendup of the Dave Matthews Band. It didn't seem right to anyone huddled backstage that the tiresome music, the 14-minute DMB jams, had reached national popularity while the Scorchers' fiery three-minutes-and-a-sneer songs only teased at mad, regional applause.

Yes, they were best as a live band, with Jason's whirling-dervish cowboy vocals, Warner's circular "alligator wrestling" dashes on the stage while spinning the guitar above his head and around his shoulders, and Perry's attacks mixed with Jeff's stoic bass lines.

But the recordings did include more than a dash of that stage madness.

Anyway, I need to credit Perry some for my hiring of Peter.

The young man from Spartanburg performed well in his interview with me. And he had to get the thumbs-up from some of the treacherous types who could sign off on my hires. Then, after they approved of my decision to hire Peter, I had to get him down to human resources (HR) before they closed up shop for the day.

I think Peter had to get back to Spartanburg for either his newspaper work or his middle school teaching (he did that either before or after his journalism stint in the Palmetto State) the next day.

With minutes to spare before the HR folks would check out for the day, I began shepherding him to those offices, which were downstairs.

Until Peter stopped short. "Tim [I had instructed him not to call me Mr. Ghianni], isn't that Perry Baggs?" he said almost breathlessly as we drew near the library.

I told him that yes, indeed, Perry Baggs, the man who created the 4/4 backbeat for the Scorchers' shuffling music, indeed did work as a librarian for the newspaper.

"That's Perry Baggs!" (or words similar), he repeated with the true fan flavor in his voice. He began pushing toward the library kind of like one of those TV zombies moving toward human prey.

I thought I was going to have to grab him by his Windsor-knotted purple tie to divert him. "We've got all these papers you need to fill out by 5, before HR leaves," I told him.

"I'll introduce you to Perry when you are done."

I don't think that went over well. All I remember is Peter saying that a newspaper that had Perry Baggs as a librarian was the place he wanted to work. We did make it to HR, and I kept my promise afterward to put Peter together with the librarian.

I have to report that Perry was, by nature, welcoming to the young man from Spartanburg.

"That's Perry Baggs of Jason and the Scorchers," Peter said again, taking one more look back at the library before he left to drive back to Spartanburg. I'm not sure if the first thing he told his fiancée, Charlotte, when getting back to his hometown was that he had gotten the job or that he had met Perry Baggs, who had become a librarian.

When Perry died (he hadn't shown up for church activities and his girlfriend summoned help), I first called Andy McClenon, who was a part of Praxis International, with Jack Emerson, the company that helped launch the Scorchers.

No longer at the newspaper, I felt compelled to write something for my *They Call Me Flapjacks* blog. I knew the newspaper would not give him his due and that the Scorchers' most ardent newspaper fan, Peter Cooper, was playing a tour of small taverns and the like across Europe with his cohorts Eric Brace and (I think) Thomm Jutz.

So my conversation with Andy, a close friend, was in part to feel out what I could say in a blog post.

While Andy was not surprised that the clock finally had played out on Perry, he was shaken.

"He was a soulful little guy. He was really focused, really sweet, a joy to be around," said Andy, adding that medication Perry had to take "would affect his moods" and perhaps influence the tension that existed between him and other members of the band.

"But I know those guys love him," he added of the drummer. "Jeez Warner was like his big brother and protector from the real world.

"Perry was very lovable. He just got confused about reality sometimes."

Andy continued heaping on praise and adding a bit of texture to his description of Perry.

"If you look back and look at the songs he wrote early on, it's interesting. He had this musical melody thing. He was really melodic in his writing."

"Jason would write the lyric, and Perry would add the fetching melody on some of the great, early songs," McClenon said.

"Jason wrote a lot by himself, but the ones that Perry was involved in tend to be the more catchy tunes," Andy said.

Along with cowrites on two of the best-known Scorchers' songs— "White Lies" and "If Money Talks" among others—Perry's musical and vocal contributions were a part of the chemistry of this, the toppermost rock band ever to come out of Music City.

Andy then compared that duo to another pair of rock songwriters.

"When you listen to Jagger and Richards, you know those are two guys whose vocals are not technically great, but when they are together, with Richards making harmony, well, I loved when Perry would sing with Jason. It was very soulful and very distinctive and very melodic."

And then there was the true country side of the Nashville hometown boy.

I'm not talking about the revolutionary, three-minutes-and-a-growl cowpunk that has Jason & the Scorchers honored with a display in the Country Music Hall of Fame and Museum in downtown Nashville.

"One of the interesting things is that in the '80s, before it was cool to do such things, Perry created this alter ego, Austin Taylor, who would record these really country demos, things like 'If Heaven's Just a Fairy Tale, then What's the Story Here,'" Andy remembered.

"He would sing it so intensely. Seriously, they were very strong vocals. Before the hipsters—and Perry was never a hipster—thought George Jones was cool, Perry Baggs instinctively knew he was and tried to emulate him in his alter ego."

In the conversation with Andy that occurred in the day or so after Perry died, he pointed out that Perry never fully left the southern gospel tradition in which he was raised.

Later in life, after fashioning different lineups of country-fried rock efforts—like the gunslinger with the chaps I mention above—Perry found his truest calling at Scottsboro Baptist Church, which is where he first was missed. When he was found, alone at home, he was dead.

His girlfriend, Katrina Cornwell, who had worked at the newspaper, wrote his obituary. It kind of shows a bit about Perry's evolution.

"Perry was kind, compassionate, funny, generous, loving and high-energy. He was someone who enjoyed life.

"Perry loved home-cooked meals, movies, music, surfing big waves at the beach and to spend time with people he considered family: blood relatives, church members, friends and his significant other.

"Most of all, he loved God, and he lived his life for Jesus Christ every day."

Of course, that's an obit written by the one who loved him most. Andy's assessment, while not loaded with religion, also is pretty accurate: "Perry never really had a rock-'n'-roll heart. He had a big heart."

I tracked down Jason, who was playing in England, at about 5 a.m. UK time a day after Perry died to talk about the loss of his old bandmate and, most of the time, friend.

"Perry had a magic, elfin-like personality that drew people to him," Jason said. "There would have been no band without Perry. Period.

"Warner brought Perry into the band in the fall of '81. At the time, we were using Barry Felts on drums, and he quit. Perry came to my house to jam with us. From the first measure of 'Gone Gone Gone,' an old Carl Perkins song, we took off on, I knew Perry was the missing piece."

Warner—a genuinely great rock guitarist when he's not doing his "straight job" as head man of Hodges Renovations, a construction firm from which he has "built a lot of houses . . . monster houses . . . in Brentwood and South Nashville. . . . Thank God I've got another skill other than making a racket"—again reflects on his friend and their first meeting.

"He was an ungodly singer even then," said Warner, who I regard as a friend.

"Perry's impact on the band is incalculable," Jason told me. "He wrote some of our best songs, played drums, sang harmonies, and was a huge part of the arrangements of the songs. . . .

"I actually think of Perry more as a great all-around musician rather than a great drummer, although he was that as well.

"Perry was a volcano of ideas. The job when writing with Perry was mostly as an editor. His creativity drove the sessions."

Even though Perry left in 2002, he was still, in most peoples' minds, the Scorchers' drummer.

Late in his life, he got back together with Jason and the boys, once for a fund-raiser for the ailing drummer and another time for an Americana Music Awards tribute.

Perry knew he was dying at the time, but he said he'd just as soon die playing with Jason & the Scorchers as die quietly (as if Perry could do anything quietly).

Jason said that those "last shows with Perry will always stick in my mind. We all knew how hard it was for him to play drums like that with his poor health."

As noted, Perry participated as a vocalist in the superb 2010 Jason & the Scorchers album *Halcyon Times*, the band's last (though perhaps not final) album.

Perry was too weak to play the drums, according to Jason. But "he sang those brilliant harmonies on four of the tracks. It was a wonderful experience to be with him again. . . .

"I spent 25 years with Perry. We had our good times and our bad ones. However, I count myself a fortunate man to have made music with him."

For a moment, Warner is, in his mind, back onstage with the Scorchers, who still play a few shows, particularly in Europe. "If the money is right, Jason and I pull that out," says the 61-year-old, whose tours with the Warner E. Hodges Band were interrupted by the pandemic. He continued building houses, though, and returned to the road as the world opened up.

Warner told me that the band officially was born with Perry on the sticks at a New Year's Eve gig in 1981. And he said there always is the chance that a fortieth-anniversary gig could be organized if things smooth out after the pandemic.

Part of the band's soul forever will be missing, though.

"It's sad to look back there [to the drummer] and Perry's not there," Warner says. "Perry was a founding member of the band. He didn't want to stop doing it. He had to stop doing it.

"It was yanked away from him. Cruel and not very nice. A lot of emotions happen when we play without him."

Duane Eddy

H E ALMOST WAS A TRAVELING WILBURY—a member of that elite corps of musicians that included his pals George Harrison, Bob Dylan, Roy Orbison, Jeff Lynne, and Tom Petty—but Duane Eddy has no regrets.

Oh, he does wish his body hadn't been invaded by cancer. But, he said, the treatment is "going good."

Sure, the treatments have affected his immunity, and that COVID pandemic was especially worrisome, but Duane was happy to talk about some of his career highlights as he sat with his wife, Deed, in their home in Franklin, Tennessee, perhaps 20 miles south of Nashville.

If not for his cancer battle and the damned virus threat, Duane could have been filling halls in England—where his guitar playing remains much in demand—during the cold, cruel COVID holiday season in 2020, when this conversation took place.

And he'd like to get back there sometime, health and strength permitting.

He and I have had many flowing conversations over the years—after all, once someone says his name is Duane Eddy and invites me to call anytime, an old rock-'n'-roll relic like me is going to follow up.

I'd talked with him about guitarists, about records, and about his fallen colleagues over the years, and it not always was published.

Heck, early in the year of the pandemic, I had called him for a story I was doing about the forecast shutdown of the concert industry worldwide. Because of his health, he hadn't any plans to be out on the stages of England and Europe anyway.

But he felt for those who were losing their already irregular stream of income. "My heart is with them because I used to do the same damn thing. I used to play honky-tonks around Phoenix," he said.

Then he made reference to a friend, Waylon Jennings, who married Jessi Colter after she had been divorced from Duane in 1968. She was Waylon's fourth and final marriage in 1969. Duane married his own third wife, Deed, in 1979. It had taken these two great and gentle men a while to find their soul mates.

"Waylon used to say 'skull orchards,'" Duane said, quoting the greatest country outlaw's phrase for the clubs and honky-tonks, where a flood of bobbing heads is about all that is visible to the men and women in the spotlights.

In one of our conversations around Christmas 2020, Duane said he hadn't given up on the idea of playing live concerts but added, "I may be retired and I just don't know it."

He paused. "Then the phone will ring, and here I go again."

Hope always reigns in the voice of this great man.

Two years before our Christmas 2020 conversations, I'd done a story on Duane's incredibly rich rock-'n'-roll history for the *Nashville Ledger*.

For that story, Duane covered a lot of territory, including an off-the-cuff, find-a-Beatle decision he made as a 30-year-old guitar sensation who was in London for shows and other business.

Duane, the master of a rugged and twangy guitar sound that gave a bit of a masculine edge to American rock music in the 1960s, had some time to kill, and he was curious.

He called a cab and rode to 27 Ovington Square in London, a casual, unannounced journey to see one of those lads from Liverpool. Those fellows, The Beatles, borrowed heavily from American masters, like Chuck Berry, the Everly Brothers, Fats Domino, Elvis, and Duane Eddy, to change the world sonically and culturally.

That building was the home of Apple Records: The Beatles' label with the Granny Smith apple logo (full on the front, halved on the flip side). The fellas, who had grown out of their prefabricated Fabs disguises, established the label for themselves—as a group and individually—and to help worthy struggling artists.

Duane hoped to hook up with Paul McCartney, the so-called cute Beatle until he let his face grow long.

"Guys I was working with knew Paul, so I thought I'd talk to him," says Duane, whose 45s, stuff like "Rebel Rouser," "Dance with the Guitar Man," "Peter Gunn," "Because They're Young," and "The Lonely One," ended up in my record collection in the late 1950s and early 1960s.

Duane, who produced his own stuff, figured he and Paul could have a nice converation since the latter had taken on some production himself and overused that expertise to offer often-unwanted critiques to Beatles' mastermind producer George Martin, Beatles leader John Lennon, and Fabs guitarist George Harrison. I don't even think the generous Ringo escaped Paul's stubborn ways of conducting recording.

Duane didn't expect to see any of the other Fabs around the office that day.

"It's back when George was doing his Indian thing" with musical magician Ravi Shankar, the Hare Krishnas, and his spiritual mentor Maharishi Mahesh Yogi, so no telling in what place or on which plane he might be.

"John was in the studio in the basement. His paisley Rolls-Royce was parked outside," Duane continues, recalling that half-century-old day. Likely the band's founder and leader was working on one of his "artsy" recordings with Yoko Ono, stuff that makes the so-called *White Album*'s strident "Revolution 9" seem almost melodic, especially if you play it backward.

"I called up [from the front desk] to see Paul. They said Paul wasn't there, 'but George is, and he wonders if you'd like to see him?'"

Guitar players love to commingle with their breed and share notes, literally and figuratively, so Duane obviously wanted to meet The Beatles' lead guitarist.

"He gave me a *White Album* and introduced me to this skinny, young blues singer who was hanging around named James Taylor," whose first, self-titled album was released by Apple and includes work by Paul and George.

It was one of a host of great musical afternoons for a wonderful man whose trek through rock history, helping and meeting other great musicians, could be called "Gumpian" (with an always ready Gretsch rather than a box of chocolates).

"I just hung around, and George was playing me the *White Album*. He was telling me that Eric [Clapton] had played a couple of solos on it," Duane recalls.

"He called Eric while I was there. He didn't put me on the phone. He said, 'Guess who I've got here?'

"They [George and Eric, whose soaring guitar work on "While My Guitar Gently Weeps" is among the album's highlights] were one-upping each other," basically showing off their kinship with the guys from whom they'd borrowed. Eric might return the favor by telling George he was hanging out with Chuck Berry or Howlin' Wolf, for example.

"It was just a couple-of-hour visit in the afternoon. I left, and that was that," Duane said of his time with the youngest Beatle, a man whose very existence in the band had, in a way, been at least informed by the king of twang.

"George apparently played one of my songs ["Ramrod"] when he auditioned for The Beatles. That's what I heard, anyway," said Duane. "He got the gig."

This adds a footnote to the often-reported tale of George playing Bill Justis's "Raunchy" while riding atop a Liverpool double-decker bus with John and Paul. Actually, of course, George had been tagging along a lot with school chum Paul, playing his guitar and demonstrating his knowledge of chords, skill that far outshone both the two older "men."

George was just a kid, as both Paul and John are quoted in *Anthology*.

"If we wanted to do anything grown-up, we worried about George looking young. We thought, 'He doesn't shave. . . . Can't we get him to look like a grown-up?'" reflected McCartney.

As for John, well, he said "George looked even younger than Paul—and Paul looked about 10, with his baby face. . . . We asked George to join because he knew more chords."

John didn't need to audition any other lead guitarists for the group that later was called Johnny and the Moondogs and that tried on other monikers before settling on The Beatles.

"George gave me the *White Album* and gave me John and Yoko's album with them naked on the cover" (*Unfinished Music No. 1: Two Virgins*).

These great treasures were soon robbed from George's new friend. "Someone stole them from my house," said Duane of the two Apple Records treasures.

"They saw them, and they took them, thought they were very cool to be had because of the fact I got them direct from The Beatles, and they somehow smuggled them from my house. That was back in the '70s, the early '70s."

While our conversation was coming at the time of the fiftieth anniversary of *Abbey Road*, The Beatles' best album (my educated opinion), Duane enjoyed talking about the day he spent with George, hearing that so-called *White Album*, whose own golden anniversary was celebrated in typical Beatles merch-hawking style two years before.

"It was very cutting edge at the time," said Duane as he recalled the listening session with George at Ovington Square.

He remembered Beatles publicist Derek Taylor being at the listening session, along with the other Taylor, the skinny singer whose first album George also gave to Duane.

It also was a victim of the LP heist. "I never got to play that album" before the thief struck, Duane adds.

Of course, James Taylor left Apple and came home to become "Sweet Baby James," the mostly gentle-acoustic force who saw "Fire and Rain" and worldwide acclaim.

Duane adds that *White Album* producer Martin and the Fabs unveiled something new, by Brit standards, in their only double album. (There have been multiple-disc compilations put out in the years since The Beatles split, but the *White Album* was their only double album as a unit.)

"I thought it was a great album. And I realized The Beatles had finally caught up [by using an eight-track recording method]. When they started, they had used four tracks, and we had 16 and 24 tracks back in the U.S.A.," said Duane.

That album, actually titled *The Beatles* but nicknamed after its pure white cover with the band name embossed in white and numbered on the original releases, is a crazy-quilt mishmash of the different styles that both made up that little quartet and drove the four men apart.

Personally, I purchased that album and The Rolling Stones' *Beggars Banquet* on the same school day afternoon in the Chicago area. I regard *Abbey Road* as The Beatles' best record and even the best record of all time, but *Beggars*—the last with troubled band founder and visionary Brian Jones still living—is The Stones' best. Brian, who drowned in his pool with or without some help from some friends after leaving The Stones, was featured posthumously on two cuts of 1969's *Let It Bleed*.

Duane didn't see George again until 1986, when mutual pal Electric Light Orchestra leader Jeff Lynne, who was producing Harrison's *Cloud Nine* album, got the two men together in a British studio for a new Capitol Records album called *Duane Eddy*.

The two guitar heroes did three tracks: "Rockabilly Holiday," "The Trembler," and "The Theme for Something Very Important." Duane also recorded "Rockestra Theme" by and with McCartney for that album. "We recorded it live. I remember him dancing around in the studio, playing his Hofner bass [his Beatles instrument] and thinking, 'How many people would want to trade places with me?'

"But I never met John. I did meet Ringo in the early '80s, talked to him [at the Hollywood Bowl] before he married [Barbara Bach] and got sober. I didn't talk to him long. He said he saw me at a show I did at the Albert Hall. He said, 'I saw you with Bill.' I was wondering who 'Bill' was. I had done so many shows. And he said 'Bill *Haley*,' like he was saying 'Bill *Haley*, you dumb ass.' Like I should have known that. If he had given me the year when he saw that show [1968], it probably would have helped."

Later, after Ringo reached a more sober point in life, "I had a nice conversation with him in England."

In March 1986, shortly after the Capitol album was finished back in Hollywood (where John Fogerty sat in on "Kickin' Asphalt") and Duane finished the mastering, Harrison—"George and I had built up a friendship"—came calling or at least looking.

"George came over to Hollywood. . . . He and Jeff [who in addition to Electric Light Orchestra is an acclaimed producer for the likes of Harrison, McCartney, Orbison, the Traveling Wilburys, and Tom Petty, with and without the Heartbreakers] came over, and they used to hang out with Bob Dylan there.

"The three of them wanted to find me, so, since they knew I liked country music, they went out to the Palomino, a country music club in North Hollywood.

"Everybody from George Jones to Waylon to Freddy Fender played there. Waylon said, 'I worked the Palomino a year one night,'" Duane says, laughing a bit about the since deceased club and comrade.

The trio in hot pursuit of their twang-master buddy found plenty of friends at the club. "They went there, and Taj Mahal was playing there. John Fogerty was there. They all got up on the stage with Taj Mahal and Fogerty. That was back when John wasn't doing any of his Creedence [Clearwater Revival] stuff [due to a royalties scuffle]."

That didn't stop the stage invaders, though, and Dylan insisted the fellows, including Fogerty, try on one of Creedence's biggest hits, "Proud Mary" (which also was a breakthrough hit for a little R&B group called the Ike & Tina Turner Revue, and if you ever saw them do it live, it changed you).

"John said [later], 'When Bob Dylan says 'Play Proud Mary,' you play 'Proud Mary,'" Duane explains. "They did a few verses; unfortunately, I wasn't there.

"Later, I did hook up with them, and we hung out. Then we went to see Dave Edmunds [of the group Rockpile and a recording history much richer] on Vine Street. . . .

"I was giving them all a ride home in this big Suburban I had at the time," Duane added with a laugh.

"I looked around, and there was Jeff Lynne and Bob Dylan in the backseat. And George Harrison was in the front seat with me.

"I thought, 'Man, I hope no one hits us. There's a lot of rock-'n'-roll history in this car.'"

Duane managed his voluntary chauffeuring duties fine, and as the evening wound to an end, he pulled off the road at a restaurant to let his first passenger, Dylan, out.

"Bob was riding his motorcycle. He had parked it around the corner from the restaurant door. We waited to make sure he got onto his motorcycle. It was a big Harley. Bob walked over and looked at it. He stood it up, then set it back down and went into the restaurant.

"George said, 'I wonder what he's thinking?'"

Deciphering what Bob Dylan is thinking probably is a tough task even for late-night rambling rock-'n'-roll stars, so they decided to leave him to his own devices with his two-wheeled gypsy queen (or whatever) and continue their trip to their various abodes.

Since three of the four future Traveling Wilburys had shared Duane's company (and his car) that night, I figured I should ask Duane about that fraternity.

The Wilburys actually were a little "pickup" band that was hatched during a recording session for one of George's best solo albums, *Cloud Nine*. The only one of his albums that surpassed it, in my view, was *All Things Must Pass*, a sprawling, God-tinged, three-record farewell to his Fab life.

When the group—Lynne, Dylan, Petty, and George—got together in Dylan's garage studio and finished a Harrison song called "Handle with Care," which was the label on a box they saw there, they decided that instead of its being a George song, they should use it as the first recording in an album's worth of songs by an invented group they named the Traveling Wilburys.

The history of that band and, of course, its members would go on for many paragraphs, and it lasted for two fine albums. What people don't know is that Duane was a handshake away from being a member of that band made up of his superstar cohorts.

"They considered it for a while, and we had a little conversation," Duane recalled, adding that it really wouldn't have worked out well, as the Wilburys' main attraction was the mixture of such iconic voices rather than instrumentals, his stock-in-trade.

He did ponder the pleasure of doing a bit of Wilbury-accompanying guitar work, mainly for the joy of "hanging out with those guys," but it never worked out.

Instead of Duane Eddy, the vocal group recruited the man who likely is the best vocalist in rock history, Roy Orbison.

Duane won't say this, but it may have worked out best for him to not be a Wilbury. That band may have been jinxed a bit, as three—Harrison, Orbison, and Petty—died before they got old.

"I was the first person ever to headline a rock-'n'-roll show at the Hollywood Bowl," Duane added in the long and happy conversation with this old journalist and record collector. "1958. Frankie Avalon. Annette [Funicello]. The Coasters. The Drifters. It was a big show. . . .

"In 2008, we celebrated the fiftieth anniversary of [the Hollywood Bowl]." On the bill that night were B.B. King, flutist James Galway, and Liza Minnelli as part of a showcase of important acts who had played there during the half century.

B.B.'s friendship is another that Duane continued to cherish long after the iconic bluesman had died.

"I first met him in Oakland. I got there late. Jerry Lee Lewis and some other people were on the bill. I'm backstage. We did our bit, and it turned out to be all right.

"This well-dressed black gentleman came in the backstage dressing room and said to me 'Duane, I love that blues [you do]. I gotta hug you. I loved it so much, I gotta kiss you on the cheek.'

"Then he stepped back and let me go, then he introduced himself: 'I'm B.B. King.' I said, 'Omigosh, it's now my turn to hug you and kiss you on the cheek.' Then we proceeded to have a long talk. We had a great time.

"He always told me I was a good guitar player.

"I found out years later that this group of young guys sitting and watching from front-row center was Creedence Clearwater Revival, the whole group. I remember that because as I was out there, I said, 'I wonder if those guys are musicians?' They were enjoying the show as musicians would. Turned out they were."

This gentle soul spends a lot of time with his thoughts (and, of course, with Deed) out at their Franklin house. The COVID scare and the cancer contribute to keeping him holed up.

But he loves to reflect on a life well lived and incredibly musical.

"I've been fortunate to work with the best musicians in the world, everybody from Paul Shaffer to Paul McCartney.

"One of the little bonuses that have come along in later years is having these guys who are giants in the music business tell me how they grew up on my records.

"Jimmy Page [of the Yardbirds and founder of Led Zeppelin] said, 'I saved up my money from my paper route to buy 'Three-30-Blues.''"

Bruce Springsteen had his E Street Band play "Because They're Young" "over and over again" to set the mood before they recorded melancholy rocker "Born to Run."

"I did the Stagecoach [big California roots festival] a couple years ago. Wayne Kramer of MC5 sat in with me just for the fun of it."

Everybody, it seems, enjoys picking up their guitar and playing with the aptly nicknamed "Hemingway of the guitar."

Duane doesn't dwell on his cancer battle. Nor does he worry too much about the fact his well-earned role as one of rock-'n'-roll's icons and prototypes is largely overlooked in the digital, streaming era of music.

"I keep happy. If you get bitter or unhappy about the past things, it only hurts more. I don't dwell on it.

"Just forward blunder."

Carl Smith and Goldie Hill

ARGOLDA VONCILE HILL, a beautiful blonde from Texas, helped me draw Carl Smith—of "Loose Talk," "You Are the One," and "Hey Joe!" fame—out of hiding.

Nobody called her Argolda, though. She was Goldie Hill, "The Golden Hillbilly," who came with her boss, Webb Pierce, from Texas to Nashville in 1952 and quickly signed with Decca, where she, at first anyway, specialized in answer songs. Her first single, "Why Talk to My Heart," was a female answer to Ray Price's big hit "Talk to Your Heart."

That song didn't make her a star, but the next year, she went to the top of the charts with "I Let the Stars Get in My Eyes," an answer to Slim Willet's "Don't Let the Stars Get in Your Eyes."

While I had spoken with her on the telephone from her farm/ranch out in Franklin, the first time I saw her in person, she was singing with Tommy Cash at a banquet for veteran performers held at a downtown Nashville hotel. I was there in part because I wanted to use my smile and blue eyes to charm her into helping me get her husband, Carl Smith, out of retirement long enough to do his first interview in decades.

It was important because Carl was going to be inducted into the Country Music Hall of Fame later that year, and, so far, he had ducked interview requests from me and from others.

"I finished doing that back in '78" (or words to that effect), he told me on the phone, a gentle but firm refusal to be interviewed. Usually, by the way, Goldie answered the phone and said Carl "is outside."

I found out later, when I had the pleasure of spending a full day with the couple, that when Goldie told a caller that "Carl is outside," he may just be at the kitchen table firing up a Marlboro. If anyone I've met in country music could have passed for the Marlboro Man of 1960s and 1970s TV commercials, it was Carl Smith. I wouldn't be surprised if Marlboro—which used "Theme for the Magnificent Seven" as its commercials' soundtrack— was one of his sponsors when he pioneered country music on television.

As for his smoking, he was considerate about turning on the stove's vent fan, pushing his chair as close as possible, and exhaling his smoke-filled lungs in that direction, away from his guests.

Anyway, I turned to his proud wife at the banquet for our first "face-to-face." And I really liked her, a wonderful talent and beautiful woman who didn't look anywhere near as old as the bulk of the folks at the Golden Voice Awards. That annual banquet celebrated the bypassed veterans while the CMA held its annual Music Fest in the big arenas and auditoriums of Music City.

Country fans back then flocked to town to see the likes of Darryl Worley or perhaps Rascal Flatts in the big venues. Meanwhile, folks like Goldie Hill, Tommy Cash, Little Jimmy Dickens, Porter Wagoner, and others went unnoticed. The same thing happens today, with the names changed. So the old stars hold their own little party for their generation of fans. Justin Tubb, the son of the great Ernest Tubb and a talented fellow himself, had been among the most active in getting the veterans celebrated. Sadly, Justin died of a stomach aneurysm in 1998. He was only 62.

I did go to that Golden Voice banquet—I was entertainment editor, and I assigned myself to that while sending Peter Cooper and Brad Schmitt to see Kenny Chesney and Brooks & Dunn (remember, this was 2003, so the beer-and-pickup-and-perky-boob formula to country success had not yet taken over Nashville). Of course, Brad, my gossip columnist, did his best to hang out with Terri Clark, Jo Dee Messina, Buddy Jewell, and other headliners of the day. I wonder if they'll join the Golden Voice crowd now? Anyway, I once met Buddy at George Jones's house, and he seemed like a decent guy, a fine example of what happens when hillbilly bar singers win talent competition shows.

Not all of them fade away. Miranda Lambert, who remains a force in good country music, finished third to him on that first season of *Nashville Star*.

I enjoyed being around the old-timers and had attended some of these banquets before.

And, I have to admit, I was looking forward to seeing Goldie in person to see how far she'd gotten in breaking down Carl, perhaps at least enough so I could shine a spotlight on him in the newspaper.

So I took in the show and waited for my chance to snag Goldie. Like I said, she'd left Carl down at the farm and came to pair up onstage with

Family was the most important thing to Carl Smith and Goldie Hill, who left music to spend time with their kids. In this shot from the early 1970s: Carl Sr., Lori Lynn, Carl Jr., Dean, and Goldie. Photo courtesy Dean Smith

Tommy Cash was never able to approach the heights of his big brother, Johnny, but he had been able to hammer around the edges of fame with "Six White Horses" and "I Recall a Gypsy Woman," among others, while also selling real estate.

He had a voice a lot like John's but not with the "cigarettes, speed, Holy Land, dust-flavored" voice, with its comforting mix of carnal arrogance and stern declaration. But he was a good fellow, and Goldie Hill had left her husband down at the farm to meet up with Tommy at the downtown Nashville hotel so they could perform for the other old-timers and their fans from places like Oshkosh and Poughkeepsie.

I think it was the Sheraton—or whatever the name of the hotel with the circular restaurant on top was called at the time. I'd walked the mile or so from *The Tennessean* on that June day because I hate downtown Nashville traffic. And that was before it was dubbed the "It City" by city sales slickers and other well-paid sycophants to the city's power players.

While I was there to talk Goldie into helping me get to Carl—who had been one of my long-time favorites, at least from the oldies bins—it was something of an unretirement for her that day as well.

Carl had been retired for decades. And Goldie, 70 at the time, was interrupting a 40-something-year vacation to participate in the Golden Voice Awards.

She and Tommy Cash shared the stage to perform "Lookin' Back to
See (If You Were Lookin' Back at Me")), the Jim Ed Brown–Maxine
Brown hit that had been covered by the likes of Grandpa Jones and Ruby
Wells, Goldie Hill and Justin Tubb, and even Guy Lombardo and His
Royal Canadians, all in 1954, before later being recorded by other stars.

The song came during the three-plus-hour brunch and show for the
Performer's Benefit Fund, which tends to the medical needs of veteran
entertainers.

As I reported in *The Tennessean*, the next day, the pairing was one of
the highlights of the show, which repeatedly brought the approximately
800 fans jamming the hotel's Capitol Ballroom to their feet. This is the
kind of crowd that can fill in the lyrics when Stu Phillips asks them to sing
along on "Crystal Chandelier."

Others in attendance included rhinestone-suited Hank Locklin and
cohost Jimmy (the "sausage guy") Dean, who obviously was feeling no
pain, even at that late-morning hour. I always admired the singer of
"Big Bad John" until that day. Guess it's hard to be humble when you
are living on ground pig, some sort of whiskey (apparently), and a story
song with the great intro: "Every morning at the mine, you could see
him arrive, he stood 6-foot-6 and weighed 245." Of course, by the end
of the song, Big Bad John has been turned to sausage meat at the bottom
of the mine:

> Now, they never reopened that worthless pit
> They just placed a marble stand in front of it . . .
> At the bottom of this mine lies a big, big man

While the show was ongoing, I snuck off to the performers' break
room—really just a hallway with a few tables and soft beverages and coffee
urns out the side door from the ballroom.

Goldie finished her stage time and came in there, where she said, with
a laugh, that this was one of the few times she had elected to take a break
from the vacation she began in 1957 after marrying Carl. Her career lasted
four years after she left the Louisiana Hayride to come along with Webb
to Nashville.

"I decided I didn't want to be on the road anymore," said Goldie as I
nursed a glass of icy water.

She was sweet and, dare I say, alluring as she talked about her decision
to leave showbiz almost at the beginning of what could have become a
superstar career. At her peak, she had the looks and the chops for it but not

the desire to give up a family life. "I didn't want to be in New York and him [husband Carl] in Florida. So, I let him do his job."

Her husband joined her "on vacation" in 1978. "He said if anyone asks where he is today to tell them he is on a world tour playing fiddle with an all-jug band." We shared a laugh.

An example of the incestuous nature of country music (or perhaps life in general) is the fact that the showcase put Johnny Cash's little brother on the stage with the wife of June Carter Cash's first husband, although all reports are that John and Carl had a good relationship.

I can't remember the details now, but my police reporter at the old *Nashville Banner* once wrote a story about a group of probably inebriated country stars, led, it is said, by Johnny Cash as he, Tom T. Hall, and George Jones and others raided Carl's produce patch out in Franklin. I may be misremembering that. Perhaps they stole watermelons. And it probably isn't even true, but the mental image of Cash, Tom T., and Jones deciding to play a trick on Carl Smith always gives me faith in the humanity of the country community.

Hell, I'll throw my pal Bobby Bare in there, too, since I'm probably making this up from purple haze in my brain. I know from our friendship that he has a sense of good mischief, dating back at least as far as 1972, when he and Shel Silverstein helped me liberate some bricks. That story is in the beginning of the book.

Back at the Golden Voice Awards that day, Hank Locklin, 85, told me his singing was "better than I ever have. My nose is not stopped up now." I was not given the opportunity to find out just how long the singer of "Why, Baby, Why?" and "Please Help Me I'm Falling" had been suffering from a stopped-up nose. He was frail but a good-natured sort. I sat down with him and let him brag, softly, to me—no story there, just an old man reliving his glory by sharing his memories with a fellow who relished the opportunity to hear them. I indeed felt lucky.

I'll note that the crowd in the ballroom, of course, would have loved to have had Goldie's husband there, but he was committed to his farm and the good life and Marlboro Light 100s.

Carl had retired from the spotlight decades before. He and his lovely wife had a glorious oasis in the Williamson Country countryside. He had become reunited with his amazingly talented and formerly estranged daughter, Carlene Carter, who had fled Nashville to hang out with the Southern California rock stars, and with her lover Howie Epstein, bassist for the Heartbreakers, she was basically a part of the Tom Petty entourage. She was a good girl and loved her mama (and Jesus and America, too).

Carl had difficulty understanding the West Coast culture that had enveloped his amazingly talented and beautiful singing daughter. His great friend and advocate, Waylon Jennings, who himself had succumbed to various temptations, helped mend fences by trying to get Carl to understand what Carlene was going through.

As Goldie hugged me and turned to reenter the banquet room, where I think she and Tommy had been hoodwinked into performing the Johnny–June sex-tease "Jackson," she told me to keep calling her from time to time.

Apparently, I'd passed some sort of spousal test, and she was going to put in a good word with Carl that this Ghianni character wasn't as bad as you might think.

It was kind of a busy summer in the entertainment business in Nashville—and not because of Buddy Jewell and Daryl Worley.

After June Carter Cash died in May, there was sort of a death watch on John. At her funeral, he had revealed himself to the public for the first time, really, in years. He was an old, feeble man with a need to live long enough to finish up some of the great work of his career. The video he and June had done of Trent Reznor's "Hurt" seemed to be on an endless TV loop since June was dead and there were tombstones in the eyes of the very thick-lensed Man in Black.

There was sort of a daily dread at the newspaper or just in the town itself. Would this be the day Johnny Cash died? I talk about that in another chapter.

My friend Peter Cooper, who was the chief music writer but now is a musician and historian, spent a lot of time gathering information for a full section that was to be published when John died.

I didn't let my worries about Cash stop me from continuing to pursue Carl Smith, though. I'd call occasionally and have words with Goldie. "No, Tim, he's not ready yet," she'd say before we went on to other general chitchat about her life on the farm, her family, and the latest in the music community death count.

When Johnny Cash finally did die in September, no one really was surprised. But then at the same time, we were stunned. Goldie and I talked about John and June and about Waylon Jennings, a big fan of Carl's, who had died the year before (February 13, 2002).

Finally, in the autumn, I guess toward the middle part of October, I got a call at my house from Goldie.

With his Hall of Fame induction coming in November 2003, Carl had finally succumbed to his wife's constant pleas to talk with this Ghianni guy.

She asked me if I could be out at the farm/ranch in Franklin at 10 the following morning. Of course, I agreed.

The classy crooner from Maynardsville, Tennessee, explained his decision to hang up his stage costumes in 1978 after 35 years of stardom that included such hits as "Let's Live a Little," "Let Old Mother Nature Have Her Way," and "It's a Lovely, Lovely World."

"I'd been deciding for two or three years," he said, fishing out a Marlboro Light, popping it into his mouth, and then leaning down over an electric stove burner to light it.

"It wasn't spur of the moment. I just wanted to play cowboy [raising horses on the ranch]. I wanted to quit while I was still in demand. I didn't want to wait until nobody wanted to come to my shows.

"I took early retirement."

Goldie laughed. "Sometimes he tells people he went on vacation," she said, adding that her own departure from show biz wasn't nearly as dramatic.

"I just kindly faded from one career to another," she said, adding that she did perform a bit after her 1957 "retirement," but her desire really was to be home for her husband and their family.

"There was never any question it was what I wanted to do," she said. "I'm fortunate I didn't have to leave the business. I still had the same friends because Carl was still in the business."

"When I married her, I thought she was going to support me," Carl said, laughing as he leaned over to pet his other constant companion, Bronco, an 85-pound German shepherd. "Instead, I had to support her."

While Goldie lunched every Thursday with music industry women— a chatty, fun group called the "Lah-Di-Dah Girls"—her husband separated himself from the music business, with a couple marvelous and loyal exceptions.

"My friends, well, I hung out with Waylon a lot until after he passed," he says. "And I'm still close with Little Jimmy Dickens."

Jennings, it should be noted, often said he would not go into any Hall of Fame that didn't have Carl Smith in it. And, true to his word, when Jennings was inducted and Carl still ignored, he did not attend the ceremonies.

"Waylon gave 'em a rough time when they finally got around to inducting him," said his old friend with a chuckle.

His reason for not being inducted sooner may be politics, or perhaps, he figured, it was because he left the business, so it turned its back on him.

"There probably were some people who didn't think I should be in the Hall of Fame," Carl said. And he didn't show any bitterness. "I'm mostly glad for Goldie and the kids."

In fact, he would consider skipping the induction altogether but for his desire for domestic bliss.

"I'd probably be in trouble if I didn't [go to the ceremony]. It'll be easier to go on and make that five-second speech on television," he said, looking at Goldie.

"I'll put on my jeans," he said, shaking off his wife's suggestion he wear one of his flashy hillbilly crooner costumes.

"Couldn't fit in them now," said the fit 76-year-old.

It should be noted here that he didn't even get that five seconds. The Hall of Fame class had, up until that year, been presented live and onstage during the CMA Awards. That year, the show—and the CMA pushing for its younger demographic and the sillier songs—didn't have that segment.

In fact, the only national exposure Carl got during the show was when his name was called out from the stage. He stood up and waved his cowboy hat. It really was an insult, but Carl let it go. He didn't ever have much need for grudges.

I can't remember if they even mentioned his co-inductee, Floyd Cramer, whose slip-note piano style—in which an out-of-key note slides into the correct note—is a unique feature of many country recordings. Floyd, a good fellow, died in 1997. Oh, since I mention Hank Locklin earlier, it likely should be noted that Floyd developed that unique style for the recording of Hank's "Please Help Me I'm Falling."

Waylon, it should be pointed out, would have been really pissed by that basic snub of Carl. In fact, enough people who had shared that great outlaw's view of the CMA's Hall of Fame politics complained, and that led to change the following year.

No, there wouldn't be tons of TV time during the glitzy and silly awards show itself. But a Medallion Ceremony, recognizing the inductees, was begun by the actual Hall of Fame.

That first Medallion Ceremony honored my friend Kris Kristofferson in 2004. I had the privilege of being there with my wife. World War II hero, music executive, and kind fellow Jim Foglesong went in the same year. He was a humble man and didn't object that during the TV awards show, the "hip" CMA featured Kris getting recognized onstage, alone. That's another story.

Carl and Goldie, at the time of this interview, had three children and nine grandchildren. And then there was Carlene, his daughter with June Carter Cash, who in the years since has moved from the West Coast to Middle Tennessee.

Here, she is trying hard to live up to her own musical legacy. She is a beautiful, spirited soul.

Carl told me he had no regrets about his decades out of the spotlight. "When I retired, I made the right decision for me," he said. "My childhood dream was to be a hillbilly singer and to be a movie cowboy."

And he even did appear in a couple of B westerns such as *The Badge of Marshall Brennan*. And, yes, he got to gun down the bad guys. "Yep, I whupped a lot of people. I started out as a wimp, but I got tough in the end."

There were offers for him to stay in Hollywood, but a studio chief told the navy vet (he enlisted at the end of World War II) that he was better off in Nashville than hanging around on a $275-a-week contract, waiting for someone to call and say, "Hey, you're gonna fall off a horse on *Maverick* today," he said.

Smith did whatever it took to keep going in showbiz, including radio shows. He was on the first live television broadcast from what was then WSM Channel 4. "They were going to have some congressional hearings or something when they went on that day. But something went wrong."

Instead, Smith and other cohorts who had been on the WSM radio station were asked to grab their instruments and stand in front of the TV cameras. The blue-eyed singer found himself at ease on TV and served stints as host of country music showcases, including a long-running network program in Canada.

And, of course, there were the constant stage appearances as he trekked from one end of the world to another peddling his particular brand of country.

"I guess I was known for adding drums. They wouldn't let me use drums on the *Grand Ole Opry*, but I used them in a show before that.

"Ernest [Tubb] raised Cain with me for using drums. Ernest and Roy [Acuff] said I'd ruin my sound. Then I came back to the Opry one time and saw Roy with a snare drum. And in his later years, when Ernest was playing dance halls, he always had to have drums."

The stories could go on forever, almost like the road. But he stepped off that road in 1978.

"I wanted to play cowboy," he said. No, not the kind who falls off a horse on a James Garner TV western but the real deal.

Smith began a second career, breeding and showing champion cutting horses. "I showed cutting horses from the time I retired until two or three years ago," he said. "I had real good success."

Cutting horse competition basically has the cowboy working with cows, singling one out, and keeping it from rejoining the herd.

"There's a lot to it. Details would bore you. It's a challenge."

He retired from that career as well. "It takes a lot of athletic ability. I got too old. It hurt too much."

Even though he was retired from competition, the great cowboy crooner continued to ride every afternoon—after he and Goldie began their days with a mile-and-a-half walk before going "into town" for breakfast.

"Well, I ride every day. I got two of the horses still. And I ride around here, look at the cows and look at the rocks and see if any of them have moved overnight.

"My philosophy is doing what I want to. I don't make appointments. I get up when I want to, go to bed when I want to, do what I want to for the rest of the day."

Carl and Goldie walked me to the front door of their house, where we exchanged hugs.

By the time I'd driven 100 yards from their house, I looked in the rearview mirror. Carl and Goldie were walking, hand in hand, down the narrow lane with their dog, Bronco, keeping them company and a small cloud of Marlboro smoke rising above them.

Harold Bradley

Harold Bradley, a Country Music Hall of Famer whose specialty was in making others sound their best, was always was chirpy when I called, no matter how much he'd been struggling physically.

Maybe it was his World War II veteran status or his early-in-life baseball dreams that kept him going. Or perhaps he was in solid shape, at least mentally, from his acrobatics on water skis, and that kept him going.

I called him dozens of times during a quarter century or more. Our generally cheery conversations ended sometime before January 31, 2019, when his history of shrugging off serious health woes finally ended. He was 93.

His Legacy.com obituary was pretty basic: "Harold Bradley was a Country Music Hall of Fame guitarist who was instrumental in creating 'the Nashville sound.' The session player was part of the famous A Team, a group of musicians who played on hit songs by Elvis Presley, Roy Orbison, and Loretta Lynn. Bradley led the local musicians union, helping bring about better working conditions, and was a key person in the creation of Nashville's music district, Music Row."

The family's longer paid obituary that appeared in *The Tennessean* is much more personal: "Harold Bradley, a kind, gentle soul and the best dad and grandfather died peacefully in his sleep Thursday morning, January 31, 2019, at the age of 93.

"Known worldwide as a music icon and the most-recorded guitarist, the Hall of Fame musician was foremost a dedicated family man. Harold Bradley married Eleanor Allen Bradley in 1952. Over their 66-year marriage, Bradley cherished family time with his wife and two daughters saying he would practice his guitar while they went to the grocery store to have time to spend with them when they returned. Later, Harold Bradley enjoyed grandchildren whom he took pride in encouraging in their own musical pursuits."

Harold was always generous and kind, but he also wasn't hesitant to get right to the point. I could be talking to him about his late brother Owen (who I did not really know but who, with Harold and Chet, pretty much formulated the so-called Nashville Sound that Waylon and Willie and the boys at first rebelled against). Or perhaps I could be talking about his work with Elvis or Patsy Cline or maybe his guitar playing on sessions with Perry Como, Joan Baez, Buddy Holly, Ivory Joe Hunter, Pee Wee King, George Morgan, Hank Williams, Burl Ives, Henry Mancini, Connie Francis, George Beverly Shea, Hank Snow, Jim Reeves, Charley Pride, Leon Russell, The Everly Brothers, Gene Watson, Marty Robbins, Freddie Hart, Conway Twitty, Roy Clark—the list goes on.

He was sorry he didn't work on the famous Bob Dylan sessions that yielded some landmark albums, but he praised the Hibbing, Minnesota, native and wordsmith for bringing outside attention to the capabilities of the Nashville Cats and studios.

Back when Harold was head of the musicians' union in Nashville, he jumped in full speed if I needed help locating a musician for a story or a comment, often for an obituary. He also would suggest musicians I should get to know. Sometimes I did.

More often the case in his post-union years, we'd just be talking about his health. I liked to call him, more than occasionally, at his home in Goodlettsville, north of downtown Nashville. He was old and frail, but our conversations always perked at least one of us up. I hope they perked up the old water-ski-jumping and slaloming enthusiast (he and his wife, Eleanor, were experts) as well. While he didn't enjoy his 10 hours of overnight kidney dialysis, he still found the bubbly energy to talk about playing the guitar and about the Nashville of his memory, a place where a gentle Music City frame of mind presided—long gone, of course.

As I've noted elsewhere, for years, I maintained the practice of calling older musicians, the ones no one was writing about anymore, in Nashville. There were several reasons for these calls. First, I wanted these folks to know that somebody genuinely still cared about them and their contributions. Second, I enjoyed it: there are worse things than having, for example, Uncle Josh Graves, Scotty Moore, Harold Bradley, Little Jimmy Dickens, Mac Wiseman, and Jimmy Otey as friends.

Occasionally, there was a third reason for my calls. Generally, against bosses' wishes, I would turn out a story or column about these people, kind of shoving these old-timers in the faces of folks who basically thought that unless musicians still were churning out hits, they didn't matter.

"You and your [entertainment] staff are writing too much about people like Johnny Cash, Waylon Jennings, and Chet Atkins," I'd be scolded frequently. And yet I applauded and encouraged my staff's archival predilections. After all, wasn't Cowboy Jack Clement just a tad more important to Music City and the culture here than Trace Adkins? (Trace: You're a big fella, so please know I like your music and your personality fine, but, well, "Honky Tonk Badonkadonk" is neither "Your Cheatin' Heart" nor "Ring of Fire.")

After that sort of thought and stubborn determination to do the right thing, I was turned out on my own. I've written about that earlier. Even so, I continued to make those calls. I still do, though the list is getting too short.

The last time I talked to Harold for a column actually began with one of these "health checks." When I called in the late morning, he was having some difficulty. He asked me to call him back ("don't forget it") later in the day. He was sure he'd be feeling better.

"I was having some fluctuation in my blood pressure this morning," he told me when I fulfilled my "callback" promise later that day.

"My blood pressure was down to 81 or something like that. It was supposed to be 120. Didn't feel so good."

Most of the phone calls I had with Harold included an inquiry from me about whether he would like his CDs back. A few years before, I was working on a Kindle book that answered the question, who do Nashville's top pickers think is or was the greatest guitarist in Music City history?

I was calling those who were still alive and gathering a few quotes. Mostly, they talked not just about themselves but about other guitarists as well.

Harold, whose history really was as a rhythm player, had high praise for the other guitarists. And he spoke at length about his own story and the wide variety of people he'd played with during his lifetime.

A couple of days after that conversation, a small box arrived in the mail. Inside were 15 CDs of Harold's music.

Some were commercial recordings on which he'd had extensive roles. Others were snippets of his guitar work that he'd put together on various CDs, simply to illustrate his work. There was no index for the music. It was just his music that he wanted to do the talking.

I called him then to thank him but added that he shouldn't have gone to the trouble and expense. I'd send them back to him soon, I said.

"No," he said. "I did those for you. No one else would want them." There was no hint of bitterness, no hint of his feeling forgotten in there. All he was saying is that I had shown interest in his work, so he wanted to share it with me.

"As far as I know, I'm the most recorded guitar player in the world," he said fairly often when we spoke.

Starting when he was 20 back in 1946—just after serving as a code breaker in the navy during World War II, duty to his country that cut short his ambitions with the Chicago Cubs—Harold was a constant in Nashville music.

I'm sure there is no accurate count, but he is said to have participated on more than 1,000 recordings. While he could play lead guitar, Harold, more often than not, was signed on as rhythm guitarist, but he was ready for anything. On many, many recordings, he played with lead guitarists Hank Garland and Grady Martin.

After Garland had a debilitating auto accident, Harold often became the go-to lead guitarist, with Ray Edenton taking over session rhythm duties. Of course, they swapped back and forth. Harold could handle any guitar task assigned.

Harold, at 90, admitted to having a pretty good memory for things he'd done in the studio but also said there was a bit of haze when it came time to detail the earliest days.

"I know I played a lot, and I remember a lot since 1946. But there is a gap of sessions back in that time. I have a pretty good [grasp of] history from then on."

The stacked-up pages of a musicians' union written chronicle of his sessions "is 46 inches thick. I've got a list of songs that's unbelievable," he told me.

Along with the stash of recordings he sent, there was a partial list of some of the hits and highlights of his long career.

Perhaps his best-known work is the rhythm guitar on Roy Orbison's number 2 pop hit "Crying" in 1961.

But, according to the Country Music Hall of Fame and Museum bio of Harold, he certainly wasn't always in the background, lending his reliable hand to the texture of the recording.

"Occasionally, Bradley did play lead parts that stood out. For example, he played the opening banjo notes on Johnny Horton's 1959 hit 'The Battle of New Orleans.' Bradley's electric bass guitar can be heard on hits such as Patsy Cline's 'Crazy.'"

Just about everywhere you look in Music Row history, you can find Harold in the session credits.

The Hall of Fame picks out some highlights from his massive list of recorded contributions: Eddy Arnold's "Make the World Go Away," Brenda Lee's "I'm Sorry," Roger Miller's "King of the Road," Orbison's "Running Scared," Ray Price's "Danny Boy," Jeannie C. Riley's "Harper Valley P.T.A.," Bobby Vinton's "Blue Velvet," Burl Ives's "Holly Jolly Christmas," Faron Young's "Hello Walls," Tammy Wynette's "Stand by Your Man," and Conway Twitty's "Hello Darlin'."

And he was far from done. In fact, when I was talking to him late in the afternoon of his blood pressure battle, he was getting ready for a three-night symphony gig with Mandy Barnett, a skilled singer whose Patsy Cline stylings had captured the attention of Harold's brother, Owen, who had produced Patsy.

Owen's swan songs were recording sessions with Mandy, and, if I remember correctly, Harold picked up where his brother left off after Owen died.

Some of what we spoke about that day ended up in a September 23, 2016, story I wrote for the *Nashville Ledger*.

In that story, I noted that Harold *was* among the few remaining from the time when real country music and Bob Dylan and Elvis and Ray Charles crossed paths down on Music Row.

He continued to work sessions almost seven decades after he worked with Red Foley to record "Chattanoogie Shoeshine Boy."

"Red changed it from 'Chattanooga,' so now the song title is 'Chattanoogie.' My first million seller,'" Harold said, repeating "Chattanoogie" and laughing.

Harold was a member of the so-called A-Team of studio musicians in Nashville, musical wizards who were called on to do four three-hour sessions a day.

Just to name a few, the A-Team included bassists Bob Moore, Norbert Putnam, and Junior Huskey; drummers Buddy Harman, Jerry Carrigan, and Kenny Buttrey; keyboardists Floyd Cramer, Hargus "Pig" Robbins, and Owen Bradley; guitarists Harold Bradley, Chet Atkins, Grady Martin, Hank Garland, and Jerry Kennedy; fiddlers Johnny Gimble, Buddy Spicher, and Vassar Clements; steel players Lloyd Green, Buddy Emmons, and Pete Drake; banjo players Earl Scruggs and Bobby Thompson; Jethro Burns on mandolin; Boots Randolph on sax; and Charlie McCoy on harmonica (and about anything else that needed playing).

The list goes on, but you get the idea.

While Harold played with just about anyone in show businesses, he admitted to me, "I have two favorites: 'Crazy' with Patsy Cline and 'Crying' with Roy Orbison."

He told me that Patsy's session was among the toughest he'd worked. "Patsy had broken ribs in an automobile wreck, and she couldn't work that session."

Owen directed, while Harold and his instrumental colleagues did their parts, waiting for her to heal.

"First of all, a normal recording session is three hours long, but we had gone on to four hours on 'Crazy'," he said.

Background singers and A-Team pickers filled their tracks that night.

According to pages from his session calendar that he sent me, the "Crazy" session ran from 7:15 p.m. to 11:15 p.m. on Monday, August 21, 1961. Harold took home $73.16 for that session. If I'm reading it right (there are several dollar amounts on the page), Harold took home $87.60 earlier in the day for a session with Webb Pierce. That same week, he worked sessions for Willie Nelson, Marion Worth, Grandpa Jones, and Kitty Wells, among others.

It's fun to look at the session logs. For example, on Thursday, March 15, 1962, he worked sessions with Conway Twitty, two with Clyde McPhatter, and one with Les Paul and Mary Ford, with whom he had several sessions that week. On Sunday, March 18, he worked three sessions with Elvis Presley. His take-home pay was $154.72.

"We had the middle left for her vocal," he said of the "Crazy" session. "Patsy came in and did it in one take. When she got through, none of us wanted to do it again." I'm sure the strain was at least as bad on Patsy.

Owen, the players, and Patsy knew that on this recording, they'd captured what remains the perfect country song (and perhaps the best ever written by Willie Nelson and, as noted earlier, the singer of my favorite recording of the song).

"Back then, we had no music, no headphones, and Owen kept coming out [of the production booth] and reworking the arrangement," said Harold.

"What Owen did with 'Crazy' was a formula he used the rest of his life," Harold said.

As for "Crying," he said the biggest memory is that Orbison, who finished his career as a Traveling Wilbury, barked out the tempo and the tone to get the Fred Foster–produced song going.

Harold said he and his fellow pickers and grinners thought they'd worked it up pretty well when Roy took over the session: "Harold, play this: 'bah, bump-bump, bump."

"That was it," Harold said, noting that Orbison, who owned perhaps the most flexible voice ever to haunt Nashville studios, knew exactly the sound he sought before he sang, "I was all right for a while."

"Both of those artists have to be among my favorites," Harold said. "But somewhere you'd have to include Elvis."

He recalled that once in an interview, he was asked of all the singers he worked with, which two would he like to hear do a duet?

"I thought for a moment and said 'Patsy and Elvis' . . . 'Patsy Meets Elvis,'" he said, mixing mirth with the realization that the passage of time made such a teaming impossible.

"Elvis was a wonderful guy," he says. "When I knew him, he wasn't on drugs. He never raised his voice in the studio. He was always really calm, and he loved to record more than anything.

"When he walked into the studio, you could tell he was in heaven." Like Orbison, Elvis also had an innate sense of how a song should sound.

Harold stopped a second, drawing a happy breath. He had to get some rest for the show with Mandy and the Nashville Symphony.

But before he went to stretch out, he wanted to put his own contributions in perspective.

"I'm the last person going back to before it happened," he said of a noble life that helped create the sound of the stars who birthed the reputation and the place that is Music Row.

"I played the first session here. . . . I've literally seen it all; and my part in it turned out to be huge."

Tyrone "Super T" Smith

T HE FIRST TIME I MET SUPER T, he was sitting in the gym of a
Nashville elementary school, talking about his retirement from a
career as a physical education teacher.

Tyrone Smith was only 60 back in May 2004, but he'd been pushing
hard as a teacher on weekdays and a super soul revue bandleader on weekends for several decades.

Something finally had to give. He loved teaching (he planned on doing
some substituting as necessary), but there was something about the allure of
putting on that Superman-like Super T costume, those blue tights with the
red cape, and flying off into full show band style that he couldn't give up.
The last time I checked, he was still doing it, just like the Tyrone Smith
Revue (aka the Super T Revue) did it for George W. and Laura Bush at
the White House not long before the day we met at the school from which
he was retiring.

He smiled broadly—he pretty much always does when talking about
delighting gym students and presidents—as we spoke on that late-spring
day.

I joked that most teachers, particularly at inner-city schools, are super-
heroes. The difference between Tyrone and the rest is that most of his
colleagues didn't wear capes and tights and didn't have bold initials embla-
zoned on their chests.

And, he told me, at his "retirement" party from teaching, the kids, who
called him "Mr. Smith," "Super T," or both, were going to get a full dose
of his show band persona.

He was planning on climbing into his form-fitting costume and shaking his rear and attached parts—"I call it the Super T Booty Green," he

said—while horns wailed, guitars flailed, and voices sailed in a school filled with kids who loved him.

In his gym-teaching clothes decorated by that coach's whistle, Tyrone didn't appear to be the kind of guy who put on tights and shook his booty for the president of the United States. But just a few months before we met up, this Nashville R&B original was doing just that.

He was at the White House with his big soul revue band, teaching President George W. Bush how to do the "Super T Booty Green."

"It goes like this," the gym teacher said after pushing himself up from his coach's desk and beginning his demonstration.

"Right hand, right knee. Then left hand, left knee. … Then *break it down*," he said as he went into the main part of the shuffle, shaking his rear end.

As he shook his booty, he cheerily hollered, "President Bush did this!"

"W" even referred to the bandleader as "Super T" as he and Laura and the family and staff enjoyed the 2003 Christmas party.

It was not the last encounter between Tyrone, his great band, and the guy who then was the "most powerful man in the world."

Tyrone grabbed national headlines by playing at Jenna Bush's wedding near the lake at the W clan's Crawford, Texas, compound. He can be seen on YouTube hollering to the bridegroom that "George W. Bush ain't got nothing on you" during the fever-pitch, dance-heavy reception.

Other video shows his "move that body" exhortation in action, as a line of blond and blue-eyed bridesmaids unashamedly do just that, shaking and shimmering body parts scarcely disguised beneath glistening gowns, I noted in a story I did October 21, 2011, for the *Nashville Ledger*.

I was writing about the show band business—Super T and Jimmy Church are the main purveyors in Nashville—in which exuberant front men lead their troupes of saxes, drums, trumpets, harmony singers—the whole works. If you've never seen a great R&B show band at work, think the Blues Brothers without the nonsense of Belushi and Aykroyd. Jake and Elwood are a lot of fun but are celluloid heroes, not "real" soul men comin' to you down a dusty road.

Super T and Jimmy Church (featured elsewhere in this collection) will make even old white guys like me and a Republican president claim "mission accomplished" after being urged and instructed in the art of booty shaking.

That presidential tie (it developed into a friendship, really) began when the band was on its normal runs through the frat party scene, stopping in Austin, Texas.

The Bush girls—Jenna and Barbara—became hooked on this show-man's enthusiastic agility and vocal charm back in their "Hook 'em Horns" days at the University of Texas.

That school in Austin was just one of Super T's stops as he conquered the frat party circuit and the corporate retreat world as well.

As noted above, the revue played the White House Christmas party as well as at "the big" inaugural ball at Bush's second coronation.

"It was the Texas-Wyoming Ball," said Tyrone, who, when not squirming and squealing like James Brown or belting it out old school in front of his large band, reverts to the soft-spoken gentleman, who, during our conversations even years after his retirement, still missed the inner-city youngsters he taught and coached.

While Super T became a Nashville institution, his roots actually are in Memphis, where the son of a preacher and church pianist began perform-ing with high school chums Booker T. Jones and Maurice White.

"The longer we played, the more money people would throw at us. I guess that's why I still play so long now."

Booker T., of course, went on to lead the MGs and produce phenom-enal music: good, danceable stuff.

The same could be said for Maurice, an original member of Earth, Wind & Fire. The three remained friends for life, even after Tyrone left the Bluff City to get his teaching degree at Tennessee State University in Nashville.

His high school sweetheart, Helen, also attended Tennessee State and spent her career as a teacher.

Tyrone was a road warrior from the outset. First came Tyrone Smith and the Invaders, a staple on the Chitlin' Circuit and then the Jefferson Street R&B scene.

Jefferson Street, which ends at the Tennessee State campus, was long a mecca for R&B before Interstate 40 cut through its heart, opening the way for urban decay. Now it is changing again, as a neighborhood for white hipsters and the like pushes down the blocks.

"I knew all of them," Tyrone said of the guys who made Jefferson Street hop.

"Jimi Hendrix. Billy Cox. Johnny Jones. . . . Once I was on a show with Ike and Tina in Clarksville [Tennessee, about an hour northwest of Nashville].

"They were very young. We played at the American Legion, right by the funeral home."

Then came the Tyrone Smith Super T Revue and a virtually nonstop, high-energy tour of campuses, clubs, and weddings. "We go wherever there's money. There's not a weekend we aren't out on the road. Some weeknights, too."

One summer afternoon, I caught up with him and his band as they tuned up for a road trip—playing a wedding in the Hamptons—by playing for a Nashville-based health care corporation's barbecue in Centennial Park.

The costumed superhero stepped from the black E-450 Super Duty Ford bus while his band blanketed a crowded corner of the park with brassy, thumping Earth, Wind & Fire funk.

The caped crusader leaned back and nodded to the beat as scores of company employees finished their lunch and settled into folding chairs.

I was there to do a story for the October 21, 2011, *Nashville Ledger*. I also was there to enjoy more time with this genuinely warm, soft-spoken man, who turns into a howling, dancing, spinning superhero once his feet get moving.

"You have to love it to do it," he had told me a bit before the show, as he relaxed in the bus in his plaid shorts and T-shirt, clutching the bag that contained the Super T suit.

"When I hit that stage, the band pumps me up."

He excused himself to go to the back of the bus and climb into his costume.

"Gotta get ready so we can do our stuff," he said, adding that this would be only a short performance. Normally, he puts Bruce Springsteen to shame with a pair of two-and-a-half-hour sets. The costumed superhero appears for only about 45 minutes. The rest of the time, it's simply Tyrone out there in showbiz civvies while the sweat-drenched Super T costume dries out in the bus.

"Gotta keep their feet moving the whole time," Tyrone said as we listened to the brass-heavy underpinning that the band is already laying down outside as the boss climbed into his costume.

As that thumping beat built toward climax, Tyrone stepped softly across the parking lot, conserving his energy for the last few steps, when he climbed up the stage steps and grabbed a microphone, and the metamorphosis was complete: "I am Super T," he hollered into the microphone he really didn't need.

"We're getting ready to get this party started."

Stutter-stepping and high-kicking, he negotiated the entire stage front, commanding all to "work that body . . . work that body."

Bobby Hebb

"Thanks for doing such a great thing for Johnny in the paper today," said the sunny voice on the other end of the line after I picked up my newsroom telephone at around 8:30 a.m. on September 2, 2004.

"I appreciate that sir," I said to the anonymous caller, who would, I was glad, go on to become a good friend, a guy I'd call often or (if I had the time) whose tidy, airy home I'd visit in the new subdivision off the Clarksville Highway in the Bordeaux section of Nashville.

"This is Bobby Hebb," he said, softly. "I sang some with Johnny back in the day."

Bobby Hebb. Robert Alvin Von Hebb. "Sunny." Calling me?

Any music enthusiast knows who Bobby Hebb was: perhaps the greatest R&B singer to come out of Nashville's old Jefferson Street rhythmic melting pot that had served as the training ground for Roscoe Shelton, Earl Gaines, Marion James, Jimmy Church, Tyrone "Super T" Smith, Billy Cox and his roommate and best pal Jimi Hendrix (back when he was "Jimmy"), Frank Howard & the Commanders, and Johnny Jones.

Other top black touring acts—like Little Richard, Gorgeous George, and Lou Rawls—were known to stop and play in that flourishing club district that was "murdered" when the federal government put Interstate 40 right through the heart of Nashville's then mostly black north side. The Del Morocco club, where Hendrix and Cox were regulars, and even the next-door beauty college, with the apartment upstairs the two men shared, were among the things bulldozed when that neighborhood was gutted. Progress.

Jimi and Billy had a single light bulb dangling from the ceiling of the apartment they found as their refuge after Hendrix washed out of his 101st

Airborne paratrooper profession. That friendship is explored in another chapter.

Bobby Hebb, who left the South for success as a jazz singer on the East Coast and especially in Europe and in Japan, composed and sang many great songs, most notably, as noted, "Sunny," which holds at least a full page in the fabled great American songbook.

I later found out that in addition to being an important singer, he was a believer in world peace and meditation, and he spoke in riddles and rhymes while enjoying cosmic conversation with anyone who could stay with him.

Hell, I'd interviewed members of the Grateful Dead and even Brian Wilson, so I knew about sometimes off-kilter and intergalactic conversation: it didn't take me much time at all to learn to listen and communicate with this gentle and unassuming music superman with Buddhist tendencies mixed with the rich Christian spirituality instilled by his blind, gospel-singing parents.

I quickly came to love Bobby Hebb as a close friend and spiritual booster.

He'd moved back to Nashville not that long before his first phone call to me, chronicled above. I really don't think he was seeking any publicity. He was happy in his new home, where he was working out songs for a new album and spending as much as time as possible with the family left behind when fame took him to the world.

He was just calling me to thank me for writing an obit for one of his childhood friends. It was just Bobby being gracious. I found out later, thanks to mailed notes and Christmas cards that I received, that Bobby was filled with the social graces.

But as we spoke about the death of his friend and his own return to his roots, I thought someone ought to write about his being back in town. I didn't want to waste time, so I asked for directions to his house before we hung up.

My day already was a success because this tenderhearted caller had liked the obituary for great R&B singer and ex-con Johnny Bragg.

Getting that obituary in the paper had made me proud: I had to argue long and hard all the way up the editorial ladder, perhaps even to the fat man himself, if I remember correctly, to get Johnny Bragg's final chapter published.

It was a story obituary I was pushing, and my direct boss back in the features department at *The Tennessean* had pooh-poohed the story obituary I pitched as an offering for the next day's paper. Story obits are feature stories that newspapers publish in the regular news columns, usually not far from the so-called paid deaths, the newsroom term for the agate-typed, paid-by-the-word obituaries that can cost surviving families thousands. Today, you are better off just letting the funeral homes publish the obituaries for free on their Web pages, but things were different back in the early part of this century.

Johnny Bragg's family didn't have thousands to spare, but it wasn't out of charity that I was pushing this story.

Generally, these story obituaries are done for rich businessmen and businesswomen—the types of folks who own steeplechase horses and/or play polo on the weekends—and perhaps a country star but only if it's someone the front office knows and who is selling music. Old-timers generally are forgotten, their families told to go pay for an obit.

But it used to be that newspapers had obituary writers and that these story obits were generally some of the best writing and reading in the newspaper because it was based on fact and history rather than "spin."

When I sensed there was insurmountable indifference to this story about a black ex-con who soared in the music circles, I just went ahead and wrote it. Once the editors read it, I'm sure sending it back up and down that ladder of indecision, they ran probably 10 inches' worth on the back of the "B" section, behind the paid deaths.

Here are some excerpts from that story:

> Johnny Bragg, 79, the last surviving member of a singing quintet of convicts known as The Prisonaires, died early yesterday at the Imperial Manor Convalescent Center in Madison after a long battle with cancer.
>
> The Prisonaires, which Bragg formed, gained attention and sparked some controversy by being allowed to record and perform outside prison walls in the 1950s.
>
> Bragg's rise to fame came after being sentenced in 1943 to six concurrent 99-year sentences after he was convicted of rape in Davidson County. In prison, Bragg began to write music, and he and his musical partners in the Prisonaires caught the attention of Sun Records firebrand Sam Phillips.
>
> Phillips recorded the inmates singing "Just Walkin' in the Rain," which became a rhythm & blues classic, during a temporary release for the inmates.
>
> Also in the studio that day in Memphis was a young Elvis Presley, Bragg recalled in a 1990 interview with *The Tennessean*.
>
> "I was having a lot of trouble pronouncing the words of the song," he said. "Elvis sat down with me and worked with me on my diction. It's a fact, he helped me."
>
> "Just Walkin' in the Rain," which Bragg co-wrote with fellow inmate Robert Riley, sold more than 50,000 copies for their band.
>
> It later sold more than 1 million copies for pop star Johnnie Ray.

In 1955, after leaving the Sun roster, Bragg renamed the group the Marigolds and they had a top 10 R&B hit with "Rollin' Stone," for Nashville-based Excello Records. . . .

The band's success also gave a considerable boost to fledgling Sun Records.

In addition to recording, Bragg and the band of felons made regular visits to the governor's mansion to entertain, which sparked a fair share of controversy at the time.

Gov. Frank Clement commuted Bragg's sentence in 1959. He was sent back to prison on a parole violation in the early 1960s. His yo-yo to and from prison included a release in 1967, a return to jail in 1977 and a final release that year.

In an interview at the time he was initially released from prison, he said, "One year in prison is worth four years of college if you are willin' to learn."

He said he certainly was willing to learn during his 15-year term. He also was able to earn a nest egg. According to a *Tennessean* story in 1959, Bragg received about $10,000 in accumulated royalties from "Walkin'" upon his prison release. . . .

Long before his health began to fail, he told a reporter he had one wish: "I just want to be remembered. When they think about Elvis, I wish they'd think about Johnny Bragg and 'Just Walkin' in the Rain.'"

Until his dying days, Bragg maintained that he was framed for the rape conviction that sent him to jail in the first place.

Of course, he didn't become as famous as his pal Elvis, although that is a helluva song, and Johnny's ties to Sam Phillips's Sun Records and kinship with the King of Rock 'n' Roll were and are worth noting.

As if you really need a reminder, Sam produced all kinds of great rock and country acts and was working the controls when Elvis, Scotty Moore, and Bill Black—tired from a long attempt at capturing magic—began screwing around with Arthur "Big Boy" Crudup's bluesy "That's All Right." If rock 'n' roll wasn't born then, this certainly was the neutron bomb that changed the world.

And that's all right with me, by the way.

And it is said, though not confirmed, that "Sunny" actually was written by Bobby Hebb as sort of a bright antidote to Johnny Bragg's "Walkin' in the Rain." I never asked Bobby about that, but given the two men's many connections, it does make sense. Of course, there's a lot more behind "Sunny," and I'll get us there eventually.

I had known Johnny Bragg only via a couple of phone calls when I was writing about the R&B scene (something the newspaper bosses had criticized by asking, "Don't you know any white people?" before ordering me to put those stories inside the features section rather than on the cover).

Of course, the saga of the Prisonaires is pure southern legend. I was convinced Johnny's death was worth noting, his life worth celebrating in the newspaper. I had to do a similar song and dance to get obits in on several people over the years. Among them was Roger Schutt, notorious Nashville radio personality "Captain Midnight," who was known for running fast and wild with Waylon and Willie and the boys during the Outlaws' conquest of Music Row. He was found dead in his apartment in a retirement tower a block from Music Row on February 8, 2005. We had spent a lot of time over the years talking about that era. Our last phone conversation was a day or two before he died.

"You're about the last one still alive at the newspaper who would remember that time," Midnight would say, often stumbling over syllables or leaving them out altogether.

Again, I had to write the obituary for Midnight—and I considered him a friend even if I'd never joined him in knife-throwing contests with Waylon—to prove it worthy of *The Tennessean*. And he was even white, by the way.

I think I got about eight inches for Midnight, but here's a section of it:

Donnie Fritts, a charter outlaw, broke into tears when told of Mr. Schutt's death. "I been knowing him from like the mid-1960s, when he had that radio show," said Fritts, crediting Mr. Schutt for making a Fritts-Dan Penn co-write, Rainbow Road, "real popular."

The song, recorded by Bill Brandon, was about an imprisoned singer. "The guys in the [Tennessee State] Prison would keep calling in to request it. He played it a lot," said Fritts, calling Mr. Schutt "one of the great characters that came out of the 1960s and '70s. He was very close to Waylon and Tompall [Glaser]. He was one of the ones that was there with us, with Kris [Kristofferson], Shel [Silverstein], Billy [Swan]."

Mr. Schutt also proclaimed himself "Music Row's best knife-thrower." He dueled Jennings for the title. The knife marks on the back wall of the Glaser compound are still visible today.

Of course, Captain Midnight really is far from the point of this story, but I wanted to get him in here somewhere. Even as I wrote it, I could almost smell the whiskey-soaked laughter.

Anyway, the fact was that my pushing for the published obit on Johnny Bragg triggered the phone call with one of music's true immortals, Bobby Hebb.

While Bobby and I talked about Johnny Bragg, we pretty much hit it off over the phone.

I, of course, knew his signature song so well that I could sing it word for word if anyone could stand it.

But I also knew he had worked with John Lee Hooker in Chicago and Thelonious Monk in New York and had toured with The Beatles.

He was a childhood friend of the singer Pat Boone, who lived on Granny White Pike, just a few miles south of his own family.

Before I talked to Bobby, I knew just a little bit about the Hebb Family, the gospel group that helped launch his career and that he was hoping to restart once he moved back to Nashville after years in the Northeast and in Europe and Japan, where he remained a star.

I also knew I really liked this guy on the other end of the phone, and it apparently was mutual, as the day or two after that obituary on Johnny Bragg appeared, triggering Bobby's call to me at the office, I was bouncing my old white Saab up over the curb that fronted his driveway (why don't they cut places in curbs for cars to enter on modern driveways?), and I knocked at his door.

I spent a good part of the day drinking black coffee with brown sugar in it ("I don't drink coffee much, mostly I drink tea," he told me, explaining the brown sugar treatment was something he picked up in Scandinavia).

Bobby sat down at the baby grand in his living room.

"Listen to this," he said. He began noodling on the piano, his cosmic smile fixed somehow both on the ceiling and on his visitor. Slowly (for Bobby wasn't one to hurry into anything then at 66 years of age), his noodling began sneaking into some of the chords of his most famous song.

Suddenly, he pushed himself up off the bench, fixed his eyes on the ceiling with his right hand counting out the beat as he abandoned the piano, and began an a cappella version of the classic song "Sunny," his vocal volume building as he sang the entire song: "Sunny, yesterday my life was filled with rain."

Even though there was just one person in the audience, he'd done his song as forcefully as if he was in a New York showroom, like the ones he used to work with costars Tony Bennett and Judy Garland.

Thunderstruck that I had just, by myself, heard one of America's classic songs performed by its original voice, I climbed up from the chair (he lacked much furniture as he'd just moved back to Nashville from the East Coast), and a handshake turned into a hug.

We sat down, this time with him switching to tea, and nursed our hot beverages while he talked about his life and the potential inspirations for that great song.

Our conversation was as easygoing and slightly mystic as the man himself, a sweet, sweet fellow.

One of the things we talked about was his signature song, the one that assured him lifelong prosperity.

"Sunny" was born in his apartment at 2186 Fifth Avenue in Harlem, New York, where he'd gone to seek fame and fortune after his career as a gospel singer with his family and onstage at the Grand Ole Opry, where he'd been a longtime member of Roy Acuff and His Smoky Mountain Boys.

Some writers report that Bobby wrote "Sunny" in response to the slaying of his brother, Harold, outside the Club Baron (now an Elks Lodge; see chapter 15 on Hendrix and Cox for details). Others say that the song stemmed from the death of President John F. Kennedy, whose brains had been blown out in a car the day before in Dallas.

Bobby said those interpretations were okay, but really the song had more to do with mood than history.

The day Harold Hebb died, he was a member of the Marigolds, the group sprung from Johnny Bragg's all-con band the Prisonaires.

Harold was doing time for armed robbery when his singing abilities caught the ear of the bandleader. With Bragg in control of the group, the Marigolds—the ex-con version of the Prisonaires—flourished after they were released from prison.

Harold's career and life ended as he bled to death outside the Club Baron. Harold's death was the end of a bar fight. He worked at the Club Baron. According to police reports, a man who refused to take his hat off in the club caused something of a row.

The club bouncer, toting a shotgun, chased the hat-wearing fellow outside.

According to the police, the guy with the hat hung around outside the club, and when he was approached by Harold, he went after him with a knife.

Harold was mortally wounded when the original bouncer or another club employee brought him the shotgun that he—with his dying breaths—shot, killing the hat man.

"It was so sad," Bobby told me as we talked about his brother's death. "Such loss."

So Bobby was feeling plenty of personal pain at the same time the nation was dealing with evil weasel Lee Harvey Oswald's (aided by someone on the grassy knoll) murder of Kennedy, a major blow to the American dream.

Bobby's closest friends in New York were Gerald Wilson and Thelonious Monk, both men known for exploring the "dark sounds."

Bobby was sad, but he wasn't ready to succumb to the darkness that cloaked Thelonious and the nation, from Dealey Plaza all the way to Jefferson Street.

"I needed to pick myself up. I needed an upper. It all goes back to playing with Roy Acuff and feeling the music."

His introduction to "The King of Country Music" (Acuff's unofficial title) went back to his early life.

Bobby, age three, and Harold, age nine, began performing around Nashville as a song-and-dance team, using tools they'd learned from their musical parents.

I'm not sure if both Bobby and Harold performed on a TV show hosted by Nashville music icon Owen Bradley (that's his statue in the park at the Deaderick Street end of Music Row, with Owen stoically sitting on the piano bench, looking out at the massive sculpture of well-endowed nude dancers), but it was little Bobby who earned a spot playing spoons and other instruments with Acuff's Smoky Mountain Boys (I do prefer their pre-Opry moniker: the Crazy Tennesseans).

Acuff would forever be a hero to Bobby not only because Acuff hired him but also because he refused to stay in a hotel if the black youngster was not allowed to stay, too. In that way, the iconic singer ("Great Speckled Bird," "Wabash Cannonball," and "Blue Eyes Crying in the Rain"), bandleader, fiddler, and yo-yo flinger became something of an unlikely pioneer of civil rights in the Jim Crow South.

Acuff's Dobro player Pete Kirby, better known as "Bashful Brother Oswald," gave the small black kid some advice heeded by the Smoky Mountain Boys. "The fellas could not read music, but they could learn to play it how it should feel," Hebb remembers. Oswald took the youngster aside: "He told me, 'Feel the music while you're performing it.'"

Another Opry star, Hank Williams, also gave the young man advice after Bobby approached him backstage and asked how to write with emotion.

"Hank was very friendly. . . . He says, 'You just sit down as if you were writing a letter.' My mother corrected me on that count. She said you must have a story to tell when you write. She . . . showed me the correct way to do it."

Writing "Sunny" "was therapy" for the young man trying to escape the personal loss and national darkness in his Harlem apartment.

On that first day I visited his house off the Clarksville Highway, Bobby walked across the room and dropped into an easy chair. He reached to the coffee table to rescue a ceramic cup half filled with tea.

And it ought to be noted that the most important musical teaming in history—The Beatles—were big fans of Bobby and of his song.

He smiled when he talked about how he enjoyed their musical company and the fact they heaped praise on his masterpiece when he opened for them on what ended up being their last tour.

"Whoo. I was very excited and very thrilled to get that job," he said. He played for the biggest crowds of his career (and he never played for that many again), "and the audience listened to me. Some of them sang along with me on 'Sunny.'"

The performers flew together on the charter and stayed in the same hotels.

"All of them were nice. Of course, when they sang on stage, there was so much screaming, they couldn't hear themselves. John and George, well, they were very quiet. But Ringo and Paul were more active and easier to get to know. It was just something to be with those cats," Bobby said, smiling while raising the tea cup to his lips.

He was among the opening acts during The Beatles' farewell tour, a big voice in the package of acts that preceded John, Paul, George, and Ringo all the way to the final live concert on August 29, 1966, at Candlestick Park in San Francisco.

"That's it, then," George Harrison said when the band made it into their plane after the show. "I'm not a Beatle anymore." Of course, they proved themselves the greatest of rock bands when they translated that Liverpool-bred sound, wit, and Scouse wisdom in studios rather than on stages.

Heck, Bobby had the opportunity to join the boys as the so-called fifth Beatle when that tour concluded.

"Ringo wanted me to come back to England to work in the studio," Bobby said without a dose of regret.

"I recommended that they hire Billy Preston."

Of course, a lot of people were given the "fifth Beatle" title, but none were actually members of that tightest of brotherhoods.

Billy Preston, whose best personal song was the hit "Nothing from Nothing" (unless you prefer "Will It Go Round in Circles"), did participate in the ill-fated *Get Back/Let It Be* sessions, during which the group was falling apart. If you ever see the joyful—and it really is—farewell concert by The Beatles on the roof at Apple Records, you'll see Billy pounding away on the keys. His presence with the band is further chronicled in filmmaker Peter Jackson's sprawling "Get Back" documentary miniseries.

During my only interview with Preston a few decades ago, I found him a gentle soul. He proved to have his personal demons, but he had built his pre-Beatles career by backing Little Richard, Sam Cooke, Ray Charles, and the Everlys. He also cowrote "You Are So Beautiful," a huge hit for Joe Cocker.

And he played on tours with The Rolling Stones and Eric Clapton and worked with George Harrison on his post-Fab stuff.

Enough about Billy Preston. I just always admired his work and am impressed as I write this that he was really The Beatles' second choice, behind Bobby Hebb, to carry the weight on keyboards.

Bobby reached tremendous heights in the years after he left Nashville to chase his musical muse across the continents.

But he wasn't shy about pointing out where it all started: his mother and father, blind musicians, trained all of their children to pursue musical and spiritual greatness together in family gospel groups.

"They were always my inspirations," Bobby said of his youth spent singing, spooning and dancing on the streets of Nashville with the rest of the Hebb family.

There actually were two Hebb family outfits working out of the Edgehill neighborhood, just off 12th Avenue South in South Nashville.

The four girls sang with their mother, with their focus gospel music performed at churches.

The male outfit was fit for the clubs of Jefferson Street.

"Daddy had a washboard band," Bobby continued. "Hebb's Kitchen Cabinet Orchestra."

"Daddy played the guitar. Harold played the washboard. Melvoid played the lard-can bass. I did the tap dancing and played the spoons."

Of course, it wasn't just "Sunny" that kept Bobby an international star.

Early on, Hebb sang backup on Bo Diddley's "Diddley Daddy" and played what he called "West Coast–style trumpet" in a U.S. Navy jazz band. He also replaced Mickey Baker in the R&B duo "Mickey and Sylvia (Vanderpool)" after the "Love Is Strange" duo split.

"Sunny," by the way, was named by BMI as number 25 on the list of the top 100 songs of the twentieth century.

Bobby released a disco-style version of his signature, "Sunny '76," in 1976.

In addition to his own hits, like "A Satisfied Mind" in 1966 and "Love Me" in 1967, Bobby wrote a lot of songs, including a cowrite with Sandy Baron of Lou Rawls's "A Natural Man."

He even did a 1972 remake of Acuff's "Night Train to Memphis" that was a minor regional hit in New York City, according to various biographical material.

After Bobby moved back to Nashville, he joined his siblings to recreate those gospel sounds. By the way, he remained a big draw out East (he had lived in New York City and in Rockport, Massachusetts, for decades before moving home).

Bobby showed me promo materials of performances in Europe and Asia.

On my first visit to his house, there were plenty of unopened boxes in the newly constructed home. He'd only just moved home and hadn't had time to unpack them yet. Some stuff still needed to be shipped from Rockport (a fishing village at the tip of Cape Ann, 40 miles northeast of Boston).

"What I like about this house is that it's not too big. Everything I need is here. That's not to say it's got everything I want, just everything I need.

"I didn't need much yard. I have someone cut it for me, anyway. But I also didn't need to have a really big house. I needed to have room for my things but not so much room that I needed to spend a lot of time cleaning it. I needed to spend my time on the music."

When the 5-foot-6, 130-pound man of style and grace wanted to find transportation after moving back home, he went out onto the Clarksville Highway, the main thoroughfare through black Nashville, and bought a 1991 black Mercedes.

In case you think this is a guy with just one song, well, he had a satchel filled with songs he'd written. And he also enjoyed singing songs by others, whether they were friends or just great writers and musicians. He had a particular fondness for Bob Dylan and Hank Williams songs.

"I recorded 'Cold Cold Heart' for the new record," he says, pointing out his admiration for Hank's work.

"I don't know Bob Dylan personally. I do know Pete Seeger. And Leadbelly [Woody Guthrie's folk-singing black associate of "Goodnight Irene" fame] was a cousin of mine. Used to be at all the Hebb family reunions."

When I wrote my first piece about Bobby, a former *Tennessean* editor who had moved away called me to say there is no way Bobby Hebb and Leadbelly were related. I told that editor that Bobby had no reason to lie. I was simply reporting a great man's version of his life.

Without warning, Bobby leaned back in his chair and mixed his own soft, sweet voice with Dylanesque rhythm and vocal attitude:

> Well, it ain't no use to sit and wonder why, Babe . . .
> When your rooster crows at the break of dawn
> Look out your window and I'll be gone

He laughed at himself, although I was uncommonly stirred by his rendition of that entire song.

"That's my favorite Bob Dylan song," he said of "Don't Think Twice, It's All Right."

Perhaps Dylan's tale of reckless rambling and lost love struck a chord with him because it jibes with parts of his own past, which included two divorces and a definite rootlessness.

But, for Bobby, well, the times were a-changin' once he moved back home.

At the time of my first visit to his home, he was in close contact with his daughter, Kitoto, 27, an aspiring actress and bus driver who lived in Massachusetts. "I love you, too," he said at the end of a phone conversation during which she was calling to check on her pop's health while I stirred the brown sugar into my coffee.

"My main thing now is to work with my family, get the Hebb family singing gospel together," he told me. "I want to teach it to all my nieces and nephews. I want them to carry on the family tradition."

He looked over to the piano, where the sheet music for "Will the Circle Be Unbroken" shared space with a couple of other gospel songs the family is working on.

"I loved my childhood. It was rough, but what's not rough? Life's not a piece of cake."

We had a few more visits and conversations before he died of lung cancer on August 3, 2010.

But I'll never forget that first visit to his house after Johnny Bragg died.

Bobby and I sat there, me drinking the brown-sugared coffee, him sipping his tea, reflecting on his past and sharing the occasional piece of Eastern mysticism or benevolence.

He played his new album, one that I don't think ever was released by the time he died. He gave me a copy, and I love it.

As the long and happy day drew toward a close and it was time for me to roll my car back over that curb at the end of the driveway, Bobby stopped me.

He leaned over and grabbed a guitar—I don't know which brand or model—and began noodling a bit with that instrument.

He then sat on a stool next to his piano, and the guitar noodling ended up leading into the song that will live forever:

> Oh, the dark days are done and the bright days are here,
> My Sunny one shines so sincere.
> Oh, Sunny one so true, I love you.

Uncle Josh Graves

I SPENT A LOT OF TIME IN Uncle Josh Graves's living room in Madison, Tennessee, kind of just because I could and also because I knew I'd always be welcomed by a big smile and hug. And black coffee and a bowl of beans may be involved.

The coffee was ready on arrival, and Evelyn, Josh's gracious wife, always would offer a bowl of beans from the pot that seemed to be constantly cooking on the stove near the back door.

As for the front door, well, most of the time, it was pulled open, letting in the sun, friends, and the occasional depressed journalist looking for joy. The storm door was always unlocked. Screened in the summer, it was easy to holler in to let Uncle Josh know who it was.

I probably was one of the few who came without a Dobro, mandolin, guitar, or other musical instrument. On my first three visits or so, I toted a reporter's notebook and a couple of pens (in case one ran out during the interview). After that, I'd come unarmed, no agenda other than the search for and dispensation of love.

He was a helluva guy. I had spoken with him on the phone a time or two over the years, but I never was lucky enough to be around him before his legs got cut off.

Without those legs, of course, it was hard for Josh to answer the door, and Evelyn, as noted, was always busy either in the kitchen or preparing things for her husband.

The kind woman had the patience and unfettered love required if a person is to spend a life as a road dog musician's wife. So much of their married life had him out on the road, mainly with Lester and Earl, then with just Lester, then with Earl, then Jerry Garcia and his pals, and then

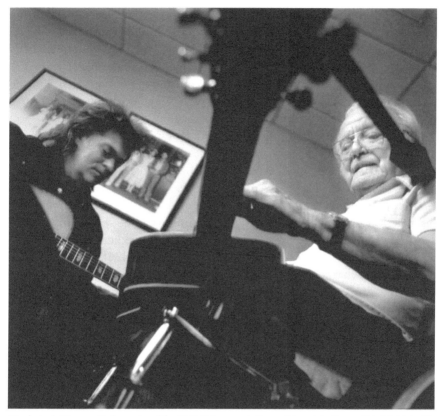

Uncle Josh Graves, Dobro wizard for Flatt & Scruggs's Foggy Mountain Boys, didn't let late-life double-leg amputations stop him. One of his collaborators and friends was Marty Stuart. © BILL STEBER PHOTOGRAPHY

with fiddler Kenny Baker. Even as life, bad habits, and poor circulation turned him legless, it was difficult to keep him off the road.

"It's just from all of those years of smoking and drinking. I smoked hard for 60 years," he answered a question I had not asked about how he lost his legs. He didn't quit smoking until he stared at himself in the bathroom mirror after his first amputation. He didn't like what he saw. The pack of cigarettes in his pajamas pocket went into the trash. It is hard to kick a 60-year habit (I had difficulty with my own 35-year turn), but Josh did it. You can't say he didn't look back because we all do.

The drinking by then was limited to an occasional beer—as long as it wasn't one of those watered-down "light" beers the amateurs seem to prefer. And perhaps he'd enjoy a glass of wine with his dinner.

Sure, he was legless, but he bragged, joyfully, that one of his great accomplishments, given his former lifestyle, was that he didn't have diabetes. With great melancholy, he rattled off the names of several of his friends, mostly poets and pickers, who suffered and died from the disease.

His eyes grew darkest and his voice thickest when he remembered his good and thoughtful friend Waylon Jennings, who died on February 13, 2002, about a year and a half before I started hanging out with Josh. I never had the fortune of spending much time with Waylon, although I had met him a few times, and I did wreck my car once in front of his house.

"Last time I saw Waylon, I didn't think he looked too good," Josh said.

He bit his lip, but he was sad to see his old friend's condition. "I didn't say that to him, but I guess it was the diabetes. That's what killed him, I guess."

Before I go on, I ought to mention that even though his legs were gone, his affection for women and his sense of humor had not been amputated.

One summer Saturday evening, he and I were together at a house party in Murfreesboro, about 45 minutes southeast of Nashville. Most of you likely know what a house party is, but these events—also called "house concerts"—are events that occur when home owners bring musicians into their homes for parties.

Party attendees generally bring a covered dish or a 12-pack or jug and put $20 in the kitty to pay the musicians. It's common in the Nashville area, with its concentration of musicians, but I have a friend in Chicago who bought a duplex just so that one-half of the house could be dedicated to house concerts and the musicians could use the attached bedrooms.

The Murfreesboro concert—which I attended as part of my research for a *Tennessean* story on August 24, 2003—was in one of those faux ante-bellum McMansions (if I recall correctly). It had drawn huge numbers of music enthusiasts, eager to hear the Dobro legend and acoustic music icon.

It was informal, with Josh playing a set on the Dobro, then taking occasional breaks. His musical sons joined him in making the glorious noise.

During one break, Josh had been given a bottle of light beer. He sipped it and then shook his head and asked for a real Budweiser, like the ones he'd seen other people enjoying.

Someone brought him an empty glass, then opened up a bottle of Bud and poured it, springing a smile on Josh's face

A woman squeezed past Josh as he sat in his wheelchair by the kitchen island, where his Bud was waiting, while we spoke.

She accidentally brushed her rear end against both of us. I didn't even think about it, as it was a crowded room.

Josh, however, lit up and called after the young and taut woman.

"You know what a legless man can do?" Uncle Josh asked her.

The woman, who sold real estate for a living, just giggled as she turned around and looked at the old man in the wheelchair.

"Nothin'," said Josh, laughing at himself.

"He's cute," or something like that, she said to me, and the Dobro man and I watched as she vanished into the crowd.

Josh told me that in his past life, even when he let his hair grow when he and Earl played with the Grateful Dead, women always looked at him that same way. Of course, he could do something about it back then if he had wanted to. He was content going home to Evelyn.

On another warm day, after my visits had become more frequent, he'd simply holler "C'mon in, Tim." Others who got the "C'mon in," no questions asked, were musical luminaries like Cash, Kris, Vassar Clements, Earl, Lester, Marty Stuart, or Kenny Baker, who always seemed to scowl while also always seeming joyous.

Hell, who knows, Jerry Garcia—one of his admirers from his Dobro playing out at the Fillmore West back when Josh's hair hung over his collar—may have come to this door. I know that Josh acolyte Jerry Douglas frequented the house.

I know a lot of folks who had or wanted to make their marks in acoustic music were smart enough to visit this comfortable ranch house occupied by the now legless man and his wife.

If you were lucky enough, Marty Stuart (mentioned already) might be here, stretching out on the couch.

"I always know where there's a pot of beans and some straight talk," Marty told me once, explaining his own "drop-in" tactics, which I sort of emulated. "He and Evelyn have raised more musicians than anyone in town.

"There's always a couch to sleep on. There's always a new song. He's always got a gangster tale, war stories, and a pot of beans."

Marty had fallen under the spell of Uncle Josh long before, back when the younger man was an acoustic music prodigy. And, despite his run of solo success, Marty dedicated much of his life to documenting (with his camera) and preserving (with his heart) the greats of acoustic music.

Madison, where Josh and Evelyn lived, is part of Metro Nashville. At the northern end of the county—you have to leapfrog the hipster-congested East Nashville and its musical geniuses and shiftless wannabe hippies—Madison had long been a home for country musicians.

I suppose it made it easier for them to get together and jam into the night or borrow guitar strings. Until Eddy Arnold pretty much "bought" Brentwood, a suburb south of Nashville, hillbillies weren't wanted in many sections of Nashville.

Country stars who for at least a while lived in Madison included Earl Scruggs, the Everly Brothers, Charlie Louvin, Floyd Cramer, Bashful Brother Oswald, Hank Snow, Jim Reeves, Charlie Rich, John Hartford, and Maybelle Carter.

Many of them spend eternity in Madison as well at Spring Hill Cemetery, the burial spot of choice for a lot of celebrities and other dead people. Jimmy Martin's massive monument—he made sure it suited him before time ultimately decided he needed to lie beneath it—is near the front entrance to the cemetery. Roy Acuff is there, too, as is George Morgan, a great voice that is all but forgotten. Bill Monroe, who chose to be buried in his hometown of Rosine, Kentucky, had his own monument constructed here, apparently just so he'd have a backup plan and nearby spots for his family to rest.

Others in that ground—the cemetery is actually across Gallatin Road from the massive Nashville National Cemetery, with its geometric rows of white headstones and heroes—include my good friend Bobby "Sunny" Hebb, Earl and the wonderful Louise Scruggs, Hank Snow, Keith Whitley, and Kitty Wells.

Another great pal of mine, Mac Wiseman, also a compadre of Uncle Josh's, is about halfway up the outside wall of the mausoleum.

If I'm at the Spring Hill Cemetery, which I visit when I'm in Madison, my favorite spot at the cemetery is the little gazebo near the back that John Hartford had constructed as his monument. The musical riverboat captain and composer of great songs like "Gentle on My Mind" wanted his pilgrims to have a place to sit, out of the sun and the rain, and write songs.

When all of them were alive, I think Kitty Wells, the undisputed Queen of Country Music, and her husband Johnnie Wright, of Johnnie & Jack fame (with his partner Jack Anglin), lived either on the same street as Josh or perhaps just a block or so over.

As background, my friendship with Josh sprung from an assignment I gave myself as entertainment editor at *The Tennessean.* A woman who worked in the composing room was a bluegrass singer on weekends, and she had performed with Josh. She told me I might want to do a story on him to let folks know he was legless but plenty healthy enough to take on more bookings to help pay his massive medical bills caused by the treatments and amputations.

I'd already spoken with Josh years before. My friend, Vassar Clements, a great fiddler and one of the kindest gentlemen I've ever met, had called me one time at the office because he was hosting an Uncle Josh fund-raiser at the World Famous Station Inn, a concrete blockhouse in Nashville's railroad gulch that was frequented by Lester, Earl, Monroe, Jimmy Martin, Josh, Vassar, and all of the acoustic greats when they came off the road.

That April 1, 2000, fund-raiser that Vassar was organizing—with Kathy Chiavola, Kenny Baker, Roni Stoneman, Jerry Douglas, James Monroe, and others—was to help with the costs of Uncle Josh's first amputation.

Josh was going to be in attendance, and he planned to pick up his Dobro. "They didn't operate on my hands," he said with a laugh when I called him to write a story promoting the fund-raiser. "I won't quit."

Back then, the squat, worn Station Inn was basically the only real structure in a desolate part of near downtown Nashville. In the years since, the club has become all but squeezed out by the condos, the gentrification, the $2,000-a-pair boot stores, organic wannabe hippie vegetable markets, and valet-fronted fancy restaurants. But that all came after Uncle Josh died, so no sense going into that here.

J. T. Gray, the longtime owner of the old blockhouse, died in 2021. For decades, he fought off the developers and their skyscraper dreams. He's gone now, a great man who always welcomed me as his guest. I hope the Station Inn remains.

Anyway, the composing room woman, Bonnie Hartle, was so convincing in her story about how kind and great this legless man was that I decided to give him a visit.

As noted earlier, after that first visit, I kept coming back, sometimes slipping out of the office of the newspaper to go "look for a story," perhaps taking me through East Nashville on Gallatin Road or perhaps out Ellington Parkway.

I did find some good stories out that way, stuff about aspiring musicians, barbers, barbecue, murders, drug raids, celebrity graves, and pawnshops.

Often, at the end of the journey, I ended up at the top of the handicapped ramp and knocking on the storm door so I could drop in and spend time with Uncle Josh.

A lot of folks found their way here. They had come to "worship" at the wheelchair where the man with no legs spent his days, sometimes wheeled up to the special table customized to aid in his music.

These pilgrims might want to pick, or they might want to talk music or ask advice.

I'm no musician. Oh, I played clarinet for 12 years or so. I still have that instrument 60 years after it was bought by my parents. It taught me how to read music and about scales and octaves. In twelfth grade, the high school band instructor one day shouted out, in front of the other 100 students in the high school symphony, that I needed to buy a better clarinet.

My folks had bought me the best they could afford, and that was good enough for me.

After the band director's attempt at embarrassing me, I quietly leaned over, picked up the case of my instrument, put it on my lap, and slowly pulled apart the clarinet, putting each piece in its spot. Then with a simple harsh expletive directed at him, I walked to the door of the practice hall and never went back. I repeated the directive to him as I shut the door (and perhaps later at graduation).

But while my playing ceased, my love for music never did. So it was a real honor to consider someone like Uncle Josh Graves a friend who looked forward to my visits.

I might add here that before Josh and Evelyn moved into this comfortable home to raise their family, they were among a settlement of Foggy Mountain Boys in a nearby trailer park.

"We all knew when they come home from the road," Evelyn told me when she recalled those days when Earl, Lester, and the rest lived in that Dickerson Road trailer park. "They were such good friends, all of them, back in those days. They came in, and they wanted to play more."

Bluegrass music, with Lester on guitar, Earl on banjo, and Josh on Dobro, used the three-finger-roll style his friend Scruggs "invented" for the banjo. The rest of the Foggys and their trailer park friends played on into the Madison night.

I never asked Mac Wiseman about it, but that gentleman, among the best flattop guitarists in the world and a charter Foggy alum (he was in the group at the start before changing course), may have dropped in as well.

After Uncle Josh died on September 30, 2006, my good friend Peter Cooper, a musician and historian, described Josh's "picking style" to perfection in his obituary for *The Tennessean*. (I was still at that paper, then, by the way, but I'd been "promoted" from entertainment editor to night cops, a move designed to make me quit. I didn't quit, but I did have to make adjustments. For example, I went to the funeral home in the morning rather than to Josh's mid-afternoon service because I had been scheduled to spend the late shift with the Metro Police Vice Squad chasing drug dealers in North Nashville.)

In our few short years as friends, I saw Josh play a lot, sometimes just for me, sometimes with others. No one ever has described his playing style better than Peter did: "Three fingers on Mr. Graves's right hand struck his Dobro strings in a rolling manner that allowed him great speed, and the silver bar that he held in his left hand produced remarkable resonance and tuneful melodies. One of only a few professional Dobro players in the 1950s when he joined Lester Flatt and Earl Scruggs's Foggy Mountain Boys, he exhibited dynamic musicianship and stage presence that reached audiences who watched Flatt and Scruggs's TV show and came to concerts."

In addition to his playing, Josh—as you can tell if you ever see the old videos of him with Lester and Earl—wore a misshapen hat and played the crowd for laughs. There was a bit of vaudeville in those old touring country concert packages.

Marty Stuart, who with Uncle Josh joined Flatt's Nashville Grass after the 1969 breakup of Flatt and Scruggs, said that the Graveses' house on Chadwell Avenue "was a 24-hour-a-day playhouse for grandchildren and stray musicians. . . . You could find an open door and an open mind there in Josh."

Marty once told me his devotion to Uncle Josh went way back to his own childhood in Philadelphia, Mississippi.

"I love him," said Stuart not long after he set it up for Josh to be the star when he invited the Dobro wizard to be rolled onto the stage at the Ryman Auditorium, where the younger man was headlining a bluegrass show.

"That really ended up being me joining Uncle Josh," Marty told me with a proud wink.

Marty added that as a kid, he'd watch Flatt and Scruggs on TV, attempting to copy Josh's notes and wearing a hat like Josh's.

Uncle Josh Graves performs as a guest of Marty Stuart in 2003 during the Bluegrass Nights at the Ryman concert series at the historic auditorium in downtown Nashville. © BILL STEBER PHOTOGRAPHY

"There has never been a time in my life when there hasn't been an Uncle Josh," he told me back at the time when I was doing that profile of the Dobro hero.

Kris Kristofferson, the great songwriter who changed the vocabulary of country music with his more graphic descriptions of life, was among Josh's greatest devotees, going back to the early 1970s at a time when Kristofferson was breaking out of Nashville and en route to the life of a movie star of sorts.

"Josh Graves is one of the finest musicians it's been my good fortune to work with," Kris told me. "The music from his Dobro is as clean and pure as a mountain stream.

"He's also one of the nicest guys you'll ever meet. I was so knocked out by his performance on 'Jesus Was a Capricorn,' I had to call out his name during the instrumental break: 'Get back, Josh!'"

If you listen to that song about the savior with the funky bunch of friends, you'll hear that Kristofferson exclamation.

His name actually was Burkett Howard Graves, but from Cash to Kristofferson to Scruggs, they all called him "Uncle Josh."

On my first or second visit during the summer of 2003, this gentle soul with the road-calloused edge looked up from his chair, the focal point of a room filled with awards and the bronze bust of his head, and told me he wanted to play something.

With precision, the "driving gloves," used to protect his resonator-stroking hands while pushing himself around in his wheelchair, came off. He tossed them on an end table.

He planted both hands on the stump where his left leg had been.

"A year ago in April, this one come off," he said, rounding a palm over that stump. The right leg, he said, had come off a year or so before that.

Even so, Uncle Josh, ever the showman, sat there in his dress clothes, his black trousers trimmed and stitched to accommodate his condition.

"After the first one came off, I got an artificial leg. I was getting to where I could use the artificial leg with the help of a walker."

When the second leg came off, he nixed suggestions to use two artificial legs. He's satisfied with a wheelchair and what he refers to as his "stumps."

He looked over at Evelyn and said he really didn't travel much, preferring to sit in the living room where the couple raised their four children. Even as I sat there, many of the 18 grandchildren dashed in and out, allowing July steam into the cool, air-conditioned house—but also raising massive smiles on this truly gentle man's face.

When he does get out, "I just use my table, put my guitar on it, and I play."

That table was why he was able to play at all after the double amputations. When a guy has legs, the Dobro generally is played while the musician stands, resonator held horizontally and propped against the upper thighs.

After the amputations, Josh, of course, no longer could stand. He tried to play sitting down, but "it hurt to play on the stumps."

Not content to live in a world without the sound of Uncle Josh Graves, bluegrass player Eddie Adcock brought a customized table out to the home in Madison. Josh could roll his wheelchair beneath the guitar on the table and play it at the same angle he did before he was legless.

"If you don't mind, I'm going to wear these," he said, pulling a pair of sunglasses from his breast pocket. "The glare bothers my eye. Got an eye infection. Got a little glaucoma, too."

Suddenly, he talked about his days with the Earl Scruggs Revue and the reputation as an acoustic magician (and musician) who earned the awe of Jerry Garcia and the Grateful Dead, who were at their very core an acoustic group.

He told me about a job he had in San Francisco at the height of the Haight-Asbury and Filmore West days.

"I was playing, and one of the guys says, 'Hey, man, let's go make a joint.'" Josh did his best Cheech and Chong imitation of a stoned hippie.

"I say, 'No, No. We're playing now. We can go to all the joints you want to for a drink when we're done.'

"He says, 'No, man, I mean weed, man.' I had no idea what that was. Never heard of marijuana.

"I hate for you to tell that story, hate for people to think I was ever that stupid."

Much of what I learned from Josh ended up in the newspaper. Other things I learned from him, though, were about grace and class.

He didn't sit in his front room, near the bronze bust of himself, and lament the past and his amputations.

Oh sure, he'd have loved to have legs.

But he also loved to tell stories of the days when he did have them, when he was with Mac or with Lester and Earl, Esco Hankins, the Pierce Brothers, Wilma Lee and Stoney Cooper, or Jesse McReynolds.

When he met Elvis backstage at the Opry, the soon-to-be-coronated king of rock 'n' roll "just jerked right through security and grabbed me and Lester. He told us we was his mother's favorites for the gospel stuff we did. Nice fella."

He also talked about feuds and friendships with people who taught him things, folks like Monroe, John Lee Hooker, and Mother Maybelle.

He cried when talking about the passing of his friend, Maybelle's daughter, June Carter Cash, just that spring.

Some of those tears likely were for her widower. Johnny Cash at that time was on a more or less deathbed recording mission. Since June's death, he had been recording as much as humanly possible out in his Cash Cabin studio by his rustic spaceship of a house in Hendersonville.

Josh, who sat in the back and "bawled" at June's funeral, was intrigued by what the Man in Black was up to and was waiting for John to call and ask him to join in on the mortal music binge that proved to be some of Cash's best stuff.

"You know, Tim, whenever you come into my house, I think of John and Kris. You've got that presence, that aura they have. It's rare," Uncle Josh told me on several occasions. It, of course, was a great compliment that I wasn't sure I deserved.

I once told Kris that, and he laughed, though he didn't disagree. After all, "if Uncle Josh said it, it was true."

Often, Josh would talk about growing up in East Tennessee and how he'd done so much more than he ever dreamed when he began playing near the Bald River in his hometown of Tellico Plains.

Josh pushed his wheelchair near that table and positioned himself and his Dobro.

Suddenly, as I had anticipated, the old man coaxed a sound as free and sparkling as that of Bald River.

He escalated into "Foggy Mountain Breakdown" before stopping and looking over at me.

"I owe a lot to this old guitar," said Uncle Josh Graves.

Get back, Josh.

Frank Howard

F RANK HOWARD HAS THREE PAGES of his autobiography finished. He's been working on it for 10 years.

"Oooo, I'm telling you, Tim, this is some risqué stuff. I was wild back then. Never did drugs, but I loved my Seagram's gin and orange juice [a 50-50 split in a big jug]. And the women."

Sometimes, he adds, he'd switch up to Tanqueray.

I don't know if Frank ever will get the autobiography written.

Realizing that three written pages does not an autobiography make, Frank's latest scheme has him sitting down in his house packed with his memories of R&B music stardom, where he's dictating and recording his recollections. Of course, it still needs to be transcribed and edited.

"You should hear some of this stuff. I'm not pulling any punches," he said. "I recorded an hour and 20 minutes' worth the other day."

He said he's "not proud" of much of the life he lived when he was a slim, young R&B star and lead singer for influential Nashville a cappella group "Frank Howard & the Commanders."

Two school chums, Herschel Carter and the late Charlie Fite, joined him on stages throughout the South as part of touring packages that spread the other Nashville Sound—soul music—from the R&B mecca that was Jefferson Street to the white joints, like Pee Wee's Supper Club in the Midtown section of the city and then out across the region.

"We had a lot of fun," said Frank, who, when his music days ended, began a career in banking. Much of that banking career (he's a vice president) has been spent as a repo man. He has done it the old-fashioned way, going out in the dead of night to repossess a vehicle.

"I didn't go out there with an attitude," he told me in one of our conversations leading up to a story in the February 2, 2018, editions of the *Nashville Ledger*.

This gentle soul—for he is that despite his rowdy peacock personality on the stage a few decades ago—tries still to be respectful of the folks whose cars, houses, furniture, and so on he's taking back because they hadn't kept up their payments. "If someone came out and told me to get off their property, I didn't argue about it. I just told them, 'We can do this now, or I can come back with a warrant.'

"I'd be going out on all of these narrow roads in parts of Tennessee where they'd never seen a black man before," he pointed out. In addition to all the paperwork explaining the repos, he also carried with him a trunk filled with compassion that he distributed by helping people figure out how they could keep their stuff.

If people were attempting to catch up on their payments, he said he'd give them plenty of breathing room. "The bank doesn't make money from repossessing," said this man, who possesses uncommon understanding of the foibles of the human condition.

That's why whenever I visit him in his office, he's on the telephone, trying to explain to people what they need to do to keep their property.

"I've been really busy with that during this pandemic," he said in early 2021 as the deadly virus continued its hold on the nation. Most of the COVID months were spent alone at his home, where he worked the phones for the bank.

It was exhausting. "People got enough trouble, losing their jobs, dealing with COVID," he said. "We [the bank] try to help them keep their cars and their houses so when this thing's over, they can start over."

Frank insists he never had any confrontations with the folks he terms "my clients" during the repo man days that got him into the door of the banking world all those years ago.

I've known Frank since 2003. At that point, he was taking a break from his banking career to run a used-car lot in Franklin, Tennessee, about 25 miles from Nashville. These were real clunkers, rejects from a large car agency.

I'd actually learned about him from my friend, Michael Gray, who is an editor or something like that at the Country Music Hall of Fame and Museum.

Long ago, I hired Michael for his first full-time job as a music journalist for the entertainment staff at the old *Nashville Banner*.

A great young man (then), Michael was a joy to be around, especially when it came to educating me on the underappreciated history of the R&B scene that grew mostly on Jefferson Street and flourished for decades.

That wide boulevard was the main thoroughfare through the black section of Nashville. The past tense there is because that neighborhood is falling victim, block by block, to gentrification and the lamented invasion of what they call "tall skinnies," the soulless but very nice homes for mostly white people that are being cloned all over Nashville, devouring the historically black neighborhoods of one-story, middle-class homes, triggering a mournful diaspora.

Many of the black families had been renting, so they were driven out when landlords sold the land to developers when Music City became the "It City." Others who owned their homes were tempted by the big checks developers were handing out, and they moved elsewhere, depositing their fat checks in banks mostly in the southeastern Metro Nashville town of Antioch or in outlying cities like Lebanon and Ashland City.

A similar "black lives don't matter" mentality destroyed the great Jefferson Street club district, Frank's musical stomping grounds, an area that served as musical headquarters to everyone from Jimi Hendrix to Jimmy Church.

As previously mentioned, when Interstate 40 was constructed, the path of the highway that goes from coast to coast went right through the black section of town, separating neighbors and cutting neighborhoods in two.

As noted in earlier chapters, it also killed the club district, extinguishing the neon lights and music roaring from each door for several blocks.

Some of the clubs, the most famous perhaps the old Del Morocco, where Jimi Hendrix and his army buddy Billy Cox were part of the house band, were bulldozed. It is said that when Joe Louis and Jackie Robinson were in town, this was their favorite haunt.

The beauty school next to that club, a fine professional school for those who wanted to take care of hair and the like for the women of the area, also went down. Jimi and Billy had lived in an apartment above that school. Reportedly, they only had one light—a bare bulb hanging on a cord—along with guitars and dreams.

The area has never recovered. And most of the people who worked those clubs died or took on "real" jobs.

The spirit of Jefferson Street, the black version of a Las Vegas strip of clubs and restaurants, died.

And so much of that music was forgotten.

Michael and a friend of his, Dan Cooper, then also a Hall of Fame worker, began exploring how they could right that wrong, and, with the full support of the great monument to mostly white hillbilly music, they mounted a *Night Train to Nashville: Music City Rhythm & Blues, 1945–1970* exhibit at the Country Music Hall of Fame and Museum.

Michael, whom I love despite his music dork persona, had a second job working weekends at Phone-o-Luxe, a used music store in the middle of what now has become known, not disparagingly, as "Little Mexico" in Nashville.

If I had CDs I no longer wanted, I would go visit Michael on Saturdays, cashing in the used discs or, occasionally, swapping them for stuff I might listen to.

One day, Michael, who had told me of his ongoing research for the museum show, pulled out a picture of a happy fellow singing into a microphone, sidekicks by his side.

"You really need to meet this guy," he said. "It's Frank Howard. And he's rounding up a lot of things for the museum exhibit."

On that slow, cold day in Music City, Michael pulled out a batch of some of the photos and other paraphernalia Frank had rounded up from his days on the Chitlin' Circuit.

Two days later, I was in Frank's basement watching videos of the music produced by Frank Howard & the Commanders as they appeared on TV R&B variety shows: *Night Train* in Nashville and *The Beat!!!!* in Dallas. The shows were similar, featuring the same acts, like the serious-minded guitar player Hendrix and the Commanders finishing up their performances with flying splits. No more flying splits, though, vowed age-thickened businessman and gospel singer Frank.

My first visit included a guided tour of the basement. "I never throw anything out," said Frank, a quote I included in a story that appeared on March 21, 2004, in *The Tennessean.*

Frank picked up items and explained them along the way, each item triggering memories of Nashville R&B faces and places.

He summarized each picture. Here's the Del. Here's the Club Baron, where Jimi Hendrix engaged in a guitar duel (and supposedly lost) to my late friend Johnny Jones and which has been turned into an Elks Lodge.

He talked about the Stealaway, a favorite haunt for Frank, Herschel, and Charlie. The New Era, over on Charlotte, is gone, too.

The Bijou Theater was Nashville's equivalent of Harlem's Apollo. Bessie Smith sang there. Trumpet virtuoso Doc Cheatham played in the pit. It vanished when Municipal Auditorium was built.

"Urban renewal," Frank said, as sourly as this gentle soul allows his voice to get.

All the while, during our hours in his basement, tapes of the old R&B shows played on the television. Frank stopped and laughed when his old friend and backing guitarist, Hendrix, swung his instrument erotically.

"I asked that they [TV producers] not let him do that behind us," he said. "People would be watching him and not us. Distracting."

Frank and the fellas not only lit up the Club Stealaway, the Del Morocco, and other Jefferson Street hot spots and dance clubs but also, often in package shows with their comrades, filled up barrooms, showrooms, and saloons, the Chitlin' Circuit, all over the South "back in the day" (as Frank says).

That Country Music Hall of Fame exhibit mentioned earlier included Grammy-winning CDs; archival compilations of the music of Jefferson Street that included "Just Like Him," a chart hit for Frank, Charlie, and Herschel; as well as music from Bobby "Sunny" Hebb (who also became my beloved friend), Johnny Jones, Earl Gaines, Roscoe Shelton, the Jimmy Church Band, Marion James, and so many more. Many of those folks appear elsewhere in this book.

The massive exhibit—Frank's image was the model for the logo, and a performance shot of him appeared on the first of the two volumes of CDs lovingly curated by Michael Gray and Daniel Cooper—revitalized interest in Nashville's R&B scene.

It also lured from the shadows the performers, many of whom had parked their soulful music a quarter century before for "straight jobs" at car lots, barbershops, liquor stores, and banks.

They reunited for a few shows to revitalize their music or at least make sure it got its due spot in Nashville's history.

Always there during that revival at the Hall of Fame or for affiliated promotional concerts, Frank Howard & the Commanders displayed their chops.

Heck, Herschel, as thin and lanky as ever, could even do the flying splits, like the group used to do in unison in the old days. Charlie also was in fine form.

Charlie died a few years ago, ending the Commanders' rebirth.

"It was like losing my brother. Me and Charlie were best friends all our lives," Frank said.

Frank went on to join the Valentines, another historic Nashville outfit, but when the pandemic came, "we lost a year, like everyone else."

Where he hasn't stopped using his rich baritone is as part of the gospel choir male chorus at Patterson Memorial United Methodist Church in Flat Rock, another of Nashville's historic, now gentrifying neighborhoods. I took my late father, Em J. Ghianni, with me to a couple of services there, and those two became mutual admirers. Frank, who offered up his gospel group for my dad's Downtown Kiwanis Spiritual Aims luncheon, was one of the first to call me and offer counsel, dashed with the Lord, after my father died.

"Dad wouldn't want you to be sad for a long time," he said. "He'd want you to miss him but to have fun, get on with your life."

Frank will tell you, with some levels of joy, about his past life, that of one-night stands, both in segregated barrooms and in bedrooms.

Yet, 40 years after his Seagram's-guzzling nights and offstage conquests, you'll instead find him on Sundays, sipping from a communion cup while kneeling near the altar. Perhaps, as his daddy told him, he did run with the devil. Now, he's putting Beelzebub in his place.

"The R&B music is bar music," says the Baptist by birth, who strayed during the hip-swiveling and pelvis-thrusting days of synchronized dancing and harmonizing with his old band, the Commanders. "What I'm singing now is about salvation."

The star tenor lifts his voice to the church rafters and to the Lord as he and the Men United choir sing, "I'm just waitin' on Jesus. I'm just waitin' on Jesus."

"Yes!" "Say that!" and "Amen!" respond members of the congregation.

I think back to our first meeting back in 2003. He finished his guided tour of his basement and sat down at an electric keyboard that he struck into action.

He cocked his head back and launched his rich voice toward the basement ceiling and beyond.

"Let him in your life. Today. Today. So you had times and troubles, and you tried to make it on your own," he sings, a song that I'd later hear him sing with brothers Bruce and Jerry in their Howard Brothers gospel group, as I reported in the story for *The Tennessean*.

Tears streamed down his face at song's end. "When you been out there as long as I been out there, I know that God has blessed me so much. I didn't get on drugs. I used to make Seagram's work overtime in my day.

"But now I know I'm blessed."

Scotty Moore

T HE LAST MAN STANDING who was in the room on July 5, 1954, when rock 'n' roll was birthed in a steamy Memphis studio, became a great friend, a guy I'd call when I needed to talk about life and music. It was a pleasure and a privilege, as this man's guitar playing was highlighted on the 45-rpm records that hooked me on rock 'n' roll in early elementary school.

"There were four of us that day that for some reason were brought together," Scotty Moore said, looking across his living room, its wall filled with guitars, during one of the visits I made to his home.

"Me, Bill, Sam, and Elvis," Scotty said.

Sam, of course, was wild-eyed Sun Records producer Sam Phillips.

Bill was bassist Bill Black, who was killed by a brain tumor on October 21, 1965. I'm fortunate that I have a Bill Black Combo 45 in my record collection. That was post-Elvis.

Everyone knows Elvis and his story. Dying on August 16, 1977, was his earthly ending, but the music and magic continue. I was lucky enough to see him in concert back in the summer of 1973 at Nashville's Municipal Auditorium. I saw Sinatra once, too, at the Grand Ole Opry House. Those last two details prove nothing except that I'm old.

Of course, all of the guys who were in that room on Union Street in Memphis are dead now.

The subject of this story, Scotty Moore, died on June 28, 2016.

Sam died on June 30, 2003.

Sinatra died on May 14, 1998, but he has nothing to do with this story other than that he was, even as an old man, the definition of cool, the stuff that made him the pre-Elvis teenage idol.

Here is a footnote to the "That's All Right" story of that steamy recording session on Union Street. Drummer D. J. Fontana, who joined Elvis, Scotty, and Bill in the Blue Moon Boys, died on June 13, 2018. D.J. became a band member at a pretty important time: his first playing is heard on the RCA session that produced "Heartbreak Hotel" on January 25, 1956. Many consider "Heartbreak Hotel" the perfect rock-'n'-roll song, the sonic definition of the genre.

But on July 5, 1954, the day in question, Scotty Moore's electric guitar fused hillbilly sensibility with something edgier and further out. When matched with Presley's hiccupping, bluesy voice and with Bill on bass, the sound was captivating enough to herald a cultural shift. Some make the case that what occurred was nothing less than the birth of rock 'n' roll. Chuck Berry and Ike Turner might have disagreed about that being the actual birth of rock 'n' roll, but it was the day that the music was launched into the cosmos.

"I never think much about that," Scotty said when he and I would talk about that first day, that "birth of rock 'n' roll" sonic boom, with Sam and Bill and the skinny kid from the projects.

But when you stop to think about it, what Scotty did, without anyone to mold it for him, was invent the role of rock-'n'-roll lead guitarist.

Keith Richards, the rock historian and scholar and later a drinking partner of Scotty's and a fellow who also occasionally plays guitar with The Rolling Stones, famously said, "When I heard 'Heartbreak Hotel,' I knew what I wanted to do in life. It was as plain as day. All I wanted to do in the world was to be able to play and sound like that. Everyone else wanted to be Elvis. I wanted to be Scotty."

Richards not only became his own version of Scotty (to Mick Jagger's Elvis) but also befriended and recorded with Moore on *All the King's Men*, a 1997 album celebrating Moore's and D.J.'s work for the King of Rock 'n' Roll. Of course, Bill Black would have been included as one of the King's Men had he been alive. The King himself would have been a welcome addition.

On the subject of Richards, it probably ought to be noted that if there is a number 2 most identifiable riff in rock music behind Scotty's, it surely is the "younger" man's intro to "Satisfaction," which Keith formulated in his sleep.

But this chapter isn't all about guitar riffs. It's about Scotty, not only as a musician but also as a human being, a humble man who didn't need much celebration, unlike his old friend, who liked to thrust his pelvis, shoot TVs, and figuratively (as far as I know) lie in bed with Richard Nixon.

Scotty became my friend sort of by accident but also due to my love of old Elvis records and old musicians in general.

It seemed to me, as entertainment editor of *The Tennessean* in Nashville, that Scotty Moore being inducted into the new "sideman" category at the glitzy Rock & Roll Hall of Fame induction ceremonies in New York City was a big deal.

It was a tough sell at a newspaper that didn't really like stories about old musicians who the "new" demographic didn't care about. To the folks buying the paper (or at least it was assumed by the bean counters), the important celebrity news involved the sexual and drunken adventures of Titans players and the second-rate country acts who were selling records.

And I guess they were right. Scotty Moore—who lived on Blueberry Hill, a winding and remote stretch of road in the extreme northern part of Metro Nashville-Davidson County—was a little surprised that anyone was interested.

A gentleman not much into mythic rock-'n'-roll hyperbole, Scotty answered the phone in his longtime home—a modest, almost cave-like residence that seemed a part of the hill it crowned—with a large dose of surprise in his voice.

I told him who I was and that I wanted to congratulate him on the honor and talk about covering him in New York. We later became great friends, one of those kinships I relish as I head into my own final decade or so.

He kind of aw-shucksed-it on that day in 2000, though he admitted he was proud. But he didn't think anyone would really care.

"I'm just an old man out here in the country who used to play guitar," he said, but there was a little chuckle in his voice. And a lot of pride.

Getting to know him later, I would guess he was either eating well-peppered scrambled eggs or holding onto a Gibson when I made that call. Or he may have been watching *Gunsmoke* or *Bonanza* reruns. You'll find a few others in this book who similarly enjoyed TV tales of the Old West, and those two old series topped the lists of, for example, Eddy Arnold and his running mate George Jones.

For most of the years that Scotty and I were friends, right up until he died in the summer of 2016, he always had that endearing chuckle.

"Well, if you're going to come up and see me again, it'd better be soon because I won't be here much longer," he'd say with mock caution, making fun of his age and precarious health while at the same time being appreciative of the regular phone calls I made. It was several years, of course, before he stopped answering those calls or welcoming me into the house on Blueberry Hill.

I probably mentioned elsewhere in this book that Scotty's name was atop a list of old-time musicians I kept in contact with until they died, folks I miss still to this day. Some are in this book, others I will keep in my heart for a while.

There still are a couple on that list that I call, but most of them are dead. Scotty Moore, Uncle Josh Graves, Bobby Thompson, Vassar Clements, Mac Wiseman, Johnny Cash (I'd call his niece, Kelly Hancock), Boots Randolph, Eddy Arnold, Charlie Dick (Patsy Cline's widower), Chet Atkins, Bobby Hebb, Jimmy Otey, D. J. Fontana, Earl and Louise Scruggs, George Hamilton IV, Tom T. and Dixie Hall, Carl Smith, Goldie Hill, Marshall Grant, Harold Bradley—those are just a few of them I'd call.

No need to mention the ones who are still with us, but I try my best to make those calls.

When I was still working at the newspaper, as I waited for my staff to finish churning out copy for me to edit and move to the copy desk, I'd call folks on that list just to chat.

I'd already begun calling some of those folks, especially Chet Atkins, but Scotty's reaction to my first call to him is what made me realize how important these calls could be to me of course, but more so to the folks I called. He triggered me to that realization when he downplayed, seriously, his Rock & Roll Hall of Fame induction. I mean, if Scotty Moore thought no one cared about him, what are these other musical veterans feeling?

I asked Scotty if he was going to New York. He said he thought so. "Yes, he is," yelled Gail Pollock, both joyfully and insistently, the voice who always was on the speakerphone when I called Scotty.

Gail Pollock, who had her own house in Nashville, spent as much of her free time as possible up at Scotty's tending to him.

She'd help with his meals, talk with him, make sure he got to his doctor's appointments, and go on trips with him. They particularly liked to go to New Orleans and Memphis (if I remember correctly) because his guitar playing was such an undying part of the music in those cities. And when I first knew him, as I mention above, he still could play. That ability diminished, then vanished, but he still liked being around music and musicians.

Scotty, who had a hematoma on his brain, couldn't travel alone or really stay by himself. He didn't need to. He slept at night. During the day, beginning mighty early. Gail arrived to make sure he got to where he needed to be. She spent most of her waking hours at Scotty's place, and, in fact, I occasionally called her at her house if I hadn't heard from Scotty in a bit. It was rare to catch her at home, but when she was, she almost always was getting her stuff together or perhaps cooking meals to drive up to Blueberry Hill.

Gail's daughter, Margi Lane, took over the care and feeding of this great man after Gail's death to cancer in November 2015, and she kept it up until Scotty died on June 28, 2016.

During Gail's decline, Scotty spent as much time as possible trying to help her at her bedside. He was a kind and gentle man who loved that woman. I spoke with him then, calling mostly to see how she was doing, and he did his best, sometimes failing, to be upbeat.

Gail was an amazing woman, and while I won't write much about her, you should know that my friendship with Scotty grew along with my friendship with Gail, I think mainly because she appreciated that I really cared for her beloved guitar man.

Back to 2000 and the Hall of Fame announcement. After I was sure that Scotty was going to be in New York, I asked if I could call him every morning—there were other activities ongoing in the Big Apple—to get his reactions to all of the hubbub.

"It's okay with me if it's okay with my keeper," he said, laughing at how dependent he was on Gail. She got on the phone and instructed me, kindly, on what I should do: she gave me the number and said I should call it anytime, and she'd get him on the phone.

I figured those calls were the only way Scotty would get the recognition he deserved. As I noted, the newspaper where I worked wasn't that much interested in old musicians like Scotty Moore (or even the rest of the people in this book), not when there was so much to report about Faith Hill, Tim McGraw, Deana Carter, Kenny Chesney, Sara Evans, Travis Tritt, Wynonna Judd, Sammy Kershaw, and Lorrie Morgan. I imagine you remember some of them.

That was the basic content of the celebrity columnist's daily rundown, and I don't really make fun of it or him here because he was giving the newspaper the stuff that focus groups and high-nosed editors had decided people wanted, and his writing was breezy and fun.

Besides that, Scotty needed to be called early in the morning, and most of my staff didn't come in until 10-ish.

So, every morning during his Hall of Fame trip to Gotham, I'd call the number Gail gave me and get Scotty's Hall of Fame report, which I would write up and give to the celebrity columnist, Brad Schmitt, to insert into his popular column.

I liked Scotty so much that I began calling him regularly after he got home from the induction and celebration, something I did right up until he died 16 years later.

On more than one occasion, I took the hour-long trip up to Blueberry Hill just to visit. And a couple of times, I got stories about him published.

I wrote the last, long feature story on Scotty, a cover story for *The Tennessean*'s Sunday arts and entertainment section.

He called me after it was published to say it was the best story ever written about him.

Since we were friends and I was a huge admirer, I told him maybe we could get together some more and I could write a book or at least a long magazine piece on him.

He just laughed that off. "Nah, Tim. C'mon up anytime you want. But I really don't want to be interviewed any more. And I don't want to tell the story in another book.

"What's left for me to say after that last story you wrote? I guess I could begin making stuff up."

Since he grew up with Elvis, Scotty wasn't dazzled much by fame. The Beatles, whom he knew, "were nice guys. And they wrote and played great songs," was his assessment of that band one day when I was doing some sort of fortieth-anniversary Beatles-conquer-America story.

Before his hematoma caused him to cease even picking up a guitar (he sold them all to collectors in his final years), Scotty used to noodle on a Gibson sometimes when we spoke. One night, I was going to join him and Gail at a Gibson celebration in Nashville (the guitar company had a large café and corporate office building in Nashville's Gulch district, where the railyard was located and where the tracks split through downtown, for a while). Scotty had a seizure or some sort of setback, and he didn't make it anyway.

Again, I tracked his recovery to make sure that when he was released from the hospital, it was reported. I also wrote an advance obituary for "Winfield Scott Moore." In the newspaper business, they used to stock up on obituaries of well-known people, leaving blanks for dates of death, burials, and so on.

It wasn't that anyone at the paper was hounding me for one—a copy editor named Kevin Paulk was the only one who seemed to care—but I was sure Scotty wasn't going to make it. I don't have that obituary, which included quotes from Sam, D.J., Keith Richards, and other rock luminaries. Happily, I instead reported he had recovered, again probably a column note I wrote for Brad Schmitt.

By the time he died many years later, that obituary had disappeared from the computer files at the newspaper, and I had disappeared from the newspaper—probably better for Scotty, anyway, as what I had written was old, and some of the folks quoted already had their own obits published.

But that's all right as the friendship was much more important to me than news value.

There were plenty of stories I didn't share with anyone, stuff that came with a wink and a nudge. He didn't want me to write about it at the time, but Scotty at one point really enjoyed his Viceroy cigarettes and single-malt scotch.

A triple-bypass surgery in the late 1990s put an end to most of such shenanigans. But he loved to tell me stories of hanging with The Rolling Stones. His best Stones pals were Ronnie Wood and Keith Richards, the guitarists for the legendary outfit.

Scotty laughed about the hours spent in Ronnie's basement, where the three great rock guitarists poured down the scotch until they could no longer stand.

His really close friendship with The Stones flourished after 1988, when Ronnie called to invite him to see the band in St. Louis, the closest that tour was coming to Nashville.

Scotty didn't really know much about The Stones, but he was flattered and excited by the prospect offered by the "World's Greatest Rock-'n'-Roll Band."

Gail laughed when she recounted the day of Ronnie's call to the Music Row office where she worked for Scotty.

"I told him [Scotty], 'There's a Rolling Stone on the telephone.' He said, 'Who?'"

He took the call, and it apparently gave him great satisfaction because he agreed to go hang out with the Gibraltar of rock bands at their next tour stop.

That Scotty had accepted the invitation stunned Gail, but it also delighted her. She went home and scooped up all her Stones albums so Scotty could learn a bit more about his hosts, who were all admirers of the man from Blueberry Hill.

The Stones flew their new friends in and put them up in the same hotel where they stayed.

"After the show, they enlisted Scotty into the room [where one of The Stones, likely Richards, was staying]," Gail said.

She added that Scotty, Ronnie, and Keith "were getting skunky-drunky and decided they wanted Scotty to teach them the licks to 'Mystery Train.'"

The alcoholically impaired trio didn't get very far when trying to handle their guitars.

"They stayed up most of the night. I don't think they ever got to learn to play the licks to 'Mystery Train.'"

She laughed at the recollection of the three blind-drunk guitarists, all rock legends of the first order.

But she noted that the friendships were just beginning and that there were plenty more alcohol-fueled jam sessions and meetups of the too-tight trio of guitar greats.

In fact, Scotty went to tons of Stones shows before his health started to slow him down. And if he couldn't get to the shows, The Stones would come to him if they were in the neighborhood.

"When Scotty had his heart attack, Keith sent Scotty a fax from Jamaica, saying, 'Scotty, you are scaring me to death, you are my bad example.'"

Gail and Scotty continued the tale, noting that the next time they met up, "Keith says, 'Some people are always telling me "you're going to drink yourself to death." I say, 'No, I'm not, look at Scotty.'"

Some point after that, Richards fell out of a tree (a palm he was climbing in Fiji) and suffered a subdural hematoma like Scotty had, and there were some dire predictions circulating as to whether the seemingly indestructible Keefer was going to survive.

Scotty sent his errant pal a fax saying, "Musicians sit on the beach and watch the monkeys. The monkeys climb the tree."

"Scotty has been in contact with the guys now for 27 years, and he always has enjoyed their company every time he's seen them," said Gail back in 2015, when The Stones were coming to Nashville to play a sellout show at the stadium of the National Football League's Tennessee Titans.

"He's always been given utmost respect from these guys. They tease and laugh at each other, and they enjoy being together."

"I just like these boys, really," said Scotty. Those boys, he said, also included Mick Jagger and drummer Charlie Watts. But those two were "more reserved," and he'd spent much time bonding over scotch with Ronnie and Keith. I know he also spent time with bassist Bill Wyman, who likely emulated Scotty's own bass-playing chum Bill Black. The Stones bassist left the band in 1992, so he wasn't around Scotty much, particularly in the latter adventures.

"All of them are real nice guys," Scotty said. "We always have a good time when we're together."

This is probably a good place to revisit the *All The King's Men* sessions and happy participant Richards, who said he first heard Elvis, Scotty, and Bill on pirate radio broadcasts into London.

The sessions were held at Levon Helm Studios in Woodstock, New York. Drummer Helm was, according to most (except perhaps Robbie Robertson), the best voice and, indeed, the heart of the Band.

The sessions, which produced 1997's star-studded *All The King's Men* tribute to Elvis on the twentieth anniversary of his death, was a project starring Scotty and D.J. But it included Richards swapping guitar licks with Scotty and joining Helm and the Band to sing "Deuce and a Quarter," written by Nashville's Gwil Owen and Kevin Gordon.

Ronnie Wood also was in the great band of backup players, teaming up with Jeff Beck on "Unsung Heroes."

I tried to get front-office approval to send music writer Jay Orr to cover the sessions. I think he'd been invited but perhaps not.

I put in a word for myself as well. But the *Nashville Banner* brass didn't recognize the momentous nature of the event and turned us down. I would have loved hanging around in that magical musical stew of pickers and pilgrims.

There's a little more to say about that last song, "Unsung Heroes," according to the July 1997 issue of *Guitar Player* magazine: "In early December, Moore and Fontana traveled to Ron Wood's Sandy Mount Studio outside Dublin, Ireland, to record the album's final track with Wood, Beck and bassist Ian Jennings. 'It feels really good to know these guys remember us,' says Scotty, relaxing on a bar stool in Wood's private pub while Ron, Jeff and others watch a tape of Elvis and the boys in action. 'Makes you feel like what we did counts for something after all these years.'"

The song "Unsung Heroes" actually sprung from a little noodling Scotty was doing on his Gibson after that Dublin gathering had warmed up with Blue Moon Boys classics, beginning with "Blue Moon of Kentucky," according to the magazine's coverage of the event.

Wood was inspired by Scotty's fiddling around.

From *Guitar Player* comes this description of Ronnie's reaction and the resulting work: "'Well, that's it! Keep that going!' With that Ron grabbed a '54 Strat and started chunking rhythm and ad-libbing lyrics about meeting his two heroes. Beck suggested an occasional line between otherworldly bends and fills. Eventually, 'Unsung Heroes' became a song. 'This is incredible. It's just the way they used to do things—somebody gets an idea and they just go with it. The amazing thing to me—and Jeff was saying this too—is that Scotty and Bill came up with that original stuff completely out of the blue. They didn't have any real precedent to go on, and that's the very last time that happened in rock 'n' roll. Everyone who came along after that had those guys to listen to. You take Jeff Beck—he and the Yardbirds were a big part of the British Invasion, and he'll tell you they were bouncing off what they'd heard from America. Then American bands bounced it back, and so on and so on. And the guy sitting right in there (points through the control room window to Scotty) started it all.'"

The article's author, Rusty Russell, continues, "Later, over pints of Guinness, Scotty and his host listen to a working mix of 'Unsung Heroes.' He and his contemporaries, Scotty says as Ron Wood's eyes begin to mist, have done their part. 'You guys have to carry the torch now—you and the younger guys. We did our thing.'"

Of course, most of the recording activity took place at Levon's place in Woodstock. And while the album was a tribute to Elvis, it wasn't the norm as far as such things go. This was not a group of admirers remaking Presley classics. Instead, these fellows took new stuff and played it in full roots-rock Hillbilly Cat style.

And while the lineup is amazing, the stars really are Scotty and D.J.

I was visiting with Scotty just before he went to Memphis to help celebrate the fiftieth anniversary of rock 'n' roll's "big boom," with a July 5, 2004, ceremony marking the first, almost accidental notes of "That's All Right."

The city had celebrations planned throughout the year, but the Global Moment in Time was simultaneously playing "That's All Right," the song on which Scotty and the rest "invented" rock 'n' roll.

Of course, they loved Scotty over in Memphis. And in November 2003, it had been announced that for all of 2004, the yearlong celebration of that golden anniversary of the big boom at Sam's place, Scotty had been appointed one of the musical ambassadors for Memphis.

And, while he was my friend and I judged him to be the topmost on that list, the other ambassadors that year weren't too shabby: Stax records legend Isaac "Shaft" Hayes, Beale Street guitar genius B.B. King, and Memphis native and NSYNC member and solo artist Justin Timberlake. The latter, of course, has gone on to be a huge solo star and even a so-so movie actor after earning international attention for exposing Janet Jackson's right breast to 114 million viewers during the Super Bowl halftime show earlier that year.

True to form, Scotty was caught off guard when I called his house to tell him about the appointment after a fax from the Memphis mayor landed on my desk announcing that fact.

"I knew they'd asked me, but I didn't know I'd been appointed," he said. I read him the mayor's certificate before his arrived in the mail.

"I don't know what I gotta do yet," he said, adding that he thought the other ambassadors were a great bunch, mostly his pals.

"B.B.'s a friend of mine. I'm an admirer of Isaac's talents. I don't know Justin Timberlake, though."

As for his own contributions to the birth of rock 'n' roll, "The thing I'm so proud of is how the music has held up all of these years."

Memphis celebrates everything Elvis and banks on the fact that tourists will gravitate to participate in anything having to do with that weird Presley kid who grew up in the projects. Elvis is Bluff City's version of Mickey Mouse.

There is the annual "Dead Elvis Week" in Memphis, with all sorts of fun and merriment set to a rock-'n'-roll beat and some somber declarations. That takes place around the anniversary of his death on August 16, 1977.

Scotty used to attend and participate in concerts at the Overton Park Bandshell, the place where Memphians got its first really good look at Elvis. But he stopped once he lost his taste for their goings-on and out of his deep love and loyalty to the greatest rock-'n'-roll hero of them all.

"Nah, I don't go any more," he told me. "It's like a circus. Everyone wants to make money off him."

"Him" of course is the skinny kid who changed the world, with Scotty and Bill (and later D.J.) setting the tone and the beat.

But Scotty was going to the celebration of the half century since he invented what lead rock guitarists should be. He and Gail were going to leave the Moore property—21½ glorious, wooded acres—the day before the celebration (if I remember correctly).

It's about three hours from Nashville to Memphis if you're pushing it. They likely were going to take U.S. 70 rather than Interstate 40, trekking a route that would have been familiar to him during his hillbilly rambling days. It also passes within a few miles of his rural hometown of Humboldt, so it likely took them longer.

His main duty at the celebration in Memphis was to push a button at a radio station at 11 a.m. Hillbilly Cat time, triggering the playing of that song on stations around the world: the Global Moment in Time I mentioned earlier.

Since he still could handle that Gibson back then, Scotty was going to perform two or three songs at the station and probably go to eat at the Rendezvous or go watch the ducks at the Peabody.

It was his last-man-left status that had him (rather than Sam, Elvis, Bill) pushing that button for the worldwide broadcast. I imagine it made him feel lonely.

On a day I was with him—a full, eight-hour day—as he prepared for that journey to Memphis, Scotty really didn't want to dwell on his role in that historic session. He didn't like sitting alone on the throne. He was endlessly proud of what he and his friends had accomplished. It was a team.

As he sat with me, the Gibson he was noodling on comfortably was a Chet Atkins–signature instrument given him by Dire Straits ("I Want My

MTV" and "Sultans of Swing") front man Mark Knopfler, who had lived in Nashville for a few years so he could worship at Chet's altar and spend some time with the guy who invented the role of rock guitarist.

"He traded me [the guitar] for an old RCA microphone," said Scotty, smiling as he played and dipping slightly into his "deet-deet-dee-deet" blistering run for "That's All Right."

Scotty was only 72½ (he added the ½) on that visit.

Scotty didn't say it, but Knopfler, Richards and Wood, the late George Harrison, Paul McCartney, John Lennon, Eric Clapton, and Jimmy Page are just a few of the rock luminaries who know just how revolutionary was Moore's part of the doings in the Sun Studio on July 5, 1954. There also is the mutual love of guitarists. My friend Fats Domino, who played piano, of course, also sang the praises of Elvis and his band when he and I spoke a few times.

"It's always hot in Memphis in the summer," Scotty said, shrugging off my mentions of his glory while he fiddled with the Gibson, allowing himself to "deet-deet-dee-deet" and travel back a half century.

He again shrugged when I mentioned that on that particular hot night, a half century before, he and the other three were brewing up a hillbilly-jump stew that would change the world for the better.

If he, Bill, Elvis, and Sam hadn't done it, he said, somebody else would have.

There were a bunch of guys hanging around Memphis who could have sounded that first shot in the rock revolution if they'd been in the right place the right time, Scotty said.

He listed Roy Orbison and Jerry Lee Lewis and put a special emphasis on his beloved friend Carl Perkins, who lost even the chance to be the main voice associated with his own signature song, "Blue Suede Shoes," because of timing and a horrible traffic wreck while en route to do *The Perry Como Show* in New York City.

Carl, a really nice man I met a few times when he was opening for Johnny Cash and then taking Luther Perkins's place in the Tennessee Three when John hit the stage, didn't complain that his friend, Elvis, got the glory. He had plenty of money and could get home to Jackson whenever he wanted to, and Beatles guitarist George Harrison was among his best friends and greatest admirers. Meanwhile, of course, Elvis was dead.

As Scotty leaned back with Knopfler's guitar, he talked about how he—leader of the Starlite Wranglers country band at night and hatter/milliner by day—had befriended Sam Phillips and had hoped to earn his way into work as a Sun session player during his "free time."

Scotty also was looking for a vocalist, someone who could expand the Wranglers' sound. Phillips responded by passing him the "strange name" of "that boy," who had recorded a birthday wish for his mother at Sun.

"I want you to call him and get him to come over to your house" (or words to that effect), Phillips said to Scotty, who said/asked "Elvis Presley? What kinda name is that?"

Anyway, you know the rest of the story.

The young Presley kid went to Scotty's Memphis house on July 4, 1954, where the host and his pal, the bassist Bill Black, a member of the country band, were waiting.

Scotty recalled an instant chemistry among the three musicians.

"We spent a couple of hours, maybe an hour and a half, playing one song after another. Elvis knew all kinds of songs. He may not have known how to play all of them."

He said he and Bill sized up the kid after he left. "Me and Bill both agreed that he had a good voice, he was young, and he sings in key." So why not start a band?

As he told me for a story I wrote for *The Tennessean*, the three men met up the next evening at Sun, where Sam Phillips was in the control room, and they began playing, sort of feeling each other out.

"We went in, and Elvis started to do every song he knew. We were tired. Me and Bill were taking a break. Truth is, we both were ready to call it a night. We had our day jobs to get to the next morning.

"Then Elvis stood up, started playing 'That's All Right,'" the song Arthur Crudup had composed and first recorded back in 1946. The blues man's title for the song was "That's All Right Mama."

Scotty told me that Sam was so excited that he stuck his head out from the control room and demanded of the trio of tired musicians, "Do it again!"

The three musicians then had to figure out just how they concocted that magical accident, then worked out the chords before recording it five times.

"It was a real simple tune," Scotty told me 50 years later.

While we spoke, he kept noodling on the guitar, emulating his actions of a half century before, when he composed rock's first guitar solo. "Deet-deet-dee-deet."

"We got through the song, and then we listened to it. We all liked it."

Two nights later, the three men, with Sam at the controls, borrowed another classic, speeding up Bill Monroe's classic "Blue Moon of Kentucky." Monroe is said to have liked it so much that he speeded up his own version.

Before long, Elvis Presley and the Blue Moon Boys were traveling the South and changing the world, but the great guitarist didn't give himself a lot of the credit for the worldwide success of the strange boy from the Memphis projects.

"I think Elvis would've happened anyway," Scotty told me. "Whether he would have made it and had the popularity he gained, I don't know. All I know is that he was just eaten up with music like we all were."

As for that immortal guitar solo?

"Rather than just play a few notes, I was trying to fill up space," he said, adding that he was a little bit worried that when he got to Memphis for the golden anniversary celebration, he'd have to dust off that old nugget for the crowds. The fans wouldn't have it any other way. But Scotty was no longer a young and healthy man, so he was a little worried.

"When I get on the stage, I hope I can still play it."

He was not completely joking, as he had suffered that subdural hematoma, necessitating surgery and a month's hospital stay, the previous winter, as noted earlier.

He didn't use what he called a "bleed" as an excuse for his diminishing guitar playing, though.

He admitted that it slowed him down. But he also was getting older. "If I can't think of the right words, give me a minute," he said. As usual, Gail was sitting by his side for most of our conversations, always ready to fill in the blanks.

As for their relationship, well, she just laughed. "We're too old to call ourselves boyfriend and girlfriend. How about calling me his 'keeper'?"

We talked about his history in the years since he left the road and settled down into a second career as a music producer and engineer, first with Fernwood Records in Memphis and then at Music City Recorders and Belle Meade Records in Nashville. His work also included a long stint at Opryland Productions.

Among his favorite janitors at his Nashville studios was a former army helicopter pilot and Rhodes scholar named Kris Kristofferson, who had immersed himself into Nashville's music and grit to help reshape both his life and, eventually, country music.

A prime engineering credit for Scotty in Nashville was Ringo Starr's country album *Beaucoups of Blues*, which came out during the splintering of The Beatles.

Key Scotty recordings—other than most Elvis recordings through the heralded 1968 comeback special—include his own 1964 effort, *The Guitar That Changed the World*.

Scotty recorded with just about anyone who needed a guitar player with tasty licks. His sessions included work with Carl Perkins, Jerry Lee Lewis, Alvin Lee, Sonny Burgess, Ronnie McDowell, Ann-Margret, Charlie Rich, Ernest Tubb, the Tractors, Billy Swan, Lee Rocker, and more.

Carl Perkins and Nashville bassist Billy Cox, Jimi Hendrix's best friend and—with Jimi and Buddy Miles—part of the Band of Gypsys that came after the Experience packed up, were among those who climbed up Blueberry Hill to record or just jam with their hero and friend.

Old Experience hands Mitch Mitchell (drums) and Noel Redding (bass) also came to Nashville to hook up with Cox and go up to Blueberry Hill to play with Scotty, Carl Perkins, and whoever was available. I was fortunate enough to talk with both of these gentlemen—despite the ferocity of the Experience, these were, in real life, subdued Brits—when they came to town.

For a good while, Scotty recorded those sessions with Carl and the boys on Blueberry Hill and sold a few discs, but he stopped. "No one wants that music anymore," he said with not a hint of bitterness in his voice. I guess the only bitterness was in my heart when I listened to this great man say that folks didn't want to hear what he and his friends could cook up there in his studio.

On that day just before his fiftieth-anniversary trip to Memphis, Scotty nodded at the window into his home studio, which he transplanted there on his economic downfall–enforced departure from Music Row.

"I love to play music," he said, adding that top blues, rock, country, and jazz players from Nashville would come up there to swap notes and record "the old-fashioned way, with everyone in the room at the same time."

New recording technology wasn't welcome on Blueberry Hill. "There's no spontaneity" of the sort that bore such society-changing fruit that night in Memphis.

"Elvis didn't care if the music had warts, as long as it felt good," he said.

"The only real beef I have is when they call Elvis the King of Rock 'n' Roll. If he was king of anything, Elvis was the king of music. We did gospel. We did country. We did all kinds of music.

"Course, I don't think Elvis ever thought of himself as the king of anything." To Scotty, Elvis was an old friend, an equal in the "Elvis, Scotty, and Bill" outfit that first rolled out of Memphis with Black's bass strung to the roof.

I was the last person to do a long interview with Scotty, and we remained friends, which, of course, carried with it the heartache when he died.

"Scotty now is back with his old friends, making some beautiful noise with that weird teenager with pink shirts and greasy hair and the more subdued bassist," I wrote in a personal obit/reflection on my *They Call Me Flapjacks* personal blog. "And it's sure that Sam is wild-eyed as he watches what's transpiring."

I then called Gail's daughter, Margi Lane, who was up at Scotty's house organizing the possessions, and she said one thing she'd heard in the media was that Scotty had died crippled up and feeble. And it really angered her.

"He was still with us," she said, adding that while Scotty did suffer slightly from dementia, he still was up and about, walking with the aid of a walker (needed because of his degenerating disc disease) and watching cowboy shows.

He also spent some time on the phone with an old journalist. And his old friends from the music business kept coming up to Blueberry Hill, where they swapped yarns.

But the old hematoma and other health woes eventually caught up with him, and he was no longer able to play guitar, even when his musical friends came by.

"People occasionally would bring a guitar over to the house, but he wouldn't play it," she said. "He wasn't sad about it. He said he was through with it. He had done it. And it was over."

I couldn't help but think about one of the many conversations we'd had over the years since that Hall of Fame induction ceremony in New York City. The man who invented rock-'n'-roll guitar looked up from the Gibson, his eyes focused on memories of Sam, sure, especially Bill and Elvis, and not only on the big bang of 1954 but also all the time on the road, joking with each other, fighting like brothers, chasing women, and even standing near each other in cheesy "Elvis" movies on Hollywood soundstages.

"I think about being the only one left," Scotty said, as he picked on the Gibson. "I miss those guys.

"I mean, I don't sit around and think about it all the time. I like to watch TV. But when you spend so much time together, there's a lot of stuff you know that no one else does.

"We had some good times."

Billy Joe Shaver

B ILLY JOE SHAVER WAS THE KINDEST, gentlest, Bible-toting and scripture-espousing man who ever shot a man in the face at a bar and drove away.

I can't help but think about what happened March 31, 2007, outside Papa Joe's Texas Saloon. That's when and where Billy Joe Shaver, reacting to an argument inside the bar, shot a man in the face. A nice guy, he asked the fellow where he wanted to be shot before he pulled the trigger on the .22.

Three days later, Billy Joe was arrested on charges of aggravated assault with a deadly weapon.

It took about three years for Billy Joe to be labeled "not guilty"—he's definitely not "innocent," nor would he claim to be. But he did like me, and I liked him, a big, gentle man, scripture always at the ready, who sometimes found himself in trouble.

My good friend Peter Cooper, the historian and musician and more, said that his first reaction to hearing that this gentle giant had shot a man was sadness. "Poor Billy Joe. Why do things like that happen to this gentle guy? Poor Billy Joe."

I have to admit that I felt pretty much the same way when I heard of that shooting by Billy Joe, who died on October 28, 2020, from a massive stroke.

Oh, Billy Joe was a devout Christian (or something like that). Christ is obviously a man who gathered around him his era's version of lovable losers, no-account boozers, and honky-tonk heroes like Billy Joe wrote about. Most of his tales, like that one, *Honky Tonk Heroes*, came from a life that he lived vitally and viscerally, and he poured the sad songs, the melancholy rambles, and the occasional perky lament out with a guitar in a soft voice that carried the gristle of age and disuse.

"I've got holy ghost power, and I'll really ring your bell," he sings to a would-be aggressor on his "If You Don't Love Jesus."

I don't know if that fight ever really took place.

The shooting-a-guy-in-the-face did.

"I am very sorry about the incident," he told *Rolling Stone* magazine for a story published on April 12, 2010, that covered the trial in Waco, Texas.

Willie Nelson was there. Willie was perhaps Billy Joe's greatest friend and took the great songwriter into his house to heal after his son, Eddy Shaver, a fiery guitarist, died of a drug overdose.

"I don't think Billy Joe would do anything wrong. Whatever happened, I don't think it was Billy Joe's fault," *Rolling Stone* reported Willie as saying as he stood outside the courtroom.

As for Billy Joe, he was found not guilty on the charges. His comments after the trial was done?

"I am very sorry about the incident. Hopefully, things will work out where we become friends enough so that he'll give me back my bullet."

When he was on the witness stand, Billy Joe testified that he did indeed shoot Billy Bryant Coker after the two retreated to the back porch of Papa Joe's Saloon, near Waco, after the man stirred his drink with a pocket knife, wiped it on Billy Joe's shirt, and told him they needed to go outside.

"I thought he was going to kill me," Billy Joe told the packed courtroom, according to the *Rolling Stone* coverage of the big doin's. "He was a big bully, the worst I ever seen—a big, bad one. And I been all around the world."

He also told prosecutors that he could not just leave the bar and take off, avoiding the tussle altogether.

"I'm from Texas. If I was a chicken shit, I would have left."

The Texas "chicken shit" defense is tried and true in the Lone Star State. I think it may have aided in the acquittal of Johnny Rodriguez in a later murder case near San Antonio. I should note that Johnny Rodriguez's house, across the street from Waylon Jennings's sprawling Flying W compound at the southern edge of Nashville, was where I was allowed to use the phone a long time ago when I needed to call the police about a car wreck. I've always liked Johnny, who used to work the Tejano edge of the so-called Outlaw movement.

Back to Billy Joe, though. He did leave the bar. But, because he was no "chicken shit," he shot Coker in the cheek with a .22 pistol first.

The incident involved beer, poor manners, and a smoky old roadhouse, all things Billy Joe eloquently celebrated in his wondrous life in song.

The argument began because Coker was rude to Billy Joe's companion, his former wife, Wanda, whom he married twice.

Billy Joe didn't take kindly to the Coker comment. I don't know what this great Texas wordsmith had to say, but the guy responded by telling the great songwriter to "shut the f—— up" and invited Billy Joe outside.

Sometime after, they reached their outside destination, and the ever-polite Billy Joe pulled out a gun and pointed it at Coker, asking, in his gentle Texas drawl, "Where do you want it?"

I'm not sure if he waited for an answer before he pointed at Coker's cheek and pulled the trigger. He and his most recent ex-wife disappeared into the soft Texas night in his truck.

The bullet went through Coker's lip, knocked out a tooth and a crown, and ended up in the back of the guy's neck. Docs left the bullet in place because it was near the carotid artery, according to a March 31, 2010, piece by Michael Hall in *Texas Monthly*.

That story goes on to say that a witness to the gunplay reported he overheard Billy Joe say to Wanda, "I'm tired of this crap happening every time we go somewhere. I'm leaving. You coming?"

In a 2018 interview with David Greene on National Public Radio, Billy Joe further described the "gunfight."

"I hit him right between the mother and the [expletive]. That was the end of that. He dropped his weapons and said, 'I'm sorry.' And I said, 'Well, you know, if you'd have said that inside, it wouldn't have been no problem.'"

I'd go on, as I find this tale a good representation of the "bad side" of a guy I truly liked and for whom I felt more than a dash of pain when I found out he had died of a stroke on October 28, 2020, at a rehab center where he was recovering from surgery to repair a hip he broke earlier in the month. He had fallen off a swing.

The eventually fatal swing-set accident came just months after he suffered the COVID plague.

His was a life of picking himself up, dusting himself, and starting all over again, as the old song goes.

A case in point is his almost lifelong devotion to the love of his life, his teenage girlfriend, Brenda. Their love was so strong that he married her three times, and he had been nursing her, then an ex-wife again, for four years leading up to her death from cancer in 1999, the same year his mom fell to cancer.

As usual, he found solace in his music, particularly the teaming with his son, Eddy. The two worked together on record and on tour until heroin claimed Eddy on December 31, 2000. He was only 38.

The loss of Eddy—the two were playing successfully together in a rockish country band called Shaver—pretty much permanently hobbled the songwriter.

"We always figured I'd be the one to go first," said this gentle giant, who the next year had a heart attack onstage at an Independence Day show at legendary and historic Gruene Hall in New Braunfels, Texas. This honky-tonk hero of a Jesus freak said to the heavens, "Thank you Lord, for letting me die in the oldest honky-tonk in Texas."

Before I go much further, I ought to note that Billy Joe Shaver was acclaimed by many of his contemporaries as the best lyricist in country music. Just ask Willie Nelson.

Or perhaps Bob Dylan, who name-checked Billy Joe in his "I Feel a Change Comin' On" on the 2009 album *Together Through Life*:

> I'm listening to Billy Joe Shaver
> And I'm reading James Joyce

I need to add, though, that Dylan shares cowriting credit with Robert Hunter, who died in 2019 after his words, coupled with Jerry Garcia's, pretty much composed the Grateful Dead songbook. It doesn't matter if it was Dylan or Hunter who put in that line about Billy Joe; the recognition is well deserved, and I'm sure James Joyce wouldn't have minded sharing a verse with a great country songwriter.

I first met Billy Joe—"met" may be too strong a word, as all I did was shake his hand and congratulate him on a great show—back in 1973.

I was at the old Exit/In on Elliston Place in Nashville. It was a quiet listening room, with maybe 20 tables, a bar, and a small restaurant nook at the time. It later expanded to become just another cavernous rock hall.

Having been captivated by Waylon Jennings's *Honky Tonk Heroes* album, I was at the club to see the author of all those songs (except for out-of-place last track, "We Had It All," by Troy Seals and my late friend, Funky Donnie Fritts, "The Alabama Leaning Man").

I should note that it has been reported that Billy Joe, getting frustrated by the roadblocks put up by hangers-on and executives while trying to get the songs to Waylon, finally exploded. "I got these songs, and if you don't listen to them, I'm going to kick your ass right here in front of God and everybody." (The quote varies by source, and at least one account has Waylon in the company of bikers who didn't want their black-clad pal threatened.)

Regardless, Waylon didn't let the violence erupt among the songwriter and his "protectors."

Waylon took the skinny kid into a back room and cautioned him about his reckless outburst—"Hoss, you don't do things like that." After listening to one song, "Old Five and Dimers," Waylon decided to do an entire album by the Wacko from Waco.

As far as the night in 1973 when I first met Billy Joe at the Exit/In, I think Doug Kershaw, the Ragin' Cajun, was the warm-up act (although it could have been Billy Swan, the guy of "I Can Help" fame, who was tending bar or at least hanging out there).

I got there early enough—I'm always early to a show out of respect for the performers and my own disdain for tardiness—I got a two-chair café table in the front, pretty much center stage.

In fact, I got there even earlier than Waylon, who sat at the table next to me and gave me his lonesome, on'ry, and mean grin. I really liked Waylon but never got to really know him. He enjoyed the show that night.

Billy Joe ran through every song from that monumental country album. My favorite lines are in the title song of the album that leaves me fulfilled and melancholy on every listen:

> Them neon light nights, couldn't stay out of fights
> Keep a-haunting me in memories

I've always been crazy, so when the show was over, I didn't slide out into the night, instead sticking around to tell the songwriter just what magic he had created.

Of course, he wrote a lot of great songs. "Old Five and Dimers Like Me," for example, is one classic. "Ride Me Down Easy" is another. And I could go on.

I talked with Billy Joe a few times over the years on the telephone. I never formally met him until the day of June Carter Cash's funeral. Two fellows I admired a lot—the great American actor Robert Duvall of *Godfather*, *The Great Santini*, and *Apocalypse Now* fame and Billy Joe—were leaning against a wall at the side of the narthex after the funeral.

Since there were so many people here, many of them just fans of the Cashes who wanted to do some star spotting, I knew that if I grabbed one of the two men to speak with, I'd lose the other one to the crowd. Quickly, I was clutching the right hand (or at least what was left after he lost two fingers and a part of the third in a youthful sawmill accident) and talking to Billy Joe.

Duvall, the consigliere, smiled and listened. He was a nice guy, too, and unforgettable in film. No one who ever saw *Apocalypse Now* can forget Duvall's Lieutenant Colonel Bill Kilgore's celebratory "I love the smell of napalm in the morning."

But this chapter is my ode to Billy Joe. Waylon is quoted by Saving CountryMusic.com about Shaver and their shared adventures.

"He was sitting on a bed one time playing guitar, and a guy who worked for me came in and said, 'Billy Joe, if you don't mind me asking, what happened to your fingers?'

"Billy started glancing around and digging in his pocket. 'Damn,' he said. 'They were here just a while ago.'"

Even though I knew and liked Billy Joe, the opportunities to write about him generally were just quick notes about his music or carryings-on that I punched out for the newspaper's celebrity gossip columnist, Brad Schmitt.

However, I finally had the opportunity to write a story when in August 2004 we shared some time together, talking about an upcoming concert out at the Grand Ole Opry Plaza, his dog, and the future.

I was the newspaper's entertainment editor, and most such assignments went to Peter Cooper, who is the best music historian and part-time entertainer I know. Ask him to sing to you sometime.

But I took this assignment, published on August 6, out of a love of Billy Joe and his music, his lyrics, really.

Billy Joe had just returned from spreading his honky-tonk fervor across Europe and had spent the night at an Austin, Texas, Red Roof Inn, calling me when he woke up.

His main motivation that day was to roll back to Waco and pick up his beloved dog.

"I'm picking up Shade at the veterinarian," he said, referring to his "8- or 10-year-old" pit bull mix.

"Born in the shade of a rose bush. She's white. Has a little ring around an eye. Cute as she can be. Little ol' ball of fire."

Good sidekick for a man who had labeled himself the "Wacko from Waco."

In addition to the upcoming performance at the Opry Plaza in Nashville (they referred to the afternoon outdoor functions as Plaza parties), he told me he was going to perform a song or two inside the actual building as part of the *Grand Ole Opry* radio program.

There was cheer in his voice as he shared his excitement over reuniting with Shade.

And, I can't remember how, but his Bible thumping slipped into the conversation. His was a honky-tonker's Christianity: devout, as good as possible to his fellow man (unless he has to shoot him in the face), and one who believed in God with all his heart.

The dog, Shade, and Jesus helped him through the toughest part of his life: He was awash in death back at the turn of the twentieth century.

As noted earlier, his wife, Brenda—"We'd been married three times"—died in July 1999 after the struggle with cancer that had Billy Joe at her side nursing her.

His mother, Victory Shaver, and Brenda's mother, Mildred Tindell, also died of cancer around that time.

It is probably worth noting that when he was a youngster, Billy Joe's mom had to rely on work at honky-tonks, often leaving him and his sister with their grandmother in Corsicana when she went off to tend bar in Waco.

A man with an eye for ladies, Billy Joe's eventual benefactor, Waylon Jennings, once talked about Victory, who was running Waco's Green Gables, a joint made famous in *Honky Tonk Heroes*.

"She was a good-looking woman, red-headed, and tough, and it was a classic dive, a dance hall with sawdust on the floor, spittoons, and a piano in the corner," Waylon said.

And then on New Year's Eve 2000, Eddy Shaver, a rocker with inherited musical chops, died of a heroin overdose in a motel at the edge of Waco.

"I didn't even know he was in town," his dad said.

Bad companions were one factor, Billy Joe said.

He also blamed himself and the example he set while fighting for redemption.

"I had to forgive myself at first. I'd done a round or two of that stuff myself. Back in 1977, I went completely cold turkey on smoking, booze, drugging. I lost down to 172 pounds from 230. Almost died because I couldn't keep anything down."

Sometime around then, he was "born again," a subject that likely drew weariness and eye rolls from some of his Nashville outlaw peers.

"At first, I jumped around like a rabbit [and preached Christianity]," he said. "Then I figured I'll just settle down and live my life."

My friend, Peter Cooper, a Spartanburg, South Carolina, expatriate, knows something about that town's biggest rock outfit, the Marshall Tucker Band. George McCorkle, guitarist, founding member, and author of the band's best song, "Fire on the Mountain," once returned from a night of partying in Nashville, according to a story Peter related.

It seems George couldn't quite make it to his apartment, and he passed out in the front yard. He was still there the next morning, a Sunday, when he woke up to see his neighbor, Billy Joe, firing up his pickup to go to church.

"I'm going to pray for your sorry ass," Billy Joe said. There likely was a smile on his face when he made that vow. And I have no doubt he kept it.

He said his faith helped him cope with the spate of death that surrounded him in 1999 and 2000.

"We were planting them right and left. If it hadn't been for my Lord and Savior Jesus Christ, I wouldn't have made it."

And "my dogs helped me out a lot," he said.

Those dogs included Etawna ("Brenda was Indian, you know, and she named the dog that. Her name meant 'wanderer, a gypsy-type' dog"). And the brindle-colored pit bull had the pup, Shade.

"They really helped me. I love my dogs."

He paused, his voice breaking. "I had to put the old mama dog down this summer. She was 16. Couldn't walk. It was the humane thing to do.

"But I cried like a baby."

We talked a bit about his writing, including *Honky Tonk Heroes*, a beer and nicotine–stained "country music opera," he said, about lovable losers, no-account boozers, and Nashville's storied Lower Broadway life (before the strip was sold by greedy city promoters as the place where tourists come and buy their boots and get drunk, a sort of neon-lit Honky-Tonk Disney World).

Of course, Waylon loved Billy Joe's writing, as did Cash, who employed him as a staff writer for a couple of years (Brenda was Cash's hairstylist; "she also worked for Dean Martin"). And Billy Joe, the writer, was held in great esteem by Kris Kristofferson and Willie Nelson, both of whom know something about penning country classics.

He admitted that his writing, along with his God and the dogs, helped him chase away personal demons. The album he was getting ready to release back in 2004 when we spoke was *Billy and the Kid*, on which he and his late son were featured as a duo one last time.

Eddy had left several songs on tapes when he died, and Billy Joe took them to a Nashville studio and did his parts.

"It was a labor of love," he said. "Wanted people to realize what a great songwriter Eddy was."

He joked himself a bit that he had a trouble with the songs because of the style in which Eddy wrote and recorded them.

"It's rock 'n' roll. In rock 'n' roll, you just kinda go for it," Billy Joe said. "I don't know if I could sing anyone else's rock 'n' roll songs.

"I'm country as an onion."

He told me that when he got back to Waco and picked up Shade, he'd take the dog with him to the cemetery where those closest to him were buried.

"I go out there every day."

Since October 28, 2020, Billy Joe no longer has to visit the cemetery. He's there with Brenda and Eddy. Knowing him, he probably figured out a way to take his dogs along with him.

The obituary, posted on the Waco Memorial Park and Mausoleum website, is simple, but it's pure Billy Joe.

"Billy Joe Shaver, 81, a resident of Waco, Texas, passed away Wednesday in a local hospital after a brief illness. Born in Corsicana, Texas, he had been a resident of Waco since 1950. He had started out with a rough life which he wrote about in his songs. He lost his mother and his wife, Brenda, in 1999 and his only son, Eddy, in 2000.

"His faith sustained him throughout his life."

Yes, he boasted "three fingers whiskey pleasures the drinkers" and "now, ladies, we'll surely take of your favors" in "Willy the Wandering Gypsy and Me."

He always said he wrote the truth, the truths, really—whether those of a life hard-traveled or those of the man who hits his knees on Sunday. "Ain't no way to get around it, you just can't beat Jesus Christ," he sang.

Then Billy Joe Shaver shot a guy in the face, took his most recent ex-wife, climbed into his truck, and drove home to see his dog, Shade.

Funky Donnie Fritts

O N A HOT SUMMER EVENING IN 2007, looking forward to some
time with a Muscle Shoals legend, I nursed my 1985 Saab up to
the door of the motel room through which a maid was pushing
her aluminum cart filled with dirty towels and fresh laundry, miniature
tubes of toothpaste, and one-shower shampoos.

"C'mon in!" hollered the voice inside the door just on the other side
of the maid. Then he thanked the woman for her toil in the small, generic,
double-queens room of the old-fashioned motor inn, the vanishing sort
where guests nose their cars right up to the door (unless they are on the
second floor, of course).

I smiled at the maid, who said something kind (or at least I think it was
kind) in a language I take to be Kurdish as I squeezed between my old car
and the blue Pontiac (if I remember correctly) driven by Funky Donnie
Fritts, the thickly mustachioed guy in blue jeans and a red-heavy floral
Hawaiian shirt, sitting at the foot of the bed that was closest to the door.
His white, straw cowboy hat and stray clothing were lined up on the other
bed. (By the way, I guessed the woman was speaking Kurdish because
Nashville has a huge population of Iraqi refugees, folks who escaped mad-
man Saddam in the years before he was hanged, live and in dying-color,
on our living room TVs.)

"She does a good job," said Donnie as the maid departed, pushing her
cart to the next room. "They do a good job here at the Fritts Carlton."

On this day, he told me, the maid didn't need to replace the sheets
because he was here for "three, four nights" to visit friends, check on his
song publishing, and, on this visit, do a set at the old Douglas Corner, a
shotgun bar that much later was a COVID victim.

Douglas Corner was, for decades, a singer-songwriter's haven in a section of Nashville I long ago dubbed "the city's antique district" in newspaper notices about offerings at the club or at Zanie's Comedy Showplace across the street. I was referring to the six or eight antique stores that shared that stretch of town. Some of those were, like the bar itself, victims of the pandemic.

The bar and small showroom stage were, like hundreds or perhaps thousands of similar joints, a victim of the times, closing midway in the year of COVID.

I had always figured I'd write an obituary for Douglas Corner sometime, as I'd done for other classic honky-tonks trampled by progress and unable to compete for tourist bucks with the sea of neon-decked, class A honky-tonk showplaces on Nashville's Lower Broadway. And progress likely would have gotten it if the virus hadn't stepped in.

Regardless, Douglas Corner was one of the great venues where songwriters showed off their stuff. Alan Jackson, Trisha Yearwood, Mr. Yearwood (Garth Brooks, who broke in there), Blake Shelton, the great Townes Van Zandt, Guy Clark, Mac Davis, Cowboy Jack Clement, and even COVID-murdered John Prine all were known to play and to haunt the confines.

Donnie—whose history of health woes and heart trouble finally ended his drawling, good-times-with-a-strong-dash-of-Christ life on August 27, 2019—was going to Douglas Corner on that trip in the summer of 2007 to showcase some of the songs from his upcoming *Down in the Groove* album. He also wanted to celebrate the kinship between Nashville and his hometown of Muscle Shoals, Alabama. I may have the dates off, but the story happened, and that's what's important.

Spooner Oldham and Dan Penn—and many members of the musical pride of Muscle Shoals, named and misspelled for the mussels that are harvested as the Tennessee River passes through—were in the crowd or the stage that night.

A guy from Germany who said he wanted to do a documentary on Funky Donnie also was in the crowd (if I remember correctly). I don't believe that documentary ever was produced. If it was, that German fellow never called on me for input, as he'd previously promised. In Music City, promises are as enduring as pissin' in the wind, to borrow a song title from the great Jerry Jeff Walker.

I actually sat with my friend, Peter Cooper, and just behind Billy Swan. Billy, Donnie's old sidekick in Kris Kristofferson's Border Lords outfit, sometimes put his old pal up for the night in his Nashville house (I suppose

if the Fritts Carlton was full). Billy made his biggest musical contribution
with the catchy "I Can Help":

> If you've got a problem, I don't care what it is
> If you need a hand, I can assure you this
> I can help, I've got two strong arms, I can help.

Billy's a good guy, and one time when I called his house to track down
Donnie, I asked how much help the guest offered. "Oh, he can help,"
Billy vowed with a tuneful laugh.

Anyway, back to the afternoon/evening in the summer of 2007, as
I entered the hotel room at the Fritts Carlton, Donnie nodded to the
chair next to the dresser. "We'll go in a minute," he said. "I need to call
Donna."

His wife of a half century, who sometimes accompanied him on his
jaunts from Muscle Shoals to Nashville, where they always stayed at this
motor inn between Radnor Railyard and Interstate 65, had stayed home.
He just wanted to tell her I was there to pick him up and we were going
out to dinner.

He had chosen P. F. Chang's, a high-priced China fusion restaurant
out in the Cool Springs area between Brentwood and Franklin, south of
Nashville.

I guess he figured I was on an expense account, or else he'd have chosen something more reasonable. "Donna and I always go out there when
she's with me," he said. "It's one of our favorite places. We get everything,
the works, starting with those lettuce wrap things."

Those lettuce wraps are made from a secret family recipe (or something
like that), according to the menu. There are protein options available.
They are good, as Donnie attested, but since I was nose-diving toward
unemployed status, they cost too much for what essentially is fancy lettuce.

But that's not the point here. We had a great time, although my car was
in its non–air-conditioned years, so, with windows wide open, we could
hardly hear each other talk during the 15 miles up and down the interstate
from the hotel, which is within a mile of where I live in the Crieve Hall
section of South Nashville. Yes, I can hear the trains a-comin' down the
track during the night.

Donnie, who by then had become a dear friend—primarily from phone
encounters but also from some songwriters' Christian luncheons I attended
mainly to meet people—told me that for a while, he had changed from
the Fritts Carlton—in reality a Red Roof Inn of the older variety—to a La
Quinta up by the Waffle House and nearer the Cracker Barrel.

But he changed back, at least in part because he found the pillows more comfortable. It also pleased him that everyone from desk personnel to the maids and maintenance guys treated him special.

And he was—special, that is.

I probably ought to mention that one time I was with my friends, Kris and Lisa Kristofferson, and they said they expected to see Donnie. They were worried he'd be delayed in the traffic up from the Shoals. When I told them their pal was staying at what he called the "Fritts Carlton" they laughed, with Lisa adding, "We'd have paid for him to have a room here" at a decidedly non–Red Roof near Vanderbilt University. "But he just loves the Fritts Carlton." Funky Donnie Fritts made everyone he met happy as far as I could tell.

Funky Donnie Fritts was given that nickname by Kris Kristofferson. He was a link between the R&B of Muscle Shoals, Alabama, and the steel-guitar-and-heartbreak of Nashville. PHOTO COURTESY CARY MARK PASSEROFF

I mentioned those Christian lunches where I occasionally bumped into Donnie. They were potlucks staged by a group of Bible-toting musicians calling their group Giving in Faith Together (GIFT). I think they still have them, and they are hosted by great songwriter and entrepreneur Buzz Cason, who has operated a recording studio in the Berry Hill section of town—pretty much right next to what I'd guess is Nashville's biggest cemetery—for a half century.

Buzz went to Berry Hill before it was cool, as that traffic-ticket town, an island inside Metro Nashville, now bustles with studios and musicians night and day. Big corporations and ugly condominiums have gobbled up Music Row, the formerly musical strip of studios where everyone from Bob Dylan to Paul McCartney to Ringo to Ray Charles to George Jones to Eddy Arnold to Chet Atkins had made historic music. Some of those folks even have chapters in this book.

Those Christian luncheons are called "First Tuesday" for the day of the month when they meet. And Donnie always tried to make it. I have been there when he tore in, sweaty and breathless after the two-plus hours from the Shoals. He would check into the Fritts Carlton after lunch and then go catch up with old running buddy, Billy Ray Reynolds.

Other regulars at these prayer-and-hope meetings included Clifford Curry ("She Shot a Hole in My Soul"), Billy Swan ("I Can Help"), Dickey Lee (among his writing credits is the immortal "She Thinks I Still Care"), and every sort of Nashville Cat.

Kenny Buttrey, the great drummer who appeared on countless recording sessions, was being remembered at one of those Tuesday gatherings I attended. I was there because I really liked his wife, Cheri, whom I had phone conversations with after Kenny died.

Kenny died of lung cancer. He and I spoke on the phone some during his decline. If you don't know of Kenny, you really don't understand the heart of Nashville, where musicians of all flavors make landmark recordings for artists from just about any genre.

After Kenny died of the lung cancer on September 12, 2004, I had written the obituary for *The Tennessean* after fighting with editors to get me a few inches of space. That's where Cheri helped me out, tracking down friends and history and arrangements.

Here's just a piece of the obit: "Kenny Buttrey—who made a career of literally pounding down barriers between country, pop, rock, R&B and folk music—died late Sunday at his Bellevue home after a long battle with cancer.

"The drummer—who played with Bob Dylan, Neil Young, Elvis, Simon & Garfunkel and more—was 59. His wife of 20 years, Cheri, and their two daughters, Kenzie, 16, and Keri, 6, were with him when he died.

"Because he worked in Nashville, some might call him a country session drummer. But that hardly tells his story. He was a member of groundbreaking Nashville groups, including Barefoot Jerry—among the early 'Southern rock' outfits—and Area Code 615, a combination of Music Row aces."

I went on to note that Kenny's musical credits included Dylan's Nashville albums—*Blonde on Blonde, John Wesley Harding,* and *Nashville Skyline*—as well as on Neil Young's career-high-point *Harvest.*

"He told me the other day that the two songs that were his favorites were 'Lay Lady Lay' with Bob Dylan and 'Heart of Gold' with Neil Young," Cheri told me the day after her beloved died.

I throw Kenny in here only because he is indicative of the types of guys who made it to Cason's gatherings and who rubbed noses and talked Jesus with guys like Funky Donnie Fritts and also because Kenny was a really nice guy when he would call me at the paper to chat, amiably, about Dylan, Neil, and the like.

Of course, Donnie knew him. Donnie knew everybody. And he, like Kenny and countless Nashville musicians, could travel the spectrum of music, from Muscle Shoals funk—mostly a sound gestated in Memphis and birthed in Alabama—to the Nashville Sound. Throw in some steel, and you've got a honky-tonk weeper.

I have to admit it was a great honor to be considered a friend by Funky Donnie Fritts. No, he wasn't a star. He was a poet, a picker, a prophet, and a preacher.

At least that's how he was when I made his acquaintance back in 1971 when I first played *The Silver Tongued Devil and I* album, which I bought at the discount house down at the corner of Waukegan and Lake-Cook roads in the northern suburbs of Chicago, where I did my time as a junior high and high school student.

I'll talk about those years some other time, but it was while in Deerfield that I really nurtured the habit of buying music. As a third grader in Grand Rapids, Michigan, I began buying records, starting out with singles, then I hit the harder stuff. The LPs started piling up in Deerfield. The late 1960s and early 1970s were the golden age of albums, as artists often tried to string themes out through both sides.

That's what Kris did on "Silver Tongued Devil."

It remains one of my favorites a full half century later, and I always identify with "The Pilgrim, Chapter 33," a song about loss and lost opportunity, busted dreams, and dusty determination dying.

Kris begins that album title song with a litany of characters the song could be about, from Chris Gantry to Dennis Hopper to Johnny Cash to Funky Donnie Fritts.

Of course, I knew who Hopper and Cash were. I later made the acquaintance of Gantry, who is a good fellow. But the name "Funky Donnie Fritts" stayed with me for the decades. "I wonder what Funky Donnie Fritts would say about this?" I'd ask myself with no knowledge of who I was talking about.

So one day, I dialed up Muscle Shoals, Alabama, and asked for the Fritts phone number. That's before technology made tracking down a phone number nearly impossible.

"Hello, this 's' Donnie," crunch syllabled the man with the welcoming drawl.

"Funky Donnie Fritts!" I proclaimed (I hardly ever use exclamation points in my writing, but one is warranted here, as I'd waited a half century to say those words).

He laughed and said, "Yeah, this is him."

I had always wanted to call him but never really had a reason to until a homemade demo by Donnie had arrived in the mail at the newspaper office, accompanied by a note to call if I was interested in talking about it. He said his friend, Kristofferson, had recommended he contact me.

Anyway, we began a friendship that lasted until he died, although I will have to say that Donnie was much more friendly and outspoken when he had a project to push. Otherwise, he spent his time quietly, writing songs, looking after his mother-in-law (she lived a block away from him), and maybe going over to Shoals' FAME studios to hang out with Spooner or Penn.

One thing that developed out of our friendship was that I asked *Journal of Country Music* editor Michael Gray if he'd like a story about Funky Donnie Fritts.

Michael, whom I had hired for his first full-time job as the number 2 music journalist when I was entertainment editor of the old *Nashville Banner*, was excited by the prospect and gave me the go-ahead.

"We Had it All," a song Donnie had written with Troy Seals, is the finale on Michael's favorite country album, Waylon's *Honky Tonk Heroes*. It's a great song, but I always felt it was out of place on an album that was written primarily by another great friend, Billy Joe Shaver.

The story on Donnie was going to be the cover story of the magazine published by the Country Music Hall of Fame and Museum, where Michael is an editor. I'll have to say here that the story was good enough to be his cover story. It was laid out, photos in place, everything ready to rip. Just before the presses ran, though, in early 2008, the magazine stopped publishing, the story appearing for a while on the Hall of Fame's website before disappearing (the curse of digital journalism).

Still, it did appear online for a while. Now I think the only printed record of it is in my blog *They Call Me Flapjacks*, again thanks to Michael, who rescued the story from the deep computer archives at the museum for me when Donnie died.

The whole story is many thousands of words, but the basic point of it is and was that Donnie was an underrated musical force, a loyal friend, and one of the most likable fellows in the music business—the kind of guy you could imagine putting peanuts in seven-ounce Cokes and handing you one if you caught him at City Drug Store in Florence, Alabama, where he was among those concocting the Muscle Shoals sound.

Donnie and other "good ol' boys"—Rick Hall, Dan Penn, Norbert Putnam, David Briggs, and Spooner Oldham—were color-blind.

They also believed the music coming from Nashville to be too vanilla. They at first even discounted The Beatles, putting them in the same category as Music Row fodder at least until they wised up. "Oh, I ended up liking a lot of The Beatles stuff, but we preferred black music, a lot of the stuff that was coming out of Memphis," Donnie said during one of our long interviews or lettuce-chewing or coffee-drinking sessions. Maybe a Coke. Hold the peanuts.

Donnie was 15 when he started drumming in a space atop the City Drug, and he and his pals listened to WLAC radio out of Nashville, which played R&B music into the night. He admitted that they also liked to check in on clear channel WSM for the sounds of the Hanks (Williams and Snow), Ernest Tubb, Lefty Frizzell, Roy Acuff, and Bill Monroe on the *Grand Ole Opry* radio show.

In the story I wrote for Michael's magazine, I summarized what transpired from the mix of music styles: "As a result, these good ol' boys from small-town Alabama made music that was a loose mix of Hank Williams heartache and chicken shack R&B, like that produced by Fritts's lifetime friend Arthur Alexander."

That musical stew turned the Shoals into a recording capital. The Rolling Stones, who covered Alexander's "You Better Move On" in 1963, were among those who used the studios down there.

Others to sample the musical magic of the Shoals included Aretha Franklin, Otis Redding, and Neil Young.

Donnie was deadpan and normal/humble when asked about all of those great sessions.

"I can't take credit for any of them coming down to record," he said. "I was there [in the room] when The Stones recorded 'Brown Sugar' [for the 1971 *Sticky Fingers* album, perhaps the band's last great album, although

I personally prefer 1968's *Beggars Banquet*, the last album to fully feature Brian Jones].

The Stones also recorded "We Had It All," which they planned to include on 1979's *Emotional Rescue*, but it kicked around, turning up mostly on bootlegs.

I'm sure there are well-produced versions out there by The Stones, and Donnie was thrilled in 2004 when he saw Stones songwriter and coleader Keith Richards sing it with Willie Nelson on a *Willie Nelson and Friends— Outlaws & Angels* TV special.

Donnie recalled, "I knew he [Keith] was going to do the song because Connie Nelson [Willie's ex-wife] called me about 1 in the morning during a rehearsal a few days before, and she said, 'You'll never guess what I'm listening to right now. I'm listening to Willie and Keith Richards sing 'We Had It All.'"

Anxious to hear the final result, Donnie tuned in the TV broadcast and was filled with glee. "I was floored when Keith Richards said it was a song by Donnie Fritts and Troy Seals. He was the only artist that mentioned the writers."

The fact musicians like his songs should never have caught Donnie by surprise. He wrote or cowrote songs covered by Sammy Davis Jr. ("You're Gonna Love Yourself [in the Morning]"), Lulu ("Where's Eddie"), Dusty Springfield and UB40 ("Breakfast in Bed"), the Box Tops ("If I Had Let You In" and "Choo Choo Train"), Robert Plant ("If It's Really Gotta Be This Way"), Muscle Shoals sensation Percy Sledge ("You're All Around Me"), and so many others.

"We Had It All" was recorded by Seals, Dobbie Gray, Dolly Parton, Tom Jones, Rita Coolidge, Bob Dylan (who performed it regularly during a tour with Tom Petty and the Heartbreakers), Tina Turner, Willie, and Conway Twitty.

Donnie's favorite version, though, was sung by his hero, Ray Charles. I called Donnie when my colleague Brad Schmitt and I were tasked with the *Tennessean* obituary on the day Brother Ray died, June 10, 2004.

The fact Ray did his song still echoed disbelief in Donnie's voice. "I mean Ray Charles, man," he said. "I'd been listening to his music my whole life. That was the high point of my songwriting career."

And, though Donnie had been a running buddy of Waylon, Willie, Cash, Bare, Tompall, Kristofferson, Billy Ray Reynolds, and Captain Midnight and had hung out with The Rolling Stones, he said he succumbed to the sucker punch of hero worship when he met Ray.

Donnie, who was clear-eyed and relatively holy when I met him had, he admitted, lived fast and hard. He did cocaine with Waylon and pills with anyone who had them. He didn't like marijuana, he allowed, leaving that to Kris and the other guys.

His health suffered. He said he prayed he'd make it when a bout with pneumonia almost took him in the winter of 2006–2007. But his wife, Donna, nursed him back to health.

But the real cost of his lifestyle was displayed back around the turn of the century, when he was emerging from about five years of hell that included open-heart surgery, four angioplasties, dialysis, and a kidney transplant.

"They told me at one time that I was going to need both a heart transplant and a kidney transplant. In other words, 'Hey, you're dead,'" Donnie recalled.

His heart held out for the rest of his life, anyway.

He was a man with a mighty big heart, a loving bear of a fellow who admitted he'd done plenty of wrong but was able to celebrate that he did plenty of right as well.

I could go on and talk more about Funky Donnie Fritts, also known as "The Alabama Leaning Man," though there's a dispute as to how he got that nickname.

There's no doubt that the "Funky" crown came from Kristofferson, as he ad-libbed the intro to "The Pilgrim, Chapter 33" in the studio.

I could talk about the fact his best friend was Arthur Alexander, and Donnie was with him in a Nashville hospital when the soul man died.

By then crippled by his own health woes, Waylon planned on attending a medical bill fund-raiser for Donnie in Florence only after Donnie had surgery. But Waylon got up and sang anyway.

Donnie celebrated and seldom lamented the wild days and nights with Kristofferson and the Border Lords. The deep loyalty, the love, the two men had for each other was mutual and unabashed and reflected in the songs they crafted.

"We've enriched each other's lives with our particular mixture of music and creative friends. We even quit smoking for each other (each of us thought the other was going to die if we didn't) and shared some of the best moments in our lives, and some of the saddest," Kris told me when I was doing the magazine piece.

That sadness came through when Kris's one-time lover, Janis Joplin, also a Fritts friend, died of a heroin overdose on October 4, 1970.

"Back when we were just getting started, Janis died, and then they released her 'Me & Bobby McGee,' and I couldn't listen to it," Kris told me. Of course, Janis's version of Kris's landmark song was a huge point in Kristofferson's own rise to fame.

"When the producer played it for me the day after her farewell 'party,' I walked out of the studio before it was finished. I couldn't listen to it," Kris said.

"So, when I had a night alone in Nashville, I thought I'd listen to it over and over until I got used to it.

"I was alone in the building until Donnie showed up, and we talked about Janis and the sad 'party' she had instead of a funeral. And he was fooling with some chord progressions and a melody on his electric piano, and we started writing this song—'Epitaph: Black and Blue'—I was the words, he was the music. And it truly expressed the emotions we were feeling.

"I guess that's the purpose of soul music. And that's why it's worth committing your life to, like Donnie has. He has created some of the most beautiful music on the planet."

There's a lot more to say about Donnie and about his movies (Kris became a star, of course, and took his mates along for the ride). Donnie told me about drugs and "disappearing" for days of fun. He told me about the wild times on the movie sets and crazy times with Sam Peckinpah, Bob Dylan, and Kris.

He told me a lot of tales about Cash and Kris, Dylan, and especially his friend, Arthur Alexander. It was a full life, as folks say, comforting themselves when they stare down at open caskets.

Instead, I'll end this chapter by quoting his lovely wife, Donna, who hung on as her husband went for a wild ride and still clung to him, lovingly, to the grave. One day, we were talking on the phone while Donnie was gone from home, looking out for Donna's mother, a block of so away.

Donna didn't want to be quoted much, opting to leave that part to her husband. "He'll call you when he gets home," she said. But she did tell me what she found special about Funky Donnie Fritts.

"I married him because even when he was crazy, he still was the kindest and most compassionate person I'd ever met."

Epitaph and Postlude

"**D**ON'T LOOK BACK. Something might be gaining on you," said Leroy "Satchel" Paige, arguably the greatest baseball player who ever lived.

He also said, "Avoid fried meats, which angry up the blood" and "If your stomach disputes you, lie down and pacify it with cool thoughts."

There was more from this wise man. In fact, his "Don't look back" quote and attitude was the reason for the title of D. A. Pennebaker's long-ago, handheld-camera, black-and-white documentary about a young, often-churlish Bob Dylan.

As much as I relish baseball and Satch's wisdom and agree with his view on fried meats and as much a role as Dylan has played in my life, I threw this "don't look back" concept out when I began writing this book and instead focused on life's rearview mirror.

Yesterday may indeed be "dead and gone," as my treasured friend Kris Kristofferson wrote and sang in one of the masterpieces: "Help Me Make It Through the Night." And, indeed, "tomorrow's out of sight."

But he also wrote, "I'd trade all my tomorrows for a single yesterday" in "Me and Bobby McGee" and lamented the "disappearing dreams of yesterday" in "Sunday Morning Comin' Down."

I really didn't want Nashville music's "dreams of yesterday" to disappear. The same goes for the people who chased those dreams and for the city where many landmarks of those dreams have been altered or obliterated. Developers have turned Dylan's *Nashville Skyline* into something unrecognizable and as generic as much of the music now being created here.

And Nashville's once nationally known R&B scene clings to life only as "oldies" exhibitions for conventions, a president, or weddings and at a meat 'n' three on Murfreesboro Road. The men and women of R&B not only coexisted with Hank's Nashville but also chased the same dreams and worked together.

I am fortunate in that I have been able, in my career as a journalist, to learn about and love many of the people who created the complex musical texture of Nashville.

"The Silver Tongued Devil"—Kristofferson and the title character in a real-as-dirt album—introduced me more than a half century ago to the city I now claim as my hometown.

The more I read all those years ago about this Oxford-educated rascal and the "hard-luck Dylan" comparisons, the more of his music I consumed.

Because of Kris's lyrics and those of fellows like Cash, Waylon, Willie, and Bare, the then low-slung river city seemed not foreign when I first hit town in 1972. Indeed, it felt like home, even as the fog from the Cumberland River settled in on Lower Broadway's scattered honky-tonks, peep shows, and tippling Opry stars in my first days here.

I had come from Chicago, the Windy City—with its massive towers and rattling trains overhead, traffic jams on the Dan Ryan, gangland myths and facts, slaughterhouses, and my beloved Cubs—when I first parked my old Falcon on Fifth Avenue South and wandered across Lower Broadway to greet "Tootsie" (Hattie Bess) and her famous knitting needle at the infamous Orchid Lounge.

Weeping steel, blue yodels, and resonator guitars offered up a far different soundtrack than the rock 'n' roll and blues of my former home. Sure, I was and remain a "rock" guy, which is why I was quietly celebratory when I drove down dirty, old Music Row—now cleaned up, punctuated by condos, and rebranded—and saw Elvis's Memphis Mafia and others, dressed head to toe in black, joking around in front of RCA Studio B. Years later, I found out that often, while the King was recording, his guys and perhaps Elvis himself went for all-night snacks at Virginia's Market over on 18th Avenue.

They may have stopped in to see Waylon and Willie and the boys, like Billy Ray Reynolds, Chris Gantry, and Captain Midnight, at their all-night pinball and knife-throwing competitions at and around Bare's 18th Avenue offices. Bare wasn't there because he went home to sleep at night.

I long ago met Virginia, the market namesake, and enjoyed her stories. The last time I stopped in that storefront, though, a pleasant gentleman who said he was the proprietor told me he had never met her and had no idea about the market's history. He knew nothing of the corner market's past and the fact that Marty Robbins used to keep the door to his nearby office flung open so that he could holler out to market-bound singers and songwriters to come on in and pick and lie. I'm sure the modern Virginia's boss never met Elvis, though I'd guess he heard of him.

In Nashville in 1972, the state capitol—now obscured to all but the occasional demonstrators or right-wing politicos—could be seen from just about anyplace. When I first rolled in, Interstate 65 was a work in progress and didn't completely bisect the city, so I viewed the spotlighted capitol as it stared down from atop the city-center hill while I drove my old Falcon down U.S. 31 West, which I didn't realize at the time was notoriously carnal Dickerson Pike.

On some nights, you'd see crumpled newspapers and trash bounce along Lower Broadway like so much sagebrush a half century ago. That was the city I embraced and still love, even as that strip has changed to sort of a honky-tonk Disney World. Purple and yellow neon has displaced the quiet darkness of the "we close at 6" furniture showrooms and the late-night glare of Linebaugh's Restaurant and Merchants Hotel. And too-often-drunken bachelorettes—relinquishing their flimsy dress hems to the wind—sing along to modern country music and Buffett and Eagles songs blasting from pedal taverns and party buses. "Nobody eats at Linebaugh's anymore," sang late great fiddler and riverboat Captain John Hartford. I am glad I had the opportunity—and to meet Hartford, too.

A valued friend of mine, the singer-songwriter Bill Lloyd (of Foster & Lloyd, part-time Cheap Trickster, and solo success) has a song, "Pedal Tavern Girl," which is a tongue-in-cheek observation of two modern Lower Broadway staples: the bachelorette party and the pedal taverns. Omnipresent in Nashville's Lower Broadway drinking district, the former has an affinity for riding on the latter, and adult beverages consumed make things both sightly, when skirts fly up, and unsightly, notes Bill in my favorite lyric: "One more shot, you'll be ready to hurl, bachelorette bay-baaay. Pedal tavern girl."

Not all that has happened is bad. We have an NFL team that lost the Super Bowl by a yard and an NHL team that made it to the Stanley Cup Finals in 2017 (only to have dreams dashed by Sidney Crosby and the Pittsburgh Penguins). There is talk of a Major League Baseball team, the Stars, coming here. And Major League Soccer has a team and a stadium, and there was even World Cup speculation.

Heck, there are big-time NASCAR and Grand Prix events here now.

Progress and city officials and boosters really don't look back.

But I liked the lonesome, on'ry, and mean feel of Lower Broadway a half century ago.

A common enough euphemism for the unsightly skyline scarring caused by the stampeding herd of condo and office towers is that Nashville is "growing vertically." The capitol, as I note earlier, is obscured and dwarfed, robbed of its proud prominence.

One constant, though, has been the music of Nashville. Sure, today's country music is not necessarily as much to my liking as the tunes of Waylon and Willie and the boys. The assembly-line songwriting style of today is often quite successful, however. But does it compare to the work of Kristofferson, Tom T. Hall, Billy Joe Shaver, Mac Wiseman, or even contemporary genius song-crafter Don ("The Gambler") Schlitz? The legacy of Hank Williams?

And while you may be able to spot a star once or twice a year at high-priced restaurants bearing their names on Lower Broadway, it's not quite the same as seeing Roger Miller writing 3 a.m. songs at Linebaugh's or listening to Ernest Tubb and Lefty Frizzell swap "road stories" about Mel Tillis and Little Jimmy Dickens in the back of Tootsie's while Hattie and her knitting needle enforced good behavior in the lower bar. Honky-tonks weren't high-rises back then. Tootsie's sprouted floors to deal with "It City" growth, but a half century ago, this most famous of bars on the strip had a street-level floor that held the bar and a second floor up a half flight of stairs, leading to a backdoor that emptied into the alley by the Ryman.

That half flight of stairs could prove tough to negotiate, by the way. But it was worth it to hang out with Bobby Bare, Lefty Frizzell, and the rest who convened by the backdoor. They could set down their beer, walk across the alley to sing for the Opry fans, and then come back to the bar and finish up before the foam disappeared.

Yesterday may be dead and gone, but the memories of those times in Music City remain—of times when you might run into Johnny Cash, dilated pupils punctuating tired eyes after an all-night Columbia recording session, enjoying breakfast served by my late friend Hap Townes at his long-defunct meat 'n' three by the railroad overpass. Baseball great Reggie Jackson ate at Hap's when he was in town for Yankee exhibition games, but that's another long story.

Memories are pretty much the inspiration for this book. I'd had the opportunity to befriend and spend time with so many great musicians who talked about the old days and about change, and I wanted to put the half century into perspective by using their voices and observations.

In my telling of their stories, I am telling the story of this city (or at least the musical part of it), illustrating the change as they—and I—have witnessed it.

I do not attempt to be an encyclopedia or even a Wikipedia in this collection. These are not scholarly biographies but rather snippets of things said and done, stories told, tears and laughter shared with me in an afternoon or some other measurement of time.

Most of these folks I met in my role as a journalist. But our conversations transcended the scattered words on a newspaper or magazine page.

There were frequent conversations, sometimes just health checks as they got older, and other times long and sunny afternoons in their living rooms—not for stories but simply out of friendship. I mention in these pages that I had a list of musicians, mostly old and ailing, whom I called at least every three weeks or so for years. Not all of them made it into these chapters. Maybe I can get to bluegrass pioneer Bobby Thompson, Hank and Hank Jr.'s favorite "cleanup man" Merle Kilgore, Grateful Dead crony and fiddle wizard Vassar Clements, and many more friends in the future.

Even as I wrote this book, some of the featured friends died. Others have seen their health, physical and mental, battered by the maladies of age.

A half century ago, George Harrison, the so-called quiet Beatle and the Traveling Wilburys' ringleader, sang "All Things Must Pass" as a melancholy farewell to the Fab Four. And that song's sentiment, which soothed baby boomers like me, stunned by the band's breakup, is correct. All things do pass away. But just as we remember George, John Lennon, Paul McCartney, and Ringo Starr and honor their cultural impact, we need to remember the voices, the guitars, and the three-chords-and-the-truth beauty of Nashville's past.

The subjects of these conversations—on the phone, in alleyways, over coffee, at funeral homes, or by kitchen tables—ranged from Dobro to Thoreaux.

Yes, I am the guy traveling through this half century by tapping these precious memories. But this isn't my story—it's their story. I'm just the tour guide because I love these people and want to remind others of what they still mean to Nashville.

So sometimes you have to look back, against Satchel's advice, although, like I said earlier, I do think the fried meat advice still stands.

Yesterday may indeed be dead and gone, as I quote my friend Kris Kristofferson earlier.

My purpose is to paint the people of those yesterdays before tomorrow is out of sight.

These are the people Kris was talking about in "The Pilgrim, Chapter 33," which I refer to in the introduction. That was the song that first let me know that—against stereotype—wisdom, wit, warmth, and words were more prevalent than hay bales and hate in this southern mecca:

> But if this world keeps right on turnin' for the better or the
>   worse . . .
> The goin' up was worth the comin' down.

He adds, "There's a lotta wrong directions on that lonely way back home."
I'm just glad the direction I followed got me to Nashville.

Index